GROUPTHINK

GROUPTHINK

Psychological Studies of Policy Decisions and Fiascoes

A revised and enlarged edition of *Victims of Groupthink:*
A Psychological Study of Foreign-Policy Decisions and Fiascoes (1972)

IRVING L. JANIS
Yale University

HOUGHTON MIFFLIN COMPANY • BOSTON
Dallas   Geneva, Ill.   Hopewell, N.J.   Palo Alto   London

Contents

Preface

The main theme of this book occurred to me while reading Arthur M. Schlesinger's chapters on the Bay of Pigs in *A Thousand Days*. At first, I was puzzled: How could bright, shrewd men like John F. Kennedy and his advisers be taken in by the CIA's stupid, patchwork plan? I began to wonder whether some kind of psychological contagion, similar to social conformity phenomena observed in studies of small groups, had interfered with their mental alertness. I kept thinking about the implications of this notion until one day I found myself talking about it, in a seminar of mine on group psychology at Yale University. I suggested that the poor decision-making performance of the men at those White House meetings might be akin to the lapses in judgment of ordinary citizens who become more concerned with retaining the approval of the fellow members of their work group than with coming up with good solutions to the tasks at hand.

Shortly after that, when I reread Schlesinger's account, I was struck by some observations that earlier had escaped my notice. These observations began to fit a specific pattern of concurrence-seeking behavior that had impressed me time and again in my research on other kinds of face-to-face groups, particularly when a "we-feeling" of solidarity is running high. Additional accounts of the Bay of Pigs yielded more such observations, leading me to conclude that group processes had been subtly at work, preventing the members of Kennedy's team from debating the real issues posed by the CIA's plan and from carefully appraising its serious risks.

Then in Joseph de Rivera's *The Psychological Dimension of Foreign Policy,* I found an impressive example of excluding a deviant from Truman's group of advisers during the period of the ill-fated Korean War decisions. De Rivera's comments about the group's behavior prompted me to look further into that series of decisions and soon I encountered evidence of other manifestations of group processes, like those apparently operating in the Bay of Pigs decision.

By this time, I was sufficiently fascinated by what I began to call the groupthink hypothesis to start looking into a fairly large number of historical parallels. I selected for intensive analysis two additional United States foreign-policy decisions and again found consistent indications of the same kind of detrimental group processes. Later I added a case study of a president's criminal conspiracy to obstruct justice, which I now regard as the most impressive example of groupthink.

This book presents five case studies of major fiascoes, resulting from poor decisions made during the administrations of five American presidents—Franklin D. Roosevelt (failure to be prepared for the attack on Pearl Harbor), Harry S Truman (the invasion of North Korea), John F. Kennedy (the Bay of Pigs invasion), Lyndon B. Johnson (escalation of the Vietnam War), and Richard M. Nixon (the Watergate cover-up). Each of these decisions was a *group* product, issuing from a series of meetings of a small body of government officials and advisers who constituted a cohesive group. And in each instance, the members of the policy-making group made incredibly gross miscalculations about both the practical and moral consequences of their decisions.

The second section, for comparative purposes, presents two case studies of well worked out decisions made by similar groups whose members made realistic appraisals of the consequences. One of these is the course of action chosen by the Kennedy administration during the Cuban missile crisis in October 1962. This decision, made by almost the same cast of characters that had approved the Bay of Pigs invasion plan in 1961, was arrived at very carefully, in a group atmosphere conducive to independent critical thinking, unlike that which prevailed in the earlier decision. Similarly, the second counterpoint example deals with the hardheaded way that planning committees in the Truman administration evolved the Marshall Plan in 1948. These two case studies indicate that policy-making groups do not always suffer the adverse consequences of group processes, that the quality of the group's decision-making activities depends upon current conditions that influence the group atmosphere.

Except for the Watergate cover-up (for which transcripts of tape recorded meetings in the White House are available), the case studies are based mainly on secondary sources—memoirs and published documents, such as the Pentagon Papers. What I try to do is to show how the evidence at hand can be viewed as forming a consistent psychological pattern, in the light of what is known about group dynamics. Consequently, well-known historical facts, along with some less well-known observations that have generally been passed over as unimportant, are interpreted in a way quite different from how such facts are treated in the writings of historians and political scientists who have studied the various policy decisions.

Since my purpose is to describe and explain the psychological processes that are at work, rather than to establish historical continuities, I do not present the case studies in chronological order. The sequence I use was chosen to convey step-by-step the implications of group dynamics hypotheses.

When writing a book about historic errors, one can hardly avoid becoming preoccupied with the errors of written history. I was repeatedly reminded of George Bernard Shaw's remark that when an historian had to rely on one document he was safe, but if there were two to be consulted he was in difficulty, and if three were available his position was hopeless. For each case study in this book, many more than three historical documents are available, and more than three historical accounts were consulted. And, of course, major fiascoes resulting from apparent errors of judgment invite controversies about what happened and why. Furthermore, the relevant documents are likely to be distorted to some unknown extent by partisan bias. One must rely mainly on the contemporary and retrospective accounts by the group members themselves—minutes of the meetings, diaries, memoirs, letters, and prepared statements given to investigating committees—many of which are likely to have been written with an eye to the author's own place in history. The documents most needed for testing group dynamics hypotheses are verbatim records of formal group meetings and of informal conversations among the members. But such records, if they exist, usually are safely locked up in government files, doomed, like the ghost of Hamlet's father, to remain confined for a certain term, until the foul crimes of those earlier days are purged away.

Ultimately, the psychological explanations inferred from the imperfect historical materials will have to be checked carefully in the same way that social scientists check any other type of explanation—and rechecked as new evidence comes to light. For purposes of *hypothesis construction*—which is the stage of inquiry with which this book is concerned—we must be willing to make some inferential leaps from whatever historical clues we can pick up. But I have tried to start off on solid ground by selecting the best available historical writings and to use as my springboard those specific observations that appear to be solid facts in the light of what is now known about the deliberations of the policy-making groups. (In order to avoid burdening the general reader with large numbers of footnotes giving the references for the historical observations and quotations cited in the text, I have added a set of source notes for each chapter at the end of the book.)

Many general readers, social scientists, and students appreciate the importance of the psychology of emotion and personality dynamics when they are trying to understand why a president, a prime minister, a revolutionary leader, or some other leading actor on the stage of history has played his role in a wayward fashion. A major purpose of this book is to increase awareness of social psychological phenomena in decisions of historic importance, so that *group dynamics* will be taken into account by those who try to understand the performance of the leading actors and members of the supporting cast. Their collective actions, as will be seen in the case studies of major fiascoes, can be responsible for staging an appalling comedy of errors that ends up as a tragedy.

A final note for scholars: This book obviously is at the intersection of three disciplines—social psychology, political science, and history. I hope that the interpretations and theoretical conceptions suggested in the case studies will add something to the thinking of scholars in each of these disciplines. For students of social psychology, this book raises some new questions (and reformulates some old questions) about the conditions under which group processes will interfere with effective decision-making by fostering shared illusions and misjudgments. For students of political science and history it points the way to making use of a psychological dimension suggested by de Rivera for analyzing how and why gross errors arise in foreign-policy decisions. For all those concerned with budding developments in the policy sciences, this book presents a number of suggestive leads concerning constructive interventions in the government's decision-making process that should improve the quality of policy decisions, if the hypotheses about conditions fostering groupthink are correct.

I presume that every reader will have some interest in the practical implications of the case studies discussed in the last chapter, which gives a tentative answer to a crucial question: *How can groupthink be prevented?* In the nuclear age, perhaps all of us might justifiably feel slightly less insecure if definitive answers to this question could quickly be pinned down and applied.

Acknowledgments

My decision to pursue the groupthink hypothesis was crystallized shortly after my daughter, Charlotte Janis, decided to accept my suggestion to prepare a term paper on the Bay of Pigs fiasco for her senior high school course in history. Her perceptive culling of the relevant evidence that she turned up in her library research encouraged me to take the hypothesis seriously enough to begin examining additional fiascoes. She continued to play a major role in the enterprise by seeking out new source materials, by constantly expressing her doubts about the validity of a group dynamics interpretation of historic events, and finally by preparing detailed editorial critiques of the initial drafts of all the chapters.

Subsequently, I had the benefit of highly skilled assistance in library research and editorial suggestions from Susan Block. Valuable editorial advice for improving the final manuscript was generously given by Judith Greissman. I am also indebted to Gale Tenen, who, as a student in one of my graduate seminars, called my attention to the potential value of examining the decisions leading up to the Korean War fiasco and the contrasting positive qualities of the decisions made during the Cuban Missile Crisis.

Special thanks are due Alexander George, who from the outset gave me constant encouragement, posed crucial questions that needed to be answered, supplied cogent references from his intensive knowledge of the political science literature, and then unselfishly devoted considerable time and thought to preparing a thorough critique of an early draft of each chapter. I also wish to thank other social scientists who have read one or more chapters for their valuable suggestions and criticisms, which I used in successive revisions of the manuscript—Robert P. Abelson, Clayton Aldefer, Chris Argyris, James D. Barber, George C. Byrne, Craig Comstock, James Dittes, John Dollard, James Fesler, Joseph Goldsen, J. Richard Hackman, Marjorie Graham

Janis, Edward Katkin, Richard Lazarus, Richard Longaker, Leon Mann, John McConahay, James C. Miller, David Musto, Richard Nisbett, Zick Rubin, Nevitt Sanford, David Sears, Cyril Sofer, G. Gaddis Smith, Daniel Wheeler, and Roberta Wohlstetter.

I want to express my gratitude to Yale University for a Senior Faculty Research Fellowship, enabling me to spend a full year at the University of California at Berkeley, which provided the opportunity to carry out extensive library research and to write the initial draft of the book. Finally, I wish to thank the director, Dr. H. A. J. F. Misset, and the staff of the Netherlands Institute for Advanced Study. During a subsequent sabbatical year (1981–82) as a Fellow-in-Residence at that Institute, my work on the final revision of this book was greatly facilitated, and I benefited greatly from the critiques I received of the new chapters from the other Fellows-in-Residence—especially from Robert R. Alford, Graeme C. Duncan, Lewis R. Goldberg, Jan van Herwaarden, and Cornelis J. Lammers.

I
Fiascoes

1

Introduction:
Why So Many
Miscalculations?

Nobody is perfect

Year after year newscasts and newspapers inform us of collective miscalculations—companies that have unexpectedly gone bankrupt because of misjudging their market, federal agencies that have mistakenly authorized the use of chemical insecticides that poison our environment, and White House executive committees that have made ill-conceived foreign policy decisions that inadvertently bring the major powers to the brink of war. Most people, when they hear about such fiascoes, simply remind themselves that, after all, "organizations are run by human beings," "to err is human," and "nobody is perfect." But platitudinous thoughts about human nature do not help us to understand how and why avoidable miscalculations are made.

Fiasco watchers who are unwilling to set the problem aside in this easy fashion will find that contemporary psychology has something to say (unfortunately not very much) about distortions of thinking and other sources of human error. The deficiencies about which we know the most pertain to disturbances in the behavior of each individual in a decision-making group—temporary states of elation, fear, or anger that reduce a person's mental efficiency; chronic blind spots arising from a person's social prejudices; shortcomings in information-processing that prevent a person from comprehending the complex consequences of a seemingly simple policy decision. One psychologist has suggested that because the information-processing capabilities of every individual are limited, no responsible leader of a large organization ought to make a policy decision without using a computer that is programmed to spell out all the probable benefits and costs of each alternative under consideration. The usual way of trying to counteract the limitations of individuals' mental functioning, however, is to relegate important decisions to groups.

Imperfections of group decisions

Groups, like individuals, have shortcomings. Groups can bring out the worst as well as the best in man. Nietzsche went so far as to say that madness is the exception in individuals but the rule in groups. A considerable amount of social science literature shows that in circumstances of extreme crisis, group contagion occasionally gives rise to collective panic, violent acts of scapegoating, and other forms of what could be called group madness. Much more frequent, however, are instances of mindless conformity and collective misjudgment of serious risks, which are collectively laughed off in a clubby atmosphere of relaxed conviviality. Consider what happened a few days before disaster struck the small mining town of Pitcher, Oklahoma, in 1950. The local mining engineer had warned the inhabitants to leave at once because the town had been accidentally undermined and might cave in at any moment. At a Lion's Club meeting of leading citizens, the day after the warning was issued, the members joked about the warning and laughed uproariously when someone arrived wearing a parachute. What the club members were communicating to each other by their collective laughter was that "sensible people like us know better than to take seriously those disaster warnings; we know it can't happen here, to our fine little town." Within a few days, this collective complacency cost some of these men and their families their lives.

Lack of vigilance and excessive risk-taking are forms of temporary group derangement to which decision-making groups made up of responsible executives are not at all immune. Sometimes the main trouble is that the chief executive manipulates his advisers to rubber-stamp his own ill-conceived proposals. In this book, however, I shall be dealing mainly with a different source of defective decision-making, which often involves a much more subtle form of faulty leadership: During the group's deliberations, the leader does not deliberately try to get the group to tell him what he wants to hear but is quite sincere in asking for honest opinions. The group members are not transformed into sycophants. They are not afraid to speak their minds. Nevertheless, subtle constraints, which the leader may reinforce inadvertently, prevent a member from fully exercising his critical powers and from openly expressing doubts when most others in the group appear to have reached a consensus. In order to take account of what is known about the causes and consequences of such constraints we must briefly review some of the main findings of research on group dynamics.

Effects of group cohesiveness

In applying the concepts of group dynamics to recent historic policy decisions, I am extending the work of some pioneering social scientists. The power of a face-to-face group to set norms that influence members was emphasized by two leading sociologists early in the twentieth century—Charles Horton Cooley and George Herbert Mead. During that same period, William Graham Sumner postulated that in-group solidarity increases when clashes arise with out-groups.

Kurt Lewin, the social psychologist who began using empirical methods to study group dynamics during the 1940s, called attention to the prerequisites for effective group decisions. He described the typical dilemmas faced by executive committees, including wartime groups of military planners who select bomb targets and peacetime groups of policy-makers who try to improve relations between nations. Lewin emphasized the need for fact-finding and objective appraisal of alternatives to determine whether the chosen means will achieve a group's goals. He warned that the lack of objective standards for evaluating goal achievement allows many opportunities for errors of judgment and faulty decisions. Lewin's analysis of the behavior of small groups also emphasized the importance of group cohesiveness—that is, members' positive valuation of the group and their motivation to continue to belong to it. When group cohesiveness is high, all the members express solidarity, mutual liking, and positive feelings about attending meetings and carrying out the routine tasks of the group. Lewin was most interested in the positive effects of group cohesiveness and did not investigate instances when members of cohesive groups make gross errors and fail to correct their shared misjudgments.

The potentially detrimental effects of group cohesiveness were emphasized by another theorist, Wilfred Bion, an eminent group therapist. Bion described how the efficiency of all working groups can be adversely affected by the preconscious myths and misconceptions of their mutually dependent members—that is, by shared basic assumptions that tend to preserve the group without regard for the work at hand.

Under the influence of Kurt Lewin's pioneering work, Leon Festinger, Harold Kelley, Stanley Schachter, and other social psychologists have carried out experiments and field investigations on the consequences of group cohesiveness.[1] Summarizing a large body of research findings that had accumulated during the 1950s and 1960s on the ways members of cohesive groups influence each other, Dorwin Cartwright concluded that the evidence converges on three main types of effects:

> Other things being equal, as cohesiveness increases there is an increase in a group's capacity to retain members and in the degree of participation by members in group activities. The greater a group's cohesiveness the more power it has to bring about conformity to its norms and to gain acceptance of its goals and assignment to tasks and roles. Finally, highly cohesive groups provide a source of security for members which serves to reduce anxiety and to heighten self-esteem.

Also under investigation are the causes of group cohesiveness—how and why group identification and feelings of solidarity develop. It has long been known that group solidarity increases markedly whenever a collection of individuals faces a common source of external stress, such as the threat of being injured or killed in military combat. Some researchers are beginning to consider the effects on group solidarity of subtler sources of stress, such as those that beset groups of harried policy-makers in large organizations.

Conformity to group norms

In studies of social clubs and other small groups, conformity pressures have frequently been observed. Whenever a member says something that sounds out of line with the group's norms, the other members at first increase their communication with the deviant. Attempts to influence the nonconformist member to revise or tone down his dissident ideas continue as long as most members of the group feel hopeful about talking him into changing his mind. But if they fail after repeated attempts, the amount of communication they direct toward the deviant decreases markedly. The members begin to exclude him, often quite subtly at first and later more obviously, in order to restore the unity of the group. A social psychological experiment conducted by Stanley Schachter with avocational clubs in an American university—and replicated by Schachter and his collaborators in seven European countries—showed that the more cohesive the group and the more relevant the issue to the goals of the group, the greater is the inclination of the members to reject a nonconformist. Just as the members insulate themselves from outside critics who threaten to disrupt the unity and esprit de corps of their group, they take steps, often without being aware of it, to counteract the disruptive influence of inside critics who are attacking the group's norms.

The norms to which the members of a cohesive group adhere, as Bion's analysis implies, do not always have a positive effect on the quality of the group's performance. Studies in industrial organizations indicate that while the norms of some work groups foster conscientiousness and high productivity, the norms of other, similar work groups foster slowdowns and socializing activities that reduce productivity. The same type of variation in norms that facilitate or interfere with the group's work objectives may be found among policy-making groups in large organizations.

Much of the current research on group dynamics is an effort to pinpoint the causes of the crucial differences in group norms that make for good or poor performance on group tasks, especially tasks pertaining to decision-making. Among the phenomena that have been intensively investigated in recent years are two detrimental tendencies arising under certain conditions not yet adequately understood—the tendency of groups to develop stereotyped images that dehumanize out-groups against whom they are engaged in competitive struggles and the tendency for the collective judgments arising out of group discussions to become polarized, sometimes shifting toward extreme conservatism and sometimes toward riskier courses of action than the individual members would otherwise be prepared to take.

Conceptions of political decision-making

Group dynamics is still in the early stages of scientific development, and much remains to be learned. At present there are only a few concepts and generalizations in which we can have confidence when we are trying to understand the behavior of policy-making groups. Nevertheless, social scientists concerned with policy-making in the government—most notably, Karl Deutsch, Alexander George, and Joseph de Rivera—have started to use group dynamics concepts that hold the promise of enriching political science. The rapprochement between the two fields, however, is still mainly a perspective for the future rather than a current reality. My hope is that the case studies in the present book will help to concretize and give added impetus to this new development within the social sciences.

The use of theory and research on group dynamics is intended to supplement, not to replace, the standard approaches to the study of political decision-making. Three conceptual frameworks have been described and applied by Graham T. Allison in his analysis of the resolution of the Cuban missile crisis. First is the classical approach—Allison refers to it as the rational actor model or The Theory of International Relations, with a capital "T"—which is rooted in the work of well-known scholars such as Hans Morgenthau, Arnold Wolfers, and Raymond Aron. Analysts using this approach construct a set of objectives that the statesman responsible for a policy is intending to achieve, "presuming always," as Morgenthau puts it, "that he acts in a rational manner." The aim of this type of analysis is to determine the ends the political actor is trying to attain by means of the policy he has chosen.

The second framework described by Allison grows largely out of the work of Herbert Simon, James March, and their collaborators. The organizational process model emphasizes factors that limit rationality in decision-making by individuals and organizations. These factors include the limitations of man's capacity to process information, constraints on attempts to obtain the information necessary for calculating maximal gains, and the tendency to find a course of action that will satisfy the most minimal goals instead of seeking for the action with the best consequences (this is known as a satisficing strategy). This approach takes account of "organizational rigidities" such as routines and procedures of bureaucratic organizations that grind out platitudes about what can be done to attain objectives.

The third framework, called by Allison the governmental politics model, derives from the work of Gabriel Almond, Charles E. Lindblom, Richard Neustadt, and other political scientists. It focuses on the intrusions of the games of domestic and local bureaucratic politics into the dangerous competitive games of international relations. In Lindblom's variant of this approach, governmental policy-making is a matter of "muddling through": Policy-makers take one little step after another and gradually change the old policy into a new one, all the while making compromises that keep every politically powerful group that enters the bargaining reasonably satisfied, or at least not dissatisfied enough to obstruct or sabotage the new trend.

Allison presents the three approaches as conceptual models to help social scientists generate hypotheses and discern important features that might otherwise be overlooked when they are trying to explain how and why a new foreign policy decision came about. He points out, "The best analysts of foreign policy manage to weave strands of each of the three conceptual models into their explanations." At the very least, according to Allison, these conceptual models can pose the questions to be answered in a systematic way in case studies of foreign policy decision-making.

> Most theorists have little respect for "case studies"—in large part because of the atheoretical character of case studies of the past. . . . What we need is a new kind of "case study" done with theoretical alertness to the range of factors identified by Models I, II, and III (and others) on the basis of which to begin refining and testing propositions and models.

In order to use the three conceptual models, analysts must take as the unit of analysis either the individual decision-maker or a large group such as the State Department, the government's intelligence community, or the various coalitions within the bureaucracy that participate in bargaining. The group dynamics approach—which should be considered a fourth conceptual model—uses a different unit of analysis. When we are trying to understand how certain avoidable policy errors happen to be made, we should look into the behavior of the small group of decision-makers, because all the well-known errors stemming from limitations of an individual and of a large organization can be greatly augmented by group processes that produce shared miscalculations.

What is groupthink?

The group dynamics approach is based on the working assumption that the members of policy-making groups, no matter how mindful they may be of their exalted national status and of their heavy responsibilities, are subjected to the pressures widely observed in groups of ordinary citizens. In my earlier research on group dynamics, I was impressed by repeated manifestations of the effects—both unfavorable and favorable—of the social pressures that typically develop in cohesive groups—in infantry platoons, air crews, therapy groups, seminars, and self-study or encounter groups of executives receiving leadership training.[2] In all these groups, just as in the industrial work groups described by other investigators, members tend to evolve informal norms to preserve friendly intragroup relations and these become part of the hidden agenda at their meetings. When conducting research on groups of heavy smokers at a clinic set up to help people stop smoking, I noticed a seemingly irrational tendency for the members to exert pressure on each other to increase their smoking as the time for the final meeting approached. This appeared to be a collusive effort to display mutual dependence and resistance to the termination of the group sessions.

Sometimes, even long before members become concerned about the final separation, clear-cut signs of pressures toward uniformity subvert the fundamental purpose of group meetings. At the second meeting of one group of smokers, consisting of twelve middle-class American men and women, two of the most dominant members took the position that heavy smoking was an almost incurable addiction. The majority of the others soon agreed that no one could be expected to cut down drastically. One heavy smoker, a middle-aged business executive, took issue with this consensus, arguing that by using will power he had stopped smoking since joining the group and that everyone else could do the same. His declaration was followed by a heated discussion, which continued in the halls of the building after the formal meeting adjourned. Most of the others ganged up against the man who was deviating from the group consensus. Then, at the beginning of the next meeting, the deviant announced that he had made an important decision. "When I joined," he said, "I agreed to follow the two main rules required by the clinic—to make a conscientious effort to stop smoking and to attend every meeting. But I have learned from experience in this group that you can only follow one of the rules, you can't follow both. And so, I have decided that I will continue to attend every meeting but I have gone back to smoking two packs a day and I will not make any effort to stop smoking again until after the last meeting." Whereupon, the other members beamed at him and applauded enthusiastically, welcoming him back to the fold. No one commented on the fact that the whole point of the meetings was to help each individual to cut down on smoking as rapidly as possible. As a psychological consultant to the group, I tried to call this to the members' attention, and so did my collaborator, Dr. Michael Kahn. But during that meeting the members managed to ignore our comments and reiterated their consensus that heavy smoking was an addiction from which no one would be cured except by cutting down very gradually over a long period of time.

This episode—an extreme form of groupthink—was only one manifestation of a general pattern that the group displayed. At every meeting, the members were amiable, reasserted their warm feelings of solidarity, and sought complete concurrence on every important topic, with no reappearance of the unpleasant bickering that would spoil the cozy atmosphere. The concurrence-seeking tendency could be maintained, however, only at the expense of ignoring realistic challenges (like those posed by the psychological consultants) and distorting members' observations of individual differences that would call into question the shared assumption that everyone in the group had the same type of addiction problem. It seemed that in this smoking group I was observing another instance of the groupthink pattern I had encountered in observations of widely contrasting groups whose members came from diverse sectors of society and were meeting together for social, educational, vocational, or other purposes. Just like the group in the smoking clinic, all these different types of groups had shown signs of high cohesiveness and of an accompanying concurrence-seeking tendency that interfered with critical thinking—the central features of groupthink.

I use the term "groupthink" as a quick and easy way to refer to a mode of thinking that people engage in when they are deeply involved in a cohesive in-group, when the members' strivings for unanimity override their motivation to realistically appraise alternative courses of action. "Groupthink" is a term of the same order as the words in the newspeak vocabulary George Orwell presents in his dismaying *1984*—a vocabulary with terms such as "doublethink" and "crimethink." By putting groupthink with those Orwellian words, I realize that groupthink takes on an invidious connotation. The invidiousness is intentional: Groupthink refers to a deterioration of mental efficiency, reality testing, and moral judgment that results from in-group pressures.

Selection of the fiascoes

When I began to investigate the Bay of Pigs invasion, the decision to escalate the Korean War, and other fiascoes, for purposes of studying sources of error in foreign policy decision-making, I was initially surprised to discover the pervasiveness of symptoms of groupthink. Although the symptoms that could be discerned from published accounts of the deliberations did not seem as obtrusive as in the face-to-face groups I had observed directly, nevertheless signs of poor decision-making as a result of concurrence-seeking were unmistakable.

After noting the first few examples of grossly miscalculated policy decisions that seemed at least partly attributable to group processes, I began collecting instances of similar fiascoes from a variety of sources, such as Harold Wilensky's *Organizational Intelligence* and Barton Whaley's *Stratagem*. In a short time, with the help of suggestions from colleagues in political science and library research by students in my seminars on group dynamics, I compiled a list of several dozen fiascoes. I cut the list to about two dozen that appeared appropriate for an analysis of group processes. I was looking for instances in which a defective decision was made in a series of meetings by a few policy-makers who constituted a cohesive group. By a defective decision, I mean one that results from decision-making practices of extremely poor quality. In other words, the fiascoes that I selected for analysis *deserved* to be fiascoes because of the grossly inadequate way the policy-makers carried out their decision-making tasks.

At least seven major defects in decision-making contribute to failures to

[handwritten margin notes: "symptoms", "Seven Defects:", "few alternatives", "1", "2", "3", "No 4 reeval", "5", "info", "bias 6", "excludes →", "7", "No post war plan", "use →"]

solve problems adequately. First, the group's discussions are limited to a few alternative courses of action (often only two) without a survey of the full range of alternatives. Second, the group does not survey the objectives to be fulfilled and the values implicated by the choice. Third, the group fails to reexamine the course of action initially preferred by the majority of members from the standpoint of nonobvious risks and drawbacks that had not been considered when it was originally evaluated. Fourth, the members neglect courses of action initially evaluated as unsatisfactory by the majority of the group: They spend little or no time discussing whether they have overlooked nonobvious gains or whether there are ways of reducing the seemingly prohibitive costs that had made the alternatives seem undesirable. Fifth, the members make little or no attempt to obtain information from experts who can supply sound estimates of losses and gains to be expected from alternative courses of actions. Sixth, selective bias is shown in the way the group reacts to factual information and relevant judgments from experts, the mass media, and outside critics. The members show interest in facts and opinions that support their initially preferred policy and take up time in their meetings to discuss them, but they tend to ignore facts and opinions that do not support their initially preferred policy. Seventh, the members spend little time deliberating about how the chosen policy might be hindered by bureaucratic inertia, sabotaged by political opponents, or temporarily derailed by the common accidents that happen to the best of well-laid plans. Consequently, they fail to work out contingency plans to cope with foreseeable setbacks that could endanger the overall success of the chosen course of action.

I assume that these seven defects and some related features of inadequate decision-making result from groupthink. But, of course, each of the seven can arise from other common causes of human stupidity as well—erroneous intelligence, information overload, fatigue, blinding prejudice, and ignorance. Whether produced by groupthink or by other causes, a decision suffering from most of these defects has relatively little chance of success.

The five major policy fiascoes I have selected for intensive case studies are the ones of greatest historical importance among the defective decisions by the United States government I have examined. Each clearly meets two important criteria for classifying a decision as a candidate for psychological analysis in terms of group dynamics: Each presents numerous indications that (1) the decision-making group was cohesive and that (2) decision-making was extremely defective. (Other fiascoes in my original list also meet these criteria and are discussed briefly in the last part of the book, where I talk about candidates for subsequent investigations bearing on the generality of groupthink phenomena.)

When the conditions specified by these two criteria are met, according to the groupthink hypothesis there is a better-than-chance likelihood that one of the causes of the defective decision was a strong concurrence-seeking tendency, which is the motivation that gives rise to all the symptoms of groupthink.

The imperfect link between groupthink and fiascoes

conclusion

Simply because the outcome of a group decision has turned out to be a fiasco, I do not assume that it must have been the result of groupthink or even that it was the result of defective decision-making. Nor do I expect that every defective decision, whether arising from groupthink or from other causes, will produce a fiasco. Defective decisions based on misinformation and poor judgment sometimes lead to successful outcomes. We do not necessarily have to accept at face value the well-known thesis—eloquently put forth by Leo Tolstoy in *War and Peace* and elaborated by Norman Mailer in *The Naked and the Dead*—that the decisions made by military commanders have nothing to do with military success. But we must acknowledge that chance and the stupidity of the enemy can sometimes give a silk-purse ending to a command decision worth less than a sow's ear. At the outset of World War I, the French high command made incredible errors, repeatedly ignoring warnings from their military intelligence officers about the Schlieffen plan. But the German high command made even grosser errors while executing the plan, preventing the Germans from capitalizing on the French rout and depriving them of the quick victory that was within their grasp.

Groupthink is conducive to errors in decision-making, and such errors increase the likelihood of a poor outcome. Often the result is a fiasco, but not always. Suppose that because of lucky accidents fostered by absurd command decisions by the Cuban military leaders, the Kennedy administration's Bay of Pigs invasion had been successful in provoking a civil war in Cuba and led to the overthrow of the Castro regime. Analysis of the decision to invade Cuba would still support the groupthink hypothesis, for the evidence shows that Kennedy's White House group was highly cohesive, clearly displayed symptoms of defective decision-making, and exhibited all the major symptoms of groupthink. Thus, even if the Bay of Pigs decision had produced a triumph rather than a defeat, it would still be an example of the potentially adverse effects of groupthink (even though the invasion would not, in that case, be classified as a fiasco).

Hardhearted actions by softheaded groups

At first I was surprised by the extent to which the groups in the fiascoes I have examined adhered to group norms and pressures toward uniformity. Just as in groups of ordinary citizens, a dominant characteristic appears to be remaining loyal to the group by sticking with the decisions to which the group has committed itself, even when the policy is working badly and has unintended consequences that disturb the conscience of the members. In a sense, members consider loyalty to the group the highest form of morality. That loyalty requires each member to avoid raising controversial issues, questioning weak arguments, or calling a halt to softheaded thinking.

Paradoxically, softheaded groups are likely to be extremely hardhearted toward out-groups and enemies. In dealing with a rival nation, policy-makers comprising an amiable group find it relatively easy to authorize dehumanizing solutions such as large-scale bombings. An affable group of government officials is unlikely to pursue the difficult and controversial issues that arise when alternatives to a harsh military solution come up for discussion. Nor are the members inclined to raise ethical issues that imply that this "fine group of ours, with its humanitarianism and its high-minded principles, might be capable of adopting a course of action that is inhumane and immoral."

Many other sources of human error can prevent government leaders from arriving at well worked out decisions, resulting in failures to achieve their practical objectives and violations of their own standards of ethical conduct. But, unlike groupthink, these other sources of error do not typically entail increases in hardheartedness along with softheadedness. Some errors involve blind spots that stem from the personality of the decision-makers. Special circumstances produce unusual fatigue and emotional stresses that interfere with efficient decision-making. Numerous institutional features of the social structure in which the group is located may also cause inefficiency and prevent adequate communication with experts. In addition, well-known interferences with sound thinking arise when the decision-makers comprise a noncohesive group. For example, when the members have no sense of loyalty to the group and regard themselves merely as representatives of different departments, with clashing interests, the meetings may become bitter power struggles, at the expense of effective decision-making.

The concept of groupthink pinpoints an entirely different source of trouble, residing neither in the individual nor in the organizational setting. Over and beyond all the familiar sources of human error is a powerful source of defective judgment that arises in cohesive groups—the concurrence-seeking tendency, which fosters overoptimism, lack of vigilance, and sloganistic thinking about the weakness and immorality of out-groups. This tendency can take its toll even when the decision-makers are conscientious statesmen trying to make the best possible decisions for their country and for all mankind.

I do not mean to imply that all cohesive groups suffer from groupthink, though all may display its symptoms from time to time. Nor should we infer from the term "groupthink" that group decisions are typically inefficient or harmful. On the contrary, a group whose members have properly defined roles, with traditions and standard operating procedures that facilitate critical inquiry, is probably capable of making better decisions than any individual in the group who works on the problem alone. And yet the advantages of having decisions made by groups are often lost because of psychological pressures that arise when the members work closely together, share the same values, and above all face a crisis situation in which everyone is subjected to stresses that generate a strong need for affiliation. In these circumstances, as conformity pressures begin to dominate, groupthink and the attendant deterioration of decision-making set in.

The central theme of my analysis can be summarized in this generalization, which I offer in the spirit of Parkinson's laws: *The more amiability and esprit de corps among the members of a policy-making in-group, the greater is the danger that independent critical thinking will be replaced by groupthink, which is likely to result in irrational and dehumanizing actions directed against out-groups.*

2

A Perfect Failure:
The Bay of Pigs

leads to missile crisis
conversion ? Cuba to Soviet base

The Kennedy administration's Bay of Pigs decision ranks among the worst fiascoes ever perpetrated by a responsible government. Planned by an overambitious, eager group of American intelligence officers who had little background or experience in military matters, the attempt to place a small brigade of Cuban exiles secretly on a beachhead in Cuba with the ultimate aim of overthrowing the government of Fidel Castro proved to be a "perfect failure." The group that made the basic decision to approve the invasion plan included some of the most intelligent men ever to participate in the councils of government. Yet all the major assumptions supporting the plan were so completely wrong that the venture began to founder at the outset and failed in its earliest stages.

The "ill-starred adventure"

Ironically, the idea for the invasion was first suggested by John F. Kennedy's main political opponent, Richard M. Nixon. As Vice President during the Eisenhower administration, Nixon had proposed that the United States government secretly send a trained group of Cuban exiles to Cuba to fight against Castro. In March 1960, acting on Nixon's suggestion, President Dwight D. Eisenhower directed the Central Intelligence Agency to organize Cuban exiles in the United States into a unified political movement against the Castro regime and to give military training to those who were willing to return to their homeland to engage in guerrilla warfare. The CIA put a large number of its agents to work on this clandestine operation, and they soon evolved an elaborate plan for a military invasion. Apparently without informing President Eisenhower, the CIA began to assume in late 1960 that they could land a brigade of Cuban exiles not as a band of guerrilla infiltrators but as an armed force to carry out a full-scaled invasion.

Two days after the inauguration in January 1961, President John F. Kennedy and several leading members of his new administration were given a detailed briefing about the proposed invasion by Allen Dulles, head of the CIA, and General Lyman Lemnitzer, chairman of the Joint Chiefs of Staff. During the next eighty days, a core group of presidential advisers repeatedly discussed this inherited plan informally and in the meetings of an advisory committee that included three Joint Chiefs of Staff. In early April 1961, at one of the meetings with the President, all the key advisers gave their approval to the CIA's invasion plan. Their deliberations led to a few modifications of details, such as the choice of the invasion site.

On April 17, 1961, the brigade of about fourteen hundred Cuban exiles, aided by the United States Navy, Air Force, and the CIA, invaded the swampy coast of Cuba at the Bay of Pigs. Nothing went as planned. On the first day, not one of the four ships containing reserve ammunition and supplies arrived; the first two were sunk by a few planes in Castro's air force, and the other two promptly fled. By the second day, the brigade was completely surrounded by twenty thousand troops of Castro's well-equipped army. By the third day, about twelve hundred members of the brigade, comprising almost all who had not been killed, were captured and ignominiously led off to prison camps.

In giving their full approval, President Kennedy, Dean Rusk, Robert McNamara, and other high-level policy-makers in the United States government had assumed that "use of the exile brigade would make possible the toppling of Castro without actual aggression by the United States." The President's main advisers certainly did not expect such an overwhelming military disaster. Nor did they anticipate that the United States government's attempts to disclaim responsibility for the initial air assault would be thoroughly discredited, that friendly Latin American countries would be outraged, that protest meetings would be held in the United States and throughout the world to denounce the United States for its illegal acts of aggression against a tiny neighbor, that intellectuals who had regarded the new administration with bright hopes would express disaffection in sarcastic telegrams ("Nixon or Kennedy: Does it make any difference?"), or that European allies and United Nations statesmen would join in condemnation. None of them guessed that the abortive invasion would encourage a military rapprochement between Castro and the Soviet leaders, culminating in a deal to set up installations only ninety miles from United States shores equipped with nuclear bombs and missiles and manned by more than five thousand Soviet troops, transforming Cuba within eighteen months into a powerful military base as a satellite of the Soviet Union. Had the President and his policy advisers imagined that this nightmarish scenario would materialize (or had they even considered such an outcome to be a calculated risk), they undoubtedly would have rejected the CIA's invasion plan.

We are given a vivid picture of the President's reactions in Sorensen's *Kennedy,* described by a *New York Times* reviewer as "the nearest thing we will ever have to the memoirs Kennedy intended to write." When the first news reports revealed how wrong his expectations had been, President Kennedy was stunned. As the news grew worse during the next three days, he became angry and sick at heart. He realized that the plan he thought he had approved had little in common with the one he had in fact approved. "How could I have been so stupid to let them go ahead?" he asked. Sorensen wrote, "His anguish was doubly deepened by the knowledge that the rest of the world was asking the same question."

Arthur Schlesinger, Jr., in his authoritative history of the Kennedy administration, recalled that "Kennedy would sometimes refer incredulously to the Bay of Pigs, wondering how a rational and responsible government could ever have become involved in so ill-starred an adventure." The policy advisers who participated in the deliberations felt much the same way, if not worse. Allen Dulles, for example, was "still troubled and haggard" several days later and offered to resign as chief of the CIA. Secretary of Defense McNamara, when he left the government seven years later, publicly stated that he still felt personally responsible for having misadvised President Kennedy on the Bay of Pigs. All who participated in the Bay of Pigs decision were perturbed about the dangerous gap between their expectations and the realities they should have anticipated, which resulted, as Sorensen put it, in "a shocking number of errors in the whole decision-making process."

Qualifications of the core members of the advisory group

It seems improbable that the shocking number of errors can be attributed to lack of intellectual capability for making policy judgments. The core members of Kennedy's team who were briefed on the Cuban invasion plan included three cabinet members and three men on the White House staff, all of whom were well qualified to make objective analyses of the pros and cons of alternative courses of action on vital issues of government policy.

Dean Rusk, Secretary of State, had been recruited by John F. Kennedy from his high-level position as head of the Rockefeller Foundation because of his solid reputation as an experienced administrator who could be counted on to have good ideas and sound judgment. He had served in policy-making positions in the State Department under Dean Acheson, first as head of the office of political affairs and later as deputy undersecretary in charge of policy coordination. During the Truman administration, Rusk became a veteran policymaker and exerted a strong influence on a variety of important decisions concerning United States foreign policy in Asia.

Robert McNamara, the Secretary of Defense, was an expert statistician who had worked his way up to the presidency of the Ford Motor Company. He enjoyed a towering reputation for his intellectual brilliance and cold logic combined with personal integrity. Early in his career he had been on the faculty of the Harvard Business School. Later he developed his expertise in the statistical control unit of the United States Air Force, where he helped to work out a successful system for surveillance and control to facilitate decision-making about the flow of materials and production. During his years at Ford Motor Company, McNamara had also devised new techniques for improving rational methods of decision-making.

Then, too, there was Robert Kennedy, the Attorney General, one of the most influential members of the President's team. According to his close associates in the government, the President's brother was a bright young man whose strengths far outweighed his weaknesses. The Attorney General had been briefed on the invasion plan from the beginning. He did not attend the entire series of formal meetings of the advisory committee but was brought in as an active participant about four or five days before the President made his final decision. During that week, according to his memorandum dictated six weeks later, "I attended some meetings at the White House. Afterwards I said to Jack that I thought that . . . based on the information that had been given to him . . . there really wasn't any alternative to accepting it." On one occasion during that same crucial week, he used his personal influence to suppress opposition to the CIA plan.

Also on hand was McGeorge Bundy, the President's Special Assistant for National Security Affairs, who had the rank of a cabinet member. A key man on Kennedy's White House team, Bundy was one of the leading intellectuals imported to Washington from Harvard University, where he had been Dean of Arts and Sciences. His background in decision-making was not limited to the problems of a great university; earlier in his career, as a scholar, he had made a close study of Secretary of State Acheson's decisions.

The White House staff also included Arthur Schlesinger, Jr., an outstanding Harvard historian whom the President asked to attend all the White House meetings on the invasion plan, and Richard Goodwin, another Harvard man "of uncommon intelligence." Goodwin did not attend the policy-making meetings but was informed about the invasion plan, discussed it frequently with Schlesinger, and conferred with Rusk and others during the weeks preceding the final decision.

The President asked five of the six members of this core group to join him at the White House meetings of the ad hoc advisory committee on the Cuban invasion plan. At these meetings, Kennedy's advisers found themselves face-to-face with three Joint Chiefs of Staff, in full, medaled regalia. These military men were carry-overs from the Eisenhower administration; throughout the deliberations, they remained quite detached from the Kennedy team. Also present at the meetings of the advisory committee were five others who had fairly close ties to the President and his main advisers. Two of the most active participants were the director and deputy director of the CIA, Allen Dulles and Richard Bissell. They, too, were carry-overs from the Eisenhower administration, but President Kennedy and his inner circle welcomed them as members of the new administration's team. According to

President Kennedy meeting in the Oval Office with two key
members of his advisory group, Secretary of Defense Robert
McNamara and Secretary of State Dean Rusk.

Roger Hilsman (director of the intelligence branch of the State Department), Bissell "was a brilliant economist and government executive whom President Kennedy had known for years and so admired and respected that he would very probably have made him Director of the CIA when Dulles eventually retired." Bissell was the most active advocate of the CIA plan; his eloquent presentations did the main job of convincing the conferees to accept it.

Three others who participated in the White House meetings as members of the advisory committee were exceptionally well qualified to appraise the political consequences of the invasion: Thomas C. Mann, assistant secretary of state for inter-American affairs; Adolph A. Berle, Jr., chairman of the Latin American task force; and Paul Nitze, assistant secretary of defense, who had formerly been the director of the policy planning staff in the State Department.

The group that deliberated on the Bay of Pigs decision included men of considerable intellectual talent. Like the President, all the main advisers were shrewd thinkers, capable of objective, rational analysis, and accustomed to speaking their minds. But collectively they failed to detect the serious flaws in the invasion plan.

Six major miscalculations

The President and his key advisers approved the Bay of Pigs invasion plan on the basis of six assumptions, each of which was wrong. In retrospect, the President's advisers could see that even when they first began to discuss the plan, sufficient information was available to indicate that their assumptions were much too shaky. They could have obtained and used the crucial information beforehand to correct their false assumptions if at the group meetings they had been more critical and probing in fulfilling their advisory roles.

Assumption number 1: No one will know that the United States was responsible for the invasion of Cuba. Most people will believe the CIA cover story, and skeptics can easily be refuted.

When President Kennedy was first told about the plan by the CIA representatives, he laid down one firm stipulation: The United States armed forces would not overtly participate in an invasion of Cuba. He repeated this essential condition each time the matter was discussed. He would not consider accepting the CIA's plan to use the armed Cuban brigade unless it could be safely assumed that the United States government would not be held responsible for initiating a military attack against its small neighbor. On the assumption that this requirement could be met, the plan was seen as a golden opportunity to overthrow Castro. The Castro regime had been a source of irritation to the United States government, even though the President and his advisers did not consider it a direct threat to American security.

In response to the President's questions about the plan, Allen Dulles and Richard Bissell assured Kennedy and his advisory group that all the world would believe that Cuban dissidents were the sole initiators and executors of the invasion. They said that highly effective precautions would mask completely the fact that the United States was engineering the invasion. The brigade of Cuban exiles would be quietly and unspectacularly landed in their homeland. The only noisy part would be the preliminary air attacks against Cuban airfields, but these would be handled by a clever cover story. The United States would be able to deny all complicity in the bombing of Cuban bases. The planes used in the bombing raids would be B-26s of World War II vintage, without any United States markings. They would look like planes in Castro's air force and could plausibly be claimed to belong to Cuban defectors.

During the weeks preceding the invasion, it became increasingly apparent that the cover story would not work. The President's press secretary, Pierre Salinger, has called the plan "the least covert military operation in history." A week before the invasion, President Kennedy complained heatedly, "I can't believe what I'm reading! Castro doesn't need agents over here. All he has to do is read our papers. It's all laid out for him." American newsmen had gotten wind of the invasion plan. They were reporting "secret" details about what was going on in United States military training camps in Guatemala, where the Cubans were being readied for the invasion, and describing efforts being made in Miami to recruit more Cuban volunteers. Yet, according to Schlesinger, "somehow the idea took hold around the cabinet table that this would not much matter so long as United States soldiers did not take part in the actual fighting."

Thus, despite evidence at hand, the policy-makers ignored the old adage that one must expect any secret known to a large number of people to leak out. Apparently they never discussed the obvious danger that a secret act of military aggression against a neighboring country might be revealed by one or more insiders, particularly when the invasion plan was known to hundreds of Cuban exiles who were being recruited and trained to carry it out. It was also known to a large number of foreign politicians, who might have had their own reasons for revealing it. Leaders of the Cuban exiles' political movements (each of whom had his own ideas about what should be done), government officials in Guatemala (who had allowed the CIA to set up camps to train the Cuban brigade), and officials in Nicaragua (who had agreed to allow the United States to use Nicaraguan air bases to launch air attacks against Cuba)—all knew what was being planned. Furthermore, members of the policy-making group were warned on several occasions by Senator J. William Fulbright, chairman of the Foreign Relations Committee, and by other prestigious men that an invasion attempt would probably be attributed directly to the United States and would seriously damage United States relations with Latin American countries and European allies. Despite all warnings, the members of Kennedy's advisory group failed to question the assumption that the secret would not be revealed. President Kennedy was so confident that he publicly promised at a press conference on April 12, 1961 (five days before the invasion), that "there will not be, under any conditions, any intervention in Cuba by United States armed forces, and this Government will do everything it possibly can . . . to make sure that there are no Americans involved in actions inside Cuba."

The world did not immediately learn that the first invaders to land on Cuban soil were, in fact, United States Navy frogmen (in violation of the President's orders), but the United States nevertheless was blamed for the invasion from the outset. The CIA's cover story was quickly torn to pieces by the world press. The credibility of Adlai Stevenson, the United States representative to the United Nations, was also sacrificed, despite President Kennedy's solemn statement to his intimates only a few days earlier that "the integrity and credibility of Adlai Stevenson constitute one of our great national assets. I don't want anything to be done [in handling the cover story] which might jeopardize that." The truth having been carefully withheld from him, Stevenson solemnly denied United States complicity in the bombings at a meeting of the United Nations General Assembly. His statements were immediately seen by foreign observers as inconsistent with news reports about the air attacks and were soon labeled outright lies when some of his alleged facts were disproved twenty-four hours later by authentic photographs. Stevenson later said that this was the most humiliating experience of his long years of public service.

Assumption number 2:   The Cuban air force is so ineffectual that it can be knocked out completely just before the invasion begins.

The invasion plan called for a surprise attack by American bombers, which would destroy Castro's air force on the ground before the invaders moved in. The conferees at the White House thought that the obsolete B-26s used to do the job would be able to destroy Cuba's military planes. They did not make sufficient inquiries to find out that these lumbering old planes would have limited capabilities and would frequently develop engine trouble. The first attack was a surprise, but only a small percentage of Cuba's planes was destroyed. Consequently, the invasion plan went awry at the outset because the Cuban air force was able to assert air control over the landing site. Cuban jet training planes, which were fast and efficient, prevented the freighters containing ammunition and supplies from reaching their destination. The supposedly ineffective Cuban air force shot down half of the American B-26s attempting to protect the invaders and repeatedly bombed the ground troops as they arrived on shore.

A second air strike by United States planes was called off by President Kennedy because it would have revealed too clearly that the planes belonged to the United States and that the entire invasion was an unprovoked attack by the United States. But even if the second air strike had been carried out, it would probably have been even less effective than the first, because there was no longer any element of surprise and the Cuban air force was well dispersed in hidden airfields.

Assumption number 3:   The fourteen hundred men in the brigade of Cuban exiles have high morale and are willing to carry out the invasion without any support from United States ground troops.

In line with his firm policy of no direct intervention by the United States, President Kennedy explicitly asked the CIA planners if the members of the Cuban exile brigade were willing to risk their lives without United States military participation. The President and his advisers were given a strong affirmative answer, and Dulles and Bissell repeatedly assured them that morale in the brigade was superb. Had the conferees asked the CIA representatives to present evidence supporting this assurance, they might have discovered that they were relying on biased information. CIA agents in Guatemala were sending reports conveying a rosy overall picture to Dulles and Bissell without informing them about exactly what was going on. In order to build morale, the agents deliberately misled the men in the exile brigade by assuring them that they were only a small part of the invading force, that other Cuban brigades were being trained elsewhere for the same mission, that diversionary landings would draw most of Castro's troops away from their invasion site, and that the United States Marines would be participating in the invasion. Furthermore, one month before the invasion, when the policy-making group in Washington was being assured about the magnificent morale of the exile brigade, the men were actually bitterly discontent and beginning to revolt. They objected to being saddled with officers who had been in the army of the reactionary Batista regime and had been recruited and promoted because of their willingness to take orders from CIA agents. When discontent finally broke out in a full-scale mutiny, the CIA agents arrested a dozen of the ringleaders and confined them in a prison camp deep in the Guatemala jungle. Such was the high morale of the exile brigade.

Ironically, one of the most convincing "demonstrations" of high morale to President Kennedy and his advisers was the fact that sons of the political leaders of the Cuban exiles volunteered for the brigade. But both the fathers and the sons had been hoaxed by CIA agents into believing that the invasion would not be allowed to fail, that the United States government was committed to using armed forces to back them up.

When the invasion took place, the men in the brigade fought well, and their morale was sustained for a time by false hope. They thought that despite all the official "propaganda" put out by the United States government to the contrary, a large number of American troops would land to reinforce them. They had also been led to expect that American ships would bring them the supplies they so urgently needed and would remain offshore to rescue them if necessary.

Assumption number 4: Castro's army is so weak that the small Cuban brigade will be able to establish a well-protected beachhead.

Another question frequently discussed by President Kennedy and his advisers was whether the small exile brigade could achieve its initial goal of establishing a firm beachhead without United States military participation. Again, without looking into the evidence, the conferees accepted the optimistic picture presented by Dulles and Bissell, who described Castro's army as poorly equipped, poorly trained, riddled with dissension, and unable to cope with even a small-scale invasion. These assurances happened to be directly contrary to reports of Castro's military strength by experts in the State Department and in the British Intelligence Service. The CIA planners chose to ignore the experts' reports, and Kennedy's policy advisers did not pursue their questions far enough to become aware of the contradictory estimates, which would have revealed the shakiness of the CIA's assumptions.

As it turned out, Castro's army responded promptly and vigorously to the invasion, even though the invaders fought well. A militia patrol, guarding the coastline because of the invasion alert, was on hand to shoot at the vanguard of the invading force the Navy frogmen sent out to mark the landing site. Soon large numbers of well-equipped Cuban troops were shelling the beachhead with 122 mm howitzers, 37 mm cannons, and rocket-throwers. Cuban armored tanks began moving in within one day after the invaders landed. By the following day, the exile brigade was surrounded by twenty thousand well-equipped Cuban troops, backed up by more than two hundred thousand troops and militiamen who could have been brought to bear if needed.

Having grossly underestimated Castro's military capabilities, President Kennedy and his advisers belatedly realized that a successful beachhead could not be established in Cuba without a military force at least ten times larger than the one they had agreed to send in. According to Sorensen: "The President thought he was approving a plan rushed into execution on the grounds that Castro would later acquire the military capability to defeat it. Castro, in fact, already possessed that capability."

Assumption number 5: The invasion by the exile brigade will touch off sabotage by the Cuban underground and armed uprisings behind the lines that will effectively support the invaders and probably lead to the toppling of the Castro regime.

When first asked by President Kennedy to appraise the CIA's invasion plans, the Joint Chiefs of Staff asserted that the chances for successfully establishing a beachhead were favorable but that "ultimate success would depend on either a sizeable uprising inside the island or sizeable support from outside." Since American intervention was ruled out by the President, victory would depend on anti-Castro resistance and uprisings behind the lines. A second appraisal by the Joint Chiefs of Staff, just one month before the invasion, made this assumption explicit. Without the support of the Cuban resistance, they reported, there would be no way to overcome the hundreds of thousands of men in Castro's army and militia.

Although skeptical at first about relying on mass insurrection against the Castro regime, President Kennedy was encouraged by his advisory group to set his doubts aside, and he ended up accepting the assumption. Shortly after the Bay of Pigs debacle, he told Sorensen that he had really thought there was a good chance that the landing of the exile brigade, without overt United States participation, would rally the Cuban people to revolt and oust Castro. According to Schlesinger, this view was shared by Kennedy's closest advisers: "We all in the White House considered uprisings behind the lines essential to the success of the operation; so, too, did the Joint Chiefs of Staff; and so, we thought, did the CIA."

Once again the CIA spokesmen had misled the other conferees in the White House by neglecting to say that they were aware of strong reasons for not going along with this assumption. As advocates of the CIA plan, Allen Dulles and Richard Bissell confined their remarks almost entirely to the positive side of the picture. They relayed the unsubstantiated reports of their secret agents claiming that more than twenty-five hundred people were in the resistance organization in Cuba, that at least twenty thousand more were sympathizers, and that CIA contacts inside Cuba were requesting a large number of arms drops.

Long after events had shown that the assumption of a Cuban uprising was completely mistaken, Allen Dulles revealed that from the beginning the CIA had not expected much support from the Cuban resistance. In fact, the CIA had no intelligence estimates that the landing would touch off widespread revolt in Cuba. The intelligence branch of the agency had not been asked to estimate the chances of an invasion's being supported by the resistance movement or by popular uprisings behind the lines. Nor were any of the experts on the Cuban desk of the State Department, who kept a daily surveillance of political activities in Cuba, asked for their judgments. Most of the participants in the White House meetings did not know this and simply assumed that the estimates mentioned by Dulles and Bissell had the full authority of the government's intelligence agency behind them.

Had the policy advisers asked more penetrating questions, some of the excluded experts might have been consulted. In the absence of impartial briefings by nonpartisan experts on Cuba, no one reminded the group of the results of a carefully conducted poll, reported in the preceding year, that had shown that the overwhelming majority of Cubans supported the Castro regime. These poll results had been circulated throughout the United States government and were generally believed to indicate relatively little hope of inducing widespread action against Castro inside Cuba. This evidence was either forgotten or ignored by the political experts in the advisory group.

Even a few skeptical questions put to Dulles or Bissell might have corrected gross misconceptions. The President and his advisers might have learned that the CIA planners realized (without mentioning it in their briefings) that the pre-invasion air strike would allow Castro plenty of time to move against the underground and to round up political dissidents. This was a necessary sacrifice, the CIA men had decided, in order to knock out Castro's air force.

The lack of detailed questioning about these matters is remarkable when we consider that President Kennedy started off with strong misgivings about the amount of anti-Castro support that could be mustered on the island. His misgivings were shared by at least one other member of his White House staff. Arthur Schlesinger, Jr., in the memorandum he gave the President during the crucial week of decision, stated his doubts about uprisings behind the lines and argued that there was no convincing evidence that mass revolt would be touched off or that Castro's regime was so weak that it could be toppled by the exiles' landing. He warned that if the brigade established a secure foothold in Cuba, the operation would at best lead to a protracted civil war and then Congressmen and other influential politicans in the United States would demand that we intervene by sending in the Marines. Others, including a well-informed journalist just returned from Cuba who was invited to the White House, made similar pessimistic forecasts. Apparently none of these dissenting views was taken seriously enough by the President or his advisers to lead them to ask the intelligence community for an objective assessment of the effectiveness of the Cuban resistance.

Within twenty-four hours after the first air strikes, it became apparent that there would be no sabotage or rebellion and that Castro's regime had the domestic situation firmly in hand. Just as had been expected by the CIA (but not by the main body of the policy-making group), the Cuban police force was alerted by the initial air strike and moved swiftly against internal sources of resistance. In Havana alone, some two hundred thousand political suspects were promptly rounded up. Elsewhere in Cuba anyone suspected of having underground connections was jailed. Even organized resistance units that were already armed and waiting for a favorable opportunity to strike out against Castro's regime were ineffective, initiating only sporadic incidents of token resistance.

The Revolutionary Council composed of exiled political leaders of the Cuban resistance movement, who were supposed to set up the new democratic government after the beachhead was established, complained bitterly after the invasion that no effort had been made to coordinate the invasion with underground activities. They said that the CIA in Cuba had failed to provide supplies for organized resistance units, thus preventing them from executing long-standing plans to cut power lines and blow up factories. The CIA was also charged with gross negligence for ignoring the armed guerrillas in the Escambray Mountains, for not using the channels available for contacting underground groups throughout the island, and for sending in their own unknown agents, who succeeded only in confusing the entire underground movement. Sorensen concludes that there was no cooperation between the planners and the Cuban underground because the CIA mistrusted the exiled left-wing leaders, just as the right-wing leaders supported by the CIA were mistrusted by most members of the underground. Consequently, "No coordinated uprising or underground effort was really planned or possible." The members of the White House advisory group might have found all this out in advance if they had been sufficiently vigilant to require the CIA representatives to present full details about their plans (or lack of plans) for mobilizing the resistance movement in Cuba.

> *Assumption number 6: If the Cuban brigade does not succeed in its prime military objective, the men can retreat to the Escambray Mountains and reinforce the guerrilla units holding out against the Castro regime.*

A major reason for approving the CIA's plan was the decision-makers' expectation that even if the invasion failed to establish a new goverment in Cuba, there would still be a net gain. At worst, the invaders would join up with the rebels in the Escambray Mountains and strengthen the anti-Castro forces on the island; so in one way or another the Cuban exiles, who were already showing signs of unrest about getting back to their homeland in order to fight against the Castro regime, supposedly would be put to good use. Dulles and Bissell, when summarizing the CIA's plan, told the advisory group on more than one occasion that the entire operation was safe because the invaders could, if necessary, escape from the beaches into the mountains. President Kennedy and others in the group were greatly reassured by this argument.

Toward the end of their deliberations, any qualms the policy advisers may have had about the mission were put to rest. They believed the CIA was planning a small invasion (rather than a large-scale amphibious assault) that would enable the brigade of exiles to infiltrate the mountains. But they never had the most relevant information, which they could have obtained. The essential facts contradicted the reassuring view that was being conveyed to the group. Evidently none of the policy-makers at the White House meetings asked to be fully briefed.

After the fiasco was over, President Kennedy and his advisers learned for the first time that the CIA officers in charge of the operation in Guatemala had not planned for an escape to the mountains and had discontinued training for guerrilla warfare long before most of the Cuban exiles in the brigade had started their training. In any case, the escape to the Escambray Mountains was a realistic backstop only as long as the plan called for landing at Trinidad, near the foothills of the mountains. When, as a result of the deliberations of the White House advisory group, Trinidad was judged too conspicuous and was replaced by the Bay of Pigs, there was no possibility that the invaders could retreat to the mountains. Schlesinger acknowledges that he and the others attending the White House meetings simply overlooked the geography of Cuba: "I don't think we fully realized that the Escambray Mountains lay 80 miles from the Bay of Pigs, across a hopeless tangle of swamps and jungle.'' This oversight might have been corrected if someone in the advisory group had taken the trouble to look at a map of Cuba, available in any atlas.

The cost of sending an invading force without an escape route soon became measurable in human lives as well as in dollars and cents. Within two days after landing on the shores of Cuba, the men in the brigade found themselves completely surrounded and learned for the first time that they had no option but to be killed or captured. Twenty months later, Castro struck a hard bargain with the United States State Department and allowed the twelve hundred men who had been imprisoned to be released for the ransom price of $53 million in food and drugs.

The suffering of the twelve hundred imprisoned men and the ransom money were only part of the losses sustained because of the policy-makers' false assumption that the invaders could easily join guerrillas in the mountains. Had they learned beforehand that there would be no way of escaping from the beaches, President Kennedy's advisers might not have been so complacent about the net gain they were expecting, and they might have decided to drop the entire invasion plan.

Why did the advisory group fail?

Why so many miscalculations? Couldn't the six false assumptions have been avoided if the advisory group had sought fuller information and had taken it into account? Some of the grossest errors resulted from faulty planning and communication within the CIA.[1] The agency obviously had its own serious defects, but they do not concern us in the present inquiry. Nor are we going to try to unravel the complicated reasons for the Joint Chiefs' willingness to endorse the CIA's plan.[2] The central question is: Why did the President's main advisers, whom he had selected as core members of his team, fail to pursue the issues sufficiently to discover the shaky ground on which the six assumptions rested? Why didn't they pose a barrage of penetrating and embarrassing questions to the representatives of the CIA and the Joint Chiefs of Staff? Why were these men taken in by the incomplete and inconsistent answers they were given in response to the relatively few critical questions they raised? Schlesinger says that ''for all the utter irrationality with which retrospect endowed the project, it had a certain queer logic at the time as it emerged from the bowels of government.'' Why did the President's policy advisers fail to evaluate the plan carefully enough to become aware of ''its utter irrationality''? What was the source of the ''queer logic'' with which the plan was endowed?

Even with the apparently unqualified endorsement of the military sector of the United States government, the six assumptions behind the Bay of Pigs invasion were not so abstruse that military expertise was needed to evaluate

Santa Clara

LAS VILLAS

Trinidad

SIERRA DEL ESCAMBRAY

Cienfuegos

CUBA

MATANZAS

ZAPATA

Bahía de Cochinos

PENÍNSULA DE

Matanzas

CARIBBEAN SEA

CUBA

BAY OF PIGS
(Bahía de Cochinos)

Prisoners captured by Castro's militia during the Bay of Pigs
attempt to invade Cuba. These men were among twelve hundred prisoners taken by Castro's forces who were later ran-
somed by the United States government for $53 million in
food and drugs.

Even a schematic map of Cuba reveals that the Sierra del
Escambray would not be an accessible place of retreat for invaders who land in the region of Bahia de Cochinos. (The
symbols representing three blades of grass, shown throughout
the Peninsula de Zapata, designate swamp lands.)

them realistically. Sorensen points out that a communication gap between the military and civilian sectors of Kennedy's administration led to a gap between the concept of the Cuban invasion and actuality:

> With hindsight it is clear that what in fact [the President] had approved was diplomatically unwise and militarily doomed from the outset. What he thought he was approving appeared at the time to have diplomatic acceptability and little chance of outright failure. That so great a gap between concept and actuality should exist at so high a level on so dangerous a matter reflected a shocking number of errors in the whole decision-making process.

But why did the *civilian* policy advisers—especially the core group of key cabinet members and White House staff—fail to close the gaps by picking to pieces the faulty assumptions? They did not put Dulles and Bissell through the kind of cross-examination that would have required the two men to reveal the inadequacies of their estimates and to go back to their agency to seek out better information. They did not make adequate use of the military and political experts who sat with them on the advisory committee. The Joint Chiefs of Staff could have been encouraged to spell out the military pros and cons of the invasion plan and to state their misgivings; the three State Department officials could have been encouraged to do the same about the chances for armed uprisings inside Cuba and the prospects of a provisional government's mobilizing popular support for the overthrow of the Castro regime.

Schlesinger acknowledges that because no one voiced any opposition at the meetings of the advisory committee, the members of the White House staff—himself included—"failed in their job of protecting the President," and "the representatives of the State Department failed in defending the diplomatic interests of the nation."

The official explanation

Why did the brilliant, conscientious men on the Kennedy team fail so dismally? The answers given by Schlesinger, Sorensen, Salinger, Hilsman, and other knowledgeable insiders include four major factors, which evidently correspond closely with the reasons John F. Kennedy mentioned in postmortem discussions with leading members of the government.

Factor number 1: political calculations

When presenting the invasion plan, the representatives of the CIA, knowingly or unknowingly, used a strong political appeal to persuade the Kennedy administration to take aggressive action against the Castro regime. The President was asked, in effect, whether he was as willing as the Republicans to help the Cuban exiles fight against the Communist leadership in Cuba. If he did nothing, the implication was that Castro was free to spread his brand of communism throughout Latin America.

The political consequences were especially obvious when the CIA representatives called attention to the so-called disposal question: What can we do with a trained brigade of Cuban exiles who are clamoring to get back to Cuba? The problem seemed particularly acute because the Guatemalan government had become embarrassed about the publicity the exiles were receiving and had asked that the men be removed. If we don't send them to invade Cuba, Allen Dulles in effect told the advisory committee, we will have to transfer them to the United States. He declared, "We can't have them wandering around the country telling everyone what they have been doing." Obviously they would spread the word, loud and clear, that Kennedy had prevented them from trying to overthrow Castro's dictatorship, and Kennedy might be accused of being soft on communism when it became known that he scuttled an anti-Castro operation. Furthermore, Castro would soon receive jets from the Soviet Union, and Cuban pilots were being trained in Czechoslovakia to fly them. Once the new planes arrived, a successful amphibious landing by the exile brigade would no longer be possible. After June 1, 1961, according to the CIA, the massive power of the United States Marines and Air Force would be required for a successful invasion of Cuba. Anyhow, the invasion could not be postponed for long because the rainy season was coming. This was the last chance for a purely Cuban invasion, and if Kennedy postponed it he would be seen as hampering the anti-Communist exiles who wanted to return to their homeland to fight for a democratic Cuba.

Factor number 2: *a new administration bottled in an old bureaucracy*

Slightly less than three months elapsed between the day the ill-fated CIA plan was presented to the leading members of the new administration and the day the CIA operatives tried to carry it out. The pressures to arrive at a decision during those early months of the Kennedy administration came when the President and his senior advisers were still developing their decision-making procedures, before they were fully familiar with each other, with their respective roles, and with the ways of circumventing bureaucratic obstacles that make obtaining relevant information difficult. The new cabinet members and the White House staff had high esprit de corps but had not reached the point where they could talk frankly with each other without constant concern about protocol and deferential soft-pedaling of criticism. Kennedy himself did not yet know the strengths and weaknesses of his newly appointed advisers. For example, the President did not realize, as he did later, that the new Secretary of State was inclined to defer to the military experts and to withhold his objections to Defense Department toughness in order to avoid charges of State Department softness. Nor had he yet learned that it was wrong to assume, as he put it later, "that the military and intelligence people have some secret skill not available to ordinary mortals."

Factor number 3:   secrecy—to the point of excluding the experts

As happens with many other vital decisions involving military action, the clandestine nature of the plan to invade Cuba precluded using the usual government channels for shaping a foreign policy decision. Ordinarily, all relevant agencies would have been allowed to study the proposed course of action, suggest alternatives, and evaluate the pros and cons of each alternative. Bureaucratic requirements of secrecy are likely to exclude from decision-making many of the most relevant experts. When the Bay of Pigs invasion was being planned, at least two groups of experts in the United States government were not consulted—those in the intelligence branch of the CIA and on the Cuban desk in the State Department. Schlesinger commented:

> The same men . . . both planned the operation and judged its chances of success. . . . The "need-to-know" standard—i.e., that no one should be told about a project unless it becomes operationally necessary—thus had the idiotic effect of excluding much of the expertise of government at a time when every alert newspaper man knew something was afoot.

The requirements of secrecy even extended to the printed matter distributed to the inner circle of policy-makers. The memoranda handed out by the CIA and Joint Chiefs of Staff at the beginning of each session were collected at the end. This made it impossible for the participants to ponder over the arguments and to check out details by collecting information from resources available in their own offices. In short, the expert judgment of the policy-makers who participated in the Bay of Pigs decision was impaired by the secrecy imposed.

Factor number 4:   threats to personal reputation and status

Government policy-makers, like most executives in other organizations, hesitate to object to a policy if they think their forthright stand might damage their personal status and political effectiveness. This is sometimes referred to as the effectiveness trap. In his account of the Bay of Pigs fiasco, Schlesinger admits that he hesitated to bring up his objections while attending the White House meetings for fear that others would regard it as presumptuous for him, a college professor, to take issue with august heads of major government institutions.

Is the official explanation complete?

Do these four factors fully explain the miscalculations that produced the invasion decision? It seems to me that they do not. Because of a sense of incompleteness about the explanation, I looked for other causal factors in the sphere of group dynamics. After studying Schlesinger's analysis of the Bay of Pigs fiasco and other authoritative accounts, I still felt that even all four factors operating at full force simultaneously could hardly have given rise to such a faulty decision. Perhaps the four-factor explanation would be plausible if the policy advisers had met hurriedly only once or twice and had had only a few days to make their decision. But they had the opportunity to meet many times and to think about the decision for almost three months.

Here are the main reasons for this judgment:

1. The political pressures mainly stemmed from the realization that the Kennedy administration might be accused of having prevented the Cuban exiles from carrying out an invasion against the pro-Communist government of Cuba. But if Kennedy and his advisers had examined the six assumptions carefully enough to see how faulty they were, wouldn't they have realized that permitting the Bay of Pigs fiasco to materialize would be at least as embarrassing, both at home and abroad? Moreover, even if the political pressure centering on disposing of the trained exile brigade was an overriding consideration, we are still left with a puzzling question: Why didn't the policy-makers explore some of the obvious alternatives for solving the disposal question without resorting to a full-scale invasion? They might have negotiated for another camp elsewhere in Central America and allowed the exile brigade to infiltrate Cuba in small groups, going to landing places where they could easily join up with the guerrilla units in the mountains. Evidently this solution to the disposal problem, which would have had less damaging political repercussions than the all-out versus all-off alternatives that were considered, was never seriously examined.

2. Although the Kennedy administration was indeed new, most of the men who participated in the decision were old hands at policy-making. How probable is it that R. Kennedy, Bundy, McNamara, Rusk, Berle, and Nitze would suppress their objections and risk allowing the nation to suffer a grave setback merely because they were uncertain about the proper way to behave? Moreover, isn't it improbable that all these men would share Kennedy's naive assumption—which he undoubtedly was expressing in greatly exaggerated form—that the military had special skill unavailable to other assessors of the invasion plan? Some of the false assumptions on which the plan was based—such as keeping United States involvement a secret—were more political than military, and the advisers knew that in these matters they had more expertise than the military men. Most likely, R. Kennedy, Bundy, McNamara, and the top State Department officials concluded that nothing really important was wrong with the invasion plan. Otherwise, regardless of their new roles and other considerations that might have made them hesitate to communicate their objections, at one of the many sessions in which the invasion plan was discussed they would undoubtedly have managed to call attention to the unacceptable grounds for the assumptions on which it rested.

3. Many experts in the government were certainly excluded in a futile effort to keep the plan secret. But wouldn't the President's key advisers have in-

sisted on consulting their own experts if they had carefully inspected the shaky grounds on which the CIA planners were basing their judgments? A few incisive questions about the evidence for the CIA planners' estimates of Castro's military and political strength might have quickly revealed that they were relaying uninformed estimates made without consulting the intelligence experts in their own agency or in the State Department. Wouldn't the President and his advisers then have realized that there was "a need for them to know," and wouldn't experts have been asked to provide the policy-makers with an objective appraisal? With the experts excluded, outside criticism of the CIA's plan was kept to a minimum. But why was there so little criticism from inside the group of high-level government officials who were sufficiently expert to evaluate at least some, if not all, of the assumptions?

4. Even the highest government officials may become concerned about potential damage to their status and future effectiveness that might result from criticizing a plan proposed by the military. Still, it was by no means clear that agreeing to the plan would be more advantageous than calling attention to gaps in the CIA's rationale and raising valid objections. If any advisers had realized that the invasion was going to be a fiasco, wouldn't they also have realized that acquiescing would be much more damaging to their reputation than raising critical questions to force the others, however reluctantly, to reexamine their assumptions? Would the policy advisers remain silent at meeting after meeting if they thought the President was being misled into making a stupid decision, damaging to his administration and to the country as a whole? When given the responsibility of forming a judgment about vital matters of national policy, such men are not likely to be intimidated by vague threats of damage to their careers. Moreover, the four members of the Kennedy team who had worked with the President before and during the election campaign—Bundy, Schlesinger, Goodwin, and Robert Kennedy—would not have felt such constraints when they talked among themselves about the plan to invade Cuba. They knew the President well enough to realize that he valued fresh viewpoints and independent thinking, that he was ready to change his mind in response to strong arguments, and that he would support them against backbiting from anyone in the executive branch on whose toes they might be stepping.

Sensitized by my dissatisfaction with the four-factor explanation, I noticed in Schlesinger's account of what the policy-makers said to each other during and after the crucial sessions numerous signs of group dynamics in full operation. From studying this material I arrived at the groupthink hypothesis.

Groupthink does not replace the four-factor explanation of the faulty decision; rather, it supplements the four factors and perhaps gives each of them added cogency in the light of group dynamics. It seems to me that if groupthink had not been operating, the other four factors would not have been sufficiently powerful to hold sway during the months when the invasion decision was being discussed.[3]

Symptoms of groupthink among President Kennedy's advisers

According to the groupthink hypothesis, members of any small cohesive group tend to maintain esprit de corps by unconsciously developing a number of shared illusions and related norms that interfere with critical thinking and reality testing. If the available accounts describe the deliberations accurately, typical illusions can be discerned among the members of the Kennedy team during the period when they were deciding whether to approve the CIA's invasion plan.

The illusion of invulnerability

An important symptom of groupthink is the illusion of being invulnerable to the main dangers that might arise from a risky action in which the group is strongly tempted to engage. Essentially, the notion is that "If our leader and everyone else in our group decides that it is okay, the plan is bound to succeed. Even if it is quite risky, luck will be on our side." A sense of "unlimited confidence" was widespread among the "New Frontiersmen" as soon as they took over their high government posts, according to a Justice Department confidant, with whom Robert Kennedy discussed the secret CIA plan on the day it was launched:

> It seemed that, with John Kennedy leading us and with all the talent he had assembled, *nothing could stop us.* We believed that if we faced up to the nation's problems and applied bold, new ideas with common sense and hard work, we would overcome whatever challenged us.

That this attitude was shared by the members of the President's inner circle is indicated by Schlesinger's statement that the men around Kennedy had enormous confidence in his ability and luck: "Everything had broken right for him since 1956. He had won the nomination and the election against all the odds in the book. Everyone around him thought he had the Midas touch and could not lose." Kennedy and his principal advisers were sophisticated and skeptical men, but they were, nevertheless, "affected by the euphoria of the new day." During the first three months after he took office—despite growing concerns created by the emerging crisis in Southeast Asia, the gold drain, and the Cuban exiles who were awaiting the go-ahead signal to invade Cuba—the dominant mood in the White House, according to Schlesinger, was "buoyant optimism." It was centered on the "promise of hope" held out by the President: *"Euphoria reigned; we thought for a moment that the world was plastic and the future unlimited."*

All the characteristic manifestations of group euphoria—the buoyant optimism, the leader's great promise of hope, and the shared belief that the group's accomplishments could make "the future unlimited"—are strongly reminiscent of the thoughts and feelings that arise among members of many different types of groups during the phase when the members become cohesive. At such a time, the members become somewhat euphoric about their newly acquired "we-feeling"; they share a sense of belonging to a powerful, protective group that in some vague way opens up new potentials for each of them. Often there is boundless admiration of the group leader.

Once this euphoric phase takes hold, decision-making for everyday activities, as well as long-range planning, is likely to be seriously impaired. The members of a cohesive group become very reluctant to carry out the unpleasant task of critically assessing the limits of their power and the real losses that could arise if their luck does not hold. They tend to examine each risk in black and white terms. If it does not seem overwhelmingly dangerous, they are inclined simply to forget about it, instead of developing contingency plans in case it materializes. The group members know that no one among them is a superman, but they feel that somehow the group is a supergroup, capable of surmounting all risks that stand in the way of carrying out any desired course of action: "Nothing can stop us!" Athletic teams and military combat units may often benefit from members' enthusiastic confidence in the power and luck of their group. But policy-making committees usually do not.

We would not expect sober government officials to experience such exuberant esprit de corps, but a subdued form of the same tendency may have been operating—inclining the President's advisers to become reluctant about examining the drawbacks of the invasion plan. In group meetings, this groupthink tendency can operate like a low-level noise that prevents warning signals from being heeded. Everyone becomes somewhat biased in the direction of selectively attending to the messages that feed into the members' shared feelings of confidence and optimism, disregarding those that do not.

When a cohesive group of executives is planning a campaign directed against a rival or enemy group, their discussions are likely to contain two themes, which embody the groupthink tendency to regard the group as invulnerable: (1) "We are a strong group of good guys who will win in the end." (2) "Our opponents are stupid, weak, bad guys." It is impressive to see how closely the six false assumptions fit these two themes. The notion running through the assumptions is the overoptimistic expectation that "we can pull off this invasion, even though it is a long-shot gamble." The policy advisers were probably unaware of how much they were relying on shared rationalizations in order to appraise the highly risky venture as a safe one. Their overoptimistic outlook would have been rudely shaken if they had allowed their deliberations to focus on the potentially devastating consequences of the obvious drawbacks of the plan, such as the disparity in size between Castro's military forces of two hundred thousand and the small brigade of fourteen hundred exiles. In a sense, this difference made the odds against their long-shot gamble 200,000 to 1,400 (over 140 to 1).

When discussing the misconceptions that led to the decision to approve the CIA's plan, Schlesinger emphasizes the gross underestimation of the enemy. Castro was regarded as a weak "hysteric" leader whose army was ready to defect; he was considered so stupid that "although warned by air strikes, he would do nothing to neutralize the Cuban underground." This is a stunning example of the classical stereotype of the enemy as weak and ineffectual.

In a concurrence-seeking group, there is relatively little healthy skepticism of the glib ideological formulas on which rational policy-makers, like many other people who share their nationalistic goals, generally rely in order to maintain self-confidence and cognitive mastery over the complexities of international politics. One of the symptoms of groupthink is the members' persistence in conveying to each other the cliché and oversimplified images of political enemies embodied in long-standing ideological stereotypes. Throughout their deliberations they use the same old stereotypes, instead of developing differentiated concepts derived from an open-minded inquiry enabling them to discern which of their original ideological assumptions, if any, apply to the foreign policy issue at hand. Except in unusual circumstances of crisis, the members of a concurrence-seeking group tend to view any antagonistic out-group against whom they are plotting not only as immoral but also as weak and stupid. These wishful beliefs continue to dominate their thinking until an unequivocal defeat proves otherwise, whereupon—like Kennedy and his advisers—they are shocked at the discrepancy between their stereotyped conceptions and actuality.

A subsidiary theme, which also involved a strong dose of wishful thinking, was contained in the Kennedy group's notion that "we can get away with our clever cover story." When the daily newspapers were already demonstrating that this certainly was not so, the undaunted members of the group evidently replaced the original assumption with the equally overoptimistic expectation that "anyhow, the non-Communist nations of the world will side with us. After all, we *are* the good guys."

Overoptimistic expectations about the power of their side and the weakness of the opponents probably enable members of a group to enjoy a sense of low vulnerability to the effects of any decision that entails risky action against an enemy. In order to maintain this complacent outlook, each member must think that everyone else in the group agrees that the risks can be safely ignored.[4]

The illusion of unanimity

When a group of people who respect each other's opinions arrive at a unanimous view, each member is likely to feel that the belief must be true. This reliance on consensual validation tends to replace individual critical thinking and reality-testing, unless there are clear-cut disagreements among the members. The members of a face-to-face group often become inclined, without quite realizing it, to prevent latent disagreements from surfacing when they are about to initiate a risky course of action. The group leader and the members support each other, playing up the areas of convergence in their thinking, at the expense of fully exploring divergences that might disrupt the apparent unity of the group. Better to share a pleasant, balmy group atmosphere than to be battered in a storm.

This brings us to the second outstanding symptom of groupthink manifested by the Kennedy team—a shared illusion of unanimity. In the formal sessions dealing with the Cuban invasion plan, the group's consensus that the basic features of the CIA plan should be adopted was relatively free of disagreement.

According to Sorensen, "No strong voice of opposition was raised in any of the key meetings, and no realistic alternatives were presented." According to Schlesinger, "the massed and caparisoned authority of his senior officials in the realm of foreign policy and defense was unanimous for going ahead. . . . Had one senior advisor opposed the adventure, I believe that Kennedy would have canceled it. No one spoke against it."

Perhaps the most crucial of Schlesinger's observations is, "Our meetings took place in a *curious atmosphere of assumed consensus.*" His additional comments clearly show that the assumed consensus was an illusion that could be maintained only because the major participants did not reveal their own reasoning or discuss their idiosyncratic assumptions and vague reservations. President Kennedy thought that prime consideration was being given to his prohibition of direct military intervention by the United States. He assumed that the operation had been pared down to a kind of unobtrusive infiltration that, if reported in the newspapers, would be buried in the inside pages. Rusk was certainly not on the same wavelength as the President, for at one point he suggested that it might be better to have the invaders fan out from the United States naval base at Guantánamo, rather than land at the Bay of Pigs, so that they could readily retreat to the base if necessary. Implicit in his suggestion was a lack of concern about revealing United States military support as well as implicit distrust in the assumption made by the others about the ease of escaping from the Bay of Pigs. But discussion of Rusk's strange proposal was evidently dropped long before he was induced to reveal whatever vague misgivings he may have had about the Bay of Pigs plan. At meetings in the State Department, according to Roger Hilsman, who worked closely with him, "Rusk asked penetrating questions that frequently caused us to reexamine our position." But at the White House meetings Rusk said little except to offer gentle warnings about avoiding excesses.

As usually happens in cohesive groups, the members assumed that "silence gives consent." Kennedy and the others supposed that Rusk was in substantial agreement with what the CIA representatives were saying about the soundness of the invasion plan. But about one week before the invasion was scheduled, when Schlesinger told Rusk in private about his objections to the plan, Rusk, surprisingly, offered no arguments against Schlesinger's objections. He said that he had been wanting for some time to draw up a balance sheet of the pros and cons and that he was annoyed at the Joint Chiefs because "they are perfectly willing to put the President's head on the block, but they recoil at doing anything which might risk Guantánamo." At that late date, he evidently still preferred his suggestion to launch the invasion from the United States naval base in Cuba, even though doing so would violate President Kennedy's stricture against involving America's armed forces.

McNamara's assumptions about the invasion were quite different from both Rusk's and Kennedy's. McNamara thought that the main objective was to touch off a revolt of the Cuban people to overthrow Castro. The members of the group who knew something about Cuban politics and Castro's popular support must have had strong doubts about this assumption. Why did they fail to convey their misgivings at any of the meetings?

Suppression of personal doubts

The sense of group unity concerning the advisability of going ahead with the CIA's invasion plan appears to have been based on superficial appearances of complete concurrence, achieved at the cost of self-censorship of misgivings by several of the members. From post-mortem discussions with participants, Sorensen concluded that among the men in the State Department, as well as those on the White House staff, "doubts were entertained but never pressed, partly out of a fear of being labelled 'soft' or undaring in the eyes of their colleagues." Schlesinger was not at all hesitant about presenting his strong objections in a memorandum he gave to the President and the Secretary of State. But he became keenly aware of his tendency to suppress objections when he attended the White House meetings of the Kennedy team, with their atmosphere of assumed consensus:

> In the months after the Bay of Pigs I bitterly reproached myself for having kept so silent during those crucial discussions in the Cabinet Room, though my feelings of guilt were tempered by the knowledge that a course of objection would have accomplished little save to *gain me a name as a nuisance*. I can only explain my failure to do more than raise a few timid questions by reporting that one's impulse to blow the whistle on this nonsense was simply undone by the *circumstances of the discussion*.

Whether or not his retrospective explanation includes all his real reasons for having remained silent, Schlesinger appears to have been quite aware of the need to refrain from saying anything that would create a nuisance by breaking down the assumed consensus.[5]

Participants in the White House meetings, like members of many other discussion groups, evidently felt reluctant to raise questions that might cast doubt on a plan that they thought was accepted by the consensus of the group, for fear of evoking disapproval from their associates. This type of fear is probably not the same as fear of losing one's effectiveness or damaging one's career. Many forthright men who are quite willing to speak their piece despite risks to their career become silent when faced with the possibility of losing the approval of fellow members of their primary work group. The discrepancy between Schlesinger's critical memoranda and his silent acquiescence during the meetings might be an example of this.

Schlesinger says that when the Cuban invasion plan was being presented to the group, "virile poses" were conveyed in the rhetoric used by the representatives of the CIA and Joint Chiefs of Staff. He thought the State Department representatives and others responded by becoming anxious to show that they were not softheaded idealists but really were just as tough as the military men. Schlesinger's references to the "virile" stance of the militant advocates of the invasion plan suggest that the members of Kennedy's in-group may have been concerned about protecting the leader from being embarrassed by their voicing "unvirile" concerns about the high risks of the venture.

At the meetings, the members of Kennedy's inner circle who wondered whether the military venture might prove to be a failure or whether the political consequences might be damaging to the United States must have had only mild misgivings, not strong enough to overcome the social obstacles that would make arguing openly against the plan slightly uncomfortable. By and large, each of them must have felt reasonably sure that the plan was a safe one, that at worst the United States would not lose anything from trying it. They contributed, by their silence, to the lack of critical thinking in the group's deliberations.

Self-appointed mindguards

Among the well-known phenomena of group dynamics is the alacrity with which members of a cohesive in-group suppress deviational points of view by putting social pressure on any member who begins to express a view that deviates from the dominant beliefs of the group, to make sure that he will not disrupt the consensus of the group as a whole. This pressure often takes the form of urging the dissident member to remain silent if he cannot match up his own beliefs with those of the rest of the group. At least one dramatic instance of this type of pressure occurred a few days after President Kennedy had said, "we seem now destined to go ahead on a quasi-minimum basis." This was still several days before the final decision was made.

At a large birthday party for his wife, Robert Kennedy, who had been constantly informed about the Cuban invasion plan, took Schlesinger aside and asked him why he was opposed. The President's brother listened coldly and then said, "You may be right or you may be wrong, but the President has made his mind up. Don't push it any further. Now is the time for everyone to help him all they can." Here is another symptom of groupthink, displayed by a highly intelligent man whose ethical code committed him to freedom of dissent. What he was saying, in effect, was, "You may well be right about the dangerous risks, but I don't give a damn about that; all of us should help our leader right now by not sounding any discordant notes that would interfere with the harmonious support he should have."

When Robert Kennedy told Schlesinger to lay off, he was functioning in a self-appointed role that I call being a "mindguard." Just as a bodyguard protects the President and other high officials from injurious physical assaults, a mindguard protects them from thoughts that might damage their confidence in the soundness of the policies to which they are committed or to which they are about to commit themselves.

At least one other member of the Kennedy team, Secretary of State Rusk, also effectively functioned as a mindguard, protecting the leader and the members from unwelcome ideas that might set them to thinking about unfavorable consequences of their preferred course of action and that might lead to dissension instead of a comfortable consensus. Undersecretary of State Chester Bowles, who had attended a White House meeting at which he was given no opportunity to express his dissenting views, decided not to continue to remain silent about such a vital matter. He prepared a strong memorandum for Secretary Rusk opposing the CIA plan and, keeping well within the prescribed bureaucratic channels, requested Rusk's permission to present his case to the President. Rusk told Bowles that there was no need for any concern, that the invasion plan would be dropped in favor of a quiet little guerrilla infiltration. Rusk may have believed this at the time, but at subsequent White House meetings he must soon have learned otherwise. Had Rusk transmitted the undersecretary's memorandum, the urgent warnings it contained might have reinforced Schlesinger's memorandum and jolted some of Kennedy's in-group, if not Kennedy himself, to reconsider the decision. But Rusk kept Bowles' memorandum firmly buried in the State Department files.

Rusk may also have played a similar role in preventing Kennedy and the others from learning about the strong objections raised by Edward R. Murrow, whom the President had just appointed director of the United States Information Agency. In yet another instance, Rusk appears to have functioned as a dogged mindguard, protecting the group from the opposing ideas of a government official with access to information that could have enabled him to assess the political consequences of the Cuban invasion better than anyone present at the White House meetings could. As director of intelligence and research in the State Department, Roger Hilsman got wind of the invasion plan from his colleague Allen Dulles and strongly warned Secretary Rusk of the dangers. He asked Rusk for permission to allow the Cuban experts in his department to scrutinize thoroughly the assumptions relevant to their expertise. "I'm sorry," Rusk told him, "but I can't let you. This is being too tightly held." Rusk's reaction struck Hilsman as strange because all the relevant men in his department already had top security clearance. Hilsman assumed that Rusk turned down his urgent request because of pressure from Dulles and Bissell to adhere to the CIA's special security restrictions. But if so, why, when so much was at stake, did the Secretary of State fail to communicate to the President or to anyone else in the core group that his most trusted intelligence expert had grave doubts about the invasion plan and felt that it should be appraised by the Cuban specialists? As a result of Rusk's handling of Hilsman's request, the President and his advisers remained in the curious position, as Hilsman put it, of making an important political judgment without the benefit of advice from the government's most relevant intelligence experts.

Taking account of the mindguard functions performed by the Attorney General and the Secretary of State, together with the President's failure to allow time for discussion of the few oppositional viewpoints that occasionally did filter into the meetings, we surmise that some form of collusion was going on. That is to say, it seems plausible to infer that the leading civilian members of the Kennedy team colluded—perhaps unwittingly—to protect the proposed plan from critical scrutiny by themselves and by any of the government's experts.

Docility fostered by suave leadership

The group pressures that help to maintain a group's illusions are sometimes fostered by various leadership practices, some of which involve subtle ways of making it difficult for those who question the initial consensus to suggest alternatives and to raise critical issues. The group's agenda can readily be manipulated by a suave leader, often with the tacit approval of the members, so that there is simply no opportunity to discuss the drawbacks of a seemingly satisfactory plan of action. This is one of the conditions that fosters groupthink.

President Kennedy, as leader at the meetings in the White House, was probably more active than anyone else in raising skeptical questions; yet he seems to have encouraged the group's docility and uncritical acceptance of the defective arguments in favor of the CIA's plan. At each meeting, instead of opening up the agenda to permit a full airing of the opposing considerations, he allowed the CIA representatives to dominate the entire discussion. The President permitted them to refute immediately each tentative doubt that one of the others might express, instead of asking whether anyone else had the same doubt or wanted to pursue the implications of the new worrisome issue that had been raised.

Moreover, although the President went out of his way to bring to a crucial meeting an outsider who was an eloquent opponent of the invasion plan, his style of conducting the meeting presented no opportunity for discussion of the controversial issues that were raised. The visitor was Senator J. William Fulbright. The occasion was the climactic meeting of April 4, 1961, held at the State Department, at which the apparent consensus that had emerged in earlier meetings was seemingly confirmed by an open straw vote. The President invited Senator Fulbright after the Senator had made known his concern about newspaper stories forecasting a United States invasion of Cuba. At the meeting, Fulbright was given an opportunity to present his opposing views. In a "sensible and strong" speech Fulbright correctly predicted many of the damaging effects the invasion would have on United States foreign relations. The President did not open the floor to discussion of the questions raised in Fulbright's rousing speech. Instead, he returned to the procedure he had initiated earlier in the meeting; he had asked each person around the table to state his final judgment and after Fulbright had taken his turn, he continued the straw vote around the table. McNamara said he approved the plan. Berle was also for it; his advice was to "let her rip." Mann, who had been on the fence, also spoke in favor of it.

Picking up a point mentioned by Berle, who had said he approved but did not insist on "a major production," President Kennedy changed the agenda by asking what could be done to make the infiltration more quiet. Following discussion of this question—quite remote from the fundamental moral and political issues raised by Senator Fulbright—the meeting ended. Schlesinger mentions that the meeting broke up before completion of the intended straw vote around the table. Thus, wittingly or unwittingly, the President conducted the meeting in such a way that not only was there no time to discuss the potential dangers to United States foreign relations raised by Senator Fulbright, but there was also no time to call upon Schlesinger, the one man present who the President knew strongly shared Senator Fulbright's misgivings.

Of course, one or more members of the group could have prevented this by-passing by suggesting that the group discuss Senator Fulbright's arguments and requesting that Schlesinger and the others who had not been called upon be given the opportunity to state their views. But no one made such a request.

The President's demand that each person, in turn, state his overall judgment, especially after having just heard an outsider oppose the group consensus, must have put the members on their mettle. These are exactly the conditions that most strongly foster docile conformity to a group's norms. After listening to an opinion leader (McNamara, for example) express his unequivocal acceptance, it becomes more difficult than ever for other members to state a different view. Open straw votes generally put pressure on each individual to agree with the apparent group consensus, as has been shown by well-known social psychological experiments.

A few days before the crucial meeting of April 4, another outsider who might have challenged some of the group's illusions attended one of the meetings but was never given the opportunity to speak his piece. At the earlier meeting, the outsider was the acting Secretary of State, Chester Bowles, attending in place of Secretary Rusk, who was abroad at a SEATO conference. Like Senator Fulbright, Bowles was incredulous and at times even "horrified" at the group's complacent acceptance of the CIA's invasion plans. However, President Kennedy had no idea what Bowles was thinking about the plan, and he probably felt that Bowles was there more in the role of a reporter to keep Rusk up to date on the deliberations than as a participant in the discussion. In any case, the President neglected to give the group the opportunity to hear the reactions of a fresh mind; he did not call upon Bowles at any time. Bowles sat through the meeting in complete silence. He felt he could not break with formal bureaucratic protocol, which prevents an undersecretary from volunteering his opinion unless directed to do so by his chief or by the President. Bowles behaved in the prescribed way and confined his protestations to a State Department memorandum addressed to Rusk, which, as we have seen, was not communicated to the President.

An additional bit of information about Bowles' subsequent career seems to fit in with all of this, from the standpoint of group psychology. During the bitter weeks following the Bay of Pigs fiasco, Chester Bowles was the first man in the new administration to be fired by President Kennedy. Some of Bowles' friends had told the press that he had opposed the Cuban venture and had been right in his forecasts about the outcome. Evidently this news annoyed the President greatly. Bowles' opponents in the administration pointed out that even if Bowles had not leaked the story to the press, he had discussed the matter with his friends at a time when it would embarrass the White House. This may have contributed to the President's solution to the problem of what to do about the inept leadership of the inefficient State Department bureaucracy. He decided to shift Bowles out of his position as second-in-command, instead of replacing Rusk, whom he liked personally and wanted to keep as a central member of his team. "I can't do that to Rusk," Kennedy later said when someone suggested shifting Rusk to the United Nations. "He is such a *nice* man."

During the Bay of Pigs planning sessions, President Kennedy, probably unwittingly, allowed the one-sided CIA memoranda to monopolize the attention of the group by failing to circulate opposing statements that might have stimulated an intensive discussion of the drawbacks and might therefore have revealed the illusory nature of the group's consensus. Although the President read and privately discussed the strongly opposing memoranda prepared by Schlesinger and Senator Fulbright, he never distributed them to the policy-makers whose critical judgment he was seeking. Kennedy also knew that Joseph Newman, a foreign correspondent who had just visited Cuba, had written a series of incisive articles that disagreed with forecasts concerning the ease of generating a revolt against Castro. But, although he invited Newman to the White House for a chat, he did not distribute Newman's impressive writings to the advisory group.

The members themselves, however, were partially responsible for the President's biased way of handling the meetings. They need not have been so acquiescent about it. Had anyone suggested to the President that it might be a good idea for the group to gain more perspective by studying statements of opposing points of view, Kennedy probably would have welcomed the suggestion and taken steps to correct his own-sided way of running the meetings.

The taboo against antagonizing valuable new members

It seems likely that one of the reasons the members of the core group accepted the President's restricted agenda and his extraordinarily indulgent treatment of the CIA representatives was that a kind of informal group norm had developed, producing a desire to avoid saying anything that could be construed as an attack on the CIA's plan. The group apparently accepted a kind of taboo against voicing damaging criticisms. This may have been another important factor contributing to the group's tendency to indulge in groupthink.

How could such a norm come into being? Why would President Kennedy give preferential treatment to the two CIA representatives? Why would Bundy, McNamara, Rusk, and the others on his team fail to challenge this preferential treatment and accept a taboo against voicing critical opposition? A few clues permit some conjectures to be made, although we have much less evidence to go on than for delineating the pattern of preferential treatment itself.

It seems that Allen Dulles and Richard Bissell, despite being holdovers from the Eisenhower administration, were not considered outsiders by the inner core of the Kennedy team. President Kennedy and his closest associates did not place these two men in the same category as the Joint Chiefs of Staff, who were seen as members of an outside military clique established during the earlier administration, men whose primary loyalties belonged elsewhere and whose presence at the White House meetings was tolerated as a necesary requirement of governmental protocol. (Witness Secretary Rusk's unfriendly comments about the Joint Chiefs being more loyal to their military group in the Pentagon than to the President, when he was conversing privately with fellow in-group member Schlesinger.) President Kennedy and those in his inner circle admired Dulles and Bissell, regarded them as valuable new members of the Kennedy team, and were pleased to have them on board. Everyone in the group was keenly aware of the fact that Bissell had been devoting his talents with great intensity for over a year to developing the Cuban invasion project and that Dulles was also deeply committed to it. Whenever Bissell presented his arguments, "we all listened transfixed," Schlesinger informs us, "fascinated by the workings of this superbly clear, organized and articulate intelligence." Schlesinger reports that Bissell was regarded by the group as "a man of high character and remarkable intellectual gifts." In short, he was accepted as a highly prized member.

The sense of power of the core group was probably enhanced by the realization that the two potent bureaucrats who were in control of America's extensive intelligence network were affiliated with the Kennedy team. The core members of the team would certainly want to avoid antagonizing or alienating them. They would be inclined, therefore, to soft-pedal their criticisms of the CIA plan and perhaps even to suspend their critical judgment in evaluating it.

The way Dulles and Bissell were treated by President Kennedy and his associates after their plan had failed strongly suggests that both men continued to be fully accepted as members of the Kennedy team during the period of crisis generated by their unfortunate errors. According to Sorensen, Kennedy's regard for Richard Bissell did not change after the Bay of Pigs disaster, and he regretted having to accept Bissell's resignation. When Dulles submitted his resignation, President Kennedy urged him to postpone it and asked him to join a special commission to investigate the causes of the fiasco. During the days following the defeat, Kennedy refrained from openly criticizing either Bissell or Dulles (this must have required considerable restraint). On one occasion when a mutual friend of Dulles and Kennedy told the President self-righteously that he was deliberately going to avoid seeing the CIA director, Kennedy went out of his way to support Dulles by inviting him for a drink and ostentatiously putting his around him in the presence of the would-be ostracizer. This is a typical way for a leader of a cohesive group to treat one of the members who is temporarily "in the dog house."

The picture we get, therefore, is that the two CIA representatives, both highly esteemed men who had recently joined the Kennedy team, were presenting their "baby" to the rest of the team. As protagonists, they had a big head start toward eliciting a favorable consensus. New in-group members would be listened to much more sympathetically and much less critically than outsiders representing an agency that might be trying to sell one of its own pet projects to the new President.

Hilsman, who also respected the two men, says that Dulles and Bissell "had become emotionally involved . . . so deeply involved in the development of the Cuban invasion plans that they were no longer able to see clearly or to judge soundly." He adds, "There was so deep a commitment, indeed, that there was an unconscious effort to confine consideration of the proposed operation to as small a number of people as possible, so as to avoid too harsh or thorough a scrutiny of the plans." If Hilsman is correct, it is reasonable to assume that the two men managed to convey to the other members of the Kennedy team their strong desire "to avoid too harsh or thorough a scrutiny."[6]

Whatever may have been the political or psychological reasons that motivated President Kennedy to give preferential treatment to the two CIA chiefs, he evidently succeeded in conveying to the other members of the core group, perhaps without realizing it, that the CIA's "baby" should not be treated harshly. His way of handling the meetings, particularly his adherence to the extraordinary procedure of allowing every critical comment to be immediately refuted by Dulles or Bissell without allowing the group a chance to mull over the potential objections, probably set the norm of going easy on the plan, which the two new members of the group obviously wanted the new administration to accept. Evidently the members of the group adopted this norm and sought concurrence by continually patching the original CIA plan, trying to find a better version, without looking too closely into the basic arguments for such a plan and without debating the questionable estimates sufficiently to discover that the whole idea ought to be thrown out.

Conclusion

Although the available evidence consists of fragmentary and somewhat biased accounts of the deliberations of the White House group, it nevertheless reveals gross miscalculations and converges on the symptoms of groupthink. My tentative conclusion is that President Kennedy and the policy advisers who decided to accept the CIA's plan were victims of groupthink. If the facts I have culled from the accounts given by Schlesinger, Sorensen, and other observers are essentially accurate, the groupthink hypothesis makes more understandable the deficiencies in the government's decision-making that led to the enormous gap between conception and actuality.

The failure of Kennedy's inner circle to detect any of the false assumptions behind the Bay of Pigs invasion plan can be at least partially accounted for by the group's tendency to seek concurrence at the expense of seeking information, critical appraisal, and debate. The concurrence-seeking tendency was manifested by shared illusions and other symptoms, which helped the members to maintain a sense of group solidarity. Most crucial were the symptoms that contributed to complacent overconfidence in the face of vague uncertainties and explicit warnings that should have alerted the members to the risks of the clandestine military operation—an operation so ill conceived that among literate people all over the world the name of the invasion site has become the very symbol of perfect failure.

3

In and Out of North Korea:
"The Wrong War
with the Wrong Enemy"

Discuss

The decision to escalate the Korean War in the fall of 1950 by authorizing General MacArthur's victorious military forces to cross the 38th parallel in an attempt to occupy North Korea was the Truman administration's Bay of Pigs. It illustrates once again how responsible leaders of a democratic nation can support each other in making gross errors of judgment that have disastrous consequences. Victory soon turned into defeat when Communist China responded by entering the war.

In a detailed analysis of the United States policy-makers' deliberations concerning the occupation of North Korea, Alexander George, a well-known political scientist, points to a number of psychological as well as political factors that make the explanation of the miscalculation "complex and many-faceted":

> The momentum of events following MacArthur's landing at Inchon, the intoxication of success, domestic political considerations, and wishful thinking no doubt abetted the miscalculation. . . . But . . . intelligence appraisals [of Chinese Communist intentions] did not challenge sharply or early enough the widespread euphoria and optimism within the administration.

Granted that inadequate intelligence reports and other nonpsychological factors contributed to the faulty decision-making, we must still try to understand how sober policy-makers with long experience in responsible positions could succumb to "the intoxication of success," indulge in "wishful thinking," and collectively take enormous risks in a state of "euphoria and optimism." The groupthink hypothesis helps to account for this cluster of psychological factors.

President Truman's harmonious advisory group

On the night of June 24, 1950, the unexpected news that the North Koreans had invaded South Korea reached government leaders in Washington. The next day, the United States government announced that Americans would aid South Korea and would not appease the Communist aggressors. Thereafter, a creeping movement toward war took place day by day, as one little emergency decision after another was made to cope with the augmented crisis created by the piecemeal collapse of South Korea's military forces.

Throughout the initial week of crisis and during subsequent months, substantially the same group of government leaders met frequently to decide what to do about the war in Korea. The members of this policy-making group, headed by President Harry S. Truman, included Secretary of State Dean Acheson and the four ranking civilians in the Defense Department—Secretary of Defense Louis A. Johnson, who was replaced in September 1950 by General George C. Marshall, Secretary of the Army Frank Pace, Secretary of the Navy Francis P. Mathews, and Secretary of the Air Force Thomas K. Finletter. In addition, the meetings were usually attended by the four Joint Chiefs of Staff (Generals Omar N. Bradley, J. Lawton Collins, and Hoyt S. Vandenberg and Admiral Forrest J. Sherman) and by several undersecretaries and assistant secretaries from the State and Defense Departments. The key members of this ad hoc group of advisers were also members of the National Security Council, which had official responsibility for making policy recommendations to the President but which met less frequently.

During the first week of daily conferences to deal with the Korean War crisis, Truman's group of advisers developed a high degree of solidarity. Glen Paige, a political scientist who has made an intensive study of the group's first six meetings based largely on interviews of the members, calls attention to the "intra-group solidarity" at all the crisis meetings. He concludes that "one of the most striking aspects [of the set of decisions that committed the United States to fight in Korea] is the high degree of satisfaction and sense of moral rightness shared by the decision makers." Paige quotes one of the participants who described the general atmosphere of a meeting at which a major decision was made as "the finest spirit of harmony I have ever known." Every time they met during the first week of the crisis, according to Paige, the advisers agreed to a recommended course of action "with minimal conflict."

The members of the group continued to display esprit de corps and mutual admiration throughout the many months they worked together. It was a group of men who shared the same basic values and the dominant beliefs of the power elite of American society, particularly about the necessity for containing the expansion of "world communism" in order to protect the "free world."

Relations between the Joint Chiefs of Staff and the President's civilian

President Truman with two advisers who were greatly influen-
tial in the government deliberations over the issue of invading
North Korea—Secretary of Defense George C. Marshall and
Secretary of State Dean Acheson.

advisers were not strained, as they were during the early days of the Kennedy administration. The military and civilian advisers in Truman's group were not only mutually respectful but participated in the "fine spirit of harmony." In a case study of Acheson's role in the decision to occupy North Korea during the fall of 1950, political scientist David S. McLellan concludes that "General Bradley and other members of the JCS shared completely Acheson's view of grand strategy.... Bradley and the Joint Chiefs were so in accord with Truman and Acheson that they earned from Senator Taft the epithet of 'political' generals." On all the major Korean War decisions, including those made during the crucial days in early November 1950 when the group decided to ignore the ominous implications of intelligence information that correctly reported the presence of Communist Chinese military units in North Korea, the civilian advisers were in substantial agreement with the Joint Chiefs.

Indications of the favorable attitude of the military men toward the civilians in the group can be seen in General Collins' account of the Korean War (insofar as his personal assessments are representative of those of the other Joint Chiefs). General Collins expresses overall satisfaction that the recommendations made by the Joint Chiefs "carried considerable weight with the President, and with the Secretaries of State and Defense." The civilian within the group with whom General Collins worked most closely was Secretary of the Army Frank Pace; their relationship, he says, was characterized by "full understanding, mutual confidence and respect." Collins is unstinting in his praise of the civilian who was the group's leader. Referring to President Truman's leadership at conferences in which he participated, Collins asserts:

> I came to have tremendous admiration for this remarkable man.... He developed a rare talent for listening to his advisers in this field [foreign affairs] and quickly getting to the root of a problem. He was ever ready to hear both sides of a proposition and would balance them objectively and finally come up with a clear-cut, fearless decision.

After General Marshall joined the group, the Joint Chiefs could feel all the more secure about their role in the President's war councils because they had a Secretary of Defense with immense prestige who, unlike his immediate predecessors, was a military man and could fully understand their way of thinking. This advantage for the generals was not at the cost of increased concern among the State Department representatives and other civilian advisers who might be sensitive about the amount of influence wielded by the men in the Pentagon. All had immense respect for General Marshall and did not perceive him as a man who would allow his loyalty to the military establishment to dominate his judgment.

Harmony within the group was increased in another way when Louis Johnson was replaced by George Marshall. Before the outbreak of the Korean War, Johnson and Acheson had been feuding over United States policy toward China, and as a result the two men "disliked and distrusted each other personally." Early in the Korean War crisis these two core members of the

President's team carefully avoided quarreling and even praised each other publicly, presumably to avoid disrupting the group; but their truce was a superficial and fragile one. In his memoirs, Acheson says that in the fall of 1950 Johnson's behavior was so bizarre that he must have already been suffering from the brain disease that ultimately proved fatal. Johnson was dismissed from his post of Secretary of Defense when President Truman learned that he had been working with Republican opposition leaders who were launching a campaign to remove Acheson from office. With Marshall in the key position, Acheson was reunited with his "revered and beloved former chief," with whom he had worked closely during 1947–1949, when the general had served as Secretary of State. "No change," Acheson asserts, "could have been more welcome to me." Acheson describes General Marshall as a man "richly endowed," supreme in the "art . . . of judgment in its highest form"—not merely in military affairs but "in great affairs of State, which require both mastery of precise information and apprehension of imponderables." Above all, he was a leader "who compelled respect."

Perhaps the closest bond of all was between President Truman and Acheson. In their memoirs, written many years later, the two men showed no reticence about expressing their mutual admiration. Truman praised Acheson for his "keen mind, cool temper, and broad vision." After devoting two pages to refuting the "noisy clamor" of those who said he should have fired Acheson, Truman concluded: "History, I am sure, will list Dean Acheson among the truly great Secretaries of State our nation has had." Acheson returned the high compliment in his memoirs by telling his readers, in effect, that history will list Harry Truman among the truly great Presidents our nation has had. "Among the thirty-five men who have held the presidential office," Acheson solemnly predicts, "Mr. Truman will stand with the few who in the midst of great difficulties managed their offices with eminent benefit to the public interest." Elaborating on Harry Truman's qualities as a leader, Acheson asserts that the President evoked esprit de corps among his lieutenants. He compares the cheerful temperament of his Harry with England's great Harry, who five hundred years earlier had cheered his men before the battle of Agincourt. "His liberal eye doth give to every one . . . a little touch of Harry in the night," Shakespeare had written of Henry V. Acheson said of Truman:

> The "little touch of Harry," which kept all of us going, came from an inexhaustible supply of vitality and good spirits. . . .
> [He had the] qualities of a leader who builds esprit de corps. He expected, and received, the loyalty he gave. As only those close to him knew, Harry S. Truman was two men. One was the public figure—peppery, sometimes belligerent, often didactic, the "give-em-hell" Harry. The other was the patient, modest, considerate, and appreciative boss, helpful and understanding in all official matters, affectionate and sympathetic in any private worry or sorrow. This was the "Mr. President" we knew and loved.

Defective decision-making

Scholars disagree about the quality of the Truman administration's initial intervention decisions, made in June 1950, authorizing American military support to help South Korea resist the North Korean invaders. Some believe the United States policy-makers overcommitted themselves in Korea on the basis of miscalculations and without having adequately explored the alternatives to armed intervention. Others argue that the decision to intervene was basically sound under the circumstances, especially because of the mounting danger that countries in the Soviet bloc might seize control of neighboring nations in Europe as well as in Asia. But historians and political scientists seem to be in general agreement about the poor quality of the risky decision made several months later—the decision to authorize pursuit of the defeated North Korean army across the 38th parallel up to the border of Communist China. At the start of the war, United States policy had been to prevent the pro-Communist government of North Korea from conquering South Korea. The escalation decision authorized a large-scale American military effort, in the name of the United Nations, to conquer all North Korea so that the entire country could be placed under the control of the pro-American South Korean government. This policy switch from "containment" to "rolling back" was made in the face of repeated threats of military invervention by the Communist Chinese government. Truman and his advisers decided to ignore the risks and took a huge gamble, without quite realizing how high the stakes would be if they lost.

Within a few weeks after the escalation decision, disaster struck. On November 28, 1950, the Chinese attacked in massive force, inflicting a major defeat on United States troops, trapping entire units and compelling the rest to withdraw hastily. During the weeks that followed, MacArthur's forces were driven out of North Korea and were almost driven out of South Korea in "the longest retreat in American history." From this point on, the members of Truman's group attempted to undo their error, to avoid further provocation of China, and to limit the war in Korea as much as possible. And from this point on, the war in Korea was marked mainly by inconclusive advances and retreats followed by a frustrating stalemate, which had devastating political consequences for the Truman administration.[1]

After the Chinese Communists entered the war, just as they had repeatedly warned the United States they would do, General Bradley, chairman of the Joint Chiefs of Staff, summed up the disillusionment of American policy-makers. America, he said, was becoming embroiled "in the wrong war, at the wrong place, at the wrong time, and with the wrong enemy."

In *Presidential Power,* Richard Neustadt describes the Truman administration's decision to occupy North Korea as ill contrived and essentially opportunistic—"a passing fancy, taken and abandoned as the war news changed." The policy-makers glossed over the opportunistic aspect of their

American troops preparing to withdraw in the general retreat
when Chinese Communist troops unexpectedly entered the
war. This occurred in late fall of 1950, after the United States
government's fateful decision to pursue the North Korean
army across the 38th parallel up to the border of Communist
China.

new war aim of using military force to achieve a unified anti-Communist Korea by justifying their decision in terms of restoring peace and security in the name of the United Nations. During the summer and fall of 1950, the United States and its allies were able to dominate the voting in the United Nations General Assembly, which promptly passed one resolution after another promoted by American representatives. With scarcely any debate, the new aim of uniting Korea by military force was approved on October 7, 1950, in a United Nations resolution worded essentially as it had been hastily drafted by the U.S. State Department. The resolution was not well planned and did not take account of the risks that George Kennan had carefully outlined in a memorandum he had submitted to the Secretary of State. Acheson later admitted: "The trouble inherent in the resolution itself and in the encouragement it gave to General MacArthur's adventurism lay in the fact that it was not thought through and it masked in ambivalent language the difficulties and dangers against which Kennan had warned."

Truman and his group of advisers evidently had complete faith in the military soundness as well as the morality of the escalation decision. In part, their misplaced faith may have been the result of a semantic trap that they had baited themselves. According to Neustadt:

> In White House memoranda and in papers for the National Security Council, in intelligence evaluations, and the like, repeated use of such terms as "the UN objective," "the decision of the UN," "the UN's purpose to unify," soon dulled awareness that the new war aim was nothing but a target of opportunity chosen rather casually (and at first provisionally) by the very men who read these words. The tendency of bureaucratic language to create in private the same images presented to the public never should be underrated. By the middle of October [1950], I would say, in their minds no less than in public, Truman and the rest were thinking of the UN aim not as a mere convenience but as a cause.

Ignoring the risks

Some grave risks should have been apparent to Truman's advisers long before the group became committed to approving MacArthur's efforts to conquer North Korea. For more than two months, the Peking government had been waging a "hate America" campaign in the Chinese press. This may have been provoked by the Truman administration's decision in late June 1950 to send United States naval forces to protect Formosa from a possible assault by Communist China. The move appears to have been interpreted by Communist China as intervention tantamount to entering the Chinese civil war on the side of the Nationalist government of Chiang Kai-shek. In late September 1950, with American and other United Nations troops poised on the borders of North Korea, the Chinese began issuing explicit warnings, culminating in a belligerent statement on October 1 that China would not

① stand aside if MacArthur's forces crossed the 38th parallel. The warning was repeated on October 3, this time relayed to Washington through the Indian ambassador to China, who stated that "if the U.N. forces crossed the 38th parallel China would send in troops to help the North Koreans." In retrospect, Acheson admitted that "Chou's words relayed by Ambassador Panikkar were a warning, not to be disregarded." But at the time, the warning was wholly disregarded as a "bluff." All the other warnings, earlier ones and subsequent ones, were also dismissed by the members of Truman's advisory group as empty threats intended only for manipulative purposes.[2] Neustadt says, "With the military opportunity before them and with diplomatic dangers out of sight, the men he [Truman] leaned on for advice saw little risk of any sort." They decided that the time was ripe to eliminate Communist control of North Korea; they recommended escalating the defensive war to protect South Korea into a full-scale offensive war of conquest.

② When the Chinese leaders failed to deter the United States from occupying North Korea by their strong verbal threats of intervening, they resorted in early and mid-October to much more ominous warnings by sending into North Korea substantial Chinese forces, which engaged in tactical contact with South Korean and United States troops. But, incredibly, Truman's advisers encouraged the President to harden his commitment to the conquest of North Korea at a time when they wanted to avoid war with China at all costs.[3] They gave more discretion than ever to MacArthur, "a general whom the men in Washington had every reason to know was malevolent in his predisposition toward them, unreliable by virtue of his vanity, and hell-bent on a showdown with communism in Asia."

During late October and early November, when Chinese military units in large concentrations began to inflict heavy casualties on MacArthur's forces, Truman's advisers still failed to recommend any real change in the United States war policy, although their complacency was temporarily shaken. Acheson says in his memoirs:

> As I look back the critical period stands out as the three weeks from October 26 to November 17. Then all the dangers from dispersal of our own forces and intervention by the Chinese were manifest. We were all deeply apprehensive. We were frank with one another, but not quite frank enough.

That they were not quite apprehensive enough is indicated by their failure to take any realistic precautionary action. The only new decisions made during this critical period were to give the conventional verbal reassurances to representatives of the Chinese government about United States intentions to respect China's borders and to "explore" the possibility of negotiating a settlement, on the wishful assumption that the Chinese had mobilized their military might solely for the limited purpose of protecting their interests in the power facilities along the Yalu River. More worrisome assumptions were also discussed—including the possibility that the Chinese might be ready to enter all-out war at the risk of starting World War III—but the danger was not taken seriously enough to initiate any change in military policy. Although there was much talk about sending messages to MacArthur to induce him to display appropriate caution and restraint, no clear-cut change in his orders was issued, and he was allowed, at his own discretion, to advance to the border of Communist China.

George and Smoke assert that Truman's advisers were worried about the risk to MacArthur's forces not because they thought the Chinese might launch a massive offensive but because of other military considerations. Poor deployment had left United Nations troops vulnerable to enemy counterattacks. George and Smoke commented on the overoptimistic miscalculations of Truman's advisory group:

> It is not often that history is generous enough to provide policy-makers with several opportunities to correct initial mistakes in perception and judgment that would lead, if unchecked, to catastrophe. But in this case it was. . . . Until [the third week in November 1950] . . . Washington could have avoided the worst damage of the Chinese attack. . . .
>
> . . . the fact that days passed without any further sign of the Chinese forces strengthened in their [the administration leaders'] minds the sanguine possibility to which they had subscribed earlier, namely, that the Chinese had decided after all to restrict their intervention to minor activity.

The lack of realistic caution displayed by Truman's group of advisers during October and November 1950 cannot be attributed primarily to defective intelligence. From a study of the documents, political scientist H. A. de Weerd has concluded that although United States intelligence reports underestimated Chinese capabilities and intentions, the evidence available to the policy-makers was good enough to have made reasonably vigilant statesmen take seriously the threat of full-scale Chinese intervention: "It was not the absence of intelligence which led us into trouble but our unwillingness to draw unpleasant conclusions from it." This unwillingness is clearly shown by the changes in outlook that characterized the meetings of Truman's advisers during November 1950.

It is surprising, Joseph De Rivera points out in his psychological study of the Korean War decisions, that the group of decision-makers did not correct each other's oversights but instead "supported each other's beliefs in a manner that increased risk-taking." Secretary Acheson, the man upon whom President Truman relied most heavily for guidance, appreciated the dangers, according to De Rivera, but had his own reasons for feeling optimistic. Acheson failed to say anything to the President to counteract the illusions created by General MacArthur's glib assurances that America would soon be completely victorious, and none of the President's other advisers called his attention to the possible dangers because they all were "collaborating in an optimistic view of the situation." In emphasizing the mutual support for excessive risk-taking that the members of Truman's advisory group provided each other, De Rivera highlights one of the central themes of the present analysis—the tendency for cohesive groups to foster a shared illusion of invulnerability, which inclines them to minimize risks.

The mutual support for risk-taking, it seems to me, was part of a more general pattern of concurrence-seeking behavior, which also fosters uncritical acceptance of stereotypes of out-groups and a sense of unanimity about the wisdom and morality of past decisions. All the main components of this groupthink pattern can be discerned in the available accounts of the group's deliberations, particularly during the critical November days when the members knew that Communist China had started to intervene in the Korean War.

De Rivera describes the advisers' use of crude stereotyped conceptions of "communism" in their diagnoses of international relations in the Far East as an independent source of error in the deliberations of Truman's advisory group. But in terms of my analysis of the concurrence-seeking tendencies of cohesive groups, the failure of Truman's advisers to correct their stereotyped misconceptions can be linked with the group members' propensity for supporting each other in taking excessive risks.

Stereotyped conceptions of Red China and Russia

On the basis of his intensive analysis of documents, supplemented by discussions with Acheson and other State Department officials, McLellan concludes that the decision to authorize MacArthur's forces to advance to the borders of China "is a prime example of an American propensity to take the righteousness of its actions for granted and to ignore the objective reality which its behavior represents to others." Whether or not it is uniquely American, such a propensity can be expected to exert an overriding influence on policy advisers in a cohesive group, particularly when their deliberations are insulated from opposing judgments of qualified experts outside the group.

The views of the members of Truman's advisory group concerning Red China's military strength and intentions were based on ideological presuppositions that they shared with all other leading members of the administration and with many other Americans as well—financiers, corporation heads, newspaper editors, and a large proportion of common citizens in both the Democratic and Republican parties. Of course we must take it for granted that any group of national policy-makers, even when they are not indulging in groupthink, will strongly resist changing any of their fundamental ideological conceptions. Most resistant of all are their justifications for pursuing policies designed to win out over their rivals in the competitive struggle for international markets and for military power. Nevertheless, reasonably intelligent men like the policy advisers in Truman's group are not completely insensitive to the winds of historic change. At times, they can modify their rationalizations and surmount the limitations on their thinking about foreign policy issues imposed by the ideological assumptions to which they are committed. Intelligent national leaders are capable of modifying some of their misconceptions about rival nations when impressive evidence indicates that their notions may mislead them into inappropriate action that could result in severe military or economic losses and drastically interfere with attaining their long-term political goals.

However infrequent it may be for policy-makers to correct their misleading stereotypes and rationalizations, it is much rarer still when they are functioning as members of a cohesive group striving to maintain a uniformity of outlook. The objective assessment of relevant information and the rethinking necessary for developing more differentiated concepts can emerge only out of the crucible of heated debate, which is anathema to the members of a concurrence-seeking group. They tend to retain all the platitudinous stereotypes that fit in beautifully with the long-standing ideology of the political elite to which they belong.

One of the dominant stereotypes shared by all members of Truman's advisory group was that Red China was a weak nation, whose main source of potency in world affairs came from its affiliation with the Soviet Union, which meant that China's foreign policy was largely dominated by Russia. The members failed to take account of obvious indications that this oversimplified conception might not apply to Red China's possible responses to American troops in Korea. It contributed to their miscalculation of the risk of provoking a full-scale military response if the United States attempted to use its military power to gain control over China's neighbor and ally. The group members' failure to scrutinize their stereotyped misconception and to consider alternative hypotheses concerning Red China's capabilities and intentions is a prime symptom of groupthink.[4]

Even within the confines of their stereotyped conception of Soviet domination, the advisory group neglected to consider whether the Soviet Union could impose such total restraint that the Chinese leaders would be utterly incapable of putting any effective pressure on the Russians to allow them to take military action to counteract the encroachment of the hostile United States forces approaching their borders. McLellan points out that "all previous experience forewarned that Red China would not tolerate the presence of hostile U.S. forces in its backyard," but the pervasive ideological tendency "shared by Acheson and his critics alike" was to belittle China's position in the world. Acheson's image of China, *"quite at variance with the facts . . . was that of a docile puppet of Moscow without a will of its own."* That this unrealistic image was shared by the entire group of Truman's advisers is indicated by Neustadt's account of a crucial meeting during the second week of November, when the members had become concerned about the large number of Chinese troops engaging in battle with MacArthur's forces. Truman's advisers, according to Neustadt, thought that "Moscow . . . did not want general war; the Chinese, then, would have to show restraint."

Failure to correct misconceptions

In contrast to the key advisers who clung to the notion that Red China was a mere satellite of the Soviet Union, with no option but to accept United States encroachments, some government experts outside the in-group had quite different views. Within the State Department was George Kennan, a leading expert on the Soviet bloc, who repeatedly made realistic predictions to Secretary Acheson and to other State Department officials concerning Red China's probable reactions to the crossing of the 38th parallel. Kennan, who had a much more differentiated conception of the perspectives and intentions of the Chinese leaders, based on careful assessment of the available evidence, exerted a marked influence on the thinking of the State Department's policy planning staff, headed by Paul Nitze. This group opposed crossing the 38th parallel and occupying North Korea. Secretary Acheson was fully cognizant of the opposing views of Kennan and of Nitze's staff but apparently did not invite these experts to brief Truman's advisory group or to discuss their alternative views in depth. Kennan abruptly left the State Department in exasperation at the end of August, when the initial steps in the decision to cross the 38th parallel had already been taken, because of his isolation from decision-making; he felt that he had become "a 'floating kidney' . . . one step removed from the real decisions."

When the Korean War began at the beginning of the summer, Kennan had expected to meet with the presidential advisers but instead found himself "relegated to the sidelines: attending the respective meetings in . . . the Secretary's office, but not those that took place at the White House level." Evidently Secretary Acheson had adopted the role of a self-appointed mind-guard, making sure that Kennan and those who shared his critical views of the risks of provoking Communist China were always kept at a safe distance from the men who had the power to shape United States policy in the Korean War.[5]

Kennan was able to discern that gross misconceptions of "Soviet communism" were playing a vital role in the deliberations of the policy-making group, and he was utterly appalled:

> All through that summer [1950] I had the feeling that the situation was slipping away not only from the control but from the influence of people like myself. I talked about this several times with Chip Bohlen [in the State Department] who I believe shared this impression. . . .
>
> Altogether, I could find no comfort in what I could observe of the general conduct of foreign policy by our government in that hectic summer. . . . Nothing seemed more futile than the attempt to infuse mutual understanding of concept . . . and above all sophistication of concept into this turmoil of willful personalities and poorly schooled minds.

To an outside observer, one of the most incomprehensible characteristics of a cohesive group that is sharing stereotypes and manifesting other symptoms of groupthink is the tenacity with which the members adhere to er-roneous assumptions despite the mounting evidence to challenge them. The members of Truman's advisory group appear to have been unable to assimilate any new information about Red China that could correct their misconceptions and provide them with a more differentiated view of China's intentions and capabilities. McLellan asserts:

> The United States had not hesitated to resist aggression eight thousand miles from its shores; why should China not be expected to react to MacArthur's hostile campaign in similar fashion?
> ... It is difficult to excuse Acheson's judgment that the United States could conduct an offensive designed to wipe out China's North Korean ally and not expect Peking to react with the maximum force at its command.
> ... [The Joint Chiefs of Staff] miscalculated China's capabilities.... Had MacArthur been held to [the] ... limitations [imposed earlier]his armies would not have been so vulnerable to the Chinese onslaught and it would certainly have prevented the campaign from becoming an unmitigated disaster whose consequences have weighed fatefully on Sino-American relations ever since.

Even after it became painfully obvious that they had made serious errors in judging what China would do, the group members continued to assume that China was participating in a Russian-inspired conspiracy. At an emergency meeting on November 28, 1950, as General MacArthur's forces were unexpectedly retreating before the massive onslaught of the Chinese Communist army, Secretary Acheson asserted that "we needed to bear in mind that the Soviet Union was behind every one the Chinese and North Korean moves." He said that the Chinese attack was a Russian "trap," an attempt to lure America to enter the war by bombing Manchuria, so that "Russia would cheerfully get in it" and "bleed us dry." President Truman, General Bradley, and other conferees echoed Acheson's idea, just as they had at earlier meetings. They spoke of China, Russia, and North Korea as a homogeneous entity and accepted the notion that "communism" had decided that China should intervene to divert the United States from its anti-Communist role in Europe.

The use of the old Soviet conspiracy notion may have enabled the group members to maintain their morale despite the shocking setback that revealed the inadequacy of their recent collective judgments about China. President Truman was able to inject some morale-building thoughts by asserting that the Chinese move was "a ruse" to bring to a halt American aid in the rebuilding of Europe, because the unity that United States leadership had achieved in Europe had become the main target for world communism's attack. The United States, he said, would make it clear that its commitments in Europe would not be abandoned for new entanglements in Asia. In other words, Soviet communism was again trying to fox us, but we would outfox them.

Muffing the last chance at a crucial meeting

Commenting on the National Security Council's meeting on November 9 and numerous subsequent meetings of Truman's advisers as the crisis posed by China's intervention continued, Acheson acknowledged that the quality of the decision-making was poor:

> Here, I believe, the Government missed its last chance to halt the march to disaster in Korea. All the President's advisers in this matter, civilian and military, knew that something was badly wrong, though what it was, how to find out, and what to do about it they muffed. That they were deeply disturbed and felt the need for common counsel is shown by the unprecedented fact that in the three weeks and three days from November 10 until December 4, when disaster was full upon us, the Secretaries of State and Defense and their chief assistants met three times with the Chiefs of Staff in their war room to tussle with the problem, the two secretaries met five times with the President, and I consulted with him on five other occasions. I have an unhappy conviction that none of us, myself prominently included, served him as he was entitled to be served.

After the November 9 meeting of the National Security Council, which the President was unable to attend, Truman was told that it was agreed that General MacArthur's directive should not now be modified and that he should be free to do what he could militarily, but without bombing Manchuria. What MacArthur chose to to, just as the men in Washington had expected, was to continue his preparations for an all-out offensive, a "victory march" directly toward the borders of China. His plans were abetted by the sudden disappearance of the huge Chinese force during the two weeks following the November 9 directive. What the Chinese chose to do, however, remained a mystery—until they struck with devastating force on November 25. As long as there was no sight of them, MacArthur assumed that the Chinese had been bluffing all along and had pulled back out of weakness. Truman's advisers did not challenge MacArthur's optimistic interpretation of the mysterious disappearance, although they were puzzled by it at first.

The push toward concurrence that produced unwarranted optimism among Truman's key advisers was apparent at a meeting on November 21 of Acheson, Marshall, Bradley, and other officials at the Pentagon. From his study of the records of this meeting and from his retrospective discussions with former Secretary Acheson, McLellan had the impression that there was "something strangely unreal . . . about this meeting." The unreality had to do with the shared illusion that MacArthur's forces would soon attain complete victory, a "prevailing confidence that MacArthur could accomplish his mission and that Chinese intervention, if it did occur, could be contained within a buffer zone along the Yalu." In contrast to the concerns that some participants had voiced less than two weeks earlier, it was now simply taken for granted that the war would soon be won and the Chinese would resign themselves to having MacArthur's forces occupy North Korea. The conferees were aware of a large concentration of Chinese troops near the border (actually there were three hundred thousand) and forty thousand guerrillas behind MacArthur's lines. The effective frontline strength of MacArthur's forces—stretched dangerously thin, as Secretary Marshall had pointed out at an earlier National Security Council meeting—numbered only one hundred thousand. Furthermore, MacArthur's plans called for even greater dispersion of his combat troops as they fanned out in approaching the Yalu River. But no one apparently wanted to spoil the prevailing mood of confidence in imminent victory by inducing the group to examine plausible alternative views of what Red China might really be up to, which could have led them to deliberate about the need for changing their military and political strategy. One neglected alternative was that the Chinese withdrawal might be an attempt to give the United States a final chance to reconsider occupation of North Korea. Another was the ominous likelihood that the withdrawal was a tactical stratagem to prepare a trap for the advancing United Nations forces, in accord with Mao's well-known doctrines of guerrilla warfare.

Earlier that day, Acheson had talked with members of his State Department staff about alternative outcomes. MacArthur might be successful in repelling Chinese intervention, but, on the other hand, "if . . . we find ourselves with a long struggle on our hands, we must turn to negotiation." He does not appear to have raised even this watered-down version of the possibility of military failure at the meeting in the Pentagon. Acheson did speak about the need for working out with the Chinese a buffer zone along the Yalu River to make clear to the Communist Chinese leaders that the United States posed no threat to their territory. Secretary Marshall urged that the announcement of America's willingness to establish a buffer zone be postponed until after MacArthur's offensive achieved victory: "The time for making political proposals would be after MacArthur had had such a success." Robert Lovett, undersecretary of defense, reported that there was no reason to expect that MacArthur could not drive the enemy forces back to the Yalu. Acheson accepted this optimistic judgment. Secretary Marshall's minutes of the meeting state that he expressed his satisfaction to the group that Acheson agreed that General MacArthur should push forward his planned offensive.

Commenting on Acheson's inappropriate lack of anxiety at this time, McLellan says that the Secretary of State's misjudgment was "shared with all the other participants [and] seems to have derived from wishful thinking." Acheson seems to have succumbed to the strong reassurances of Undersecretary Lovett, the expressed satisfaction of Secretary Marshall, and the complacent optimism of the Joint Chiefs. In the absence of these pressures from within the group, he might have pursued the line of thought he had developed earlier that day with his State Department staff, which would have led him to push for a somewhat more realistic way of coping with the Chinese intervention, one not based on wishful thinking.

The unanimous agreement at the Pentagon meeting on November 21 and the satisfaction expressed in Secretary Marshall's minutes appear to have been attained partly because the military members of the group did not voice their continuing concern about the vulnerability of MacArthur's widely dispersed forces. Evidently the military members of the advisory group did not think the risks were serious enough to warrant perturbing the President, the Secretary of State, and other civilian officials with disquieting information. Moreover, by saying nothing about their qualms, they could avoid generating possible disputes within the advisory group about whether to confront the touchy commander in Korea with new demands that he would resent and oppose.[6] Thus, during November 1950, the nation's highest military leaders, loyal and true members of Truman's advisory group, may have collectively assumed the role of mindguards.

Deflection of anger away from the group

When MacArthur launched his all-out drive toward the borders of China on November 24, 1950, he announced that the offensive would soon bring the war to an end, and he told the troops that they would be home by Christmas. But the very next day the Chinese started their massive counteroffensive, and by November 28 it had become obvious that if American troops came home by Christmas it would be only because they had been driven off the Korean peninsula in utter defeat.

At 6:15 A.M., on November 28, General Bradley phoned the President to tell him that MacArthur's forces were being attacked and driven back by an estimated two hundred sixty thousand Chinese troops. This surprising bad news, which came directly from MacArthur's headquarters, blasted all the illusions that had bolstered the decision to occupy North Korea. It demonstrated once and for all that the warning messages from Communist China should not have been dismissed as bluffs, that the engagements with Chinese units in North Korea three weeks earlier should have prompted a rapid change in policy, and that the disengagement of the Chinese troops during the preceding two weeks should have been considered an ominous prelude to a disastrous assault. Clearly Truman's decision to try to unify Korea by force of arms had been a horrible mistake that might soon lead to ignominious defeat of the United Nations forces and might even precipitate the third world war.

Truman responded to the shocking news by promptly phoning Secretary Marshall and Secretary Acheson. He also spoke with Averell Harriman and John Snyder, both of whom participated in meetings of the National Security Council, which was to assemble for an emergency session later that day. Evidently Truman felt somewhat reassured after these phone calls. "They all agree with me," he told his White House staff a few hours later, "that we're capable of meeting this thing."

Before the morning was over, Truman displayed an extraordinary outburst of anger. Given the enormous discrepancy between the expected low risks of the venture into North Korea and the reality of the danger posed by the offensive China had launched with more than a quarter of a million men, it is understandable that President Truman would become angry when he discovered how badly he had been misled. Against whom did he direct his anger? This question is of considerable psychological interest because it casts some light on the President's attitudes toward his advisers. Did he blame his military experts, who should have urged him to change his directives to MacArthur in order to curb that restless warrior's overambitious plans? Did he single out Acheson or any of his other political advisers who should have cautioned him that the Chinese Communists could really mean what they had been saying and doing ever since MacArthur began moving his troops into North Korea? He did not. Truman concentrated his vindictiveness solely against Republican newspaper publishers and other Republican "vilifiers."

Truman's emotional outburst occurred at the end of his routine morning conference with his White House staff. During the meeting, according to an eyewitness account by John Hersey—who was working on a "Profile" of the President for *The New Yorker* and happened to be present at the time—Truman seemed preoccupied but kept his feelings in check. When the routine business was finished, Truman gravely told his staff the bad news he had received that morning from General Bradley. As he spoke, his mouth drew tight, his cheeks flushed, and it seemed to Hersey that he was about to sob. Truman continued to speak in a quiet, somber voice as he gave emergency directions to his staff. Then, in an open display of "anguish," together with "irritability and disgust," Truman excitedly blurted out his hostile diatribe against the domestic enemies on whom he bitterly cast the blame:

> Well the liars have accomplished their purpose. The whole campaign of lies we have been seeing in this country has brought about its result. I'm talking about the crowd of vilifiers who have been trying to tear us apart in this country. Pravda had an article just the other day crowing about how the American government is divided, in hatred. Don't worry, they keep a close eye on our dissensions. We can blame the liars for the fix we are in this morning. It's at least partly the result of their vicious, lying campaign. What has appeared in our press, along with the defeat of our leaders in the Senate, has made the world believe that the American people are not behind our foreign policy—and I don't think the Communists would ever have dared to do this thing in Korea if it hadn't been for that belief. Why, J——[a newspaper publisher] had an editorial just yesterday claiming that he was personally responsible for the defeat of our foreign policy. He boasts about it! And the result is this news we got this morning.

Here we have what appears to be a typical example of displaced hostility in response to unexpected frustration. Truman's anger apparently was deflected away from those in his administration who had misinformed and misled him. He directed it toward a substitute target, his political opponents within the United States who he felt were undermining his well-justified

Korean War policies, rather than against any members of the in-group who had remissly advised him that the threat of Chinese intervention could safely be ignored.

Deflection of anger away from the group members is typical behavior for a frustrated leader who is loyal to his in-group. Such deflection avoids creating dissension and demoralization within the group and may even help to unify the members in the face of defeat by mobilizing them against the rival out-group to which the blame is imputed. In this case, the attacking Chinese enemy had given fair warning, and a major source of frustration was the failure of all responsible leaders in the Truman administration to expect the worst from that enemy. The domestic "vilifiers" of the administration were a target close to home, a fifth column that could be seen as inflicting a "stab in the back" and "playing into the hands of the enemy." Their alleged perfidy might incline the in-group to stand together, to continue the fight for the "good cause" to which all the members were committed. In choosing this displaced target, however, Truman was undoubtedly unaware of the psychological functions it would serve. His vindictiveness toward the anti-administration press appears to have been a spontaneous emotional response, and there is no reason to doubt that he sincerely believed what he was saying.

Truman launched a second verbal attack against the pro-Republican press later during the same day, this time in the presence of his advisers, at the emergency meeting of the National Security Council. During the meeting, there appears to have been considerable discussion about who was to blame for the debacle. Dean Acheson held the Soviet Union responsible. Vice President Barkley was deeply perturbed about the "incredible hoax" that General MacArthur had committed by announcing that the boys would be home by Christmas. "Did MacArthur know what was going on, he asked, and how could a man in his position be guilty of such an indiscretion?" The President tried to calm Barkley by telling him that this was no time "to damage MacArthur's prestige" or to "pull the rug from under the General." By handling the steamed-up Vice President in this way, the President probably conveyed to the others that he was not going to be vindictive toward anyone who had misinformed or misadvised him. In effect, he was demonstrating his unwillingness to let the arrogant commander become a scapegoat after all his obstreperousness and outright deceit. (Truman had nearly decided to fire MacArthur three months earlier when he refused to desist from his reckless efforts to propagandize for extending the war to China.) The message must have been clear that none of the generals or civilian advisers in Washington was about to be made a scapegoat either.

The President communicated a different form of the same important message to his advisers later in the meeting, when he told them, just as he had told his White House staff, that certain disloyal newspaper publishers had played into the hands of "the Soviets." Truman was accepting and elaborating on Acheson's claim that the Soviet Union was the hidden enemy behind China's unexpected move: He said that three of America's biggest publishers were dividing the nation and leading other nations to believe that the American people had no confidence in their government. The campaign of "vilification and lies and distortion of facts in so many of our papers was the greatest asset the Soviets had." When that meeting ended, Truman met with his full cabinet, which had also been convened for an emergency session. He asked General Bradley and Secretary Acheson to brief the cabinet about the unfortunate developments in Korea. Then, for the third time that day, he talked about "the damage" that had been done to America's international position by "the reckless charges and the rumor-mongering of the recent political campaign."

There is a remarkable parallel between Truman's initial reaction to the Korean War debacle and Kennedy's initial reaction to the Bay of Pigs fiasco. Kennedy, too, took pains to support his vulnerable advisers who had led him into the misadventure, displayed signs of loyalty to his team, and directed his vindictiveness toward various out-groups, including newspapers that had exposed the secret Cuban invasion plans in advance and criticized the administration for attempting to overthrow the government of a neighboring country. The press seems to be a ready-made target for the displacement of presidential wrath, in the service of preserving the unity and morale of the administration's team.

The norm sender: "I told my advisers that we had to meet their thrust"

Just as President Kennedy's group adhered to the norm of avoiding serious criticism of the Bay of Pigs invasion plan, President Truman's advisers appear to have developed a comparable norm that kept them from critically appraising their policy of escalating the war against the North Korean Communists. Throughout the summer and fall of 1950, Truman's advisers appear to have adhered to a set of norms that included approving the formula "no appeasement of Communism," accepting the stereotyped conception of a Soviet Communist conspiracy, and denying the risks of provoking an all-out war with Red China. How did this set of norms come into being?

Part of the answer, as in the case of the Bay of Pigs decision, can be found in the leadership practices of the President. Of course, Truman's way of handling his group of advisers was not quite the same as Kennedy's. During the planning of the invasion of the Bay of Pigs, President Kennedy probably quite unintentionally nudged his advisory group to accept the CIA's plan. He was not guilty, however, of a practice sometimes encountered among government leaders who are much more directive—the practice of giving not-so-subtle shoves in the direction of one particular course of action. At the outset, a powerful leader can convey a norm to his advisory group that limits all discussion to favorable comments about the policy he prefers, making advocacy of any alternative an act of deviation. Something like this seems to have happened in the case of the Korean War decision. Where John Kennedy gently nudged his advisers with the blunt end of a pencil, Harry Truman did his nudging with a cattle prod.

Of course, Truman was far from a dictatorial or authoritarian leader. Throughout his seven years in the White House, he sought to base his decisions on a group consensus of his advisers. He prided himself on his open-mindedness. He was probably quite sincere when he said that during the Korean War crisis, as always, he tried to listen to all sides before approving what he thought was the most balanced approach.

According to Paige's analysis of the documents and interviews bearing on the decision to enter the Korean War in June 1950, the President set the tone at all the meetings with his advisers, strongly shaping the group consensus as each successive step was taken to deepen America's involvement in North Korea. The President's vociferous advocacy of a hard military line during the initial meetings of the advisory group indicates that he had no hesitation about setting the norm in favor of one particular alternative. President Truman opened his first meeting with his advisers by telling the group that he had an "open mind" and wanted to know everything they were thinking about the situation. But during the meeting the President was quite uninhibited about expressing his own belligerent view, setting forth the Soviet conspiracy theory in a vigorous way that set the tone for all subsequent discussions. When General Bradley, as spokesman for the Joint Chiefs of Staff, responded by saying that the Russians were obviously testing the United States in Korea and that the line ought to be drawn now, President Truman promptly reinforced this strong military stance in no uncertain terms: "I said that most emphatically I thought the line would have to be drawn." At the crucial meeting on the next day, the President again presented his conclusion about the meaning of the invasion and what would have to be done about it: "I told my advisers that . . . the Reds were probing for weaknesses in our armor; we had to meet their thrust without getting embroiled in the world-wide war." At each successive meeting, the President reiterated his belligerent position. Several days later, for example, when Secretary Acheson had started to speak about some of the risks, stating that what had been done in the last three days might ultimately involve America in all-out war, President Truman immediately replied that he thought that the danger involved was obvious but that we should not withdraw from Korea unless a military situation elsewhere required such action. With statements like that, it could hardly escape the attention of everyone in the advisory group that the name of the game, so far as the President was concerned, was commitment to United States military action in Korea.

There is insufficient evidence of how President Truman conducted the meetings with his advisers during the late summer and fall of 1950 to ascertain whether he continued in the same exhorting manner when the decision was being made to occupy North Korea as when the initial intervention decision was made in the June meetings. It seems probable, however, that Truman's leadership style did not change markedly from June to November.

Group influence on the leader: ''I accepted the position taken by practically everyone else.''

If we assume that the President continued to urge his advisers to adopt the position he favored, it might be argued that the group's failure to examine alternatives and to explore adequately the unfavorable consequences of their decision to recommend the military occupation of North Korea did not arise from groupthink at all. Maybe the advisory group's errors can be attributed entirely to the influence of a stubborn, opinionated President, who for all his fine words about being open-minded, simply refused to listen to any ideas that disagreed with his own. Such a conclusion might appear to follow from some of the evidence of Truman's directive leadership style. But it fails to take account of other important considerations that argue strongly against a ''one-man'' explanation, including the evidence that points to the genuineness of the symptoms of groupthink among the members of Truman's advisory group.

There are many indications that the conformity of his advisers was a product of group processes rather than exclusively a matter of sycophantic yielding to the President's wishes. First of all, despite his strong advocacy of his own pet ideas at meetings with his advisers, President Truman on more than one occasion showed his readiness to accept opposing views of his advisers and to be influenced by them. During the first week of the Korean crisis, for example, Truman was responsive to his advisers' objections to his strong preference to accept an offer from Chiang Kai-shek to send thirty-three thousand Chinese Nationalist ground troops to augment the United Nations forces in Korea. On June 28, 1950, at a private conference with the Secretary of State, Truman listened to Acheson's opposing arguments but remained unconvinced. The next day, however, Truman brought up the issue at a meeting of his entire group of advisers. In his typical prodding fashion, he asked the group ''if it would not be worthwhile to accept the Chinese offer especially since Chiang Kai-shek had said he could have his 33,000 men ready for sailing within five days.'' Just in case they did not catch on to the answer he was hoping for, he added that ''Time was all important.'' But Acheson then restated his objections and others in the group, instead of bolstering the President's inclinations, voiced additional objections. Truman still felt, however, that there were strong reasons for sticking to his original position. (He asserted that he was still concerned about America's ability to deal with the enemy with the small forces available.) Nevertheless, after further discussion, the President finally gave in when it became clear to him that his key advisers did not share his view: "*I accepted the position taken by practically everyone else;* . . . namely that the Chinese offer ought to be politely declined."

Here was one occasion when the advisory group clearly showed itself capable of resisting pressures to conform to the leader's stance. This type of give and take is the expected pattern in a cohesive group of policy-makers. Much of the time the group consensus may be shaped primarily by a highly directive leader, but the leader himself, as a participant in the group, can be influenced, like anyone else, when the others happen to arrive at a consensus that differs from his own preferred position.

The foregoing incident fits in well with descriptions of Truman's general responsiveness to his advisers' recommendations, despite his tendency to prod them in the direction he wanted to go. According to Paige, President Truman's assertive leadership style was tempered by a strongly permissive element, and his handling of the Korean crisis was no exception. It seems probable, therefore, that during the fall of 1950 Truman could have been talked out of a belligerent stance if a majority of his advisory group had opposed authorizing American troops to cross the 38th parallel into North Korea, in order to avert war with Communist China.

A second line of evidence against attributing the escalation decision to just one man is the apparent sincerity of the judgments expressed by members of Truman's advisory group. The advisers genuinely agreed with Truman's point of view about Red China and the Soviet conspiracy. When the participants gave retrospective accounts years later—some in their memoirs and others in interviews conducted by Paige—they consistently argued in favor of Truman's Korean War decisions and reiterated the same arguments that they had accepted at the meetings in 1950. Obviously, such testimony is always suspect because we never know to what extent participants are trying to justify their earlier actions or are hoping to secure a favorable verdict in future accounts of their role in history. Still, it is impressive that after the Democrats—running on the record of the Truman administration—were overwhelmingly defeated in the 1952 election, none of the participants in the meetings took the opportunity to claim that he had had sufficient foresight to object to the ill-fated decision to occupy North Korea or that Truman had rejected sound advice. Such claims would enable a participant to correct the record and even to detach himself from bearing some of the responsibility for the debacle that ensued when China entered the war.

Social scientists who have analyzed the decision to occupy North Korea—De Rivera, George, McLellan, Neustadt, and others—infer that the members of Truman's advisory group genuinely believed that there were solid grounds for recommending the escalation decision and that they exerted a strong influence on President Truman. Neustadt, for example, reiterates the theme that at each stage in the escalation decision during the fall of 1950, the President was following the recommendations of his advisory group:

> The President's own course throughout October heightened every danger . . . if there should be some substance in Chou's warning. And it cannot be

said that an alternative approach was urged on Truman by his circle of advisers. Unhappily for him he chose as they advised. . . .

* * *

By November only the precise amount of loss remained in question. By then the answer rested with a government that Washington knew least of any in the world, and with a general Truman had considered firing in August. The essence of the tragedy . . . is that a President should have walked into such a corner facing front; he was not pushed, he chose. September's choices, and October's, took him there.

Truman walked in step with his advisers. . . . More realism and less appetite in Washington might have suggested [a good natural defense line at the waist of the Korean peninsula] as victory enough. But Truman did as his advisers urged and tied himself to unification.

It seems probable, therefore, that the members of the group fully collaborated with the President, sharing his optimistic outlook (although sometimes for different reasons) and believing that losses would be slight in comparison with the benefits for the United States government.

In summary, the main reason for the members' concurrence on the ill-considered escalation decision was that Truman's advisory group was adhering to a set of norms that were promoted by the leader and that all willingly accepted. These shared norms enabled the members to maintain a sense of group solidarity at the expense of suffering from many of the major symptoms of groupthink. The most prominent symptoms were excessive risk-taking based on a shared illusion of invulnerability, stereotypes of the enemy, collective reliance on ideological rationalizations that supported the belligerent escalation to which the group became committed, and mindguarding to exclude the dissident views of experts who questioned the group's unwarranted assumptions.

4

Pearl Harbor Revisited: Or, Why the Fortress Slept

When groupthink dominates, the members of a decision-making group share a sense of complacency and fail to respond to warnings. This chapter is a case study of America's lack of vigilance in 1941, which resulted in the destruction of the United States Pacific Fleet at Pearl Harbor. We examine the shared illusions, rationalizations, and related symptoms of groupthink that contributed to the wishful thinking displayed by the group of naval commanders in Hawaii during the weeks preceding the Japanese attack. This group's illusion of invulnerability seems to have been reinforced by two other interlocking groups of military decision-makers—the top-level Army officers in Hawaii and the President's War Council of policy-makers in Washington. All three groups contributed to the incredible failure to shore up the defenses of America's greatest Pacific fortress despite warning after warning that signaled imminent attack. All remained convinced that the fortress was impregnable.

"It can't happen here"

On the night of December 6, 1941—just twelve hours before the Japanese struck—Admiral Husband E. Kimmel (commander in chief of the Pacific Fleet) attended a dinner party given by his old crony Rear Admiral H. Fairfax Leary and his wife. Other members of the in-group of naval commanders and their wives were also present. Seated next to Admiral Kimmel was Fanny Halsey, wife of Admiral Halsey, who had left Hawaii a few days earlier to take his task force to the Far East. During the conversation, Mrs. Halsey said that she was certain the Japanese were going to attack. "She was a brilliant woman," according to Captain Joel Bunkley, who described the party, "but *everybody thought she was crazy.*"

Admiral Leary, at a naval inquiry in 1944, summarized the complacency at that dinner party on the eve of the attack and at the daily conferences held by Admiral Kimmel during the preceding weeks: "The prevalent opinion in the Fleet among the higher command," he stated, ". . . was that *the situation permitted of emphasizing training at the expense of security."* Leary, like other participants in the conferences with Kimmel, asserted: "There was complete and free interchange of information and opinions among the higher naval command." When asked whether any thought had been given to the possibility of a surprise attack by the Japanese, he responded, "we all felt that the contingency was remote . . . and . . . the feeling strongly existed that the Fleet would have adequate warning of any chance of an air attack."

The same attitude was epitomized in testimony given by Captain J. B. Earle, chief of staff, Fourteenth Naval District, who lived in the house next door to Kimmel and was a friend and admirer of the admiral. Earle was asked whether any account was taken prior to December 7, 1941, of a report prepared in March 1941 by two aviation officers who had concluded that a dawn patrol attack launched against Pearl Harbor from one or more Japanese aircraft carriers could achieve complete surprise: "Yes," Earle answered, "we considered this point, but somehow or other, we always felt that *'it couldn't happen here'* . . . we didn't believe the Japanese would take that chance."

From the consistent testimony given by Admiral Kimmel's advisers at inquiries following the Pearl Harbor attack, it appears that they all believed in and acted on the basis of an extreme sense of invulnerability—until the Japanese bombs began to explode. Admiral King, head of a military commission that conducted one of the inquiries, concluded that at Pearl Harbor there was an "unwarranted feeling of immunity from attack."[1]

Some of the false assumptions behind the naval commanders' feelings of invulnerability, implied by Captain Earle's testimony, were based on uninformed stereotypes about the enemy that are, by now, familiar landmarks on the road to military fiascoes. Although Japan's militaristic leaders were thought to have evil intentions toward America, they were considered too weak to implement them: No need to take seriously the possibility of a destructive attack by a blustering, little third-rate power that was noisily challenging the American colossus. Besides, America's military intelligence could keep close tabs on the Japanese and find out in advance all they needed to know about Japan's military plans.

Inside information obtained by MAGIC

Nations on the edge of war always wish that their intelligence services could break the enemy's secret codes. For once, the wish came true. The United States government achieved precisely this unique advantage in 1940, thanks to the brilliant detective work of a few American cryptographers. The intercepted Japanese messages, in the words of Herbert Feis, "gave an almost daylight picture of the mind of the Japanese government." The historian Roberta Wohlstetter has described the enormous amount of information about Japanese intentions that was obtained because America had the key to practically all Japanese codes and ciphers used in messages to Japanese embassies and consulates, which was referred to within the government as MAGIC. "Never before," she says, "have we had so complete an intelligence picture of the enemy." But MAGIC was not enough.

MAGIC supplied plenty of warning signals showing that Japan was getting ready for massive military operations, but it did not inform the Americans exactly where. This ambiguity left room for collective misjudgments based on wishful thinking. Because the military commanders stationed in Hawaii agreed that the target could not be their own naval base at Pearl Harbor, no alert was sounded when the Japanese planes arrived over Pearl Harbor until after the bombs started exploding. The attack began at about 8:00 o'clock on a Sunday morning, and the vast majority of naval officers and men were on weekend leave or just getting up from their bunks. The Japanese were able to drop their bombs at will on the ninety-six American ships at anchor. They sank or damaged all eight battleships in the harbor as well as three cruisers and four other vessels. More than two thousand men were killed, most of them Navy personnel; at least as many were wounded or missing. Most of the Navy buildings and Army aircraft installations were completely destroyed. "It was the worst military disaster in American history."

If Washington had withheld secret information about Japan's war moves, the unpreparedness at Pearl Harbor would have been understandable. But the military commanders in Hawaii were given a steady stream of warnings during 1941 based on what MAGIC revealed, and, in addition, they had obtained warning information from their own intelligence operations. Following the Pearl Harbor disaster, the warning messages were studied meticulously. Seven different governmental investigating committees and several private investigators spent years collecting the pertinent documents, interviewing the participants, and analyzing every scrap of evidence in an effort to understand how such a stupendous blunder came about. From a careful review of all thirty-nine volumes of hearings published by the congressional investigating committee and the other pertinent evidence, Roberta Wohlstetter concluded that just before the Pearl Harbor attack the intelligence information available in Washington was "close to ideal."

Misinterpreting the war warnings

The commanding officers in Hawaii were given impressive warnings by Washington indicating that they should be prepared for war with Japan. On November 24, 1941, Admiral Harold Stark (chief of naval operations in

Washington) sent Admiral Kimmel a strong warning that war with Japan was to be expected at any time: "Chances of favorable outcome of negotiations with Japan very doubtful. This situation coupled with statements of Japanese government and movements [of] their naval and military forces indicate in our opinion that a surprise aggressive movement in any direction including attack on Philippines or Guam is a possibility." Admiral Kimmel and his advisers regarded this warning as confirmation of their own expectations that the outbreak of hostilities would soon occur, but they continued to assume that no additional reconnaissance was necessary because Pearl Harbor would not be a target of Japanese attacks. Had they increased air reconnaissance to cover the totally neglected sector to the north of Hawaii, they would have had a good chance of spotting the approaching Japanese aircraft carriers well before the morning of December 7, in which case the Japanese, implementing their plan for just such a contingency, would have turned the carriers around to return to Japan without attempting any attack.

On November 27, 1941, a stronger warning was received from Admiral Stark in Washington:

> This dispatch is to be considered a war warning. Negotiations with Japan looking toward stabilization of conditions in the Pacific have ceased and an aggressive move by Japan is expected within the next few days. . . . Execute appropriate defensive deployment preparatory to carrying out the tasks assigned in WPL 46 [the Naval war plan].

Admiral Kimmel discussed this message with the members of his advisory group, and again all agreed that "there was no chance of a surprise air attack on Hawaii at that particular time." They felt certain that this was the message Washington intended to convey, for Hawaii was not specifically mentioned as a possible target of Japan's aggressive move in the current war warning or in the similar warning of November 24. They noticed that in the latter warning Guam was mentioned as a likely place where the Japanese might strike but was not on the list of possible targets in the more recent war warning, which cited the Philippines, Malaya, and other remote areas. Guam was not considered to be a likely target, according to Captain Edwin T. Layton (Kimmel's chief of fleet intelligence), but someone joked about the omission, remarking facetiously, "I guess they thought Guam was going to fall anyway, so it would not be worth while to put it in."

The advisory group's lengthy discussions of whether to conduct long-range air reconnaissance concluded, as usual, with the decision that the planes would be better used by continuing the training program for air crews. The members of the group were keenly aware of the high costs of going on a full alert with complete 360-degree air reconnaissance, which would drastically interfere with their training mission, rapidly use up their limited supplies of aircraft fuel, and in the absence of spare parts wear out their aircraft within a few weeks. They did not consider, however, the alternative of a partial increase in surveillance with some dispersal of warships, cancellation of weekend leaves, full alert of anti-aircraft units, and other precautionary measures that could have increased the security of Pearl Harbor and the fleet without being exorbitantly costly. Because they did not believe Pearl Harbor was vulnerable, they felt the limited alert conditions that had prevailed in the fleet for several months were sufficient.

The Navy officers assumed, however, that the Army command in Hawaii had gone on a full alert, including full-time use of all radar stations, which were manned at that time solely by Army personnel. This false belief was based partly on the misunderstanding of a message from Army headquarters and partly on seeing Army units moving troops, trucks, and antiaircraft weapons through the streets around Pearl Harbor. In keeping with their low degree of vigilance there was a "Let George do it" attitude, which made the naval officers quite willing to unload various defense responsibilities they felt were both troublesome and unimportant. None of them took the trouble to check carefully with their counterparts in the Army to make sure that anti-aircraft and radar units under Army control were fully activated. Consequently the naval commander did not find out until after Pearl Harbor was destroyed that their assumption about the Army alert was wrong. The Army, too, merely went on a limited alert, designed solely to cover the threat of sabotage, and was not ready for an air attack. The Army had bunched all its planes on the runways, wing tip to wing tip, to protect them with cordons of guards against saboteurs. This positioning enabled the Japanese to destroy many more American aircraft than would have been possible if the planes had remained dispersed.

On December 3, 1941, Kimmel met with two members of his staff, Lieutenant Commanders Herbert M. Coleman (fleet security officer) and Layton, to discuss newly arrived messages warning that Tokyo had just ordered all diplomatic missions in the United States and other countries to destroy their secret codes. Subsequently, both Layton and Kimmel recalled that in this conversation they had devoted a great deal of attention to the exact wording, stressing the fact that the dispatch from Admiral Stark in Washington had said "most" of the codes, not "all." From their textual analysis, the naval officers agreed that the code destruction should not be regarded as an ominous sign that the Japanese were planning to attack an American possession; rather, the Japanese were most likely just taking routine precautions in case their embassies and consulates in British or American territory were seized in retaliation for their invasion of Thailand or Malaya. At the close of the meeting, these officers felt so confident that their interpretation was correct that they thought it unnecessary to check with Washington to make sure they had grasped exactly what had been intended. Two days later, when confronted with the warning that the Japanese consulate in Hawaii was burning papers, these three men and others in Kimmel's group of advisers continued to be completely unconcerned about the threat to Hawaii, believing this was another routine precaution, like the ones the Japanese had taken earlier. "Again and again," Wohlstetter states in reviewing the dismal record of neglected warnings during the ten days before the attack, "there is this reaction, that certainly the outbreak of war with Japan was to be expected at any moment after November 27, but not to be expected at Pearl Harbor."[2]

Kimmel's congenial group of advisers

As the various warnings were received, each decision by the naval command at Hawaii was made after considerable discussion in formal conferences and informal conversations, which Admiral Kimmel regularly conducted with a group of naval officers whom he designated his "senior advisers." Included were four key men on Kimmel's staff with whom he conferred nearly every day and with whom he usually took his meals—Captains William W. Smith, Walter DeLany, Charles H. McMorris, and Arthur C. Davis. Also in attendance at the staff conferences or at private conferences with Kimmel were Marine Colonel Omar T. Pfeiffer, Lieutenant Commander Edwin T. Layton, and several other members of the admiral's staff. In addition, Kimmel asked a number of commanders of the fleet to attend conferences at his headquarters whenever they returned to Pearl Harbor from sea duty—Vice Admirals Walter S. Anderson, Wilson Brown, William L. Calhoun, William F. Halsey, Herbert F. Leary, William S. Pye, Rear Admiral Milo Draemel, and a few others. Also present at important conferences were Admiral Claude C. Bloch (commandant of the Fourteenth Naval District, which included all the Hawaiian Islands) and sometimes Bloch's chief of staff, Captain John Earle. Kimmel's advisory group was described by a knowledgeable investigator at the congressional hearings on the Pearl Harbor attack as one of the "most distinguished lists of [military] advisers that have been assembled at one time under any man's command."

There are strong indications that Kimmel's advisers formed a cohesive ingroup and shared strong feelings of loyalty to their leader. Face-to-face contact among the members of the Navy group was not limited to business meetings. All the men were part of the naval enclave in Honolulu and frequently spent time together off duty as well as on duty. Admiral Kimmel, for example, used to drop in at Admiral Bloch's house at night from time to time to talk over new developments and to obtain his advice. Kimmel combined business with pleasure when he saw members of his advisory group at social gatherings or on the golf course and he occasionally discussed his personal problems. When visiting his next-door neighbors Captain and Mrs. Earle, he sometimes talked with them about missing his wife and explained to them his reasons for not having her with him.

Although he was a hard-working man who made strong demands on everyone under his command, Admiral Kimmel maintained friendly relations with his advisers, all of whom respected him as an excellent commanding officer. Captain Smith, Kimmel's chief of staff, felt secure enough about his friendly relationship to urge Kimmel to bring his wife from the continent to

Admiral Husband E. Kimmel (commander in chief of the
Pacific Fleet during 1941) conferring with two of his "senior
advisers"—Captains Walter DeLany (left) and William W.
Smith (right).

Honolulu, as most of the other officers had done, but Kimmel explained that he felt that he could do his job better if he lived alone. Smith succeeded, however, in persuading Kimmel to take time off for recreation and enlisted Admiral Pye's help to get him to the golf course from time to time.

Staff subordinates usually had more impersonal conversations with Kimmel, but apparently looked up to him with admiration. The fleet operations officer, Admiral Good, reported retrospectively that the chief "was grand to work for: demanding but understanding." The fleet marine officer, Colonel Pfeiffer, described himself as having become an ardent "Kimmelite" following an episode in which the admiral had given him some much-needed reassurance after having erroneously castigated him. "From that time on," Pfeiffer said, "I wanted to work twice as hard for him. . . . There had been engendered in me a loyalty that nothing could shake and to this day never has been shaken."

The leader of a cohesive group who feels secure about the loyalty of the members is likely not only to give reassurance when it is needed but also to be relatively free about expressing his own personal feelings of anxiety or depression and accepting reassurance from the members. There are some indications that at times Kimmel participated in this type of mutual responsiveness. On the afternoon of December 6, 1941, for example, Kimmel expressed his anxiety to his staff officers about the safety of the fleet, having been impressed at this particular time by the worrisome signs indicating that Japan might be getting ready to launch a massive attack somewhere or other. One of them promptly reassured the admiral that "the Japanese could not possibly be able to proceed in force against Pearl Harbor when they had so much strength concentrated in their Asiatic operations" and another told him that nothing more needed to be done. "We finally decided," Kimmel recalled, "that what we had [already] done was still good and we would stick to it." So, at the last conference on the day before the attack, Admiral Kimmel missed his last chance to correct the gross unpreparedness of the fleet. He failed to follow through on his momentary misgivings after hearing members of his staff convey the usual rosy picture about the safety of the fleet. At the end of that Saturday afternoon, Kimmel "put his worries aside" and went off to Admiral Leary's dinner party.

The next day, appalled by the widespread destruction at Pearl Harbor and depressed by his failure to protect the fleet, Admiral Kimmel openly expressed his personal feelings to members of his staff. He told two of them that it would be proper for Washington to relieve him of his command. But, according to Kimmel's own account, "They both protested at once and said nothing like that would happen." Their reassurance on this point soon proved to be just as unrealistic as the reassurance they had given him on the day before the attack. Shortly thereafter, when Admiral Kimmel was demoted and relieved of his command, members of the Navy group came to the house to try to cheer up "ol' Kimmel." Most of his principal advisers remained loyal to him long afterward by defending his decisions and by acknowledging, at the numerous inquiries conducted during subsequent years, their own misleading advice.[3]

Noisy warning signals and wishful thinking

Several naval commanders in Washington placed the blame for unpreparedness squarely on Admiral Kimmel and his staff. Admiral Turner, head of Navy war plans in Washington, told the Naval Court of Inquiry that just reading the newspapers should have prompted Kimmel to order a full alert and to prepare adequately for the December 7 attack. Admiral Kimmel retorted that during the first week of December the newspapers in Honolulu continued to carry news of negotiations between the United States and Japan and that messages from Washington were at fault because they failed to mention specifically that Hawaii was a possible target of attack. As a result of their lack of explicitness, Kimmel argued, the warnings from Washington failed to correct the reasonable inferences he and his staff had drawn from the limited information available to them. His defense was deemed unacceptable. He was court-martialed, reprimanded, and demoted to a position in which he would not be required to make any important decisions.

After reviewing all the pertinent evidence, Roberta Wohlstetter concluded that, incredible as it may seem, Admiral Kimmel's defense was much closer to the truth than the accusations leveled against him by the naval commanders in Washington. From November 27 on, Kimmel and the members of his advisory group were not, in fact, the least bit complacent about the imminence of war with Japan. They were deeply concerned about training their men and preparing their equipment for a long, hard war in the Pacific. But they retained one specific complacent view, which was, in effect, that "it will happen somewhere else, not here." This unwarranted bit of optimism was never altered by the barrage of warning signals because every one of the messages, in one way or another, was sufficiently ambiguous about the local tactical situation that it could be interpreted in line with the assumption that Pearl Harbor could not possibly be a target.

Wohlstetter's main point is that along with the crucial military warning signals, there were large numbers of competing and irrelevant signals. This background "noise," as Wohlstetter calls it, often gave a confused picture and sometimes pointed in the wrong direction, obscuring the messages and signs pointing to danger. The Japanese changed the call signals of their ships and introduced smoke screens and deceptions in their messages to keep even their own diplomats from learning about the secret plan for attacking Pearl Harbor. This added to the other kinds of noise that kept obscuring the officers' perceptions of the warning messages, right up until the Sunday morning when, like the dénouement of a detective story, the enemy's unexpected action suddenly revealed for the first time the full meaning of the blackout of the Japanese carriers, the burning of codes in the Japanese consulate, and all the other clues and emergency signals. According to Wohlstetter:

> The history of Pearl Harbor has an interest exceeding by far any tale of an isolated catastrophe that might have been the result of negligence or stupidity or treachery, however lurid. For we have found the roots of this surprise in circumstances that affected honest, dedicated, and intelligent men.

The men who had responsibility for the defense of Pearl Harbor were "as efficient and loyal a group of men as one could find." The explanation of their failure, Wohlstetter concludes, lies in the

> very human tendency to pay attention to signals that support current expectations about enemy behavior. . . . For every signal that came into the information net in 1941 there were usually several plausible alternative explanations, and it is not surprising that our observers and analysts were inclined to select the explanations that fitted the popular hypotheses.

In Washington, as well as in Hawaii, the most popular hypotheses placed all the possible targets of Japanese attack thousands of miles west of Hawaii. This was reflected in the way the communications from Washington were worded, as well as in the way they were interpreted. Moreover, United States military intelligence was poorly organized and poorly coordinated, both in Washington and in Hawaii, contributing to the noisy confusion. If more adequate background information had been supplied to the high-level Navy officers in Hawaii who had to decide whether to institute an alert—which could have been done only at the cost of interrupting ongoing training programs and the high-priority mission of supplying personnel and equipment to United States outposts close to Japan—they might have relinquished their unruffled "business as usual" attitude in response to the warnings. We must remember, too, Wohlstetter points out, that so many warnings were received in Hawaii during 1941, that they "may have added up to a feeling of 'cry wolf.'"

Do the ambiguities adequately explain why the Navy was so utterly unprepared for the air attack on December 7? Apparently sensing that an explanation solely in terms of too much noise is incomplete, Wohlstetter adds a rather cryptic afterthought: "What was unreasonable was the failure [of the military commanders in Hawaii] under such conditions to consider seriously some less reasonable or less probable, but more damaging eventualities."

Here is the heart of the problem. The puzzling question that still remains to be explained is this: Why did the commanding officers at Pearl Harbor fail to take account of alternative interpretations of the warning signals in addition to what they considered the most probable interpetation? Why didn't they acknowledge that their inferences about what Japan was most likely to do were uncertain and that a threatening move against Hawaii was at least a remote possibility? After all, military leaders are supposed to be constantly vigilant and to have contingency plans ready in order to cope with low-probability events that could endanger national security if they happen to materialize, particularly at the military base for whose safety they are responsible. In the fall of 1941, all the naval officers knew, even before being told by Washington, that at any moment Japan was likely to launch "a surprise aggressive move in any direction." Doesn't "any direction" logically include their direction, an attack against Pearl Harbor? Not very probable perhaps, but still a contingency to be fully prepared for?

In his history of United States naval operations in World War II, Samuel Eliot Morison states that a reasonable condition of readiness could have been established without interfering with training schedules. At the very least, this would have allowed the naval command to reduce the death toll and prevent much of the large-scale destruction at Pearl Harbor by being fully alerted by the early morning contacts with Japanese submarines just outside Pearl Harbor (which were made an hour or more before the air attack began but were misinterpreted) and by Army radar contact with the planes. Morison, too, regards it as unreasonable for the naval command to have completely precluded the possibility of an air raid:

> After every allowance is made for the insistent training problem and the failure of Washington to let the Hawaiian commands have all the intelligence in their possession, the fact remains that Pearl Harbor was the most important United States Base in the Pacific and that war was imminent, as everyone who read the newspapers knew. It was an outpost, too, where military men are supposed to be alert at all times, like a sentry walking past his post. Admiral Kimmel need not have had so rigid a schedule of arrivals and departures that the Japanese could count on the battleships being in port Sunday morning. Normal [peacetime] weekend leaves and liberties need not have been granted when war was likely to break out any day. Distant air reconnaissance might have been very much better, as it became immediately after the heavy losses on 7 December.

Ultimately, despite all the noise that accompanied the warning signals, it was unreasonable for the Navy group to have omitted its own base at Pearl Harbor from the list of possible Japanese targets. Recognizing this, Wohlstetter has made some allusions to "wishful thinking":

> There is a good deal of evidence . . . that in conditions of great uncertainty people tend to predict that events that they want to happen actually will happen. Wishfulness in conditions of uncertainty is natural and is hard to banish simply by exhortation—or by wishing. . . .
>
> Pearl Harbor is not an isolated catastrophe. It can be matched by many examples of effective surprise attack. . . .
>
> The stunning tactical success of the Japanese on the British at Singapore was made possible by the deeply held British faith in the impregnability of that fortress. As Captain Grenfell put it, newspapers and statesmen like their fortresses to be impregnable. "Every fortress," he wrote, "that has come into the news in my lifetime—Port Arthur, Tsing Tao, the Great French defensive system of the Maginot Line—has been popularly described as impregnable before it has been attacked."

The label "wishful thinking" points in the direction of psychological causes but does not constitute an adequate explanation until the conditions that promote it are more fully elaborated. To say merely that there were conditions of uncertainty is not sufficient because men do not always succumb to wishful thinking when facing uncertain dangers. If they did, few soldiers in an active war zone would ever bother to take precautions against being bombed, mined, and ambushed; few citizens would ever have a medical checkup, take out accident insurance, or bother to eliminate fire hazards in their homes. The problem, therefore, is to specify when people take uncertain dangers seriously and when they wishfully ignore them.

The groupthink hypothesis specifies some of the conditions that give rise to collective wishful thinking and enables us to pick up where Wohlstetter's analysis leaves off. By pointing to a specific set of psychological causes, it helps to account for the extraordinary lack of vigilance at Pearl Harbor.

Shared rationalizations: why it couldn't happen here

When members of a group support each other in maintaining an illusion of invulnerability, we can expect to find them also manifesting a second major symptom of groupthink that bolsters it. They develop a set of shared beliefs that rationalize their complacency about the soundness of their policy decisions. These rationalizations, often based on stereotypes and ideological assumptions about the enemy that are widely accepted within the government bureaucracy, contribute to the members' unresponsiveness to impressive information that otherwise would incline them to rethink the pros and cons of alternative courses of action. The Navy group in Hawaii appears to have developed just such rationalizations, some of which probably could have been easily shaken if anyone had seriously questioned them. Nevertheless, those flimsy rationalizations let the members believe their policy of ignoring the warnings was rational.

One rationalization, accepted by the Navy group right up until December 7, was that *the Japanese would never dare attempt a full-scale surprise assault against Hawaii because they would realize that it would precipitate an all-out war, which the United States would surely win.* It was utterly inconceivable "that a power as small as Japan would make the first strike against a power as big as the United States," Wohlstetter writes. Six months earlier, this stereotyped view of Japanese impotence might have met with the approval of most experts in Washington, who thought it highly improbable that Japan would provoke the United States to declare war. But by July 1941 many Washington analysts realized that the outlook had changed, especially because the United States had imposed a strangling blockade that cut Japan off from supplies of oil, cotton, and other vital raw materials. None of the necessary supplies could be secured from Japan's Axis partners in Europe because they, in turn, were cut off by a British naval blockade. It was apparent that Japan was getting ready to take some drastic military counteraction to nullify the blockade.[4] But the naval commanders in Hawaii still retained a naive image of a midget that would not dare strike a blow against the powerful giant.

When the warnings from Washington called attention to imminent outbreak of war, the high-level naval officers at Hawaii agreed that *Japan would focus exclusively on the weakest targets in the Far East, taking on the British and the Dutch, one at a time; only after that, in an indirect way, might Japan challenge the United States.* Had the members of the Navy group attempted to look at the situation through Japanese eyes, instead of relying on a group-think view of the enemy, they might have realized that a knockout blow against the United States fleet at Pearl Harbor was within the realm of possible alternatives that Japanese military leaders might be considering, however much of a blunder it might be from an American or even from an objective point of view. Once it became clear that Japan was moving toward war with the United States, the argument that the Japanese would not dare attack a base like Pearl Harbor lost much of its force.

No one discussed the anticipated enemy moves from the standpoint of how the Japanese would view the risks of *not* attacking the United States, of allowing themselves to be relegated to the status of a third- or fourth-rate power, deprived of all their hard-won territories gained from years of fighting and sacrifice, divested of all national honor. By not examining Japan's alternatives from the Japanese military leaders' point of view, the Navy group was able to continue to assume that a Japanese attack against the Pacific Fleet at Pearl Harbor was not just a low-probability event but had practically zero probability.

Equally simplistic was the main question the members of the Navy group discussed when they received the war warnings from Washington in late November. "Which *one* place," they asked themselves, "will Japan strike?" They concurred, largely on the basis of information about recent Japanese ship movements, that the one place would most likely be Malaya or Thailand. Their shared misconceptions prevented the members of the Navy group from entertaining even as a remote guess what the Japanese actually did do on December 7, 1941—direct their entire fleet of aircraft carriers to attempt a knockout blow against the United States fleet at Pearl Harbor and simultaneously use the rest of their military forces to invade Thailand and to launch air attacks followed by landings at Malaya, Hong Kong, Wake, Guam, and the Philippines.

Lieutenant Commander Layton, naval intelligence expert, was aware of the possibility that the Japanese might strike at more than one place. But his thinking appears to have been influenced by the same limited conceptions of the enemy held by the others in the Navy group. On December 6, 1941, Layton discussed with Vice Admiral Pye some fresh intelligence information that fixed the location of Japanese warships in the Gulf of Siam. Layton remarked that "the only problem remaining was whether or not they would leave us on their flank as a menace or take us out on the way down.'' Such strong words about an imminent threat to the United States Navy certainly ought to have led the conversation of the two seasoned naval officers to a realistic consideration of the potential danger to all United States bases flanking Japan, including their own. But when Layton and Pye talked about the flank, according to their subsequent testimony, they had in mind only remote places—the Philippines or Guam—not Pearl Harbor. So far as their own base was concerned, these two officers, like everyone else in the Navy group, were convinced that *the Pacific Fleet concentrated at Pearl Harbor was a major deterrent against an enemy air or naval attack*. The fleet was not considered a possible target. Kimmel's advisers thought the Japanese would be unbelievably stupid to risk losing their carriers and aircraft by sending them thousands of miles over the ocean to Hawaii.

True, the warnings from Washington had repeatedly mentioned a possible surprise attack, which could give the Japanese a great advantage, but ''there seems to have been no realistic appraisal of what surprise would mean; no estimate of what such an attack could conceivably do to our fleet, air, and ground forces; and no calculation of probable damage to men and equipment—not even a tentative percentage.'' Instead of thinking through the implications of a surprise attack and working out realistic scenarios that could be used for defense planning, the Navy group relied on a crude assumption: *Even if the Japanese were foolhardy enough to send their carriers to attack us, we could certainly detect and destroy them in plenty of time*. Admiral Pye subsequently gave testimony concerning the secure feelings that he and his associates shared about detecting any attempted attack against Pearl Harbor. He put it this way: ''If we had ten minutes warning everybody would have been there [shooting the planes down], and we didn't anticipate that they could get in without ten minutes warning.'' The naval officers did not anticipate that in a state of unreadiness the significance of the warning signals occurring during the hours preceding a surprise attack—such as patrols encountering hostile submarines and radar detection of unidentified aircraft—could be completely missed or mishandled so that there would be no advance warning.

Another assumption not subjected to critical evaluation was that *no warships anchored in the shallow water of Pearl Harbor could ever be sunk by torpedo bombs launched from enemy aircraft*. This unanimously held belief seemed to be grounded in well-established facts. In 1940, the only air-launched torpedoes the United States Navy knew about required a minimum depth of about sixty feet, whereas the depth of the water in Pearl Harbor was only thirty or forty feet. Having avoided conjecturing that the Japanese might attempt a surprise attack at Pearl Harbor, the Navy group failed to consider the likelihood that an enemy intent on sinking a fleet anchored in a shallow harbor might be able to solve the technological problems involved in achieving this objective. The Navy group assumed that the Japanese could do no better than the Americans could in launching aerial torpedoes. Probably it would have violated the Navy group's stereotyped view of the enemy as inferior to themselves to assume that the Japanese might develop a weapon superior to the ones possessed by the United States Navy.

By the fall of 1941, as a matter of fact, the Japanese had devised and successfully tested a new type of wooden fin that could be attached to a regular torpedo, enabling their aircraft to sink ships in shallow water. Although this secret Japanese development had not been detected, the naval officers at Pearl Harbor had nevertheless been warned specifically about this possibility. In June 1941, Admiral R. E. Ingersoll, assistant chief of naval operations in Washington, sent the Navy headquarters in Hawaii a letter about recent developments, indicating that ships in shallow water might be vulnerable to torpedoes. No minimum depth of water in which naval vessels may be anchored, Admiral Ingersoll stated in his letter, can arbitrarily be assumed to provide safety from torpedo plane attack. He also said that deep-water attacks were much more likely, and this reassuring statement caught the eye of the recipients. After receiving this letter, according to Kimmel, "all my staff, Admiral Bloch and I considered the torpedo danger negligible." Once again, we see the tendency of the Navy group to ignore completely an uncomfortable contingency that seemed to have a low probability of materializing.

In summary, the members of the Navy group in Hawaii in 1941 bolstered their assumption that Pearl Harbor was immune from attack by accepting well-worn ideological assumptions as the basis for flimsy rationalizations, which they thought were based on hard facts: (1) Japan would first direct its military power against weak targets, such as the British and Dutch territories, before attacking any possession of the most powerful nation in the world. (2) In view of the power and efficiency of the United States Pacific Fleet, the risks involved in sending any Japanese aircraft carriers close enough to attack Pearl Harbor were so great that Japan would never decide to do so; the American fleet at Pearl Harbor was a deterrent, not a target. (3) If the Japanese were foolish enough to send aircraft carriers, the Americans could certainly detect and destroy them in plenty of time; even with only ten minutes warning from radar, practically all attacking planes could be shot down. (4) Warships anchored at Pearl Harbor could not be sunk by aircraft because the water was too shallow for torpedoes. In view of all these fortunate circumstances, there was obviously no need to waste time or equipment on flying extensive reconnaissance missions. Nor was it necessary to deprive the officers and men of the fleet of the usual peacetime weekends in port, even though war with Japan might break out any day.

These beliefs and assumptions form a typical cluster of groupthink symptoms. The sense of complete unanimity within the group concerning Japan's deficient capabilities enabled conscientious naval officers to be certain that they were doing the right thing by concentrating all their energies and resources on military training of fresh recruits and on other long-term preparations for future battles that might some day take place far off in Asia. A corollary to this group norm was that they should avoid being sidetracked from these prime missions by the steady flow of war warnings. If taken too seriously, they told each other, these warnings would inveigle them into taking costly and useless protective measures to deal with nonexistent dangers.

An unfunny joke that conveyed the norm

Most illuminating of the local norm-setting behavior that presumably contributed to the complacency of Kimmel's in-group concerning the safety of the fleet is a brief exchange between Admiral Kimmel and Lieutenant Commander Layton. Somewhat perturbed by the puzzling loss of radio contact with the Japanese aircraft carriers, Admiral Kimmel had asked Layton on December 1, 1941, to check with the Far East Command for additional information. The next day, when the admiral was again discussing the lost carriers with Layton, he remarked jokingly, "What, you don't know where the carriers are? Do you mean to say that they could be rounding Diamond Head [at Honolulu] and you wouldn't know it?" Layton replied that he hoped they would be sighted well before that.

This exchange, as Wohlstetter points out, implies an "atmosphere of geniality and security." What the two men were saying to each other, in effect, was: "According to the rule book we ought to look carefully to see if the missing Japanese carriers are heading toward us here at Pearl Harbor, but obviously we don't need to bother." The admiral's unfunny joke about the Japanese carriers' approaching Pearl Harbor, when they were in fact moving full steam ahead toward Hawaii, is reminiscent of the shared amusement at the Lions' Club meeting when, a few days before disaster struck, one man jokingly displayed a parachute as his answer to the town engineer's warning that the town might cave in. Laughing together about a danger signal is a typical manifestation of groupthink.

Having relegated the Japanese threat to Hawaii to the category of laughing matters, the admiral was making it clear, though in an indirect way, that he would be inclined to laugh derisively at anyone who thought otherwise. This cue probably would not have inhibited a conscientious intelligence officer like Layton from speaking his piece if he judged that the evidence clearly pointed to a grave threat. ("I did not at any time suggest," Layton dejectedly acknowledged at a congressional hearing, "that the Japanese carriers were under radio silence approaching Oahu. I wish I had.") But the admiral's foolish little joke may have induced Layton to remain silent about any vague, lingering doubts, which he himself did not take very seriously. Either man, especially after that joking interchange, would risk the scornful laughter of the other (whether expressed openly to his face or behind his back) if he were to express second thoughts to the effect that "Seriously, though, shouldn't we do something about the slight possibility that those carriers might *really* be headed this way?" Because this ominous inference was never drawn, not a single reconnaissance plane was sent out to the north of the Hawaiian Islands, allowing the Japanese to win the incredible gamble they were taking in attempting to send their aircraft carriers to within bombing distance of Pearl Harbor without being detected.

That joking exchange between Kimmel and Layton was merely the visible part of a huge iceberg of solid faith in Pearl Harbor's invulnerability. If a few warm advocates of preparedness had been within the Navy group, steamed up by the accumulating warning signals, they might have been able to melt it; but they would certainly have had a cold reception at first. To urge a full alert would have required presenting unwelcome arguments that countered the myth of Pearl Harbor's impregnability. Anyone who was tempted to do so knew that he would be deviating from the group norm: The others were likely to consider him foolish, if not "crazy," just as members of the in-group regarded Mrs. Halsey at the dinner party on the eve of the disaster when she announced her deviant opinion that the Japanese would attack.

During the week before the attack it would have been doubly difficult for any of Kimmel's advisers to voice misgivings to other members of the group. It was not simply a matter of taking the risk of being scorned for deviating from the seemingly universal consensus by questioning the cherished invulnerability myth. An even greater risk would be the disdain the dissident might encounter from his colleagues for questioning the wisdom of the group's prior decisions. For a member of the Navy group to become alarmed by the last-minute warning signals and to wonder aloud whether a partial alert was sufficient would be tantamount to asserting that the group all along had been making wrong judgments. At the very least, it would show lack of confidence in the group's capabilities in fulfilling one of its fundamental missions—providing adequate security at Hawaii in order to protect the Pacific Fleet, the naval base at Pearl Harbor, and the local population. Kimmel, as leader of the group, had sufficient "idiosyncrasy credit" to be able to express his last-minute gut reaction on the afternoon of December 6, but he was quickly reminded of the group's standard rationalizations for setting momentary qualms aside.

In the atmosphere of apparent unanimity, with no clear-cut warning signal indicating that the Japanese were planning a sneak attack against Pearl Harbor, even the most conscientious military adviser would find it easier to risk what seemed to be a very low-probability threat of an enemy attack rather than face the high-probability threat of social censure for questioning the validity of the group's recent reaffirmations of its commitment to a business-as-usual and a weekend-leave-as-usual policy. It is precisely under these conditions that social anxiety about violating group norms exerts its greatest inhibitory pressure, inducing sensible men to remain unsensibly lacking in vigilance, to avoid thinking about realistic scenarios not in accord with the group's assumptions. The result is a shared psychological set that involves a marked distortion in information-processing, which is a core constituent of the groupthink syndrome. The psychological set can be inferred from consistent manifestations of bias against accepting the implications of any new information that could challenge the group's preferred course of action.

Naval officers who did not accept the invulnerability myth

The assumption that the Japanese would never dare attack the Pacific Fleet anchored at Pearl Harbor was evidently not generally accepted by naval officers who were not in the upper echelons of the Navy organization. We surmise this from the evidence that among lower-ranking officers on different warships that were among the sitting ducks on December 7, the degree of concern about the possibility of a sneak air attack varied widely. According to Morison's history of United States naval operations in World War II, the poorest prepared of all the ships at Pearl Harbor was the S.S. *California,* the flagship of Vice Admiral Pye, who was commander of the battle force of the Pacific Fleet and was a member of Kimmel's in-group. (Both Pye and Bunkley, the captain of the *California,* were among those who were in no mood to accept Mrs. Halsey's pessimistic forecast at the dinner party on the night before the attack.) On the fateful Sunday morning, this ship, unlike most of the others, had more than ten minutes to get ready because it was the last one hit by the Japanese torpedoes. But the officers on board did not know what to do. The few officers who had been trained for such emergencies were away from the base on normal peacetime shore leave for the weekend. The ship was still in its "unbuttoned" condition when it was sunk by two torpedoes dropped by Japanese planes. The number of casualties and the amount of damage inflicted, according to Morison, were far greater than they would have been if the ship had been properly prepared.

In contrast, the S.S. *West Virginia,* which sustained more devastating blows from the enemy planes, had relatively few casualties and relatively limited damage "because of the excellent discipline of the crew and the prompt alert." Morison attributes the decisive action on board this ship to a group of well-trained young officers who had seriously discussed the possibility of an air raid on the fleet before December 7 and had worked out a series of control measures in preparation for it. When the first bomb hit a hangar on nearby Ford Island, one of the junior officers on the *West Virginia* alerted the entire ship; the others on board promptly put into operation the anti-aircraft control measures they had developed. While the ship was sinking, the officers and men prevented their torpedoed vessel from capsizing and kept up anti-aircraft fire against the planes that were repeatedly dive-bombing them.

None of the officers responsible for the advance preparations on the *West Virginia* were members of the high-level group of Navy officers headed by Ad-

A view of capsized and burning ships of the United States
fleet in Pearl Harbor after the Japanese had attacked in the
early morning hours of December 7, 1941.

miral Kimmel. Unlike their superior officers in the Navy group, they obviously had not accepted the myth that the fleet at Pearl Harbor was safe from attack. We do not know how many naval officers on Admiral Pye's unprepared flagship privately held the same vigilant attitude as those on the *West Virginia* but felt unable to say or do anything about it. Nor do we know how many men in the upper echelons of the naval command had doubts and misgivings about the dominant myth. All we know is that none of the high-ranking officers raised a question about the fleet's unpreparedness for an air attack or decided to take special precautions within their own domain, like those taken by the young officers on the *West Virginia*.

Kimmel's group of advisers was not alone in belittling the threat to Pearl Harbor. Strong support of their view came from military colleagues in the Army command at Hawaii and in naval headquarters at Washington.

Reinforcements from the Army

The naval officers' complacent views were undoubtedly reinforced by optimistic communications from high-level Army officers in their local social network, when they held official discussions of joint military defense problems and when they chatted together at the officers' club or on the golf course. One source of glowing optimism was Lieutenant Colonel Bicknell, the Army chief of G-2 at Hawaii, who had frequent discussions with some members of the Navy group. Bicknell confidently expressed, over and over again, the belief that Japan would never dare attack America directly. His outlook was shared by General Walter Short, head of the Hawaiian Department of the Army, and by the members of the general's staff.

In contrast to the Army's rivalry with the Navy in Washington, the high-level Army officers in Hawaii looked up to their counterparts in the Navy as models of intelligent planning, efficiency, and zeal in carrying out all essential security measures. Army officers shared the belief that the presence of the Navy at Pearl Harbor was sufficient guarantee of full protection for the Hawaiian Islands. General Short subsequently testified that he felt convinced "that the Navy was strong enough and the task forces were strong enough to be such a threat against any concentration excepting the entire Japanese fleet . . . that it would be a very decided deterrent to the Japanese ever sending a task force into that area."

This courteous and respectful sentiment among the Army leaders was probably communicated to the admirals with whom they conversed, if not directly, then by the fact that they never asked any boorish questions about how well prepared Pearl Harbor was for an air attack. When men are in frequent contact, what remains unsaid can be as eloquent as what is said. Contrary to rumors current at that time, Admiral Kimmel and General Short frequently conferred and saw each other socially on the golf course and elsewhere.[5] On December 7, 1941, as a matter of fact, they had a golf date, which neither was able to keep.

More reinforcements from Washington

Strong support for the Navy group's illusions and rationalizations came from an unexpected quarter in Washington. Admiral Stark, the chief of naval operations and a member of the President's War Council, personally regarded the danger of a full-scale attack against Pearl Harbor as extremely small. In both the formal directives and the informal letters he wrote to Admiral Kimmel he often inserted his personal beliefs about Pearl Harbor's relatively safe status; they were considerably more optimistic than the beliefs of other members of the War Council.

The dominant view in Washington during 1941 was not quite the same as the zero-probability estimate of an air attack on Pearl Harbor prevalent among the naval officers at Hawaii. The members of the War Council and the military experts in the Pentagon assumed that there was a low probability that Pearl Harbor would be attacked, because the enemy might strike in any direction, at any American base. They thought that they were alerting Hawaii to the possibility of real danger, particularly when they agreed to send out the war-warning messages in late November. Nevertheless, their low-probability estimates affected the wording of their communications to Hawaii and enabled Admiral Stark to be unperturbed about continuing to communicate his own brand of Navy optimism.

None of Stark's official warning messages was sufficiently dramatic or explicit about the danger to Hawaii to challenge the local officers' assumptions about Hawaii's immunity. Moreover, Admiral Stark promptly counteracted some of the most impressive messages by personal letters to Admiral Kimmel, which contributed to the noise that was obscuring the warning signals. Written in a friendly and confidential tone, these letters explained that the outlook was not as bad as it might have sounded in the preceding official communiqué. Kimmel regularly showed these letters to his advisers, and the personal views they contained were often discussed in group meetings.

Admiral Stark, who had close personal and professional ties with Admiral Kimmel and some of the other officers under his command, appears to have been functioning as a mindguard. By interspersing his personal optimistic letters without the official warnings, he was protecting the Navy group at Hawaii from thinking about the distressing implications of the communications from the War Council.[6]

A clear warning from the War Council to institute a full alert in preparation for a surprise attack on Pearl Harbor might have undercut the influence of Stark's personal correspondence and might therefore have succeeded in changing the outlook of the Navy group. But the War Council never authorized sending any such tactical warning. The recipients of the official war warnings of November 24 and 27, sensitized to words that fit in with their relatively placid assumptions, noted that a number of possible targets for a Japanese attack were listed—the Philippines, Guam, Thailand, Borneo—but Hawaii was not mentioned. They made much of this omission. In a way they were right to notice it, because it did indeed reflect the low-probability estimates of the War Council. But the naval officers gave an extreme interpretation to this clue. They believed it meant that the government leaders agreed with their assumption that there was no chance at all of a Japanese attack against Pearl Harbor, that the only threats to be considered were minor ones—a sabotage attempt by a local Japanese agent or a lone submarine that might slip through the guarded waters around Hawaii, both of which could easily be handled by existing military routines. When the authorities at headquarters said, in effect, that the threat was not highly probable, local groupthink evidently translated the message into "negligible probability—forget it."

Peace of mind among Roosevelt's advisers

The weak wording of the official war warnings—their frequent use of vague phrases like "hostile action possible" and their failure to list Pearl Harbor among the possible targets of a Japanese attack—correctly reflected the lack of vigilance among the members of the War Council so far as Hawaii was concerned. In May 1941, General Marshall, who was then chief of staff, informed President Roosevelt that *"the Island of Oahu,* due to its fortification, its garrison and its physical characteristics, is believed to be the strongest fortress in the world." In September 1941, the general sent a memo to the President stating that Hawaii needed no ground troop reinforcements because "Presence of Fleet reduces threat of major attack." During the months preceding the Pearl Harbor attack, General Marshall's unconcern about Hawaii seems to have matched that of Admiral Stark. These two leading members of the President's War Council, who headed up America's armed forces, evidently helped to maintain peace of mind among Roosevelt's civilian advisers.

The War Council was chaired by President Roosevelt and included, in addition to General Marshall and Admiral Stark, Secretary of State Cordell Hull, Secretary of War Henry L. Stimson, Secretary of the Navy Frank Knox, and presidential adviser Harry Hopkins. The consensus of this group was that there was only a slight chance that Japan would attack any United States possession before expanding its perimeter at the expense of British and Dutch possessions. All the members believed that Hawaii was the least vulnerable of all American possessions in the Pacific. They decided, however, that to be on the safe side adequate preparations should be made in case of a surprise attack. With this remote threat in mind, they ordered the War Department to notify the military commanders in Hawaii to be alert for a "surprise aggressive move in any direction." But even in late November 1941, when they sent out "the war warnings that failed to protect," as historian Herbert Feis describes them, the men who made the decision did not envisage the possibility that a military disaster might result from unpreparedness.

It appears that the members of the War Council were complacent about the threat to Hawaii, even though they never resorted to such extreme forms of denial as did the Navy group in Hawaii. Perhaps the War Council was also suffering from its own, somewhat milder symptoms of groupthink. This group, according to Feis, repeatedly ignored the warnings of Ambassador Grew, from his observation post in Tokyo, to be on guard against sudden naval and military attacks on American possessions. On November 3, 1941, for example, Ambassador Grew sent a strong warning to Washington from Tokyo, predicting that if conciliation attempts failed, the Japanese might make "an all-out, do-or-die attempt, actually risking national Hara-kiri, to make Japan impervious to economic embargoes abroad rather than yield to foreign pressure." Such action, he cautioned, might come "with dangerous and dramatic suddenness." If the members of the War Council and their staffs had taken these warnings more seriously, they might not have missed so completely the ominous implications of the Japanese messages that were being decoded in Washington.[7] They also would have monitored whatever warnings they sent out to make sure that the Army and Navy commands in Hawaii had instituted a full alert, instead of continuing to send somewhat vague messages telling the Army and Navy at Hawaii that maybe there will be war with Japan, maybe it will be soon, maybe something ought to be done to prepare for it.

A week before the Pearl Harbor attack, the members of the War Council became more worried than ever before about what the Japanese might be up to, but the only real source of concern was the movement of the Japanese convoy toward Thailand. While awaiting Japan's next piece of "deviltry," as they called it, the members of the War Council continued to believe that the initial Japanese attack would be against the British and perhaps the Dutch but not against the United States. Their main concern right up until December 7 was how to justify American intervention to the isolationist-minded American public when the threat to America's security seemed so remote.

On November 27, after authorizing the war warning, the members of the War Council became noticeably less tense; most of them regained their peace of mind and made plans to take the coming weekend off. At another meeting the next day, one of the members started to sound a warning note, but the others ignored it. Near the beginning of the meeting, Secretary Hull said that in his opinion the Japanese might make a surprise attack against various places simultaneously. This subject was not pursued, however. Neither the President nor any of the others asked Hull to elaborate on his remark. Had someone done so, the discussion might well have led to a reappraisal of the danger to American possessions. Instead, the group discussion remained focused on the same old oversimplified question with which the Navy group at Hawaii was preoccupied: Were the Japanese going to attack British or Dutch territory in the Far East? According to Secretary Stimson's notes on this meeting, the consensus was that the Japanese expeditionary force was going to try to "get around the southern point of Indo-China and to go off and land in the gulf of Siam, either at Bangkok or further west, [which] would be a terrific blow at all of the three powers, Britain at Singapore, the Netherlands, and ourselves in the Philippines. It was the consensus of everybody that this must not be allowed." By the end of the meeting, none of the low-probability threats, such as an attack against American islands in the Pacific, was brought up for consideration.

The extent to which the members of the War Council were unprepared for a blow against the fleet at Pearl Harbor is typified by the reaction of Secretary of the Navy Knox when his peace of mind was finally undermined by the first brief news dispatch from Admiral Stark about the Pearl Harbor attack. Knox said, "My God, this can't be true! This must mean the Philippines."

Collective groupthink among interlocking groups

When groupthink tendencies become dominant, the members of an executive group withhold from each other information about their personal doubts. They try to avoid saying anything that might disturb the smooth surface of unanimity that enables the members to feel confident that their policies are correct and are bound to succeed. A similar withholding of unwelcome information may occur when interlocking groups reciprocally indulge in groupthink. This seems to have happened among the three main groups responsible for the defense of Pearl Harbor—the Navy and Army groups in Hawaii and the War Council in Washington. All three assumed that the United States fleet anchored at Pearl Harbor was safe.

In their messages to each other, the three interlocking groups mutually reinforced their lack of vigilance, often by what they did not say. They did not exchange views about specific preparations needed in Hawaii to ward off a possible surprise attack. The Navy group said nothing to the Army group in Hawaii about activating its radar stations or its anti-aircraft guns and allowed the local Army leaders to persist in their belief that the mere presence of the fleet guaranteed protection against any form of hostile action except sabotage. The Army group, in turn, neglected to communicate to the Navy group that the radar stations and anti-aircraft installations were hardly in operation at all except for training purposes. The War Council in Washington did not inquire about the kind of alert that had been instituted in Hawaii, and the Navy group did not bother to inform anyone in Washington about its decision to make no changes whatsoever after receiving the war warnings. When the military members of the War Council were sent a relevant message from the Army command in Hawaii stating that only an anti-sabotage alert had been set up, they did not notice it. All along, their warning messages to Hawaii neglected to mention the threat to Pearl Harbor, even though the members of the War Council held a somewhat more realistic view of the necessity to be prepared for an attack. Thus, the three groups helped each other maintain a facade of complacency and set the stage for America's astounding unreadiness at Pearl Harbor.

5

Escalation of the Vietnam War: How Could It Happen?

All observers agree that a stable group of policy advisers met regularly with President Johnson to deliberate on what to do about the war in Vietnam. Fragmentary evidence now at hand gives some clues about how and why the group's policy of escalating the war was so assiduously pursued during the period from 1964 through 1967. The escalation decisions were made despite strong warnings from intelligence experts within the United States government, as well as from leaders of the United Nations, from practically all of America's allies, and from influential sectors of the American public. Even if the members of Johnson's advisory group were willing to pay a high price to attain their economic and political objectives in Vietnam, they apparently ignored until too late the mounting signs that their decisions to escalate the war were having devastating political repercussions within the United States, and that these repercussions were threatening to destroy the President's chances of being reelected. Accounts in the Pentagon Papers about the group's meetings and private statements made by individual members expose what seem to be gross miscalculations and blatant symptoms of groupthink. The evidence now available is far from complete, and conclusions will have to be drawn quite tentatively. Nevertheless, it is worthwhile to grapple with the main questions that need to be answered to discover if the groupthink hypothesis applies to these notoriously ill-conceived decisions.[1]

What needs to be explained?

More than a mere exercise in the psychological analysis of major foreign policy decisions, showing how group dynamics may have influenced America's Vietnam policy may help us to understand how conscientious statesmen could ignore the impressive voices of so many reputable Americans concerning the immorality as well as the adverse political consequences of their military actions. Perhaps even more important, an analysis of the shared illusions of Johnson's inner circle may give us insights that help explain how such men could still the inner voices of their own consciences. As Ithiel Pool, one of the few American professors of political science who supported the Johnson administration's basic Vietnam policy, points out: "It is hard to understand how intelligent men could believe that aerial bombardment, harassment and interdiction artillery fire, defoliation, and population displacement could be effective means to win a population, or how moral men could believe them appropriate means of action among the population we are defending." After all, the policy-makers in the Johnson administration were sincere democrats who prided themselves on their humanitarian outlook. How could they justify their decisions to authorize search-and-destroy missions, fire-free zones, and the use of "whatever violent means are necessary to destroy the enemy's sanctuaries"—all of which set the stage, the normative background, for the Mylai massacre and other acts of violence by the United States military forces against Vietnamese villagers?

The most thorough analysis of the Johnson administration's Vietnam War decisions is in the Department of Defense's study known as the Pentagon Papers, which was declassified and published in twelve volumes by the United States government in 1971, after *The New York Times* and other newspapers had revealed the main contents to the American public. In restrained but unambiguous terms, the historians and political analysts who prepared this secret study call attention time and again to the poor quality of the decision-making procedures used by the policy-makers who met regularly with President Johnson. They emphasize in particular the group's failure to canvass the full range of alternative courses of action and their superficial assessment of the pros and cons of the military recommendations under consideration during 1964 and 1965. For example, at a major strategy meeting on September 7, 1964, according to the Department of Defense analysts, "a rather narrow range of proposals was up for consideration." Neil Sheehan, in *The New York Times* book on the Pentagon Papers, adds that "the study indicates no effort on the part of the President and his most trusted advisers to reshape their policy along the lines of . . . [the] analysis" prepared jointly by experts from the three leading intelligence agencies of the government toward the end of 1964. According to that analysis, bombing North Vietnam had little chance of breaking the will of Hanoi. The vital decision made on February 13, 1965, to launch the previously planned air strikes against North Vietnam, the Defense Department study states, "seems to have resulted *as much from the lack of alternative proposals as from any compelling logic in their favor.*"

After leaving the government, Bill Moyers, an articulate member of Johnson's in-group, admitted: "With but rare exceptions we always seemed to be calculating the short-term consequences of each alternative at every step of the [policy-making] process, but not the long-term consequences. And with each succeeding short-range consequence we became more deeply a prisoner of the process."

Who were the prisoners and why couldn't they escape?

President Johnson's inner circle

During the Johnson administration the major Vietnam decisions were made by a small inner circle of government officials, most of whom remained for a few years and then were replaced, one at a time. In addition to the President, the in-group included Special White House Assistant McGeorge Bundy (later replaced by Walt Rostow), Secretary of Defense Robert McNamara (replaced during the last year of the Johnson administration by Clark Clifford), and Secretary of State Dean Rusk (who managed to remain in Johnson's advisory group from the bitter beginning to the bitter end). For several years Press Secretary Bill Moyers and Undersecretary of State George Ball also participated in the meetings. The group also included General Earl Wheeler, chairman of the Joint Chiefs of Staff from 1964 on, and Richard Helms, director of the Central Intelligence Agency from 1966 on.

President Johnson consulted this small group on all major policy decisions concerning the Vietnam War. Although most individual members of the inner circle were replaced before the Johnson administration came to an end, "its work was distinctively continuous because new men joined it only infrequently and always one at a time." The members sometimes called themselves "the Tuesday Lunch Group," and others have referred to the group as "the Tuesday Cabinet." At their Tuesday noon meetings, the members deliberated about the next steps to be taken in the Vietnam War and often dealt with purely military matters, such as the targets in North Vietnam to be bombed next.

Before discussing symptoms of groupthink, we must consider whether Johnson's inner circle was unified by bonds of mutual friendship and loyalty, an essential precondition for the emergence of the groupthink syndrome. Some journalists depict Lyndon B. Johnson as an extraordinarily aggressive and insensitive leader, who made such excessive and humiliating demands on everyone who came in frequent contact with him that he was cordially disliked, if not hated. With these alleged attributes in mind, we are led to wonder if perhaps the apparent unity of Johnson's inner circle was simply superficial conformity and polite deference out of a sense of expediency, with each member inwardly feeling quite detached from the leader and perhaps from the group as a whole. But if this were the case, it was not detected by Chester Cooper, J. Townsend Hoopes, Bill Moyers, James Thomson, Jr., and other observers in the Johnson administration who were in contact with members of the inner circle. Rather, the picture we get from those who observed from close at hand is that the group was highly cohesive.

Most explicit on this point is Henry Graff, who had the opportunity to conduct private interviews with President Johnson and with each of his principal advisers on four different occasions between mid-1965 and the end of 1968. Graff was repeatedly impressed by what appeared to him to be genuine friendship and mutual support among the members of the Tuesday Cabinet, which he felt characterized the group up until early 1968. Later in 1968 he noted a tone of querulousness in the comments the men made about the

A meeting in late 1967 of "the Tuesday Lunch Group"—
President Johnson's inner circle—discussing the Vietnam
War. Members include (clockwise from the President who sits
with his back turned in the foreground) Secretary of Defense
Robert McNamara (soon to be replaced by Clark Clifford);
General Earl Wheeler, chairman of the Joint Chiefs of Staff;
Clark Clifford; Special White House Assistant Walt Rostow;
Tom Johnson and George Christian, White House aides;
Richard Helms, director of the Central Intelligence Agency;
and Secretary of State Dean Rusk.

mounting barrage of criticisms directed against Johnson's war policy, as the increasingly obvious signs of its failure began to take their toll. But before that final phase, according to Graff:

> The men of the Tuesday Cabinet were loyal to each other, with a devotion compounded of mutual respect and common adversity. They soon learned, as all congenial committeemen learn, to listen selectively and to talk harmoniously even when in disagreement. Familiarity with one another's minds became an asset as well as a handicap in the years they conferred and labored. And their facility with words (laced with the Pentagonese all spoke so fluently) made the sessions memorable for the participants week in and week out.

Even in early 1968, when outstanding officials like Deputy Secretary of Defense Paul Nitze were submitting their resignations and it was hard to avoid bickering within the inner circle about whether the Vietnam War policy could be salvaged, Graff was still impressed by the "loyalty with which the men around the President defended him and the decisions they had helped him reach, regardless of any private misgivings they may have increasingly entertained." During the preceding year or two, as the members "felt increasingly beleaguered," Graff surmises, "they turned toward one another for reassurance" and became "natural friends" of their chief. He adds that the Tuesday Cabinet exerted an extraordinarily powerful influence over its leader, perhaps more than any other presidential advisory group in American history.

Bill Moyers, from his personal observation as a member of Johnson's inner circle, has corroborated Graff's conclusion that the group was highly cohesive. Directly in line with the groupthink hypothesis, Moyers mentions the concurrence-seeking tendency of the members as part of his explanation for the lack of critical debate about Vietnam War policies:

> One of the significant problems in the Kennedy and Johnson Administrations was that the men who handled national security affairs became too close, too personally fond of each other. They tended to conduct the affairs of state almost as if they were a gentlemen's club, and the great decisions were often made in that warm camaraderie of a small board of directors deciding what the club's dues are going to be for the members next year. . . . So you often dance around the final hard decision which would set you against . . . men who are very close to you, and you tend to reach a consensus.

Daniel Ellsberg's critique of the "quagmire myth"

The points just discussed lead one to suspect that groupthink was one of the causes of the Vietnam War fiascoes perpetrated by the Johnson administration. But there are, of course, other ways of interpreting the available observations, including some that provide an explanation solely in terms of political considerations. An extreme position of this type is taken by political analyst Daniel Ellsberg. In June 1971, he turned over to *The New York Times* and other newspapers the secret Pentagon Papers, which stunned the nation. Only a few weeks before, Ellsberg had published a scholarly article in which he presented his own opinions on the causes of the Vietnam War, based on his study of the secret documents.

Ellsberg challenges what he calls the "quagmire myth," which depicts the American Presidents and their advisers as stumbling into the Vietnam War during the 1950s and 1960s by taking one little step after another, without being aware of the deep quicksand lying ahead. Ellsberg denies that United States escalation decisions stemmed from unrealistic presidential hopes or failures to foresee the consequences. Each major escalation decision by President Johnson and his predecessors, he claims, was made with full awareness that either larger military steps would almost certainly have to be taken or else retreat and a Communist victory would have to be accepted. American policymakers, according to Ellsberg, regarded the measures taken not as "last steps" but rather as "holding actions, adequate to avoid defeat in the short run but long shots so far as ultimate success was concerned." Their essential purpose was to "buy time," to postpone defeat in Vietnam, with all its accompanying "political and personal consequences of charges of 'softness on Communism.'" In brief, America's Vietnam policy was largely determined by one fundamental political rule: "This is not a good year for this administration to lose Vietnam to Communism." Every year there were important programs to push through Congress, and congressional elections were always coming up within a year or so, even if presidential elections were not close at hand.

The power of this fundamental rule, Ellsberg claims, derived from a mixture of motives originating primarily from deeply ingrained memories of the defeatist charges to which the Truman administration had been subjected by Senator Joseph McCarthy and other right-wing Republicans after General MacArthur was removed from command during the Korean War stalemate. Those right-wingers had "tattooed on the skins of politicians and bureaucrats alike some vivid impressions of what could happen to a liberal administration that chanced to be in office the day a red flag rose over Saigon."

Ellsberg adds that a subsidiary rule (another legacy of the humiliations of the Korean War), was also in the minds of the policy-makers: Avoid committing United States ground troops to a land war in Asia. This second rule, he believes, accounts for the policy-makers' reluctance to use truly powerful military means against the North Vietnamese, except in a dire crisis to avert defeat.

All the main escalation decisions, in Ellsberg's view, were made in periods of deep pessimism and were intended only to restore the stalemate in order to postpone a possible Communist victory. In each instance, the President and his principal advisers allegedly knew what the costs would be and were willing to pay them, even though in their public statements they were saying that only one more small step was needed for victory.

Ellsberg claims that his explanation accounts for all the Vietnam War decisions made by five presidents—Truman, Eisenhower, Kennedy, Johnson, and Nixon. It certainly has the aesthetic beauty of supplying a relatively simple formula to explain the United States government's sorry record of involvement in Vietnam over a period of more than twenty years. But how well does it fit the available evidence?

Although Ellsberg argues that the policy-makers were generally quite realistic, he admits that there are some sticky facts concerning "buoyant hopes" during the Johnson administration: "When U.S. combat units flooded into Vietnam from 1965 on, the pessimism of later 1964 gave way increasingly to buoyant hopes, by 1967, of an essentially military victory." Moreover, in essential agreement with the observations reported by James Thomson, Jr., and other "insiders" in the Johnson administration, Ellsberg says that yes, there was a great deal of "self-deception," "inadvertence," "inattention," "lack of realistic planning," "over-ambitious aims for means used," and "over-optimistic expectations." He acknowledges that all these "flaws and limitations increasingly do characterize the executive decision-making process." But Ellsberg tries to explain away all the overoptimism as the consequence of implementing the chosen policy: The deception of Congress and the public gave rise to a tendency for the policy-makers' expectations gradually to "drift in the direction of the public optimism expressed constantly from the outset . . . eventually replacing phony and invalid optimism with genuine invalid optimism."

Thus, Ellsberg leaves open the possibility that President Johnson and his advisers were making miscalculations about their Vietnam policies as a result of wishful thinking during 1967 and perhaps before that, "from 1965 on." In addition, he suggests that when all the major escalation decisions were made, well before 1967, the policy-makers' adherence to the fundamental rule may itself have been based on a miscalculation concerning political reaction in the United States to the alternative policy of withdrawal from Vietnam: "Fear of . . . McCarthyism's power at the polls may always have been *overdrawn*. . . . Yet, what matters, of course, is what . . . officials *believe* their risks to be."

Ellsberg mentions some observations suggesting that during 1965 the fundamental rule, whether based on miscalculations or not, was used as a kind of slogan and that social pressure was put on the President to act in accordance with the slogan in a way that would deflect attention away from other serious risks:

> In the spring of 1965 President Johnson is reported to have received calls almost daily from one of his closest advisers telling him (what no one had to tell him): "Lyndon, don't be the first American President to lose a war." It is true that such advisers omitted warnings of other deadly errors.

Ellsberg adds that Johnson's advisers neglected to call his attention to the dangers of by-passing Congress, of allowing official military statements that describe the enemy forces as defeated to be issued during a lull in the fighting when those forces were readying for a major offensive, and of accepting recommendations from the Pentagon to "draft and spend and kill and suffer casualties at the rate . . . [the] military will propose."

In short, this portion of Ellsberg's account of what was going on in 1965 does not offer such convincing arguments in support of his purely political explanation that an explanation based on the groupthink hypothesis should be discarded. In contrast to more global statements he makes elsewhere in his paper, these passages certainly do not preclude the possibility that the members of Johnson's advisory group were collectively overlooking or remaining silent about some of the most unfavorable consequences of their policy recommendations.

A "colossal misjudgment" and subsequent miscalculations

As for the alleged "pessimism of later 1964," the available evidence does not show an impressive degree of fit with Ellsberg's hypothesis that the President and his advisers had a realistic view of what their escalation decisions would accomplish. When we look into the Pentagon Papers, we find that the conferees sometimes did talk about the possibility that the war might last for years, but we also find a number of direct contradictions of Ellsberg's statement that unrealistic hopes were not a prominent factor in the major escalation decisions of late 1964 and early 1965. These decisions involved accepting a military plan, known as Operation Rolling Thunder, to launch massive air attacks against North Vietnam. According to the Department of Defense study, the original purpose of the plan was "to break the will of North Vietnam." The Department of Defense study also asserts: "The idea that destroying, or threatening to destroy, North Vietnam's industry would pressure Hanoi into calling it quits, seems, in retrospect, a *colossal misjudgment.*" In the spring of 1965, when the air assaults were started, according to the study, "official hopes were high that the Rolling Thunder program . . . would rapidly convince Hanoi that it should agree to negotiate a settlement to the war in the South. After a month of bombing with no response from the North Vietnamese, optimism began to wane."

According to the Pentagon Papers, the escalation of the air war was planned secretly during the election campaign in the fall of 1964. The decision to authorize the first phase of the plan was made one month *after* Johnson's election victory; the decision to authorize the second phase was made only about two months later. In this period the administration did not need to be very concerned about the prospects of defeat of its program in Congress, and the next election was a long way off. The landslide victory itself must have shown the astute political minds in Washington that the failure of Goldwater's aggressive anti-Communist campaign meant that at least for the time being there was little realistic basis for worry about the power of the right-wing Republicans to mobilize public support. Yet precisely during the months when the election victory was still fresh in mind President Johnson and his advisers made the major decisions to authorize the Rolling Thunder program.

Tom Wicker, *New York Times* associate editor and columnist, reports that he was informed by several officials close to the President in 1964 that the same type of elated self-confidence that had pervaded the thinking of Kennedy's in-group prior to the Bay of Pigs fiasco was reexperienced following the 1964 election victory, at the time Johnson and his advisers committed themselves to escalating the air war in Vietnam:

> Several officials who were close to Johnson at that time . . . recall the sheer *ebullience* of the moment. One of them had also served Kennedy and remembers the same *sense of omnipotence* in the White House in early 1961. . . . [He said,] "*We thought we had the golden touch. It was just like that with Johnson after sixty-four.*"

These observations, if accurate, suggest that when Johnson and his principal advisers were deliberating about the escalation decisions, they shared a staunch faith that somehow everything would come out right, despite all the gloomy predictions in the intelligence reports prepared by their underlings.

By the summer of 1965, the complete failure of the air war could not be denied, especially when the Vietcong successfully carried out a major offensive and took over large amounts of territory in South Vietnam. Washington began to receive urgent requests from General Westmoreland, the United States military commander in Vietnam, for more and more ground troops. At the end of July, when the decision was made to approve a huge increase in ground forces, Washington officials had become extremely pessimistic, just as Ellsberg says. They realized the war would be long and hard and would require even more troops in the future. But even so, the conferees' intentions and expectations, described in the Pentagon Papers, only partially corresponded to the pattern described by Ellsberg. True, "the major participants in the decision . . . *understood* the consequences." But we are also told that the choice, as they saw it

> was *not* whether to hold on for a while or let go—the choice was viewed as *winning* or losing South Vietnam. . . .
> Instead of simply denying the enemy victory and convincing him that he would not win, the thrust became *defeating* the enemy in the South.

The Department of Defense study suggests that when the decision was made to increase American forces in 1965, perhaps "no one really foresaw what the troop needs in Vietnam would be," and the enemy forces may have been "consistently underrated." This could hardly be called an instance in which the decision-makers definitely foresaw the consequences.

All during the summer and fall of 1965, the air war against North Vietnam was continued. But because Operation Rolling Thunder was not achieving its original purpose of breaking the will of the North Vietnamese, its purpose was redefined. The new objective of the operation was to reduce the flow of men and supplies from the north. This change for the first time brought the policy-makers' internal rationale into line with the alleged purpose that had been told to Congress and to the public during the preceding months. In deciding to continue the Rolling Thunder program to attain this much more modest objective, however, the Washington officials were making still another misjudgment. The Pentagon Papers quote a Department of Defense document dated January 18, 1966, that states: "The program [Rolling Thunder] so far has not successfully interdicted infiltration of men and material into South Vietnam."

Here again, as in the case of the decision to increase ground troops, we see that a decision made when the policy-makers were gloomy is not necessarily free of miscalculations. In general, the mere fact that conferees find themselves in a crisis and realize they are facing the possibility of defeat does not preclude a strong element of wishful thinking and even a strong dose of over-optimism about limited hopes such as escaping with their skins intact, successfully postponing defeat indefinitely, and holding out long enough for a lucky break to turn the tide in their favor.

A major part of Ellsberg's argument about the lack of a sizable gap between expectations and reality hinges on the fact that when the major escalation decisions were made, reports from intelligence experts in the CIA, the State Department, and the Defense Department showed a "persistent skepticism . . . about proposals for improving [the long-run prospects of anti-Communist forces] . . . a pessimism almost unrelieved, often stark—yet in retrospect, credibly realistic, frank, cogent." The Pentagon Papers bear out Ellsberg's contention that the policy-makers were aware of at least some of the pessimistic estimates contained in these reports. But there is no evidence to show that President Johnson and his principal advisers personally accepted the invariably pessimistic estimates in the intelligence reports or took seriously the likelihood that further major escalations of the type outlined in the contingency plans prepared by assistant secretaries and other lower-echelon officials would actually be needed. The Pentagon Papers indicate that on some important occasions the dire forecasts were simply ignored. In the late fall of 1964, for example, the high hopes of President Johnson and his principal advisers that Operation Rolling Thunder would break the will of North Vietnam were evidently not diminished by the fact that the entire intelligence community, according to the Department of Defense study, "tended toward a pessimistic view." About a year and a half later, the CIA repeatedly estimated that stepping up the bombing of North Vietnam's oil-storage facilities would not "cripple Communist military operations," and the policy-makers were aware of this prediction. Instead of accepting it, however, they apparently accepted the optimistic estimates from the Pentagon, which asserted that the bombing would "bring the enemy to the conference table or cause the insurgency to wither from lack of support." Thus the Pentagon Papers do not support Ellsberg's contention but, instead, corroborate statements of the inside observers who say that President Johnson and his inner circle of advisers paid little attention to the pessimistic forecasts from experts in the government's intelligence agencies.

The cogency and validity of Ellsberg's explanation remain an open question. The evidence shows that even if his main arguments against the quagmire myth are subsequently verified by fresh evidence about the deliberations of the policy-makers, his analysis of the major escalation decisions made by the Johnson administration still leaves open the possibility that the President's advisory group made serious miscalculations and that the errors arose from group pressures of the type postulated by the groupthink hypothesis. Ellsberg's impressive case that the policy-makers gave high priority to the decision rule "this is not the year to allow a red flag to rise over Saigon" may prove to be well substantiated, but the evidence may also show that Johnson's inner circle used this rule in just the way that a group suffering from groupthink uses any shared ideological slogan or stereotype. Furthermore, Ellsberg's own critique of the quagmire myth presents a number of observations and inferences concerning errors of judgment, overoptimism, and wishful thinking that are essentially the same as those contained in reports made by inside observers who were located in the White House (James Thomson and Bill Moyers), in the Department of Defense (Townsend Hoopes), and in the State Department (Chester Cooper) during the Johnson administration. Nevertheless, the challenge posed by Ellsberg's analysis highlights the need to postpone drawing any definitive conclusions until we have further evidence about what the members of the policy-making group believed and what they said to each other when they were deliberating about their escalation decisions.

Major sources of error

James Thomson, Jr., a historian who was a member of McGeorge Bundy's staff in the White House, has attempted to explain the poor quality of the escalation decisions, which he calls "Lyndon Johnson's slow-motion Bay of Pigs." He addresses himself to the paradox that although the members of the policy-making group had all the attributes of well-qualified and well-intentioned leaders—sound training, high ability, and humanitarian ideals—they persistently ignored the major consequences of practically all their Vietnam War policy decisions. They repeatedly gave in to pressures for a military rather than a diplomatic or political solution; they took little account of the destructive impact of their policies on the Vietnamese people, whom they were supposedly helping; they badly bungled or sabotaged every opportunity to negotiate disengagement of the United States from Vietnam. What could cause a group of responsible policy-makers to persist in a course of action that was producing so much suffering to the people of Vietnam and so much havoc within their own nation?

In attempting to answer this question, Thomson discusses a large number of causal factors. Some are historical and political considerations, such as institutional constraints in the State Department against sponsoring policies that could be construed as "soft on communism" in the Far East; these were the legacy of America's Asia policy of the 1950s. Thomson also points out that the policy advisory group was insulated from political expertise in the government and, as the Vietnam decisions progressively involved more and more military force, it was essential for the policy-makers to consult more and more military experts, who almost always proposed escalating the war. Still, being exposed to strong pressures from the military establishment should not necessarily cause high-level civilians who preside over their country's foreign policy to move consistently in the direction of military escalation. Surely hardheaded policy-makers in the Johnson administration could raise critical questions, insist on full political briefings, assess the unfortunate consequences of military escalation, and work out alternative ways of settling the problems of United States involvement in Vietnam.

What happened to the critical evaluators, the doubters, the dissenters? Thomson answers this crucial question, again on the basis of his personal observations and experiences within the White House, by citing a number of psychological factors that he believes influenced decision-making by the group of men who shaped America's Vietnam policy. He lists about two dozen specific factors, which can be classified into six major categories: (1) excessive time pressures, (2) bureaucratic detachment, (3) stereotyped views of Communists and Orientals, (4) overcommitment to defeating the enemy, (5) domestication of dissenters, and (6) avoidance of opposing views. I shall try to show how Thomson's seemingly diverse points may be brought together into a more comprehensive explanation by giving an interpretation in terms of the groupthink hypothesis.

Applying the groupthink hypothesis

Because we still lack well-authenticated details of the way the President and his inner circle carried out their policy deliberations from 1964 to 1968, the available observations must be used mainly to point up the new questions that need to be answered in order to determine whether the groupthink hypothesis offers at least a partial explanation of the ill-fated escalation decisions made by the Johnson administration. Thomson's account of the defective ways Johnson's in-group arrived at its Vietnam policy decisions are fairly well corroborated by other inside observers (Cooper, Hoopes, and Moyers) and hint at small-group processes. But neither Thomson nor any other observer explicitly discusses any aspect of group dynamics (except for the few sentences quoted from Bill Moyers concerning the group's tendency to seek consensus instead of debating the issues). Thomson confines his discussion to two different types of causes, both of which may have played an important role in the Vietnam escalation policy. One type involves the sociological features of the large organization—the social patterns and pressures that arise in a government bureacracy. The other type pertains to individual psychology, focusing on the way the individual decision-maker reacts to the tasks and pressures imposed upon him. Do these two types of causal factors tell the whole story?

The groupthink hypothesis, when added to the sociological and the individual psychological factors, may contribute a more complete explanation and may help us understand how and why the various patterns of behavior described by Thomson became dominant reactions. The groupthink hypothesis can encompass the psychological factors he discusses but points to a different source of trouble from that of explanations focusing only on the bureaucratic organization and on the individual. Rather than assuming that each policy-maker is responding to the demands of the bureaucracy and to other pressures in his own way and that it so happens that each of them ends up by becoming detached, biased, overcommitted to his past decisions and prone to ignore challenging intelligence reports, we shall pursue the possibility that the commonality of the responses of the key policy-makers may arise from their interaction in a small group, which generates norms that all the members strive to live up to.

Effects of stress on group cohesiveness

The first factor derived from Thomson's analysis—excessive time pressure—is likely to affect the mental efficiency of any individual, whether he is functioning alone or in a group. Time pressure is, of course, one of the sources of stress that besets any group of executives in a crisis, especially if the members are required to take prompt action when they are confronted with contradictory political pressures from many different interested parties. Whenever a decision has to be made that vitally affects the security of his nation, the government executive is likely to undergo a variety of severe stresses. He realizes that a great deal is at stake for his country and for the rest of the world and that it also may be a crucial moment in his personal career. If he chooses the wrong course of action, he may lose his status, face public humiliation, and suffer a profound loss of self-esteem. These political and personal threats can have a cumulative effect, especially when the decision-maker is under constant time pressure and has little opportunity to study even the most important proposals. (Washington bureaucrats quipped that the reason McNamara looked so good, in comparison to the others who participated in the White House meetings, was that the long drive from the Pentagon gave him eight extra minutes to do his homework in the back of his limousine.) All members of a government policy-making group share these common sources of stress whenever they have to make an important foreign policy decision. Even if the President alone is officially responsible, each of his close advisers knows that if the group makes a serious error and the prestige of the administration is badly damaged, every member may in one way or another be held accountable. Any member of the inner circle might become a scapegoat and be pilloried by investigating committees or the news media. The members of Johnson's advisory group were subjected to a mounting spiral of severe stress as the threats of public humiliation and loss of prestige gradually began to materialize.

Field studies of infantry platoons, air crews, and disaster control teams bear out the findings of social psychological experiments with college students that show that external sources of stress produce a heightened need for affiliation. In times of crisis, a natural tendency arises among the harassed members of a preestablished group to meet together more often and to communicate more than ever with each other, to find out what the others know about the dangers confronting them, to exchange ideas about how the threats might best be dealt with, and to gain reassurance. The heightened need for affiliation, which leads to greater dependency upon one's primary work group and increased motivation to adhere to the group's norms, can have beneficial effects on morale and stress tolerance. But the increase in group cohesiveness will have adverse effects if it leads, as the groupthink hypothesis predicts, to an increase in concurrence-seeking at the expense of critical thinking. An executive committee like Johnson's Tuesday Lunch Group would be expected to show both the positive and the negative effects of increased cohesiveness during periods of crisis.

We can view the excessive time pressures described by Thomson as a causal factor that adversely affects the quality of the policy-makers' decisions in at least two different ways. First, overwork and fatigue generally impair each decision-maker's mental efficiency and judgment, interfering with his ability to concentrate on complicated discussions, to absorb new information, and to use his imagination to anticipate the future consequences of alternative courses of action. (This is a matter of individual psychology and is the aspect emphasized by Thomson.) The additional aspect to be considered is this: Excessive time pressure is a source of stress that, along with the even more severe sources of stress that generally arise in a crisis, will have the effect of inducing a policy-making group to become more cohesive and more likely to indulge in groupthink. Thus, in order to pursue the groupthink hypothesis, we are led to raise this question: *Did the members of Johnson's advisory group display signs of an increase in group cohesiveness and a corresponding increase in manifestations of concurrence-seeking during crisis periods, when they had relatively little time off from their jobs?* We shall return to this question shortly.

Effects of commitment to prior group decisions

Bureaucratic detachment and stereotyped views of Communists and Asians involve attitudes that affect the deliberations preceding each new decision. From the beginning, most members of Johnson's inner circle probably shared similar ideological viewpoints on basic issues of foreign policy and domestic politics. However, all of them probably did not start with the same attitude of detachment toward the human suffering inflicted by the war and the same unsophisticated stereotypes concerning world communism and the peoples of the Orient. As a historian, Thomson was shocked to realize the extent to which crudely propagandistic conceptions entered the group's plans and policy statements. He indicates that Johnson's inner circle uncritically accepted the domino theory, which simplistically assumes that all Asian countries will act alike, so that if the Communists were permitted to gain control over one country in the Far East, all neighboring countries would promptly become vulnerable and fall under Communist domination. As for the Vietcong and the North Vietnamese, the dominant stereotypes made these "Communist enemies" into the embodiment of evil and thus legitimized the destruction of countless human lives and the burning of villages. In support of Thomson's analysis, psychologist Ralph K. White has shown how consistently the public statements of Johnson, Rusk, McNamara, and others in the Tuesday Lunch Group reveal the pervasiveness of the policy-maker's black-and-white picture of the Vietnam War, which always contrasts an image of the diabolical opponents with an image of the invariably moral and virile American government.

When Johnson's Tuesday Lunch Group was formed, some members probably held these attitudes strongly and others probably had somewhat different views. In the course of interaction, the former may have influenced the latter. For example, as Thomson suggests, the few members who had spent many years participating in military planning conferences at the Pentagon may have introduced to the rest of the group a detached dehumanizing attitude toward the Vietnam War, using the euphemistic vocabulary of "body counts," "surgical air strikes," and "pacification." The members of the group who began with a more humanistic way of thinking and talking about the evils of war may have followed the lead of the military men. But why would the members holding detached attitudes succeed in getting the others to adopt their dehumanizing outlook? Why not the other way around?

One of the main psychological assumptions underlying the groupthink hypothesis is that when a policy-making group becomes highly cohesive, a homogenization of viewpoints takes place, helping the group to preserve its unity by enabling all the members to continue to support the decisions to which the group has become committed. When one of the main norms is being committed to pursuing a war policy, as in this case, we expect that commitment will be bolstered by subsidiary norms that reduce disputes and disharmony within the group. In this context, detachment toward the use of military means and dehumanization of the victims of war, as well as negative stereotypes of the enemy, have functional value for a group committed to military escalation. Sharing such attitudes tends to minimize the likelihood that any member will challenge the group's policy by raising moral and humanitarian considerations, which would stimulate bickering, recriminations, and discord. It follows from the same psychological assumption that if the same group were to commit itself to a nonviolent peace-seeking course of action, a reverse trend would appear: The members who personally think in terms of moral and humanitarian values would no longer suppress such considerations but, rather, would take the lead in setting a new fashion for using a humanizing vocabulary that bolsters the new group norm.[2]

Additional historical evidence is obviously needed in order to pursue the suggestion that the attitude of detachment toward the victims of war and the stereotyped conceptions of the North Vietnamese Communists expressed by Johnson's Tuesday Lunch Group might be interpreted as symptoms of groupthink. Among the main questions to be answered are those having to do with when, in the sequence of decisions, these adverse attitudes were manifested by most or all members of the group. *Were attitudes of detachment and stereotyped views of Communists and Asians expressed relatively rarely by members of the in-group before their first major decisions to escalate the war? Does the emergence of a dehumanizing vocabulary and stereotyped terms in the group's discussions fit the pattern of a subsidiary group norm that follows the militaristic decisions the members had previously agreed upon?*

Overcommitment to defeating the enemy—another factor described by Thomson—involves a well-known human weakness that makes it hard for anyone to correct the errors he has made in the past. The men in Johnson's inner circle, according to Thomson, ultimately convinced themselves that the Vietnam War was of crucial significance for America's future—a conviction that grew directly out of their own explanations and justifications. It became essential to the policy-makers to continue the costly and unpopular war, Thomson surmises, because they had *said* it was essential. Instead of reevaluating their policy in response to clear-cut setbacks, their energetic proselytizing led them to engage in "rhetorical escalation" that matched the military escalation, deepening their commitment to military victory rather than a political solution through negotiation with the government of North Vietnam. The members of Johnson's inner circle, according to another inside observer, remained "united both in their conviction about the rightness of present policy and the fact that all were implicated in the major [escalation] decisions since 1964."

We know that most individuals become heavily ego-involved in maintaining their commitment to any important decision for which they feel at least partly responsible. Once a decision-maker has publicly announced the course of action he has selected, he is inclined to avoid looking at evidence of the unfavorable consequences. He tries to reinterpret setbacks as victories, to invent new arguments to convince himself and others that he made the right decision, clinging stubbornly to unsuccessful policies long after everyone else can see that a change is needed. Each policy-maker, whether he has made the crucial decisions by himself or as a member of a group, is thus motivated to perpetuate his past errors—provided, of course, that his nose is not rubbed in inescapable evidence.

Like attitudes of detachment and derogatory stereotypes, the tendency to recommit oneself to prior decisions can be greatly augmented by social pressures that arise within a cohesive group. From time to time, setbacks induce a policy-maker to doubt the wisdom of past decisions in which he has participated. But what a man does about his doubts, if he is a member of an in-group of policy-makers, depends in large part on the norms of the group. If the members agree that loyalty to their group and its goals requires rigorous support of the group's primary commitment to open-minded scrutiny of new evidence and willingness to admit errors (as in a group committed to the ideals of scientific research), the usual psychological tendency to recommit themselves to their past decisions after a setback can give way to a careful reappraisal of the wisdom of their past judgments. The group norm in such a case inclines them to compare their policy with alternative courses of action and may lead them to reverse their earlier decisions. On the other hand, if, as often happens, the members feel that loyalty to the group requires unwavering support of the group's past policy decisions, the usual psychological tendency to bolster past commitments is reinforced. Following a series of escalation decisions, every member is likely to insist that the same old military drumbeat is the right one and that sooner or later everyone who matters will want to be in step with it.

Did President Johnson's group of policy-makers show signs of adhering to a norm requiring the members to continue supporting the group's past escalation decisions? Many of the characteristics mentioned by Thomson and other observers suggest a positive answer. In elaborating on the group's commitment to its past decisions, Thomson describes the group's tendency to evolve a set of shared rationalizations to justify the militant Vietnam policy. He mentions a closely related symptom that also carries a strong taint of groupthink—mutual agreement to rewrite recent history in a way that would justify the Vietnam escalation policy:

> another result of Vietnam decision-making has been *the abuse and distortion of history*. Vietnamese, Southeast Asian, and Far Eastern history has been rewritten by our policy-makers, and their spokesmen, to conform with the alleged necessity of our presence in Vietnam. Highly dubious analogies from our experience elsewhere—the "Munich" sellout and "containment" from

Europe, the Malayan insurgency and the Korean War from Asia—have been imported in order to justify our actions. And more recent events have been fitted to the Procrustean bed of Vietnam. Most notably, the change of power in Indonesia in 1965–1966 has been ascribed to our Vietnam presence; and virtually all progress in the Pacific region—the rise of regionalism, new forms of cooperation, the mounting growth rates—has been similarly explained. The Indonesian allegation is undoubtedly false (I tried to prove it, during six months of careful investigation at the White House, and had to confess failure); the regional allegation is patently unprovable in either direction.

We cannot avoid recollecting how the bureaucrats in Orwell's *1984* rewrote their own history and were able to make their new versions quite acceptable to those who remembered what really happened by requiring all loyal followers of Big Brother to practice "doublethink"—knowing and at the same time not knowing the truth. How did the policy-makers in the Johnson administration handle this problem within their own ranks? *Were the insiders who could not accept the new rationalized version of East Asian history silenced by the rest of the group?*

Conformity pressures

Similar questions need to be answered about the way in which the policy-makers handled the "loyal opposition," the government officials, Vietnam experts, and Congressmen who were arguing in favor of the alternative policy of negotiating a peace settlement. Did the members of Johnson's policy-making group consider the eminent members of their own political party who advocated alternative policies to be transmitters of potentially important ideas about how the problems of Vietnam might be solved? Or *did they gravitate toward the groupthink view that advocates of a negotiated peace were disloyal and had to be kept out of their high counsels? Did they privately brand the leading doves as despicable "isolationists" who were a threat to American security?*

We can see from the foregoing questions that from the standpoint of a groupthink interpretation, the phenomena resulting from the group's commitment to its past policy decisions include the remaining types of factors extracted from Thomson's analysis—domestication of dissenters and avoidance of opposing views from critics inside and outside the government. Both of these may be manifestations of a group process involving a constant striving for homogeneous beliefs and judgments among all members of the in-group, in line with their past commitments. Striving for consensus, which helps the members achieve a sense of group unity and esprit de corps, is, of course, the psychological basis for all the symptoms of groupthink.

We learn from Thomson that during the Johnson administration everyone in the hierarchy, including every senior official, was subjected to conformity pressures, which took the form of making those who openly questioned the escalation policy the butt of an ominous epithet: "I am afraid he's losing his effectiveness." This "effectiveness trap"—the threat of being branded a "has been" and losing access to the seats of power—inclines its victims to suppress or tone down their criticisms. In a more subtle way, it makes any member who starts to voice his misgivings ready to retreat to a seemingly acquiescent position in the presence of quizzical facial expressions and crisp retorts from perturbed associates and superiors.

Thomson also informs us that during Johnson's administration, whenever members of the in-group began to express doubts—as some of them certainly did—they were treated in a rather standardized way that effectively "domesticated" them through subtle social pressures. The dissenter was made to feel at home, providing he lived up to two restrictions: first, that he did not voice his doubts to outsiders and thus play into the hands of the opposition; and second, that he kept his criticisms within the bounds of acceptable deviation, not challenging any of the fundamental assumptions of the group's prior commitments. One "domesticated dissenter" was Bill Moyers, a close adviser of President Johnson. When Moyers arrived at a meeting, Thomson tells us, the President greeted him with, "Well, here comes Mr. Stop-the-Bombing." Undersecretary of State George Ball, who became a critic of the escalation decisions, was similarly domesticated for a time and became known as "the inhouse devil's advocate on Vietnam." From time to time he was encouraged to "speak his piece . . . and there was minimal unpleasantness." The upshot, Thomson says, was that "the club remained intact."

From the standpoint of reducing tension and bolstering morale within "the club," the subtle domestication process may work well, both for the dissenter and for the rest of the group. The nonconformist can feel that he is still accepted as a member in good standing. Unaware of the extent to which he is being influenced by the majority, he has the illusion that he is free to speak his mind. If on occasion he goes too far, he is warned about his deviation in an affectionate or joking way and is reminded only indirectly of his potentially precarious status by the labels the others give him ("Mr. Stop-the-Bombing," "our favorite dove"). The others in the group, as Thomson says, feel satisfied about giving full consideration to the opposing position and can even pat themselves on the back for being so democratic about tolerating open dissent. Nevertheless, the domesticated dissenter repeatedly gets the message that there is only a very small piece of critical territory he can tread safely and still remain a member in good standing. He knows that if he is not careful he will reach the boundary beyond which he risks being branded as having lost his "effectiveness."

In this connection, we wonder why two of the domesticated dissenters within Johnson's in-group—George Ball and Bill Moyers—unexpectedly resigned from their posts and left Washington in 1966. A similar question arises about the departure of McGeorge Bundy in 1967 and Robert McNamara in 1968. Did these men leave for purely personal reasons that had

President Johnson conferring with one of his closest aides,
Bill Moyers, who was one of the domesticated dissenters on
the Vietnam War within Johnson's inner circle.

nothing to do with their criticisms of the escalation policy? Were they perhaps fired by President Johnson—without the consent of his other advisers—because he was dissatisfied with their work or because he was offended by their criticisms? *Or was the departure of any of these formerly domesticated dissenters a result of a group process, involving collective pressures from most or all other members of the in-group because of violations of a group norm—the taboo against challenging the war policies to which the group had previously committed itself?* If the evidence points to an affirmative answer to the last question, indicating that one or more of the dissenters became casualties of group pressures, we shall have some strong support for the groupthink hypothesis.

These are not rhetorical questions. Several alternative hypotheses could account for the departure of the domesticated dissenters. The groupthink hypothesis, though one plausible explanation, cannot yet be evaluated as being more valid than (for example) the possibility that the President got rid of these men not as the leader acting on behalf of the group but solely on his own initiative, without the support of the majority of his close advisers. It is even conceivable that the inner circle was split into factions and that a coalition of (for example) the Joint Chiefs of Staff and Walt Rostow won the support of the President at the expense of an opposing faction that was pushing for deescalation. We cannot expect to be in a position to evaluate the applicability of the groupthink hypothesis to the handling of dissenters among Johnson's advisers until more candid observations become available from men who left the group and from core insiders who can describe the deliberations at the Tuesday lunch meetings. Even more valuable would be detailed minutes of those meetings, specifying who said what about each of the issues raised by the domesticated dissenters. In the meantime, we have to make do with the observations already at hand.

The ways of a transgressor: exit Robert McNamara

Fortunately, a detailed account has been published of how Secretary of Defense McNamara was precipitously removed from his position as the second most powerful member of the Johnson administration. The story comes from Townsend Hoopes, whose position as undersecretary of the Air Force brought him in frequent contact with McNamara during the Secretary's last months in office. Hoopes was in a position to make firsthand observations of events at the Pentagon, but, regrettably, he does not inform us about his sources of information concerning what McNamara and others said at high-level meetings of the President's advisory group, in which the undersecretary was not a participant. If Hoopes' statements prove to be accurate, we shall be led to conclude that McNamara was a domesticated dissenter who, despite desperate attempts to remain a loyal member of Johnson's team, was

eliminated from the government because his repeated efforts to bring about a
policy change in the direction of deescalation of the Vietnam War could not be
tolerated by what Hoopes calls the "gathering of homogeneous hawks."

In the spring of 1967, according to Hoopes, the inner group of advisers
was nearly unanimous in supporting the Vietnam War policy, the one
dissenter being McNamara. The book on the Pentagon Papers prepared by
The New York Times contains a considerable amount of documentary
evidence of McNamara's dissent:

> Mr. McNamara's disillusionment with the war has been reported previously,
> but the depth of his dissent from established policy is fully documented for
> the first time in the Pentagon study, which he commissioned on June 17,
> 1967.
>
> The study details how this turnabout by Mr. McNamara—originally a
> leading advocate of the bombing policy and, in 1965, a confident believer
> that American intervention would bring the Vietcong insurgency under con-
> trol—opened a deep policy rift in the Johnson Administration.
>
> The study does not specifically say, however, that his break with
> established policy led President Johnson to nominate him on November 28,
> 1967, as president of the World Bank and to replace him as Secretary of
> Defense.

There are many indications that throughout the spring of 1967
McNamara went through considerable turmoil after he had concluded that
the others in the group were wrong in assuming that the North Vietnamese
could be bombed into coming to the negotiating table. According to some
reports, supposedly originating with his wife, he was "at war with himself"
and up half the night trying to decide what he ought to do.

A highly revealing episode occurred shortly after McNamara had
presented some impressive facts about the ineffectiveness of the bombings to
a Senate investigating committee. President Johnson was displeased by
McNamara's statement and made bitter comments about his giving this information to the Senators. The President complained to one Senator, "that
military genius, McNamara, has gone dovish on me." To someone on his
staff in the White House, the President spoke more heatedly, accusing the
Secretary of Defense of playing right into the hands of the enemy, on the
grounds that his statement would increase Hanoi's bargaining power. "Vent-
ing his annoyance to a member of his staff, he drew the analogy of a man trying to sell his house, while one of the sons of the family went to the prospective
buyer to point out that there were leaks in the basement." This line of thought
strongly suggests that in his own mind Johnson regarded his in-group of policy
advisers as a family and its leading dissident member as an irresponsible son
who was sabotaging the family's interests. Underlying this revealing imagery
seem to be two implicit assumptions that epitomize groupthink: We are a
good group, so any deceitful acts we perpetrate are fully justified. Anyone in
the group who is unwilling to distort the truth to help us is disloyal.

Hoopes describes how with each passing month McNamara was gradually eased out of his powerful position, finding himself less and less welcome at the White House, until finally he was removed from his high office in "a fast shuffle" by the President, who was "confident that he would go quietly and suffer the indignity in silence." Once McNamara was removed from the group, Hoopes concludes, the members could once again enjoy complete unity and relatively undisturbed confidence in the soundness of their war policy. During the months following McNamara's nonvoluntary departure, increasing numbers of intelligence specialists and other experts were urging a reappraisal on the basis of new evidence following the surprise Tet offensive by the supposedly defeated Vietcong in early 1968. But, according to Hoopes, the in-group, having become temporarily homogeneous once again, avoided calling them in for consultations and apparently did not study their reports.

The member's sense of confidence may have been maintained for a time by Rostow's effective mindguarding, which went far beyond the call of duty. Hoopes claims that during the last year of Johnson's administration, as discontent with the Vietnam War was growing throughout America and even within the military bureaucracy, Rostow cleverly screened the inflow of information and used his power to keep dissident experts away from the White House. This had the intended effect of preventing the President and some of his advisers from becoming fully aware of the extent of disaffection with the war and of the grounds for it. The group managed to discount all the strong pressures from prestigious members of their own political party and even from former members of the White House group (such as McGeorge Bundy) until after a new member of the Tuesday Lunch Group—Clark Clifford, who replaced McNamara as Secretary of Defense—unexpectedly became convinced of the soundness of the deescalation position. (Clifford had been brought in as a dependable hawk who would restore unity to the group.) Relatively unhampered by loyalties to the old group, Clifford reported to Hoopes and the rest of his revitalized staff at the Pentagon that at the daily meetings on Vietnam in the White House he was outnumbered 8 to 1. But Clifford fought hard and well, according to Hoopes. During this period other powerful influences may also have been at work to induce Secretary of State Rusk and others in the group to take account, belatedly, of the numerous persuasive reasons for modifying their policy.[3] The transformation culminated in the unprecedented speech from the White House on March 31, 1968, when, with tears in his eyes, President Johnson announced that he was deescalating the war in Vietnam and would not seek reelection.

If Hoopes' account of the way McNamara and other nonconformists were dealt with is corroborated by subsequent testimony from other observers and by documentary records, we shall have strong evidence that, at least during the last half of 1967, the failure of Johnson's in-group to take account of the growing signs that its Vietnam policy required drastic revision was a product of groupthink. The hypothesis leads us to ask questions about other symptoms of groupthink, such as striving for unanimous agreement and willingness to take serious risks on the basis of a shared illusion of invulnerability.

Unanimity within the group

In the Pentagon Papers, the Department of Defense analysts say that "from the September [1964] meeting forward, there was little basic disagreement among the principals [the term the study uses for the senior policymakers] on the need for military operations against the North." Lyndon B. Johnson, however, says in his memoirs that sometimes there were marked disagreements among his advisers. But the instances he describes seem limited to periods when more than one member of the group was proposing a temporary halt in the bombing as a move toward peace. For example, at a meeting on December 18, 1965, when McNamara, Rusk, and Bundy argued for a bombing pause in order to pursue Soviet Ambassador Dobrynin's proposal for diplomatic discussions with Hanoi, the military men and others gave opposing arguments that were "equally persuasive," according to Johnson, and it was "another of those 51–49 decisions that . . . keep [the President] awake late at night." In contrast, Johnson emphasizes the unanimous agreement of the group in his descriptions of six meetings at which major escalation decisions were recommended—on September 9, 1964; February 6 and 8, 1965; July 27, 1965; January 31, 1966; and September 28, 1967. On the last of these dates, for example, the issue was whether to speed deployment of American troops to Vietnam, as requested by General Westmoreland. Johnson's only comment is, "All my advisers agreed that we should carry out this acceleration."

Henry Graff, when interviewing members of the Tuesday Lunch Group, was impressed by the repeated emphasis on unanimity expressed by each of them. George Ball, when asked in 1966 about his opposition to bombing North Vietnam, took pains to affirm his basic agreement with the rest of the group. "The one thing we have to do," Ball resolutely told Graff, "is to win this damned war." He added that until the commitment of a large number of troops was made six months earlier, other options may have been open, but now "there is no longer any useful argument to be made about current policies." Ball seems to have become so domesticated at the time of the interview that we can hardly believe he was still a dissenter.

Confidence in ultimate victory despite repeated setbacks and failures was another theme in the interviews. For example, in January 1968 Rostow told his fellow-historian with complete certainty, "History will salute us." On this point, Graff's interviews bear out an admission made by Bill Moyers after he had resigned from his post in the White House: "There was a confidence," Moyers said, "it was never bragged about, it was just there—a residue, perhaps of the confrontation over the missiles in Cuba—that when the chips were really down, the other people would fold."

Overlooking the risks

The Department of Defense study, in disagreement with Ellsberg's claim that the administration was never optimistic when major escalation decisions were made, indicates that the members of the policy-making group were overoptimistic about defeating North Vietnam by means of bombing raids during 1964 and early 1965. In the book on the Pentagon Papers published by *The New York Times,* Neil Sheehan's summary of the Defense Department study states that in November 1964 the air war against North Vietnam was expected "to last two to six months, during which Hanoi was apparently expected to yield." Despite momentary periods of pessimism and gloom about setbacks, according to Chester Cooper, a great deal of overoptimism was manifested from 1964 up until the last several months of the Johnson administration:

> The optimistic predictions that flowered from time to time . . . reflected genuinely held beliefs. While occasional doubts crossed the minds of some, perhaps all [senior policy-makers], the conviction that the war would end "soon" and favorably was clutched to the breast like a child's security blanket. Views to the contrary were not favorably received. . . . We thought we could handle Vietnam without any noticeable effect on our economy or society. . . .
> Because the war was likely to be over "soon," there was also a reluctance to make any substantial changes in the bureaucratic structure. There would be no special institutional arrangements for staffing the war, for implementing or following up decisions.

We know, of course, that Johnson's Tuesday Lunch Group did not have a carefree attitude about the dangers of extending the Vietnam War to the point where China or Russia might become directly involved. During certain periods, especially before 1966, the members were so keenly aware of the vulnerability of America's forces in Vietnam and of the possible fall of the government of South Vietnam that they wanted to avoid engaging in peace negotiations for fear of having little or no bargaining power. The members of the group continued to be aware of the precariousness of South Vietnam's cooperation with America's anti-Communist efforts throughout the entire Johnson administration. Thus it certainly cannot be said that they maintained grossly overoptimistic illusions about the overall security of the American military enterprise in Vietnam. Yet at times there may have been a more limited type of illusion that inclined the policy-makers to be willing to take long-shot gambles. Many observations suggest that the group experienced some temporary lapses in realism about the grave material, political, and moral risks of escalation. The lapses were caused by shared illusions that "everything will go our way, none of the dangers will seriously affect us."

Observations bearing directly on the risky decisions made by Johnson's Tuesday Lunch Group during 1966 are reported by David Kraslow and Stuart Loory, two well-known journalists who made a careful study of the public record of the Vietnam War and interviewed more than forty United States officials who knew something about the inside story. In their account of what went on behind the scenes when Johnson's Tuesday Lunch Group was making its crucial decisions, we can identify many clear indications of a sense of unwarranted complacency about the ultimate success of the group's chosen policy. If their account proves to be substantially verified by subsequent historical analysis, it will raise a number of additional questions concerning the role of groupthink in the policy-makers' willingness to take extreme risks with regard to provoking an all-out war with China and Russia, presumably on the basis of a shared assumption that events were bound to come out the way they hoped.

Throughout 1966 the Tuesday Lunch Group was primarily concerned about selecting bombing targets in North Vietnam. Kraslow and Loory describe how the group attempted to evaluate every proposed target by following a special procedure, which the members felt would enable them to take account of all the relevant criteria:

> As a result of all the staff work in the Pentagon and at the State Department, the authorization requests for each target were reduced to a single sheet of paper—a kind of report card—on which the suggested strikes were described in summary. Each individual sheet contained a checklist for four items:
> 1. The military advantage of striking the proposed target.
> 2. The risk of American aircraft and pilots in a raid.
> 3. The danger that the strike might widen the war by forcing other countries into the fighting.
> 4. The danger of heavy civilian casualties.
> At the Tuesday lunch, President Johnson and his advisers worked over each of the target sheets like schoolteachers grading examination papers. Each of the men graded each of the targets in the four categories.
>
> The decisions were made on the basis of averaged-out grades. . . .
>
> In this manner the President and his principal advisers, working over a lunch table in the White House, showed their intense concern with individual road junctions, clusters of trucks and structures down to small buildings in a land thousands of miles away. Their obvious concern lent great weight to the contention that never has more care been taken in making sure that limited war-making objectives were not being exceeded.

Did the group's ritualistic adherence to a standardized procedure for selecting targets induce the members to feel justified in their destructive way of dealing with the Vietnamese people? After all, the danger of heavy civilian casualties from United States air attacks was being taken into account on their checklists. Did they allow the averaging to obscure the fact that they were giving the greatest weight to military objectives, with relatively little regard for humanitarian considerations or for political effects that could have serious consequences for United States national security? *Did the members of the group share the illusion that they were being vigilant about all aspects of United States policy in Vietnam, while confining their efforts almost solely to the routines of selecting bombing targets?*

   The great need for vigilance, of course, derived from the danger that a bombing attack would provoke Russia or China to transform the Vietnam War into the third world war. Although this risk was on the members' checklist, on at least one occasion, according to Kraslow and Loory, this consideration was given less importance than the supposed advantages of striking the target. In the late spring of 1966, the Tuesday Lunch Group authorized, for the first time, the bombing of the large petroleum-storage depot in the Hanoi-Haiphong area, even though the members were informed that Soviet ships were located dangerously close to the target area in the harbor at Haiphong. The rationale for this risky decision was that the bombing might push the government of North Vietnam to begin negotiations under conditions favorable to the United States. Throughout the spring of 1966, American government officials had repeatedly tried to find out if the enemy was ready to work out a peace settlement. Ambassador Lodge reported from Saigon that he had some indications that the bombing raids and supply difficulties were creating a strong desire in Hanoi for peace talks. With this information in mind and with full awareness that Soviet ships might accidentally be sunk, the Tuesday Lunch Group decided that the time was ripe for a severe blow in the vicinity of the enemy's major harbor. This decision must have involved much more than mere wishful thinking about the ultimate military and political success of bombing North Vietnam. If Kraslow and Loory are reporting accurately, all members of the group knew the venture was precarious and could bring America to the brink of war with the Soviet Union. The Defense Department analysts who prepared the Pentagon Papers say that the execution message sent to the commander in chief of Pacific forces was "a remarkable document, attesting in detail to the political sensitivity of the strikes."

   If the air attack was so politically sensitive, why was it authorized in the first place? *Was this decision to carry out the bombing raid (despite the risk of provoking the Soviet Union to enter the war) based on a flimsy sense of invulnerability shared by the members of the group while they were conferring?*

   We are not informed about how complacent or perturbed the members felt when they were making the decision, but we are told that subsequently the leading participant, when he was alone, became deeply agitated as he thought about the riskiness of the decision: President Johnson on the night the raid was to be executed (June 29, 1966) was too upset to sleep:

> For months afterward President Johnson would tell occasional visitors how he worried that night that the raids would somehow go wrong and an errant bomb would strike a Soviet ship in Haiphong harbor and start World War III.
>
>   He worried so much that his daughter, Luci, returning home from a date with her fiance, Pat Nugent, urged the President to pray. She . . . urged her father to seek solace in the [Catholic] church [to which she belonged]. . . . At 10:30 P.M. a waiting Dominican monk saw two black limousines drive up to the entrance of the neo-Gothic building. The President, Mrs. Johnson, Luci

President Johnson making his historic television address to the nation on March 31, 1968. Johnson ordered an immediate halt to the bombing of 90 percent of the territory of North Vietnam and challenged Ho Chi Minh "to respond positively and favorably to this new step toward peace." At the end of the address he announced that he would not run for the presidency in 1968.

and Nugent stepped out of one car; a detail of Secret Service men, from the other.

The entire group entered the dim, empty church. The presidential party dropped to its knees and prayed silently.

Back in the White House, the President remained awake most of the night, awaiting the final reports on the raids. At 4:30 A.M., satisfied that no great mishap had occurred, he went to sleep.

Did the President's anxiety about the risks arise only when he was alone, when the members of the group were not available to reassure him about the dangerous action they had collectively authorized? During the day or so preceding the scheduled bombing (when it could have been called off) did he set aside his deep concerns about the danger of provoking the outbreak of World War III out of a sense of commitment to the group? Did he abstain from using his presidential powers to cancel the dangerous mission or to call another meeting of the group to reconsider the decision because he felt that any move toward reversal might be regarded as a violation of the group's taboo against raising doubts about its prior decisions? Unfortunately, Lyndon B. Johnson is less than candid in his memoirs, *The Vantage Point*. He makes no mention of the episode. Perhaps these questions will be answered later in a more revealing biography.

Destroying the elusive flowers of peace

Johnson does mention in his memoirs a series of abortive efforts to end the war in Vietnam through negotiations. His comments pose some related questions about the Tuesday Lunch Group's willingness to take serious risks with regard to sabotaging peace negotiations and losing the United States government's credibility at home and in the world community. One such abortive effort described by Johnson was the Marigold plan, which fleetingly occupied the attention of United States policy-makers toward the end of 1966, when they were assured that Hanoi for once would not demand a cessation of the bombings of North Vietnam until *after* an agreement was reached:

> In the summer of 1966 Ambassador Lodge was approached in Saigon by Janusz Lewandowski, the Polish member of the International Control Commission, who had just visited Hanoi. Talks began. Those exchanges, reported in secret cables under the code name Marigold, continued for six months. . . . After receiving assurance from Lodge [concerning the bombing halt] . . . we authorized him to tell the Polish representative on December 3 that we were ready to meet with the North Vietnamese in Warsaw on December 6, using the Lewandowski draft as the basis for discussion. . . .
> . . . [But] the North Vietnamese failed to show up for the critical meeting the Poles had promised to arrange in Warsaw on December 6, 1966.

The code name Marigold was assigned to this potential peace move by William P. Bundy, an assistant secretary of state in close contact with the policy-making members of the White House group, who was in charge of all such developments. He gave them flower names as a satirical reference to "flower children" and other supposedly disreputable elements in American society who stood for peace—perhaps in deference to the policy-makers' commitment to a hard-nosed military approach in Vietnam.

Chester Cooper, another State Department official and an active "Marigolder," told a bitter story in his memoirs, *The Lost Crusade* (1970). According to Cooper, the Marigold peace initiative was destroyed as a result of a decision by Johnson's Tuesday Lunch Group to resume bombing within the city limits of Hanoi just when the opening sessions were being held in Warsaw with Polish officials who were expected to function as go-betweens with the North Vietnamese government. Essentially the same story had been told two years earlier by Kraslow and Loory on the basis of their interviews of unnamed government officials, one of whom may have been Chester Cooper. One small part of the story is acknowledged by Johnson in his memoirs: "The Poles claimed that the North Vietnamese had failed to appear because we had bombed targets near Hanoi two days before the suggested meeting." Johnson argues that whether the Poles had any definite commitment from Hanoi was uncertain and that the bombings should not have made any difference: "If Lewandowski had reported accurately to Hanoi, the North Vietnamese knew perfectly well that the bombing would not end before the talks began." What Johnson leaves out of his account is that United States negotiations with Polish officials continued for more than a week after the first scheduled meeting date and that while those meetings were going on the United States launched two additional air attacks against Hanoi. According to the account in the Pentagon Papers, "The major result of the raids close to Hanoi on Dec. 2, 4, 13 and 14—all inside a previously established 30-mile sanctuary around the Capital—'was to undercut what appeared to be a peace feeler from Hanoi.'"

Johnson also fails to mention that he and his policy advisers had received repeated warnings that renewal of the bombing would damage the prospects of the Marigold plan. The warning messages came from the United States ambassador in Warsaw, from a leading Polish diplomat in Saigon who had been instrumental in initiating the peace move, and from the Italian ambassador to the United States, who was also one of the originators of the Marigold peace plan. At the same time, a group of influential officials in the United States State Department who were deeply involved in planning the peace talks—including Nicholas Katzenbach, acting as Secretary of State in Rusk's absence, and Averell Harriman, the official United States ambassador given a special mandate to seek peace—strongly recommended to the President and his key advisers that the Hanoi bombing program not be continued while the talks were going on in Warsaw.

Cooper does not believe that the Marigold plan was deliberately sabotaged by Johnson and his advisers; rather, the Johnson administration's search for a way out of the war at the end of 1966 was genuine, although not always "whole-hearted" and "marked by groping and fumbling." One of the main reasons for fumbling this peace initiative and other negotiations later on, Cooper suggests, was that Johnson's in-group was adhering to a norm of being tough and belligerent toward the enemy, maintaining a strong virile stance whenever the opportunity for a give-and-take political settlement arose:

> Stopping or moderating the bombing, even temporarily and even as a logical or necessary accompaniment to a diplomatic initiative was regarded as an American admission of weakness and failure. . . . It was no great mystery why, despite American protestations in favor of a political rather than a military solution, the North Vietnamese were wary and skeptical. And to compound their suspicions, many of Washington's plans for a "political solution" involved, for all practical purposes, a negotiated surrender by the North Vietnamese.

Perhaps the group norm of avoiding conciliatory acts that could be construed as signs of softness and a lack of virility accounts for the fact that during the period when the Marigold plan was germinating, "the issue of negotiations was very much a residual claimant on the time of the President's 'Tuesday Lunch' group; it was the military track, and especially the bombing targets, that virtually dominated the discussions."

Whether the United States policy-makers were sincere or insincere in their efforts to start peace talks in December 1966, they overlooked the foreseeable consequences of their decision to bomb Hanoi at that particular time, when diplomats in many different countries knew that a peace move was supposed to be getting under way. A number of influential foreign diplomats who had worked hard to bring the contending nations to the peace table in Warsaw were astounded and spoke heatedly to Secretary General U Thant and others in the United Nations about America's ruthless destruction of the frail Marigold plan, which they had so carefully nurtured for six months. Furthermore, practically all high-ranking officials in the Italian and Polish governments knew that the first steps of the secret Marigold plan were being taken, for their ambassadors were functioning as mediators. After each of the four bombings of the Hanoi area, representatives of both governments expressed their shock and did not hesitate to openly question United States representatives about their government's alleged sincerity in seeking a peaceful settlement. Thus, the Hanoi bombings had the effect of inducing distrust, unnecessarily putting a strain on relations with Italian representatives who had been allies, and creating bitter feelings of alienation in the Polish government, which may have undermined years of United States effort to wean that country away from Soviet influence.

Probably less embittered but no less demoralized than the foreign diplomats who functioned as mediators were their counterparts in the United States State Department, the officials who were given the task of pursuing the elusive flowers of peace. They could hardly be expected to continue to work assiduously on their assigned mission of trying to arrange for peace talks when their own urgent requests for a temporary halting of the air war against North Vietnam to allow the carefully planned peace negotiations to get under way were completely disregarded.

Resumption of the bombings against Hanoi in December 1966 evoked an outcry of protest and recriminations against the United States in the world press, which at that time still knew nothing about the peace initiative. Mass protest meetings were held in England and in other countries allied with the United States. Many responsible American commentators for the first time began to attack the United States war effort in Vietnam as senseless. Only one month earlier President Johnson had promised, in what he called a "declaration of peace," to try to arrange for a withdrawal of American troops from Vietnam. Again we are reminded of Orwell's *1984* "doublethink" vocabulary, in which "war is peace." Johnson's November peace statements were not forgotten when the air war against Hanoi was resumed a month later. The credibility gap widened and continued to haunt the President throughout the remainder of his administration.

If United States policy-makers sincerely intended to pursue the peace negotiations, their failure to call off the bombing of the Hanoi area resulted in a complete fiasco. It utterly ruined all chances for fulfilling that intention. We must await the declassification of the relevant documents before we can expect to find out whether the group members shared the belief that they were conscientiously pursuing opportunities for peace negotiations by denying that their militaristic decision to step up the bombing of North Vietnam would undermine the peace talks.

Even if subsequent historical research were to show that United States policy-makers were insincere—for example, that they were deliberately prolonging the war in the expectation that later they might obtain a favorable peace settlement—their decision to ignore the warnings would still have to be rated as foolish because the members overlooked the undesirable political consequences. They could have foreseen that all those who knew about the Marigold plan would point to United States leaders as the saboteurs of the attempted peace move because of their ill-timed bombing attacks. If the policy-makers were being deceitful, they should have realized that they would be exposing their disreputable intentions of prolonging the war unless they postponed the raids against Hanoi for a short time, until it became apparent that the conferees who were trying to implement the Marigold peace plan could not come to any agreement. *Did the members of Johnson's advisory group ignore the obvious risks because of their overconfidence in the military policy to which they were committed, sharing the overoptimistic belief that the renewed bombing attacks against Hanoi would succeed at long last in forcing a weakened enemy to seek peace on America's terms?*

When we consider the credibility gap in terms of the groupthink hypothesis, we are led to raise the following additional question: *Did the President and other members of the group make the mistake of destroying public confidence in their statements about the war because they were mutually sup-*

porting each other in discounting mounting evidence of the failure of the military policy to which they had committed themselves? The plausibility of an affirmative answer is suggested by Hoopes' assertion that President Johnson repeatedly issued unwarranted, optimistic statements to the press, not just because he was temperamentally inclined to oversell his policies but because he was also constantly "buoyed by the stream of glad tidings coming from his advisers." The President, during his last year in office, according to Hoopes, became

> the victim of (1) Rostow's "selective briefings"—the time-honored technique of underlining, within a mass of material, those particular items that one wishes to draw to the special attention of a busy chief—and (2) the climate of cozy, implicit agreement on fundamentals which had so long characterized discussions within the inner circle on Vietnam, where never was heard a discouraging word.

If historical research on the Johnson administration proves Hoopes to be right, we shall have strong evidence that the President, like other members of the inner circle, was a victim of groupthink. But any definitive judgment of whether this conclusion is correct will have to await the release of secret documents from the government's files and the publication of candid memoirs that provide dependable answers to the questions just posed.

Limitations of the groupthink hypothesis

Suppose the historical evidence supports the groupthink hypothesis. Will we then be led to conclude that there was really nothing wrong with the Johnson administration's foreign policy toward Southeast Asia that couldn't be cured simply by avoiding groupthink? Certainly not. Even if the policy-makers had not indulged in groupthink, the Vietnam War policies might have been essentially the same because of the political and economic values of the men who held power positions in the United States government. Still, it is probable that if they were indulging in groupthink they were prevented from becoming fully aware of the futility of their ill-conceived escalation decisions and from correcting some of their most fallacious assumptions soon enough to reconsider the alternatives open to them. It is conceivable that group dynamic factors influenced their deliberations to such a degree that if the Johnson administration had been able to set up the appropriate conditions for avoiding groupthink, the policy-makers might have renounced some of their original war aims and might at least have become willing to negotiate a peace settlement in 1966, when the Marigold plan was being pursued, if not earlier.

Careful historical analysis of United States government documents and memoirs should sooner or later yield some definitive answers to the queries raised in this chapter. The answers might prove to be negative, of course, in which case the groupthink interpretation of the Johnson administration's errors in its Vietnam War policies will have to be discarded. For example, the decisions may have largely reflected the influence of just one man, the President himself. It seems improbable, however, that his advisers exerted no real influence over him and that when they said they agreed to his policy of escalation they secretly disagreed. Men of the caliber of McNamara, Rusk, Rostow, and Bundy are not likely to be mere sycophants, like those who surround a dictator. If the alleged facts, as presented by Cooper, Hoopes, Moyers, Thomson, and other analysts, are essentially correct, it seems highly probable that group dynamics exerted considerable influence on the decisions of the policy-makers who escalated the war in Vietnam.

The Vietnam case study, even though conclusive evidence is not yet at hand for evaluating alternative interpretations, shows better than any other the potential contemporary relevance of the groupthink hypothesis. It reveals the type of inquiries that will need to be made when the historical records become more complete in order to test the validity of the groupthink hypothesis. The questions asked in this chapter are not those that historians and political analysts typically ask. Perhaps if social scientists take seriously the potential influence of group dynamics on high-level policy decisions, they will ferret out the evidence necessary to answer those questions.

II
Counterpoint

6

The Cuban Missile Crisis

A series of crucial policy decisions that provides an extraordinary counter-point to the Bay of Pigs decision was made in October 1962, during the historic thirteen days of the Cuban missile crisis. This crisis has been referred to as "the most critical in our nation's history" and "the greatest danger of catastrophic war since the advent of the nuclear age." The policy-making group included most of the same key men who participated in the Bay of Pigs decision, but this time they functioned in a much more effective way and showed few symptoms of groupthink, which were counteracted.

Background of the crisis

Within a year or so following the Bay of Pigs invasion attempt, the Soviet Union worked out an arrangement with the Castro regime to set up missile in-stallations in Cuba, presumably to be armed with nuclear warheads. More than twenty thousand Russian troops, well equipped with tactical weapons, were sent to Cuba to protect the installations. Shortly after detecting missile sites scattered throughout Cuba, United States military intelligence experts estimated that the installations represented about one-third of the Soviet Union's entire atomic warhead potential. If fired at American cities, the missiles might kill about 80 million Americans.

During the months preceding the crisis, the CIA had been receiving reports from agents in Cuba asserting that the Russians were setting up offen-sive atomic weapons, in addition to the defensive conventional weapons that they had publicly acknowledged supplying. But this information was not definitive. United States intelligence specialists and the rest of the government continued to assume that newly arrived Soviet personnel and equipment in Cuba were merely intended to reinforce the Cuban air defense system, as the Russian leaders repeatedly claimed. This shared consensus—as unwarranted

A photograph taken in October 1962 by a U-2 plane flying over Cuba showing supportive buildings for ballistic missiles, fuel tank trailers, and a missile erector in San Cristobel. Extensive vehicle trackage, coupled with the construction of cable lines to control areas, indicates the quick tempo of Soviet activity.

as the consensus about Castro's weakness that had evolved before the Bay of Pigs invasion—evidently kept the Kennedy administration from taking the initial warning signs seriously. But White House complacency was rudely shattered on October 16, 1962. On that day the President was informed that CIA photo interpreters, while routinely checking photos taken by a U-2 plane flying over Cuba, had discovered a group of recently completed buildings for ballistic missiles in San Cristóbal. In this startling photograph, specialists could clearly identify a launching pad and an offensive missile lying on the ground.

The mission of the Executive Committee

When word reached President Kennedy, he promptly called together a group of high-level advisers, which later was called the Executive Committee of the National Security Council. The membership of this group overlapped with that of the policy-making group that had approved the Bay of Pigs invasion plan. In fact, five of the key men on the Executive Committee attended most of the crucial meetings on both decisions: President Kennedy, Secretary of State Rusk, Secretary of Defense McNamara, Assistant Secretary Paul Nitze, and White House Foreign Policy Coordinator McGeorgy Bundy. Another key member was Attorney General Robert Kennedy, who had attended the initial briefing session on the Bay of Pigs plan and later had a hand in strengthening the consensus in favor of executing that plan. Other key members of the Executive Committee during the Cuban missile crisis were General Maxwell Taylor (newly appointed chairman of the Joint Chiefs of Staff), Vice President Lyndon B. Johnson, White House staff member Theodore Sorensen, and John McCone (who had replaced Allen Dulles as chief of the CIA). A few additional experts and officials, whose judgments the President wanted to consider, also attended practically all the meetings. Among them were Roswell Gilpatrick, George Ball, and Llewellyn Thompson.

When the members were called together on the first day of the crisis, "the President made it clear that acquiescence was impossible" and that the group was expected to decide on a course of action that would get the missiles out of Cuba before they became operational. A diplomatic approach, either directly to Khrushchev or indirectly through the United Nations would have been preferred by a few members of the committee, but "the President had rejected this course from the outset." John Kennedy, along with many other officials in the United States government, took the position that the Soviet missiles could not be allowed to remain in Cuba not only because of the military threat but also because of political damage to America's position in the world. Key members of the administration also believed that ignoring the missile build-up would impair Kennedy's personal prestige and would compromise his attempts to implement his foreign and domestic policies. Leading Republicans, including Senators Goldwater and Keating, had been strongly pressuring

The Executive Committee of the National Security Council
meets in the White House during the Cuban missile crisis. The
participants—identified clockwise from President Kennedy,
bending over table at right—are Secretary of Sate Dean Rusk;
Secretary of Defense Robert McNamara; Roswell Gilpatrick,
Deputy Secretary of Defense; General Maxwell Taylor, Chairman of the Joint Chiefs of Staff; Paul Nitze, Assistant
Secretary of Defense; Don Wilson (hidden), Deputy Director
of the United States Information Agency; Theodore
Sorensen, Presidential Counsel; Townley Smith (seated by
bookcase); McGeorge Bundy, White House Foreign Policy
Coordinator; Secretary of the Treasury Douglas Dillon; Vice
President Johnson; Llewellyn Thompson as the adviser on
Russian affairs; William C. Foster; (hidden) John McCone,
chief of the CIA; and George Ball (also hidden), Under
Secretary of State. Attorney General Robert F. Kennedy is
standing at far left.

Kennedy to use United States military power to put a stop to the missile build-up in Cuba. Only one month earlier, in response to these political pressures, the President had publicly stated his belief that all the missiles in Cuba were purely defensive weapons. He had pledged to take action if any offensive missiles were introduced. As one political analyst put it, "If Eisenhower had inadvertently embarrassed Khrushchev personally and politically by his clumsy handling of the U-2 affair in . . . 1960, Khrushchev foolishly repaid Kennedy tenfold and under far more dangerous circumstances."

President Kennedy's initial decision (before the first meeting of the Executive Committee) was that some form of coercive action would have to be taken to eliminate the missile threat. This judgment has been attacked by a number of political critics. They claim that Kennedy unnecessarily created a dangerous crisis to protect his prestige and that he took a serious gamble by letting the Kremlin decide whether to preserve peace by removing the missiles. Other critics, however, regard Kennedy's reasons for his initial decision to resort to coercive action well warranted by the circumstances.

Whether the President was right or wrong in setting up his objective is not relevant to a discussion of group decision-making. What is relevant is the fact that the President let the Executive Committee decide how to get rid of the missile threat. We are concerned with the decision-making activity of this group. If the participants' accounts of what happened at their meetings are correct, we are led to conclude that this policy-making group met all the major criteria of sound decision-making. The decision-makers (1) thoroughly canvassed a wide range of alternative courses of action; (2) surveyed the objectives and the values implicated; (3) carefully weighed the costs, drawbacks, and subtle risks of negative consequences, as well as the positive consequences, that could flow from what initially seemed the most advantageous courses of action; (4) continuously searched for relevant information for evaluating the policy alternatives; (5) conscientiously took account of the information and the expert judgments to which they were exposed, even when the information or judgments did not support the course of action they initially preferred; (6) reexamined the positive and negative consequences of all the main alternatives, including those originally considered unacceptable, before making a final choice; and (7) made detailed provisions for executing the chosen course of action, with special attention to contingency plans that might be required if various known risks were to materialize.

These criteria refer to the quality of the decision-making procedures, regardless of whether the outcome (which in this instance hinged largely on the way the Kremlin responded) was successful. Foreign policy decisions of "good" quality—that meet the seven criteria—generally have a much better chance of being successful in the long run than those that do not. But a decision does not necessarily have to have a successful outcome to be rated as a "good-quality" decision, according to the definition provided by these criteria. The definition carries a rather anomalous implication, which needs to be spelled out in order to indicate why the Cuban missile crisis serves as a counterpoint to the Bay of Pigs and other fiascoes. The reason is not that the

Cuban missile crisis turned out to be a success story. If the Soviet leaders had chosen to respond belligerently to the naval blockade and if, following the disaster, an objective analyst was still alive who could evaluate the same evidence that is now accessible, that analyst would be obliged to conclude, on the basis of the seven criteria, that despite the horrible outcome, the decision-making procedures of the Executive Committee were of "good quality."

President Kennedy's initial decision to resort to some form of coercive action to get rid of the missiles in Cuba may have failed to meet some of these criteria. Had he not precluded the alternative of relying upon the traditional methods of diplomacy and accommodation to negotiate with the Soviet Union and with the Castro government, President Kennedy might have succeeded in finding a way not only to eliminate the missile threat but also to terminate Cuba's military alliance with the Soviet Union. Some social scientists now regard Kennedy's two-power military approach as a serious error. Irving Horowitz, for example, claims that Kennedy's view of the missile crisis was unduly influenced by a games-theory model that led him to initiate an unnecessarily dangerous "game of chicken" in response to a relatively minor threat to America's security, forcing an unwarranted showdown between two major powers at the risk of starting an all-out nuclear war.

Whether or not Kennedy's initial decision to preclude a diplomatic approach is judged to have been an act of brinkmanship, the Executive Committee could be criticized for conforming too readily with the President's way of defining its mission. The government leaders in the group might have been able to influence the President to change his initial judgment if they had become convinced that the President was wrong in excluding a purely diplomatic approach. But, except for this possible deficiency, the Executive Committee by and large did a good job of examining and evaluating alternative courses of coercive action in order to supply the President with the answers to the policy questions he asked them to answer. Even Horowitz, who is among the most severe critics, acknowledges that the final recommendations of the Executive Committee "emerged from a political bargaining process which involved not only the military factors and strategic analysis, but also considerations of morality . . . and international political consequences."

Decisions made during the thirteen-day crisis

For five days, starting on October 16, 1962, the Executive Committee met continually, often holding formal sessions several times a day, in order to arrive at a strategic plan. At first the best choice seemed to be to threaten a surgical or massive air strike, in the hope that the verbal threat would induce the Soviet Union to withdraw the missiles. But the group recognized from the start that the Soviet leaders might refuse to acquiesce to this threat, and their refusal might lead to a rapid, uncontrolled escalation that would bring on a nuclear war. After debating the alternatives day after day, a majority of the group finally decided on October 20 that the best choice was to institute a naval blockade. This choice, they felt, had the advantage of being a low-level action that would serve as a nonhumiliating warning and would still "maintain the options," as McNamara put it, permitting a gradual, controlled escalation later on, if necessary.

The crisis continued for another eight days, and the same group continued to meet daily until the crisis was finally resolved by Khrushchev's offer to withdraw the missiles. On October 22, President Kennedy gave his dramatic speech revealing to the world the hitherto secret evidence of the offensive missile sites in Cuba and announcing the United States government's decision to quarantine Cuba. Khrushchev promptly denounced the blockade as "piracy." Eighteen Soviet ships—some of them almost certainly carrying nuclear armaments—continued relentlessly on their course toward the quarantine zone. During the next few suspenseful days the United States repeated its threat to board Soviet ships, forced several Soviet submarines to surface near the quarantine zone, and actually did board a Lebanese vessel chartered by the Soviet Union. These actions were calculated to postpone a direct military confrontation while demonstrating the firm resolve of the United States government to counteract the missile build-up in Cuba. Then, on October 24 and 25, shortly before reaching the quarantine zone, most of the Soviet cargo ships (including all those with large hatches, presumed to be carrying nuclear missiles) turned around and headed back toward Russian ports.

Despite the success of the blockade, the situation was still considered dangerous because work was continuing on the Soviet missile sites in Cuba, and they were rapidly becoming operational. The Executive Committee began to consider a response that would make its contingency plans operational. These plans involved taking further graduated steps toward more direct forms of military action, possibly resorting to air strikes against the missile sites or even an invasion of Cuba. Before taking further action, however, the committee decided that additional warning messages—but not a formal ultimatum—should be sent to the Soviet leaders, urging them to remove the missiles immediately in order to avoid the outbreak of war. As this new crisis was reaching a climax, Khrushchev made it known that the Soviet Union would respond favorably if the United States were willing to make some concessions in turn. The crisis was finally resolved on October 28, when the Soviet leaders agreed to remove the missiles in exchange for assurances that the United States would not invade Cuba.

Dissension within the group

From the various accounts of the thirteen days of agitated deliberations, it is apparent that the members of the Executive Committee continuously disagreed with each other despite strong pressures to develop a consensus. For example, on the fourth day of meetings, according to Sorensen: "The President was impatient and discouraged. He was counting on the Attorney General and me, he said, to pull the group together quickly—otherwise more dissensions and delay would plague whatever decision he took. He wanted to act soon." When the consensus was not forthcoming in the next meeting, Sorensen departed from his usual conduct at these meetings and tried to push the members toward a unified response by telling them "that we are not serving the President well, and that my recently healed ulcer didn't like it much either." Here we have an instance of strong pressure toward group concurrence of the type that frequently is observed in groups dominated by groupthink tendencies. But the members of the Executive Committee were able to resist this pressure. They continued their lively debates about the alternatives open to them, notwithstanding the impatience and ulcers that their disunity might cause.

The next day, the majority finally agreed on the naval blockade as the initial course of action. Nevertheless, the group did not develop a consensus involving shared illusions of invulnerability. On the contrary, most members thought that even the best possible alternative was fraught with the enormous danger of touching off a nuclear holocaust in which the Soviet Union and the United States might destroy each other. Nor did the members show any other sustained symptoms of groupthink, although, from time to time, there were transient tendencies to invoke stereotypes and to exert pressures toward conformity. By and large, the members of the group proved to be extraordinarily successful in retaining their critical resources as independent thinkers, despite all the strains and pressures of the thirteen-day crisis.

What can we learn about the conditions that enabled this Executive Committee to avoid becoming victims of groupthink? Part of the answer has to do with the traumatic impact of the earlier fiasco in which most of the leading personalities on the Executive Committee had participated. Bitterness still lingered from the humiliating failure of the Bay of Pigs invasion, which had been launched a year and a half earlier. The Kennedy team was no longer so naive about seemingly authoritative military briefings or so insensitive to the dangers of oversimplifying foreign-policy issues. But the changes were not simply a matter of each man's resolving to do better next time. Important procedural changes had been introduced into the organized policy-making process—changes calculated to prevent the policy-makers from accepting uncritically glib arguments put forth by enthusiastic proponents of an ill-conceived plan. Before continuing with our examination of how the Executive Committee functioned during the Cuban missile crisis, we must first backtrack a bit to consider the transformations initiated in the White House during the months following the "worst defeat" of President Kennedy's entire career, after his initial anguished question, "How could we have been so stupid?" was replaced by "What can we do to avoid being so stupid again?"

Legacy of the Bay of Pigs

At a time of shattering defeat, mutual respect and a sense of group identification have important positive functions in maintaining morale. A cohesive group can survive a catastrophically bad decision, belatedly learn the lessons of its bitter experience, and live to make better decisions next time. Just such a success story seems to fit the facts of how the Kennedy administration faced the adversities of the Bay of Pigs fiasco. Despite the barrage of justified attack against them, the President and the key men in his administration showed no signs of demoralization or ineffectual response to the shattering defeat.

One of Kennedy's first acts after the defeat of the Cuban invaders was to announce to the press that he bore sole responsibility for the fiasco. He strongly opposed any attempts to shift the responsibility to the others who had participated in the deliberations. Those who worked closely with him realized that although he seemed outwardly composed, he was deeply perturbed. With great self-control he managed to avoid lashing out at Richard Bissell and Allen Dulles, the two CIA chiefs who had cooked up the foolish plan and had misled him into thinking that it would work. (He did, however, quietly accept their resignations.) Kennedy displayed his irritation from time to time, but it was against people who were not members of the in-group. For example, he attacked newspaper reporters and editors for having failed to censor news of the impending Cuban invasion. He felt they should have done this in the interest of national security. Kennedy's biographers agree that this attack was unquestionably a mistake and embroiled the President in a lengthy, inexpedient feud with the press.

While scorn was being heaped on them at home and abroad, the key members of the Kennedy team supported each other and this mutual support helped them to avoid being demoralized. They were able to take constructive action, to repair some of the damage, and to cope with new international crises in Laos, Vietnam, the Congo, and Berlin. Their behavior after the fiasco appears to be a good illustration of the favorable consequences of group cohesiveness under conditions of temporary defeat, in contrast to the unfavorable consequences that create poor decision-making at times when nothing has happened to disrupt the group's optimism about the success of its policies.

The problem facing the leader of a cohesive group is how to obtain the morale gains of high cohesiveness without the losses caused by groupthink. President Kennedy seemed to be aware of this problem, although neither he nor any of his associates ever formulated it in this way. One of the President's first acts after the debacle was to set up a commission of inquiry to find out exactly what had gone wrong. Then, acting partly on his advisers' recommendations and partly on his own hunches, Kennedy introduced a series of sweeping changes in the decision-making procedures of his team to ensure that there would never again be a fiasco like the Bay of Pigs. An analysis of these changes is necessary to see how they might increase the problem-solving efficiency of a government administration. Many of Kennedy's innovations avoided the usual drawbacks of traditional bureaucratic practices, such as maintaining such strict secrecy that the flow of information to the decision-making body is restricted. The President's procedural changes also set up the conditions that promote independent thinking by curtailing the adverse influence of groupthink tendencies. Four major procedural changes were carefully followed when the administration subsequently had to make vital decisions that might affect national security, as in the case of the Cuban missile crisis.

New definitions of the participants' role

Members of the policy-making group were given a new and much broader role: Every participant was expected to function as a skeptical "generalist." Henceforth advisers from the various government departments were supposed to participate in policy discussions not primarily as spokesmen for the agency they represented but as critical thinkers. They were charged with examining the policy problem as a whole, rather than approaching the issues in the traditional bureaucratic way whereby each man confines his remarks to the special aspects in which he considers himself to be an expert and avoids arguing about issues on which others present are supposedly more expert than he. Furthermore, the two men whom the President trusted most—his brother Robert Kennedy and Theodore Sorensen (neither of whom had been present at the initial Bay of Pigs planning sessions)—were given a special role. As intellectual watchdogs, these two men were told to pursue relentlessly every bone of contention in order to prevent errors arising from too superficial an analysis of the issues. Accepting this role avidly, Robert Kennedy, at the expense of becoming unpopular with some of his associates, barked out sharp and sometimes rude questions. Often he deliberately became the devil's advocate. Sorensen felt his responsibility for preventing errors so keenly that he would spend many a night pondering possible flaws when new plans affecting national security were under discussion.

Changes in group atmosphere

The group meetings of government policy-makers were organized in a completely different way. In accordance with the group rule that sessions should be devoted to frank and freewheeling discussion, the usual rules of protocol were suspended. No formal agenda was imposed upon the group. To broaden the scope of information available to the core group of decision-makers, departmental spokesmen and outside experts were invited to give their views and then were carefully questioned about the grounds for their conclusions. With an eye to obtaining fresh points of view, new advisers were brought in periodically. Recognizing the usual tendency for visitors to remain silent, members of the group deliberately asked them to give their reactions during the discussions.

Meetings of subgroups

As a special device to facilitate critical thinking, the Executive Committee was sometimes broken up into two subgroups. The separate subcommittees would meet independently to work on a policy decision and then would come together for debate and cross-examination in the reassembled group. The members of the White House staff, in addition to attending the meetings of the ad hoc policy-making group, also met separately with the President, "away from the inhibiting presence of the grandees in the Cabinet Room."

Leaderless sessions

Occasionally, President Kennedy deliberately absented himself from the meetings of the policy-making group, particularly during the preliminary phases when the full range of alternatives was being discussed for the first time. One reason for his absence was to avoid exerting undue influence on the way his advisers conceptualized a problem. Robert Kennedy, who strongly supported his brother's resolve to allow some sessions to be leaderless, commented, "I felt there was less true give and take with the President in the room. There was the danger that by indicating his own view and leanings, he would cause others just to fall in line." When the President was absent, either Secretary Rusk or Robert Kennedy chaired the meeting, but each of these men seemed aware that he should not try to direct the group or attempt to replace the President as the most influential voice in the group.

A new group norm manifested during the missile crisis

Largely as a result of the four new procedures and related changes in leadership practices that consistently encouraged open-minded inquiry and debate, the members of the Executive Committee avoided succumbing to groupthink, despite the fact that they formed a cohesive group with all the usual social pressures operating to induce conformity with group norms. In effect, striving to be thorough in their appraisals of alternatives became a new type of norm. This norm was established at the initial meeting on the Cuban missile crisis, and from then on the members of the group seemed to be aware of the danger of premature closure, even though one or another of them expressed feelings of annoyance and impatience at times—as did President Kennedy—about the delays in arriving at a consensus.

At first President Kennedy, like most other government officials, was surprised and angered by the unexpected news of the offensive missiles in

Cuba, particularly because it had become apparent that Khrushchev was lying when he had recently reassured the United States government that all the weapons Russia was supplying to Cuba were purely defensive. Adlai Stevenson, who spoke with the President on the first day, was disturbed to hear the President tell him that "we'll have to do something quickly. I suppose the alternatives are to go in the air and wipe them out or take other steps to render the weapons inoperable." If the President had presented his initial position forcefully, the group members might have conceptualized their task as deciding which type of air assault to recommend—the limited surgical strikes favored by the President or the more extensive air assaults favored by the Joint Chiefs—without giving much consideration to any of the less drastic or less dangerous options. But instead of inducing the group at the opening session to focus on the air-strike action he favored, President Kennedy emphasized the need to canvass alternatives. His message was that "action was imperative," but he wanted the members to devote themselves to making "a prompt and intensive survey of the dangers and all possible courses of action." That very day the group began examining the pros and cons of the most obvious alternatives. Robert Kennedy intervened at one point, taking on his customary role of intellectual watchdog, to urge the group to add more alternatives: "Surely," he asserted, "there was some course in between bombing and doing nothing."

In response to this prod from the Attorney General, the group considerably broadened the spectrum of alternative responses to be considered. By the end of the first day of meetings the committee had seriously discussed at least ten alternatives: (1) do nothing; (2) exert diplomatic pressure on the Soviet Union by appealing to the United Nations or to the Organization of American States to set up inspection teams; (3) arrange for direct communication between President Kennedy and Khrushchev, possibly at an immediate summit conference; (4) secretly approach Castro to warn him of drastic United States action and to split him off from the Soviet Union; (5) institute low-level military action by setting up a naval blockade to prevent Russian ships from bringing missile armaments to Cuba; (6) launch an air assault that would bombard the missile sites with pellets to render them inoperable without causing any casualties; (7) carry out a limited surgical air strike, with advance warnings to allow Cubans and Soviet personnel to escape being killed while the missile installations were being destroyed; (8) carry out a limited surgical air strike without any advance warning; (9) carry out a massive air strike against all military targets in Cuba to prevent effective anti-aircraft fire and possible retaliation against targets in the United States from as yet undetected missile sites; (10) launch an all-out invasion to "take Cuba away from Castro."

The group discussed the advantages and disadvantages of each alternative, including the first two, which had been rejected from the beginning by the President. During the first day McGeorge Bundy urged a traditional diplomatic approach but soon dropped this position and later became an advocate of an air strike. McNamara also ignored the President's exclusion of a noncoercive response and argued that no coercive action was necessary because "a missile is a missile" whether it is launched from Cuba or from the Soviet Union. Nitze and others soon convinced McNamara, however, to accept the President's definition of the situation as requiring a coercive response. Their major arguments were that with a huge stockpile of atomic missiles close to the United States, the Soviet Union's capability for launching a nuclear attack would be doubled and the warning time would be drastically reduced from fifteen minutes to only two or three minutes. Perhaps the speed with which Bundy and McNamara were induced by others in the group to abandon their initial position and to conform with the leader's stricture was a manifestation of groupthink tendencies. If so, this incipient tendency must have been short-lived. After the first day all indications point to a relative absence of concurrence-seeking. The members of the group vigorously debated a variety of alternative coercive actions and freely voiced their misgivings with little regard for traditional protocol, most noticeably when the President was not there.[1] Sorensen recalled:

> one of the remarkable aspects of those meetings was a sense of complete equality. . . . We were fifteen individuals on our own, representing the President and not different departments. Assistant Secretaries differed vigorously with their Secretaries; I participated much more freely than I ever had in an NSC [National Security Council] meeting; and the absence of the President encouraged everyone to speak his mind.

When the President attended the meetings, his skepticism and his disregard for traditional deference to the military judgments of the Joint Chiefs of Staff also contributed to the atmosphere of objective inquiry and debate. For example, he was unwilling to accept the judgment of General Curtis Le May, the Air Force chief of staff, who, while arguing for a massive air assault rather than a blockade, assured the President that the Russians would not retaliate. President Kennedy's skeptical retort was, "They, no more than we, can let these things go by without doing something. They can't, after all their statements, permit us to take out their missiles, kill a lot of Russians, and then do nothing." Further questioning of the Joint Chiefs' arguments for their strong recommendation to carry out an air strike elicited answers that shook the confidence of the President and others in this alternative. In their answers the military experts acknowledged that they could not be sure that all the missiles would be wiped out even by a massive air assault or that during the attack itself nuclear missiles would not be launched against American cities before the sites were destroyed.

General Le May, however, may have deliberately given the President and his civilian advisers the impression that air strikes could not be surgical. He and the other Joint Chiefs had decided to promote a massive attack against Cuba. They were convinced that that was the only proper solution to the missile crisis. In this instance, according to Graham Allison, the information search by participants in the Executive Committee was incomplete and remained so during the first week. But by the beginning of the second week the nonmilitary participants found out independently from civilian experts that a surgical air strike was feasible, and they then added it to the list of options to consider in the event that the blockade failed.[2]

Whenever he presided, the President took pains to call on men in secondary positions such as Nitze, Ball, and Thompson, to obtain their individual views, recognizing that lower-ranking officers "would not voluntarily contradict their superiors in front of the President, and that persuasive advisers such as McNamara unintentionally silenced less articulate men." From time to time, President Kennedy brought in United Nations representative Adlai Stevenson and representatives from other government agencies along with a number of distinguished outsiders—Dean Acheson, former Secretary of State; Robert Lovett, former Secretary of Defense; and John McCloy, former High Commissioner of Germany. The President and others in the group encouraged these outsiders to go along with the same procedural norms that were being followed by the insiders—to present their own points of view frankly, to ask difficult questions, to make the others defend their assumptions. This unusual way of proceeding must have created some consternation among the outsiders. One unimpressed visitor, who evidently missed the firm guiding hand of a leader and the mutual support of a strong group consensus, was Dean Acheson. He was used to the entirely different style of presidential leadership that had characterized the policy-making groups headed by President Truman. Acheson testily complained that "discussions within the Executive Committee after a couple of sessions seemed to me repetitive, leaderless, and a waste of time."

Yet, contrary to Acheson's exasperated appraisal of the group meetings, the members managed to work out a complicated plan of action. On the basis of their probing discussions of the risks and drawbacks, they were able to spell out a series of alternative scenarios that could ensue from their blockade decision. These scenarios enabled the policy-makers to specify a graded series of stronger military actions that could be taken in response to possible counteracting moves by the Soviet leaders. For example, the group developed contingency plans specifying what would be done if the Russians refused to allow Soviet ships to be searched or if they launched a submarine attack against American ships in retaliation for the sinking of one or more Soviet ships that might try to break through the blockade.

Fortunately, none of these dire contingencies arose, and none of the escalatory steps was taken. But the fact that the backstop plans were worked out with such great care, rather than allowing them to be so vaguely defined that they would have to be improvised if the Russians were recalcitrant, may well have reduced the chances of accidental escalation arising from excited misjudgments. Indeed, there were times when it looked as though the Soviet Union was going to ignore the blockade and force the United States Navy into an armed confrontation with Soviet ships and submarines. Delicate operational handling was required in order to head off the most horrendous of all the scenarios the group had rehearsed.

As a result of the thorough review of all the drawbacks, the recommendations the group gave to the President included much more than strategic military guidelines. The group worked out in considerable detail ways of handling a variety of political, legal, and diplomatic ramifications, which, if neglected, could cause a blockade attempt to fail. In order to diminish political pressures from military-minded Congressmen, the President and his advisers planned in advance a briefing session with leading Congressmen, who, as it turned out, reacted in much the same angry way the President had when he had first learned about the nuclear missiles. Even Senator Fulbright, who had taken a firm anti-militaristic stand earlier concerning the invasion of Cuba (just as he was to do later during the Vietnam War), urged at this particular time a much stronger "military action rather than such a weak step as a blockade," because he regarded the Cuban missiles as an unprecedented threat to American security. President Kennedy, in a very distressing session with the Congressmen, had to spell out many of the contingency military plans and remind the irate Congressmen of the enormous risks that had led the group to settle on the blockade solution.

The legal aspects were painstakingly pursued by a number of lawyers in the group, who felt that accepting the strong recommendation, made by Dean Acheson, to ignore legality when vital matters of national security were at stake would be a serious mistake. At considerable cost in time and effort, a subcommittee of the Executive Committee worked out a successful plan to obtain a two-thirds favorable vote from the Organization of American States, which set up a legal, hemisphere-wide blockade. The members of the Executive Committee realized that without this vote, the blockade could be labeled as an act of war in violation of international law. Avoiding this was especially important because Soviet leaders were known to take legalistic formulations seriously in such matters and would feel justified in accusing the United States of piracy if the United States boarded Russian ships.

Recognizing that support of the major powers of Europe and other parts of the world might be essential, members of the Executive Committee spent considerable time discussing the diplomatic repercussions of United States coercive action. Turkey, for example, had to be prepared for Soviet pressure or even possible air attacks because the United States missile sites located there were likely to be equated with the Soviet installations in Cuba. African countries also became involved in the far-reaching plan, because the committee realized that the Russians could circumvent the naval blockade by flying atomic warheads into Cuba if they could refuel their planes in West Africa. Accordingly, it became necessary to dispatch United States ambassadors to see the Presidents of Guinea and Senegal in order to prevent this alternative route from materializing. In retrospect, speaking of the elaborate preparations made as a result of the group's deliberations, Robert Kennedy was able to assert, without contradiction from public affairs commentators, that "nothing, whether a weighty matter or a small detail, was overlooked."

Subjective discomfort

The Executive Committee did not give birth to its elaborate plans without undergoing a considerable amount of subjective discomfort, sleeplessness, and protracted turmoil. Of course much of the discomfort must have been evoked by the ever present threat that the crisis might escalate to all-out thermonuclear war, and it probably was augmented by the group discussions. The participants were keenly aware of the enormous risks they were taking; they repeatedly acknowledged all the uncertainties and dire contingencies that could arise from a military confrontation with the Soviet Union. This time there were none of the illusions of safety that the White House group had shared while planning the Bay of Pigs invasion, no comfortable rationalizations that minimized the dangers, no shared myths about the invulnerability of the group or of the nation.

Knowing that one misstep could precipitate a devastating nuclear war, the members' need for emotional support from the group was undoubtedly very high, but most of the time the lack of consensus frustrated this need, depriving the members of a sense of unity that would have enabled them to feel more confident about a successful outcome. Sorensen vividly described his own agonizing responses to the crisis:

> In no other period during my service in the White House did I wake up in the middle of the night, reviewing the deliberations of that evening and trying to puzzle out a course of action. Not one of us at any time believed that any of the choices before us could bring anything but either prolonged danger or fighting.

Dean Rusk spoke grimly about the possibility of "nuclear incineration" and disclosed his disquieting train of thought by professing surprise at being "still alive" the morning after President Kennedy announced the United States blockade of Soviet ships. Robert McNamara, noted for his cool, computer-like capacity to think about the unthinkable, has said that he personally experienced "the most intense strain I have ever operated under." He added a comment about the cohesiveness of the group resulting from common exposure to danger, which, as McNamara put it, "forges bonds and understanding between men stronger than those formed by decades of close association."

All accounts of the sessions are filled with comments about unpleasant arguments and distressing agitation. Robert Kennedy's memoirs of the Cuban missile crisis are punctuated by constant references to the unpleasant bickering and agitated feelings stirred up by heated debates over every course of action that anyone proposed. For example:

> And so we argued, and so we disagreed—all dedicated, intelligent men, disagreeing and fighting about the future of their country, and of mankind. Meanwhile, time was slowly running out.

* * *

> The next morning, at our meeting at the State Department, there were sharp disagreements again. The strain and hours without sleep were beginning to take their toll. . . . Those human weaknesses—impatience, fits of anger—all are understandable.

The picture that emerges is quite different from the placid sense of unanimity and the shared sense of unlimited power that had characterized the policy-making group when it approved the plan to invade Cuba a year and a half earlier.

Vigilant appraisal: the antithesis of groupthink

Along with strong subjective feelings of insecurity and exasperation, there were several unusual objective features of the Executive Committee's sessions. In all accounts of the Cuban missile crisis are consistent indications of four characteristics of vigilant appraisal, which contrast sharply with the manifestations of concurrence-seeking during the deliberations about the Bay of Pigs invasion.

Acknowledgment of grave dangers even after arriving at a decision

At every meeting during the Cuban missile crisis, the participants openly acknowledged that whatever course of action they were contemplating would be highly dangerous. The threat of catastrophic destruction of the United States by Soviet missiles, whether launched from the new sites in Cuba or from Soviet submarines or aircraft, was constantly the focus of the group's attention, particularly when the members were discussing contingency plans involving an escalation of military force. This group never attained that complacent sense of security that so often emerges when a groupthink-dominated group arrives at a consensus. After the members had decided that a blockade would be much less risky than a direct air attack on Cuba or a full-scale invasion, the members continued to discuss the possibility that the blockade might fail and leave the United States in an even more vulnerable position if the Russians succeeded in completing the Cuban missile sites. Out of the renewed discussion provoked by their vigilant appraisal of the risks, the group evolved a new set of contingency plans to follow up the blockade, if necessary, with stronger military action. But these additional contingency plans, while increasing somewhat the group's confidence in the blockade decision, still did not eliminate profound concern about "the difficulty of halting an escalation, once started."

Other potentially damaging consequences for the United States were also subjected to vigilant scrutiny. A prolonged blockade would give the Russians time to make counterthreats and stir up world opinion, which could lead to mass protests and possibly even the fall of some Latin American governments. Castro might take counteractions by executing a number of Bay of Pigs prisoners each day the blockade continued. At home, American military leaders might become frustrated and demand more military action as the unrelieved tensions built up. Reflecting all the qualms of the members of the Executive Committee, the President summed up the shaky status of the recommended course of action when he announced to the group that he reluctantly decided to accept it: "There isn't any good solution. Whichever plan I choose, the ones whose plans are not taken are the lucky ones—they'll be able to say 'I told you so' in a week or two. But this one seems the least objectionable."

On the first morning the blockade went into effect, the group was informed that Russian ships were moving steadily toward the interception line set up by United States naval vessels. This was another occasion when the participants openly acknowledged the risks. At one point during this session, according to Robert Kennedy, the President expressed "the danger and concern we all felt hung like a cloud over us" by asking, "Isn't there some way we can avoid having our first exchange with a Russian submarine—almost anything but that?" Just a few minutes before, the group had received distressing news from the Navy. A Soviet submarine was moving into position between United States naval ships and the two Russian freighters that the Navy expected to board within less than one hour. When the President asked his question, Robert Kennedy had a distressing thought—and he assumed that this was what his brother was thinking too—which took the form of a much more unnerving question: "Was the world on the brink of a holocaust?" He noticed that his brother was showing extraordinary signs of emotional tension: His face seemed drawn and haggard, drained of all color; his hand went up to his face to cover his mouth. The two brothers stared at each other across the conference table. At that moment, Robert Kennedy had a peculiar sense of dissociation, as he became wholly preoccupied with a flood of vivid memories of the worst personal catastrophes of their lives:

> For a few fleeting seconds, it was almost as though no one else was there and he was no longer the President. . . . Inexplicably, I thought of when he was ill and almost died; when he lost his child; when we learned that our oldest brother had been killed; of personal times of strain and hurt. The voices droned on, but I didn't seem to hear anything.

This momentary dissociation, during which Robert Kennedy vividly recalled experiences of overwhelming stress that he and his brother had undergone, is a typical anxiety reaction under conditions of severe stress.

Similar reactions have often been observed in combat soldiers and surgical patients at moments when they are momentarily overwhelmed with the realization that real danger is at hand.

By speaking frequently about the grave risks and reminding the group of the intolerable consequences of miscalculations when two nations find themselves approaching the brink of war, the President made it clear that he would not assume the role that members of a beleaguered group usually want their leader to assume during a serious crisis—that of a reassuring authority figure who attempts to dispel the doubts and anxieties of his followers.

In private conversations, President Kennedy referred to *The Guns of August*—in which Barbara Tuchman presents a vivid account of how the political and military leaders of Europe blundered into World War I by making one incredibly foolish decision after another—as a warning for the nuclear powers in our own time. He suggested that the Executive Committee's deliberations would provide historic material for *The Missiles of October,* which could be a sequel to *The Guns of August*. He must have realized that if the sequel had a similar ending, there might never be any readers.

Explicit discussion of moral issues

During the discussions preceding the Bay of Pigs invasion, the moral issues raised by Senator Fulbright's speech and by Arthur Schlesinger's memorandum were never discussed. As a result, the group never examined the unsavory ethical issues posed by the CIA's plan, which involved an unprovoked military attack against a small neighboring state and required the government to make false statements to the public in order to create a supposedly plausible cover story. In contrast, during the Cuban missile crisis, members of the Executive Committee explicitly voiced their concerns about the morality of the policy alternatives they were considering, thus forestalling deceitful, clandestine actions. They maintained an attitude of vigilance toward the moral risks as well as toward the military ones. For example, on the second day of the crisis, George Ball vigorously objected to the air-strike option, arguing that a surprise attack would violate the best traditions of the United States and would harm the moral standing of the nation, whether or not the attack proved to be militarily successful. To the surprise of several members of the group, Robert Kennedy continued the argument, calling attention to the large toll of innocent human lives that would result. Urging a decent regard for humanity, the Attorney General pointed out that a surprise air attack would undermine the United States' position at home and abroad by sacrificing America's humanitarian heritage and ideals. He emphasized this moral stance by stating that he was against acting as the Japanese had in 1941 by resorting to a "Pearl Harbor in reverse."

Robert Kennedy's position was challenged by Dean Acheson, who argued that, on the basis of the Monroe Doctrine and prior official warnings, the United States government would be fully justified in using any means to eliminate the threat to national security posed by the Cuban missiles. The debate on these moral issues and related questions of the legality of possible United States actions in the eyes of other nations continued throughout that day and on succeeding days, with marked effects on other members of the group. At one point, Douglas Dillon announced to the group that he had originally felt that an air attack was justified because the Russians had deceived us but that he no longer felt this position was morally justified. He went on to say that "what changed my mind was Bobby Kennedy's argument that we ought to be true to ourselves as Americans, that surprise attack was not in our tradition. Frankly, these considerations had not occurred to me until Bobby raised them so eloquently."

McNamara shared the Attorney General's position and added that it was expedient to select an initial course of action that would enable the United States government to "maintain the options" so as to "leave us in control of events." He referred explicitly to moral arguments in his retrospective comments about Robert Kennedy's contributions to the group's decisions: "His contribution was far more than administrative . . . he opposed a massive surprise attack of a large country on a small country because he believed such an attack to be inhuman, contrary to our traditions and ideals and an act of brutality for which the world would never forgive us."

According to Robert Kennedy's own account of the deliberations, the moral issue remained a central concern right up until the time that the consensus converged on a blockade as the least risky path of quasi-military action: "We spent more time on this moral question during the first five days than on any single matter. . . . We struggled and fought with one and another and with our consciences, for it was a question that deeply troubled us all."

Reversals of judgment

The placid unanimity of the White House group that had approved the Bay of Pigs invasion plan certainly did not characterize the Executive Committee during the missile crisis. In the course of daily clashes and bickering within the group, many members changed their minds about vital issues. On the third day of the crisis, for example, "Rusk spoke out . . . first as a dove, then as a hawk, and finally as an uncertain man." In many instances, individual members reversed their positions completely after hearing appraisals of the military, political, or moral risks by others in the group. Douglas Dillon's switch from favoring an air strike to favoring a blockade after hearing Robert Kennedy's moral arguments is only one of many examples that could be cited. Among those who displayed such reversals was President Kennedy. After hearing the arguments from McNamara and others in the Executive Committee, he no longer favored a surgical air strike and changed his mind in favor of the blockade.

All accounts of the Executive Committee's meetings agree that an outstanding characteristic of the group's deliberations was the frequent changes of position that occurred while the members were trying to hammer out an acceptable strategy to resolve the crisis:

> Abel: "The fact is that nearly every man in the room changed his position at least once—some more than once—during the week of brainstorming."
>
> Sorensen: "Each of us changed his mind more than once that week on the best course of action to take."
>
> Schlesinger: "Thinking aloud, hearing new arguments, entertaining new considerations, they almost all find themselves moving from one position to another."
>
> Robert Kennedy: "None was consistent in his opinion from the very beginning to the very end. . . . For some there were only small changes, and perhaps varieties of a single idea. For others there were continuous changes of opinion each day."

Nonstereotyped views of the enemy

Stereotypes of the enemy as evil, weak, and stupid—which were so much in evidence during the White House discussions of the Bay of Pigs decision—seldom, if ever, were voiced after the bitter anger of the opening session of the Executive Committee. Most members viewed their opposite numbers in the Kremlin as no less rational than themselves and assumed that their choice of action would be selected from a broad spectrum, ranging from conciliatory to belligerent, depending largely upon the words and actions of the United States government. Often the members of the group set themselves the task of trying to predict how the enemy would react to one or another course of action by deliberately trying to imagine themselves in the Soviet leaders' place. Moreover, unlike the tightly held Bay of Pigs deliberations, which excluded most of the experts who should have been consulted, the policy-makers' deliberations during the missile crisis relied heavily on expert judgments from Kremlinologists in many different agencies, with priority given to those who had a good record of correctly predicting Russia's actions in earlier crises.

In their first meeting, the Executive Committee spent considerable time trying to understand why, from the Soviet standpoint, such drastic and risky steps had been taken to build secret missile sites ninety miles from America's shores. The members examined a wide variety of plausible explanations, including the nonsinister possibility that the Russians were merely trying to increase their bargaining power for negotiating the withdrawal of American missile sites near the Soviet Union. The upshot of discussing all the alternative interpretations of Soviet intentions was a tacit recognition that no firm conclusion could be drawn about why the Soviet leaders had set up missiles in Cuba. Thus, instead of the typical groupthink assumption that the only intention behind the enemy's threatening step must be an attempt to undermine and destroy us, most members of the Executive Committee maintained a flexible, open-ended view of what the Soviet leaders might be up to. This enabled them to take seriously the possibility of working out plans for avoiding escalation.

It was not easy to maintain this open-ended view at a time when strong Soviet provocation evoked resentment and readiness to retaliate. Khrushchev had lied and made a fool of President Kennedy by deceiving the United States government with his persuasive assurances that no offensive missiles were being sent to Cuba. Despite considerable cause for anger, the President and his advisers viewed the Soviet leaders as basically reasonable men, who could be convinced to withdraw their missiles. Without denying the cunning and deceit of the Soviet leaders, the group adopted the working assumption that the Soviet Union would not be likely to initiate a war unless unduly provoked.

Rusk and other members of the Executive Committee urged the group to choose a response that the Soviet leaders could clearly see offered them a way out. One of the problems with an air attack, most of them agreed, was that no matter how well a surgical strike might pinpoint the missile installations, it would still be a provocative military move, especially because Russian soldiers, as well as Cubans, would be killed. An important argument that led the group to regard a naval blockade as much more prudent than any alternative military response was precisely that this low-level action could serve as an unmistakable indication of America's strong intention to eliminate the missile bases without confronting the Soviet leaders with a belligerent act that would be "sudden or humiliating."

The nonhumiliation theme

The nonhumiliation theme appealed strongly to President Kennedy. He reiterated it time and again when the Executive Committee was facing the problem of how to implement the naval blockade plan, especially after the Soviet Union had responded to the blockade with propagandistic denunciations and overt acts of defiance. The majority of the Executive Committee supported the strategy of avoiding any sudden or shocking act of aggression that might push the Soviet Union into making an impulsive decision to retaliate. When news came that some Soviet cargo ships had temporarily halted as they were approaching the interception line, which had been set up eight hundred miles from Cuba, the Navy representative suggested that this could be a sinister Soviet move to group the ships around the submarine escort. But the President and others in the Executive Committee felt that a more plausible explanation was that the Soviet government was trying, just as the Americans were, to postpone a military confrontation. Against objections from the Navy, the President decided to move the interception line three hundred miles closer to Cuba, again to give the Kremlin leaders more time to evaluate the crisis. Nevertheless, he did not order any other change that might look like the United States government was backing down; the Navy continued to track and harass Soviet submarines in the Caribbean, signaling strong determination to enforce the blockade.

The Navy's first boarding was deliberately postponed until a *non-Soviet* ship arrived on the third day of the blockade, a Lebanese freighter under charter to the Soviets, which, as expected, had no arms on board. This vessel was selected carefully, according to Robert Kennedy, in order to demonstrate "that we were going to enforce the quarantine and yet, because it was not a Soviet-owned vessel, it did not represent a direct affront to the Soviets requiring a response from them." In this way, as Roger Hilsman (the Director of Intelligence in the State Department) observed, ample time was allowed between each step for the Soviet leaders to weigh the consequences.

On October 26, tension increased when the Executive Committee learned from new intelligence reports that the Cuban missile sites were being completed at full speed. On this same day, however, those members of the Executive Committee who had been defending the working assumption that the Soviets really wanted a peaceful settlement if they could find a nonhumiliating way out were unambiguously supported by events. The Soviets proposed, through an informal channel, an acceptable solution to the crisis: The Soviet Union would remove the offensive missiles and allow United Nations inspection teams to verify the removal. The Russians would pledge not to reintroduce missiles into Cuba in exchange for a United States pledge not to invade Cuba. This proposal was followed by a long, emotionally worded telegram from Khrushchev, the gist of which was that both sides must reach an agreement in order to avoid the risks of a horrible nuclear war.

Hopes for a satisfactory settlement were dashed the next day when a new note from Khrushchev, broadcast by Radio Moscow, offered entirely new terms unacceptable to the United States: Khrushchev offered to trade Soviet missiles in Cuba for United States missiles in Turkey. Worse yet, an American U-2 plane was shot down over a missile site in Cuba and the pilot was killed. This overt act of aggression seemed all the more threatening because it was now clear that the Soviet Union had for the first time ordered its military units in Cuba to activate its highly effective surface-to-air missiles. Hilsman, who was at the White House on that crucial day, says "it was the blackest hour of the crisis."

Faced with this acute deepening of the crisis and the steady movement toward open warfare, the members of the Executive Committee worked out a new military contingency plan in the event that another U-2 was shot down. But still they did not succumb to the temptation to revert to a stereotyped conception of the enemy government. Instead of focusing their deliberations solely on a military response—which would be the order of the day if the enemy were viewed as recalcitrantly set on a destructive course of action—they carefully considered the nonaggressive moves that could be made in response to the Soviet messages.

Despite the setback posed by the new hard-line message from the Kremlin, the group members persisted in their assumption that a military confrontation and the outbreak of World War III might still be prevented if only they could somehow communicate to the Soviet leaders that the Americans really meant what they had been saying about their limited but nonnegotiable demand to withdraw the Soviet missiles from Cuba. They asked themselves how this could be communicated as a positive move toward peace, not as a threat. Specifically, the question was this: What could the United States do to strengthen the pro-conciliatory tendencies of the Soviet leadership, represented by Khrushchev's personal letter, rather than play into the hands of hard-liners who favored escalation, represented by the latest official note from the Soviet Foreign Office? This kind of question would never have been raised if the members of the Executive Committee had stereotyped the Soviet leadership as a homogeneous group of conniving criminals who could be stopped only by threat of annihilation.

Earlier that week, President Kennedy had quipped, "I guess this is the week I earn my salary." Before the week was over, the Attorney General had also earned his salary. During the deliberations on October 27, Robert Kennedy came up with the brilliant suggestion that the United States government should ignore the official message received that day, as if it did not exist, and simply respond to the acceptable peace-oriented message received the day before. After an exhausting debate by the Executive Committee, this suggestion was endorsed by a consensus of the group and adopted by the President. The wording of the President's letter clearly conveyed the empathic view of the members of the Executive Committee toward the Russian leaders, reflecting their efforts to project themselves into the role of their counterparts in Moscow. The letter included conciliatory statements:

> I have read your letter of October 26 with great care and welcomed your desire to seek a prompt solution to the problem. . . . There is no reason why we should not be able to complete these arrangements and announce them to the world within a couple of days. The effect of such a settlement on easing world tensions would enable us to work toward a more general arrangement regarding "other armaments." . . . The United States is very much interested in reducing tension and halting the arms race.

The President did not, however, rely solely upon a low-pressure message to inform the Soviet leaders of the sense of urgency felt in Washington about working out a settlement before the Cuban missiles were ready for use. The formal letter itself carefully avoided hinting at any threats if the offer were refused. But, without consulting the Executive Committee, the President decided to ask his brother to transmit orally to the Soviet ambassador a much stronger message, which alluded to the threats that had deliberately been left out of the formal letter. Robert Kennedy, according to his own account, told Ambassador Dobrynin that this was *not* an ultimatum *but* "if they did not remove those bases, we would remove them . . . [and] we must have [an answer] the next day." In effect, this was a tacit ultimatum, as Alexander George has pointed out, containing the two main elements of a classical ultimatum: a reference to a threat of punishment if the demand is not accepted and a time limit for complying with the demand. Yet, an attempt seems to have been made to avoid making it sound like a belligerent or humiliating ultimatum, especially because it demanded only that the bargain originally proposed by Khrushchev be adopted. Moreover, Kennedy "offered not only a conditional pledge not to invade Cuba but—as his brother's posthumous account has now made clear—he also gave Khrushchev a private assurance that the Jupiter missiles in Turkey would be removed soon."

The President and the others present at that last crucial meeting, during which the formal letter was drafted, realized that the Soviet leaders might have already moved too far along the path toward a military confrontation to back down. The dominant feeling of the group, Robert Kennedy asserts, was one of "foreboding and gloom"; many members thought that the odds were against their last-minute conciliatory effort. To make matters even worse, they had just learned that another U-2 plane, based in Alaska, had accidentally flown over the Soviet Union on the way back from the North Pole. American fighter planes sent into Soviet territory to escort the lost U-2 plane home were, in effect, invading Soviet air space. This came to be known as "the Dr. Strangelove" incident because of its resemblance to the black-comedy film showing an accidental preemptive air strike against the Soviet Union. Occurring at such a critical time, this incident could easily have been taken for a nuclear air attack and therefore, as Khrushchev later said, could have pushed the Soviets to take "a fateful step." The Soviets might have jumped to such a dire conclusion if the United States government had not been so careful to avoid any humiliating aggressive action during the preceding days of the crisis.

Why were the decisions of the Executive Committee successful?

We do not know why the men in the Kremlin decided to accept America's tacit ultimatum. The United States government must have done something right, but the historical evidence is not yet at hand to inform us what that something was. One component might well have been the low-keyed and non-provocative wording of the warning messages addressed to the Soviet leaders throughout the crisis. This is one of the components singled out by Hilsman, who has reviewed the historic events of October 1962 with an eye to explaining how the United States induced the Soviet leaders to back down. Hilsman starts with the premise that the Soviets knew they were facing vastly superior United States forces that combined enormous conventional military power with potentially devastating nuclear power. But it was the way the United States handled its overwhelming power, according to Hilsman, that enabled the crisis to be resolved without a military confrontation "awesome to contemplate . . . American ground and air forces attacking Soviet nuclear missiles poised on their pads and defended by Soviet ground combat forces equipped with tactical atomic weapons." "Flexibility and self-restraint," Hilsman asserts, were the keynotes of the United States government's handling of the crisis. This diplomatic approach, in turn, enabled the Soviet Union to react with "wisdom and restraint." In this way, Hilsman explains the paradox that the missile crisis, which brought the two superpowers to the brink of mutual destruction, had the ultimate effect of producing a marked relaxation in the cold war, culminating ten months later in a treaty that banned atmospheric tests of nuclear bombs by both countries.

Alexander George points out that the majority of the members of the Executive Committee resisted urgent pressures from the Joint Chiefs of Staff to send an ultimatum threatening an immediate military confrontation; instead, they adopted a mixed strategy of "coercive diplomacy," which "includes bargaining, negotiations, and compromise as well as coercive threats." Had the President and his Executive Committee thought about the enemy leaders in the usual stereotyped way, without considering how they would react if the roles were reversed, the necessary restraint probably would not have been achieved. This is essentially the conclusion drawn by Robert Kennedy, who said, "A final lesson of the Cuban missile crisis is the importance of placing ourselves in the other country's shoes."

Of course the fact that Khrushchev was forced to back down in response to the United States government's coercive demands was a humiliation, but in keeping with a nonstereotyped view of the enemy, President Kennedy took steps to avoid rubbing it in. In their elation following the crisis, some leading officials in the United States government could not resist gloating, as did Secretary Rusk when he remarked to a news correspondent, "Remember when you report this—that eyeball to eyeball, they blinked first." President Kennedy then in no uncertain terms asked all members of the Executive Committee and other government officials to refrain from saying anything publicly that could be construed as claiming a victory for the United States. Almost all official United States government statements thereafter expressed respect for Khrushchev's statesmanlike role for doing "what was in his own country's interest and what was in the interest of mankind."

Conclusions

The main characteristics of the Executive Committee's deliberations are at the opposite pole from the symptoms of groupthink. Had the Executive Committee succumbed to the natural tendencies toward groupthink during the harrowing days of the Cuban missile crisis, we can easily imagine what the outcome might have been. The solution worked out by the committee members during the first five days of the crisis and the restraints they observed in advising specific decisions during the next eight days were not achieved without considerable subjective distress. President Kennedy and others in the committee were frequently frustrated and sometimes exasperated by the group's failure to arrive at a stable consensus as the members vigilantly appraised and reappraised the risks. They had to undergo the unpleasant experience of hearing their pet ideas critically pulled to pieces, and the acute distress of being reminded that their collective judgments could be wrong. Over and beyond that, the acknowledgment of the awesome threat of nuclear war made them go through thirteen days of constant tension as they realized that these might be the last days of their lives. Nevertheless, instead of striving for comfortable feelings of security, they resisted the temptation to develop a set of shared beliefs that might have reassured them that their side was bound to win and that the evil enemy would give in or forever regret the consequences. Perhaps the magnitude of the obvious threat of nuclear war was a major factor that, along with the improved decision-making procedures used by the Executive Committee, operated to prevent groupthink.[3] It seems probable that if groupthink tendencies had become dominant, the group would have chosen a much more militaristic course of action and would have put it into operation in a much more provocative way, perhaps plunging the two superpowers over the brink.

The key members of the Executive Committee who so successfully avoided succumbing to groupthink tendencies—the President, the Attorney General, the White House coordinator, the Secretary of State, the Secretary of Defense, and several other high-ranking officials—were the same individuals who had formed the nucleus of the group that eighteen months earlier had shown all the symptoms of groupthink when planning the Bay of Pigs invasion. The members of the Executive Committee who had not been involved in the Bay of Pigs decision differed little in intelligence, experience, outlook, and personality from those they replaced. This implies that groupthink is not simply a matter of a fixed attribute of a group, nor is it a question of the types of personalities that happen to be dominant within the group. If the same committee members show groupthink tendencies in making a decision at one time and not at another, the determining factors must lie in the circumstances of their deliberations, not in the fixed attributes of the individuals who make up the group. The determining factors therefore seem to be variables that can be changed and lead to new and more productive norms.

7

*The Making of
the Marshall Plan*

The postwar economic crisis

Throughout 1947, several tough-minded groups within the Truman administration confronted one of the gravest crises of the century—the threat of complete economic collapse of war-devastated Europe. Their efforts culminated in the Marshall Plan, a comprehensive and detailed program for supplying American funds to aid European recovery. It was developed in the State Department, headed by General George C. Marshall, who had urged the administration to find a constructive solution to the economic plight of postwar Europe.

Historians seem fairly well agreed that the Marshall Plan succeeded because it was so carefully designed and implemented. The plan not only prevented the crisis from worsening but it also enabled England, France, Italy, West Germany, and other Western powers to rebuild their factories, to redevelop their natural resources, and to restore the other sagging features of their economic life. Perhaps the most impressive testimony to the extraordinary quality of the Marshall Plan came from Winston Churchill, whose active participation in the shaping of modern history made him acutely aware of the likelihood that the altruistic reasons given by a major power for supplying aid to another nation are merely a cover for sordid intentions. The Marshall Plan, in Churchill's judgment, was "the most unsordid act in history."

Even some "revisionist" historians, who emphasize the sordid economic motivations of United States foreign policy during the cold war years—maintaining access to international markets, preventing national revolutions that might overturn capitalism, and interfering with Soviet bilateral trade agreements—acknowledge the strong altruistic component in the Marshall Plan. William A. Williams, for example, notes that "there can be no question that it [the Marshall Plan] did represent America's generous urge to help the peoples of western Europe, and that it did play a vital role in the recovery of that region." He adds that for large numbers of men, women, and children in Europe, it "literally made the difference between life and death."

A succession of policy-planning groups

Like many other foreign policy decisions during the cold war, the plan for aiding European recovery was worked out during a period of intensifying crisis, in the face of a seemingly enormous threat of Communist domination of Europe. But the procedures used by the Truman administration to devise the plan differed in several fundamental ways from those used by government leaders in groupthink-dominated decisions, in which policy details were worked out by a single group of high-level officials, in almost total isolation from other government officials who might have offered a different but well-informed point of view. In contrast, the Marshall Plan evolved from the work of at least six relatively independent groups of policy-planners, drawing upon the talents of a large number of individuals from many different levels of the government.

In the State Department, under Secretary Marshall's leadership, three committees were set up to grapple with the issues posed by the postwar economic crisis in Europe:

1. A special committee was appointed in March 1947 to study the problems involved in extending aid to all foreign governments that needed it.
2. A Policy Planning Staff, headed by George Kennan and established in April 1947, drafted the broad outline of the long-range plans.
3. A group of senior officials at the State Department was convened in late May 1947 to evaluate the Kennan committee's report and a memorandum independently prepared by Undersecretary of State William Clayton.

On June 5, 1947, Secretary Marshall made a public statement describing the new plan in a speech at Harvard University. Two weeks later, President Truman announced that he had appointed three advisory committees to work out further details of the European recovery plan. One of the three committees, which was headed by Averell Harriman, was given the major responsibility for formulating a full set of specific policies that could be put into operation as a practical program. The recommendations of the Harriman Committee, together with reports on the domestic economy and other relevant topics prepared by the other committees and by various government agencies, were then discussed and approved at meetings of cabinet members and other high-level officials with the President. Finally, the agreed-upon policies were embodied in a comprehensive plan submitted for the approval of the Congress.

The task of Kennan's committee

Throughout the winter of 1947, Secretary Marshall had been receiving urgent warnings from leaders of friendly nations, diplomats, and foreign affairs experts: Europe was in dire economic straits and the expansionist Soviet Union—which had already taken over Poland and a number of the Baltic countries—seemed to be on the offensive, aided by internal Communist movements. American policy-makers became increasingly worried that, with practically no resources left for military defense, the non-Communist countries of Europe might topple into the orbit of the Soviet Union.

In March 1947, President Truman announced that large amounts of financial aid would be given to Greece and Turkey in the name of a sweeping new doctrine "to support free peoples who are resisting attempted subjugation by armed minorities or by outside pressures." This new Truman Doctrine committed the United States government to take an active part in settling the political, economic, and military problems of Western Europe—much too active a part, according to many critics.[1] In any case, men on the State Department staff soon realized that the grave problems of the failing European economies would not be solved by the stopgap measures that had been taken in dealing with Greece and Turkey, that a more comprehensive and imaginative solution was required. Joseph M. Jones, a participant in the intellectual ferment of the fifteen weeks during which the Marshall Plan was evolved, has depicted those weeks as a uniquely enlivened period in the usually quite dreary history of the United States State Department:

> The Truman Doctrine decision unleashed for the first time the creative effort of the State Department staff. . . . Emotion quivered near the surface as ideas surged forth. The responsible leaders made the breakthrough; but it was the State Department's staff that swept through the breach made by the Truman Doctrine and was to a very important degree responsible for the advance to the Marshall Plan.

The influential leaders in the State Department—Dean Acheson, William Clayton, Charles Bohlen, George Kennan, and Secretary Marshall—recognized that the coming winter of starvation and discontent was posing "the most compelling world situation ever to confront the nation in time of peace." Millions of people were starving in all the great cities of Europe. Britain, with its empire crumbling, would continue to withdraw from the role of stabilizer of the European economy. Food production in France was alarmingly low, with no improvement in sight. The standard of living for most people in France, Italy, and Germany would soon reach subminimal levels and would undoubtedly lead to political disintegration, with disastrous effects on the economy of the United States as well as on all Europe. With such a dire diagnosis in mind, the men in the State Department realized that palliative, piecemeal treatments would no longer suffice; a drastic cure must somehow be found.

Upon returning from an unsuccessful attempt to get Soviet cooperation in a scheme for alleviating Europe's distress, Marshall announced in a radio address on April 28, 1947, that Europe was in such economic distress that action could no longer be delayed. "The patient," he said, "is sinking while the doctors deliberate." Marshall asked George Kennan to take charge of a two-week crash program on European economic recovery. Kennan was to work with a policy-planning staff of his own choosing, to provide a detailed, integrated set of policy recommendations. According to Kennan, his group "was supposed to review the whole great problem of European recovery in all its complexity, to tap those various sources of outside advice which we would never be forgiven for not tapping, to draw up and present to the Secretary the recommendations" about what ought to be done for Europe. Marshall told Kennan that because time was running out, he wanted the State Department to take the initiative without waiting for Congress "to beat me over the head."

Avoiding trivia

Marshall gave Kennan only two words of advice for the work of the committee: "Avoid trivia." Kennan felt that he had neither the time nor the inclination to line up a staff of distinguished authorities from outside the government, so he confined his selection to the State Department. The men he selected proved to be "intellectually hard-headed people, sufficiently familiar with the department to draw at many points on the wisdom and expertise which the lower echelons of that institution always harbor (however little or poorly they are used)."

The six-man group, which came to be known as the Policy Planning Staff, included an economist (Jacques Reinstein), a colonel of the regular army (Charles H. Bonesteel, III), a Foreign Service officer (Ware Adams), and two other experienced State Department officials (Joseph E. Johnson and Carleton Savage). The members sometimes met more than three times a day. On some days, they worked separately, meeting only to integrate their independent findings. They frequently consulted experts throughout the government and had numerous informal discussions with one another. Working day and night for three weeks (they had to ask for a one-week extension of the deadline), Kennan's planning staff considered many alternatives, debated them, and made a series of decisions that were embodied in the recommended plan for the economic reconstruction of Europe, outlined in the planning staff's report to Secretary Marshall:

> We were indebted to others for many insights, even though we, in the final analysis, had to make our own opinion of their value. Our principle contributions consisted:
>   a. in establishing the principle that the Europeans should themselves take the initiative in drawing up a program and should assume central responsibility for its terms;
>   b. in the insistence that the offer should be made to all of Europe—that if anyone was to divide the European continent, it should be the Russians, with their response, not we with our offer; and
>   c. in the decisive emphasis placed on the rehabilitation of the German economy and introduction of the concept of German recovery as a vital component of the recovery of Europe as a whole.

A meeting of the Policy Planning Staff, headed by George
Kennan (seated at left), at which the members listen to one of
the outside experts consulted during the planning and formulation of the Marshall Plan.

Any judgment of the role of the Planning Staff in the origins of the Marshall Plan will have to rest on the relative importance ascribed to these three features of it.[2]

The group's report deviated markedly from traditional State Department thinking, which generally gravitates toward a course of action expected to be supported by the administration, the Congress, and the American public. This group's comprehensive, long-term plan called for the transfer of billions of dollars to countries that had not even asked for help and probably would not ask for it. Moreover, the plan proposed that the Europeans themselves take the initiative in drawing up a coordinated program of recovery, rather than asking for a series of isolated appeals from each individual nation. Thus, the plan was to give impetus to a movement for European unity, which would build a sense of basic responsibility among European leaders for working out detailed solutions of their common problems.

The group did not hesitate to take the calculated risk of mobilizing strong political opposition within the Congress and condemnation by vocal sectors of the public. The plan was going to cost the taxpayers an enormous amount of money, with no guarantee that countries leaning toward communism would not exploit American generosity. Unencumbered by shopworn nationalistic rhetoric, the report by Kennan's group did not offer any of the popular anti-Communist slogans customarily employed to rally support for a new foreign policy. In its analysis, the planning staff did not fall back on the usual stereotypes singling out Communist connivance as the root of Europe's difficulties or justify the enormous cost of the proposed plan as necessary to "contain Soviet Communist expansion." Rather, the report placed the blame for the crisis squarely on "the disruptive effect of the War on the economic, political, and social structure of Europe," with its resultant "exhaustion of physical plant and vigor." Kennan's group distinguished carefully between the basic economic causes of Europe's distress and the attempts of the Soviet Union to exploit that distress. The planning staff realized that as a consequence of unrelieved economic hardships and the persisting threat of starvation, the people in the stricken countries of Europe would be strongly responsive to the promises held forth by the Communist movement. Secretary Marshall reiterated this nonstereotyped point of view in his public announcement. The policy, he asserted, was directed "not against any country or doctrine, but against hunger, poverty, desperation, and chaos."[3]

In Kennan's group—as in the White House group that dealt with the Cuban missile crisis—realistic appraisals were made of how the Soviet Union and its satellites were likely to respond to the various alternatives being considered. The members did not assume on the basis of sloganistic preconceptions that all the countries in the Communist bloc would behave in the same way and mindlessly sabotage United States efforts to help the people of Europe. Surprising to many insiders accustomed to thinking in terms of the usual prejudices of American politicians was the open-ended invitation extended to all nations of Europe, including those with Communist regimes, to participate fully in the recovery program.[4]

A scene from postwar Germany which indicates the degree of
disruption and disintegration caused by the war and its after-
math in the economic and social fabric of Europe by the year
1947, the eve of the implementation of the Marshall Plan.

The "agony" of critical appraisal

The proposed plan did not mature without considerable human cost and psychological stress, which at times nearly strained the bonds of the policy-planning group to the breaking point. The members of the group, Kennan informs us, were tough-minded, and "stout in argument" throughout their three weeks of constant "sweat." They took very seriously their role as critical thinkers, not sparing each other the embarrassments and humiliation of having to listen to a pet idea being subjected to incisive criticism and sometimes hacked to pieces.

Kennan gives us an inkling of what went on by quoting a synthetic example of "the sort of intragovernmental debates that preceded the formulation of the Marshall Plan."

> You say: "This shouldn't be so difficult. Why don't we tell these people to draw up a plan for the reconstruction of their economic life and submit it to us and we'll see whether we can support it or not?"
>
> That starts it off. Someone says: "That's no good. They are too tired to draw up a plan. We have to do it for them."
>
> Someone else says: "Even if they do draw up a plan, they wouldn't have the internal economic discipline to carry it out. The Communists would spike it."
>
> Someone else says: "Oh, it isn't the Communists who would spike it—it is the local business circles."
>
> Then someone says: "Maybe what we need isn't a plan at all. Maybe we just haven't given them enough in the past. If we just give them more, things will work out all right."
>
> Another then says: "That's probably true, but we've got to figure out how the money is going to be spent. Congress just won't pour money down any more ratholes."
>
> Then somebody says: "That's right; we need a program. We've got to figure out just what's to be done with the money and make sure that it does the whole job this time."
>
> To that someone else replies: "Ah, yes, but it would be a mistake for us to try to draw this program up all by ourselves. The Commies would just take potshots at it and the European governments would shrug off the responsibility."
>
> Then someone says: "That's absolutely right. The thing for us to do is to tell these Europeans to draw up a plan and submit it to us and we'll see whether we can support it or not."
>
> And then you ask: "Didn't somebody say that before?" And we're off again.

As leader of the group, Kennan seems to have made it quite clear to the members that open-minded, freewheeling, unconstrained debating was precisely what they should be doing. Everyone was urged to express any idea that might embody a useful proposal and to help spell out all the drawbacks as well as the good consequences. One of the main group norms was to subject everyone's ideas to thorough criticism. The members applied this norm to Kennan's own seemingly brilliant proposals, some of which he had painstakingly developed during the months preceding the group's deliberations: "[They] put me personally over the bumps, to drive whole series of clichés and oversimplifications out of my head, to spare me no complications."

In retrospect, Kennan states in his *Memoirs,* this was a remarkably painful group experience. The members, he says, were able to "force me into an intellectual *agony* more intensive than anything I had ever previously experienced." He recounts a specific example: "So earnest and intense were the debates in our little body in those hairy days and nights that I can recall one occasion, in late evening, when I, to recover my composure, left the room and walked, weeping, around the entire building." Here we encounter a social atmosphere entirely different from the affable, nonargumentative sessions, pervaded by groupthink, that produced the fiascoes.

More groups, more ordeals

Kennan's ordeal was not confined to the critical scrutiny and endless debates of his policy-planning group. When the group finished its task and he had submitted the report, he found himself a member of another hard-headed group. This was an ad hoc review board headed by Secretary Marshall. It included Dean Acheson, Charles Bohlen, Will Clayton, and Benjamin Cohen— all senior officials of the State Department. In advance of their crucial meeting, the members were asked to study Kennan's report and a memorandum on the same subject prepared independently by Will Clayton.

At the meeting, Secretary Marshall asked the group members for their candid judgments but avoided expressing any of his own views. The members of the review board voiced specific criticisms and expressed their doubts about whether some of the potentially unfavorable consequences could be avoided. Kennan was undoubtedly well prepared for the questions raised by the critical reviewers after the ordeal of the all-out debates in his policy-planning group. The review board ended up accepting all his main recommendations.

Secretary Marshall incorporated the major elements of the plan worked out by Kennan's group, as well as some of the proposals and formulations from Clayton's memorandum, into his speech at the 1947 Harvard commencement. This speech incorporated verbatim several key passages from Kennan's report. Because Secretary Marshall had not expressed his own opinions either during or after the review board's meeting, Kennan finally learned of the Secretary's favorable decision with genuine surprise as he read an account of the Harvard speech in his morning newspaper on June 6, 1947.

About two weeks later, President Truman appointed a Committee on Foreign Aid, headed by Averell Harriman, the Secretary of Commerce. The

Harriman Committee was a nineteen-member advisory group that included distinguished heads of industrial firms, banks, labor unions, agricultural organizations, and educational institutions. At the time it was appointed, President Truman and his advisers arranged to set up two independent supplementary committees—one under the chairmanship of Julius A. Krug, the Secretary of the Interior, the other headed by Edwin G. Nourse, the chairman of the Economic Council. Krug's committee was to independently investigate United States resources and physical capabilities for furnishing economic aid. Nourse's group was to study the economic effects of the foreign aid plan on America's domestic production, consumption, and prices. The conclusions of these two groups would be reviewed and reconciled by Harriman's committee. The final report, to be prepared by Harriman's committee, would thus be a comprehensive review of divergent and sometimes clashing interests and would take into account the major forms of opposition to be expected from the Congress.

From the outset there were open disagreements among the proponents of divergent economic policies within the Harriman Committee. Differences arose on many issues, most notably on the sensitive question of whether the American economy could support a massive aid program of the type envisaged in the State Department's plan. The "hottest fight" of all, according to a member of the committee's staff, centered on the extent to which America's crude steel resources could be made available. Out of the crucible of "hot fights," the committee finally reached a consensus and forged specific recommendations that retained the core innovations of the State Department's version of the plan while presenting additional points concerning the need for reducing economic barriers within Europe and a set of guiding principles for administering the plan.

This basic groundwork, according to Jones, enabled the entire operation to be launched promptly enough to supply the vital needs of countries that were on the verge of bankruptcy. Jones concludes that the Harriman Committee, with the help of the extensive planning concurrently carried out by other government officials, produced "a body of solid preparatory work without which the Marshall Plan could not have been launched as a sound undertaking."[5]

Joys and sorrows of a noncohesive committee

When the members of a committee represent different areas of expertise and different political constituencies, chances are increased that the group will face controversial issues squarely and will debate them before reaching a consensus. This built-in adversary feature was certainly an outstanding characteristic of the nineteen-man Harriman Committee, made up as it was of representatives of clashing interests within the United States economy. Nevertheless, noncohesive committees have problems of their own, and their problems cause errors in decision-making that are just as serious as those arising in cohesive groups that indulge in groupthink. Often the only way a large group of people with divergent objectives can arrive at a consensus is through strong political pressures, which are conducive to superficial conformity to the demands of a powerful leader (or a powerful minority faction). In a noncohesive group, disaffected members may deliberately pretend to agree with a leader's proposals and deliberately withhold their objections out of fear of political or economic reprisals. This type of deliberate conformity is not the same as groupthink, which involves genuine sharing of illusory beliefs. The members of a cohesive group dominated by groupthink tendencies remain unaware of the extent to which they are conforming to the group's norms.

When a noncohesive group, like the Harriman Committee, engages in vigorous debate and avoids the pressures to arrive at a quick consensus, it runs another risk: becoming bogged down by unproductive clashes among adversaries with irreconcilable positions. Such groups are sometimes plagued by an internal power struggle, which produces bickering about all issues, large and small.

The Harriman Committee seems to have avoided successfully both sources of difficulty. The relatively high quality of the committee's deliberations may have been facilitated by the administrative practice of splitting the membership into small working subcommittees, where issues could be debated by qualified men with divergent points of view and reasonable compromises be worked out before efforts were made to obtain a consensus in the full committee. Still, we must recognize that even though the Harriman Committee did a reasonably good job, it was not a creative group. By and large, it merely echoed and endorsed the main proposals of Kennan's policy-planning group, Will Clayton's memorandum, and other State Department advice, adding only a few suggestions about implementation. This is perhaps the most that can be expected of a large committee made up of members with diverse loyalties and interests.

Group cohesiveness without groupthink

A small, cohesive group may be required if the task is to draw up a comprehensive analysis and to find a solution that synthesizes cogent concepts, assumptions, and evidence relevant to a long-standing problem. Kennan's Policy Planning Staff, made up of six men from the same department, working together intensively, seems to have been an effective problem-solving group. The members knew they would be working together on additional problems after their three-week inquiry into European reconstruction. They respected each other's competence, and appear to have developed a strong esprit de corps. Some of the main conditions that promote groupthink were present. How did Kennan's policy-planning group avoid succumbing to the strong concurrence-seeking tendency that gives rise to the various symptoms of groupthink?

We can make only some tentative surmises about the critical conditions that make a difference. One such condition involves setting up a group norm that gives highest priority to critical appraisal. In the policy-appraising committee responsible for approving the Bay of Pigs invasion, the leader, probably without realizing it, induced the group members to give the highest priority to preserving group unity by avoiding harsh criticisms of the CIA's plans. In each of the other fiascoes we have examined, the same type of norm can be detected. But in the Executive Committee that dealt with the Cuban missile crisis, no such norm developed; instead, the norm was to discuss openly all doubts about each alternative course of action. Apparently a similar norm of open critical scrutiny took hold in Kennan's policy-planning group. Adherence to this norm requires a delicate balance of mutual suspicion and mutual trust—suspicion about the soundness of each other's arguments, combined with a basic attitude of trust that criticizing each others' ideas will not be taken as an insult or lead to retaliation.

Role of the leader

Certain leadership practices probably help to create an appropriate social atmosphere that fosters healthy skepticism and open critical discussion of controversial issues. One major factor appears to be the leader's capacity to abstain from pushing his own views and to use his influence, instead, mainly to encourage genuine debate. If the leader consistently invites open discussion, he need not necessarily remain totally silent about his own preferences, as General Marshall did. Kennan did not hesitate to present his own policy recommendations to the group, but he did so in a way that conveyed to the members that their role was to be critical evaluators, whether the proposals were being made by himself or by someone else. From his memoirs, it is apparent that Kennan served as a role model, placing his own pet ideas on the block as a kind of sacrificial lamb. His own example of accepting without recriminations all the "complications," "bumps," and "agony" must have made a deep impression on the participants, decreasing the chances that the group would accept any policy proposal before all the drawbacks had been fully aired.

Another important factor might be the leadership practices encouraged by the organization or institution with which the policy-planning group is affiliated. Kennan probably would not have felt so free to encourage open discussion if Secretary Marshall had let it be known in advance what recommendations he expected the policy-planning group to make. When the chairman of a committee knows that his chief is favorably disposed toward a particular policy, he will find it difficult to avoid steering the group to give favorable consideration to the preferred choice. Freedom from such constraints is probably rare in any large organization, especially in a government hierarchy beset by constant political pressures that are often felt to be crucial for the administration's leaders to survive in office. In order to be genuinely nonauthoritarian in asking for policy recommendations on a vital issue of funding foreign aid, the Secretary of State would have to be willing to set aside temporarily such considerations and to renounce his traditional prerogatives to put his own personal stamp on the policy thinking of the people working in his department. By remaining silent until after the report from Kennan's planning staff had been evaluated by the State Department's review board, Marshall avoided imposing any obvious constraints on the free expression of critical comments in an institutional setting where all members of the staff are expected to show deference to the judgment of their superior officer, if they know what his judgment is.

Marshall's way of handling the assignment may have been characteristic of his personal style of leadership. (When inviting Acheson to be under secretary of state, Marshall told him that he would expect from him "complete and even brutal candor," without regard for personal feelings: "I have no feelings," Marshall said, "except those which are reserved for Mrs. Marshall.") But still, in order to abstain from giving strong hints about which policies should be favored when asking a committee for advice, a conscientious Secretary of State would have to feel free, in turn, from specific constraints from his chief, the President. Hence full and impartial exploration of alternatives requires an organizational setting in which all key persons in the hierarchy, from the Chief Executive down, are willing to withhold their initial judgments and to avoid exerting pressure to obtain compliance with their initial preferences.

Avoiding insulation by involving more than one group

A specific administrative device probably contributes substantially to the quality of the decision-making procedures of a group of policy-planners—the multiple-group structure used by the Truman administration in developing the Marshall Plan. There may have been strong political reasons for setting up so many different committees. Truman needed to muster all the support he could get from leading government officials, and he "lost no opportunity to widen the involvements of his own official family in the cause." But whether intended to or not, the multiple-group structure prevents the decision from falling into the hands of a single, insulated group, with no opportunity for obtaining feedback that could correct the group's false assumptions and miscalculations. With multiple groups there is less chance that unwarranted stereotypes and slogans will remain unchallenged. Also less likely is psychological inertia resulting from the members' sense of commitment to earlier policy proposals if those proposals were made by a different group.

The group that did the preliminary work on the plan for European recovery (Kennan's planning staff) was not the group that evaluated it (the State Department's review board). Further details of the plan were worked out by a completely different group (the Harriman Committee), which was expected to take account of information and recommendations from two other independent groups of policy-planners (the Krug Committee and the Nourse Committee), as well as from Congressmen and representatives of various government agencies. The Harriman Committee's policy recommendations were reviewed by a White House group headed by the President. Thus, Truman's White House group, in making its final decisions about the specific details of the foreign aid plan, had the benefit of careful evaluations of a variety of alternatives that had been hammered out by leading experts within the government and by representatives of many different constituencies. This is an entirely different story from the Truman administration's Korean War escalation decisions, made from beginning to end by an insulated White House group, which kept every aspect of policy-planning tightly within its own hands, never allowing any other group of policy-planners within the government free rein to make independent judgments about what could and should be done.

The tentative inferences I have extracted can be summarized in terms of three specific ways that groupthink tendencies might be counteracted:

1. The leader of a policy-forming group might assign the role of critical evaluator to each member, encouraging everyone to give high priority to airing his objections and doubts openly. This practice may need to be reinforced by the leader's acceptance of criticism of his own judgments in order to discourage the members from soft-pedaling their disagreements.

2. The key leaders in an organization's hierarchy, when assigning a policy-planning mission to any group within their organization, might adopt an impartial stance instead of stating preferences and expectations at the outset. This practice requires each leader to limit his briefings to unbiased statements about the scope of the problem and the limitations of available resources, without advocating any specific proposal he would like to see adopted, so as to allow the conferees to develop an atmosphere of open inquiry and explore impartially a wide range of policy alternatives.

3. The organization might routinely follow the administrative practice of setting up several independent policy-planning and evaluation groups to work on the same policy question, each carrying out its deliberations under a different leader. This would prevent the appraisal of policy alternatives from remaining in the hands of one insulated group, a prime condition that fosters miscalculations based on concurrence-seeking tendencies.

III

Theory, Implications, and Applications

8

The Groupthink Syndrome

Symptoms of groupthink

The first step in developing a theory about the causes and consequences of groupthink is to anchor the concept of groupthink in observables by describing the symptoms to which it refers. Eight main symptoms run through the case studies of historic fiascoes (Chapters 2–5) and are seldom present in the case studies of the nongroupthink decisions (Chapters 6 and 7). Each symptom can be identified by a variety of indicators, derived from historical records, observers' accounts of conversations, and participants' memoirs. The eight symptoms of groupthink include group products and processes that reinforce each other, as can be seen most clearly in the case study of the Bay of Pigs invasion plan. The symptoms can be divided into three main types, which are familiar features of many (although not all) cohesive groups observed in research on group dynamics.

Type I: Overestimations of the group—its power and morality

1. An illusion of invulnerability, shared by most or all the members, which creates excessive optimism and encourages taking extreme risks
2. An unquestioned belief in the group's inherent morality, inclining the members to ignore the ethical or moral consequences of their decisions

Type II: Closed-mindedness

3. Collective efforts to rationalize in order to discount warnings or other information that might lead the members to reconsider their assumptions before they recommit themselves to their past policy decisions
4. Stereotyped views of enemy leaders as too evil to warrant genuine attempts to negotiate, or as too weak and stupid to counter whatever risky attempts are made to defeat their purposes

Type III: Pressures toward uniformity

5. Self-censorship of deviations from the apparent group consensus, reflecting each member's inclination to minimize to himself the importance of his doubts and counterarguments
6. A shared illusion of unanimity concerning judgments conforming to the majority view (partly resulting from self-censorship of deviations, augmented by the false assumption that silence means consent)
7. Direct pressure on any member who expresses strong arguments against any of the group's stereotypes, illusions, or commitments, making clear that this type of dissent is contrary to what is expected of all loyal members
8. The emergence of self-appointed mindguards—members who protect the group from adverse information that might shatter their shared complacency about the effectiveness and morality of their decisions

Consequences

When a policy-making group displays most or all of the symptoms in each of the three categories, the members perform their collective tasks ineffectively and are likely to fail to attain their collective objectives as a result of concurrence-seeking. In rare instances, concurrence-seeking may have predominantly positive effects for their members and their enterprises. For example, it may make a crucial contribution to maintaining morale after a defeat and to muddling through a crisis when prospects for a successful outcome look bleak. But the positive effects are generally outweighed by the poor quality of the group's decision-making. My assumption is that the more frequently a group displays the symptoms, the worse will be the quality of its decisions, on the average. Even when some symptoms are absent, the others may be so pronounced that we can expect all the unfortunate consequences of groupthink.

To be more specific, whenever a policy-making group displays most of the symptoms of groupthink, we can expect to find that the group also displays symptoms of defective decision-making. Seven such symptoms were listed earlier (at the end of Chapter 1) on the basis of prior research on decision-making in government, industry, and other large organizations:

1. Incomplete survey of alternatives
2. Incomplete survey of objectives
3. Failure to examine risks of preferred choice
4. Failure to reappraise initially rejected alternatives
5. Poor information search
6. Selective bias in processing information at hand
7. Failure to work out contingency plans

A study by Philip Tetlock indicates that among the politically relevant consequences is the relatively poor quality of the thinking that goes into the public statements made by national leaders when they announce and try to explain policy decisions that are the products of groupthink. Tetlock did a comparative study of groupthink and nongroupthink decisions, using systematic content analysis techniques to assess the quality of thinking in public speeches made by the President of the United States or the Secretary of State. For the sample of groupthink decisions, he found significantly lower scores on cognitive complexity than for the nongroupthink decisions, indicating more simplistic thinking about the issues.[1]

Antecedent conditions

In addition to stating the expected observable consequences, an adequate theory of groupthink must also specify the observable *causes*—that is, the antecedent conditions that produce, elicit, or facilitate the occurrence of the syndrome. A number of such antecedent conditions have been singled out by making inferences from the case studies presented in the preceding chapters, which take account of findings from prior research on group dynamics. One major condition that I have repeatedly mentioned has to do with the degree of cohesiveness of the group. We would not expect to find the groupthink syndrome if the members dislike each other and do not value their membership in the group. Any such group that lacks cohesiveness is likely to display symptoms of defective decision-making, especially if the members are engaging in internal warfare. But groupthink is not ever likely to be the cause of their poor decision-making. Only when a group of policy-makers is moderately or highly cohesive can we expect the groupthink syndrome to emerge as the members are working collectively on one or another of their important policy decisions. Even so, the symptoms of groupthink are unlikely to occur to such an extent that they interfere with effective decision-making *unless certain additional antecedent conditions are also present.*

What are those additional conditions? Two of them, described at the end of the preceding chapter, pertain to administrative or structural features of the policy-makers' organization. One condition involves *insulation of the policy-making group,* which provides no opportunity for the members to obtain expert information and critical evaluation from others within the organization. A second feature is *lack of a tradition of impartial leadership.* In the absence of appropriate leadership traditions, the leader of a policy-making group will find it all too easy to use his or her power and prestige to influence the members of the group to approve of the policy alternative he or she prefers instead of encouraging them to engage in open inquiry and critical evaluation. A third administrative or structural factor can also be inferred by comparing the conditions that prevailed during the groupthink decisions

(Chapters 2–5) with those during the nongroupthink decisions (Chapters 6 and 7): *the lack of norms requiring methodical procedures for dealing with the decision-making tasks.* (In Chapter 10, this antecedent condition, together with additional antecedent conditions involving psychological stress, which are suggested by the case study in Chapter 9, will be discussed in detail and examined in the light of prior research on group dynamics.)

All three of the administrative or structural conditions can be regarded as factors that facilitate the occurrence of the groupthink syndrome; they involve lack of constraints on collective uncritical thinking. Insofar as they are long-standing features of the organization, each of the three conditions can be ascertained *before* the members of a policy-making group start their deliberations on whatever policy decision is under investigation. I mention this because it is pertinent to the question of whether the groupthink syndrome can be predicted in advance. My answer is that by ascertaining the presence of one or more of the three structural conditions as well as the level of group cohesiveness of the policy-making group (which can also be rated *before* the deliberations begin), such predictions can be made. If the predictions are confirmed in future studies on policy-making groups, we shall be able to conclude that the foregoing analysis of causal factors that lead to the groupthink syndrome is substantiated by empirical evidence.

How widespread is the groupthink syndrome?

At present we do not know what percentage of all major fiascoes are attributable to groupthink. Some decisions of poor quality that turn out to be fiascoes might be ascribed primarily to mistakes made by just one man, the chief executive. Others arise because of a faulty policy formulated by a group of executives whose decision-making procedures were impaired by errors having little or nothing to do with groupthink. For example, a noncohesive committee may be made up of bickering factions so intent on fighting for political power within the government bureaucracy that the participants have little interest in examining the real issues posed by the foreign policy question they are debating; they may settle for a compromise that fails to take account of adverse effects on people outside their own political arena.

All that can be said from the historical case studies I have analyzed so far is that the groupthink syndrome sometimes plays a major role in producing large-scale fiascoes. In order to estimate how large the percentage might be for various types of decision-making groups, we need investigations of a variety of policy decisions made by groups of executives who have grossly miscalculated the unfavorable consequences of their chosen courses of action. Such investigations should also provide comparative results that are valuable for helping to determine the conditions that promote groupthink.

Candidates for a casebook of miscalculations during the Nixon, Ford, Carter, and Reagan administrations

A selection of United States government decisions to be used in further research on the incidence and conditions of groupthink-dominated deliberations could include major and minor fiascoes and near-fiascoes since the time of the Johnson administration, including some that deal with domestic policies rather than foreign policies. One strong candidate is the Watergate cover-up fiasco that led to Nixon's forced resignation from the presidency. This candidate is the one I have selected for a fully detailed analysis, which is presented in Chapter 9. It provides a kind of test case with regard to the question, Does the theoretical analysis of the causes and consequences of the groupthink syndrome (as presented earlier in this chapter) help us to understand new instances of defective policy-making behavior that differ in many important respects from the foreign-policy decisions from which the analysis was originally developed?

A second candidate is the decision by President Ford and his close advisers in May 1975 to launch an attack against Cambodia to rescue the captured ship Mayaguez and its crew. Most people do not regard that relatively minor episode as a fiasco, especially because the military mission was successful. But a few well-informed political analysts do. They point out that forty-one members of the U.S. armed forces were killed and fifty were wounded in the successful rescue of the forty crewmen. Also, minutes before the United States launched its surprise attack, the Cambodian government had already started to announce that it was releasing the ship and crew. The General Accounting Office of the U.S. government released a report in October 1976 concluding that the Ford administration had made a serious error, that the entire mission was probably unnecessary because diplomatic negotiations with Cambodia might have attained the same outcome without bloodshed.

Although Ford was praised by many supporters for having demonstrated at long last that he really did possess a crucial part of the male anatomy, he was attacked by his political opponents for indulging in machismo diplomacy. The General Accounting Office's critical report was released and publicized at the height of the election campaign, on the eve of Ford's televised debate with Carter on foreign policy. It may have resulted in Ford's losing the support of a very small percentage of voters, but perhaps just enough to make a critical difference in the narrow margin of his defeat a few weeks later on election day.

On close examination, according to Roger Morris, a former member of the National Security Staff under Henry Kissinger, the Mayaguez rescue was far from the success it seemed at first. He concludes: "Running through the Mayaguez crisis was much of the muddled, impulsive policymaking that marked the worst and the most ineffectual of the U.S. intervention in South-

Groupthink? President Ford, Secretary of State Henry Kissinger, and two White House aides (Donald Rumsfeld and
Brent Scowcroft) cheering their victory—the rescue of the
Mayaguez and its crew of forty Americans. The cost was
forty-one American servicemen killed and fifty injured.

east Asia over the last decade.'' Among the many observations and surmises that Morris offers to support his conclusion that the Mayaguez decision was muddled and impulsive are the following:

> Washington operated in the Mayaguez seizure with almost no diplomatic intelligence on the possible intentions of the new Cambodian regime. Lower level State Department officers with long experience in Cambodia were excluded from the center of the crisis management, much as the handful of officials analyzing Hanoi or the Vietcong were absent from the critical decisions by President Johnson and Nixon on the war. Gerald Ford in 1975, as his predecessors had so often before him, seems to have struck in Southeast Asia not as a last resort after exhaustive diplomacy, not in some genuinely informed calculus of the adversary's intentions, but by what must have been a largely intuitive judgment that he had no other choice.
>
> Whatever the timing and motivation for the raids, the tactical military planning turned out to be as questionable as the diplomacy.
>
> All this must be fairly weighed, of course, against the administration's perspective on the crisis. The President and his advisers were no doubt in the grip of the Pueblo tragedy, whatever the differences between the two cases. They were anxious to avoid further ''defeat'' in Indochina.

If Morris's analysis is correct, the decision to use military force to rescue the Mayaguez crew is a strong candidate for a groupthink analysis.

Another is the decision by President Carter and his advisers in April 1980 that led to the ill-fated attempt to use military force to rescue the American hostages in Iran. The news media called it a fiasco comparable to the Bay of Pigs. Government spokesmen claimed that it was all a matter of unforeseeable accidents and bad luck that helicopter failures forced the military commander to abort the entire mission on the desert sands of Iran hundreds of miles from Teheran. Informed critics, however, said that it was probably lucky that the risky mission had to be called off at an early stage with the loss of only eight American lives, because if it had proceeded to Teheran, it still would have failed badly and the losses would have been enormous.

Drew Middleton's military analysis in the *New York Times* concluded that:

> Even if the militants had been overcome and the hostages freed, the noise of the operation would surely have awakened the neighborhood. Iranian reinforcements could have brought the hostages and their rescuers under fire, and attacks on the helicopters flying in from Damavand might have made this crucial part of the planned operation unworkable.

A report prepared by the staff of the Senate Armed Services Committee, released in June 1980, concluded that ''major errors'' were made in the planning as well as in the execution of the military operation. Poor contingency planning and inadequate intelligence were among the specific criticisms. A similar conclusion was reached in a less controversial report by a high-level military review panel for the Joint Chiefs of Staff. The report, released in August 1980, concluded that although the concept of a small clandestine operation

President Jimmy Carter and Secretary of State Cyrus Vance
leaving the White House. Both became deeply perturbed in
April 1980 when the military mission to rescue the American
hostages in Iran ended in a fiasco. All the President's advisers
had met and concurred on the military rescue mission while
Vance—who had favored a diplomatic solution through negotiation—was away from Washington. When Vance returned,
he opposed the decision as "ill conceived," but no one took
his cogent arguments seriously and he resigned in protest.

was sound, there were many flaws and misjudgments in the planning, attributable at least in part to overzealous secrecy: The Joint Chiefs of Staff never had a written plan "to study and review in the privacy of their own offices," and "the hostage rescue plan was never subjected to rigorous testing and evaluation by qualified independent observers."

More fundamental criticisms of the military plan were put forth by Secretary of State Cyrus Vance who regarded it as "ill-conceived" and resigned in protest when the mission was launched. One of his objections was that even if the military mission succeeded in rescuing all fifty American hostages held in the U.S. Embassy and the three others held at a distant building in the Foreign Ministry, Iranian militants could retaliate by capturing and perhaps harming over two hundred other Americans still in Iran. Another of his major concerns was that the secret military mission would drastically impair the United States' relations not only with Moslem nations but also with America's European allies, who had just agreed to cooperate on a boycott of Iran to prevent the United States from endangering world peace by resorting to a dangerous military solution.

Vance opposed a military solution in favor of trying to work out a diplomatic solution through negotiations (which, in fact, turned out to be quite possible). Roger Fisher, an expert on international conflict, concluded in his analysis in the *New York Times* that if President Carter was led to believe diplomatic possibilities had been exhausted, his assumption was just plain "wrong."

Evidently, all the President's advisers except Secretary of State Vance concurred on the military rescue plan. Agreement was reached at a meeting held, without Vance's knowledge, on the day after his long-planned departure on vacation. When he returned, after the decision had already been made, Vance was permitted to present his objections at a meeting of the President and his national security advisers. "When he finished, he was greeted by 'deafening silence' [but afterwards] when it was too late, some of its participants conceded privately that he had raised serious questions."

Was Secretary Vance excluded from the crucial meeting in which the final decision was made because, as a lone dissenter who would not give in, he was being "treated as a deviant who was violating the group's norms"? Had those who admitted—after it was too late—that he was raising important objections been suppressing their own doubts, as loyal members of an in-group often do when they are prematurely striving for concurrence rather than for a critical evaluation of the available options? Were other symptoms of groupthink also manifested? These are not intended as rhetorical but as genuine questions that might profitably be pursued along with other key questions essential for a complete examination of the groupthink hypothesis in a detailed case study.

A fourth candidate is a minor and much less dramatic decision that marred the early months of President Reagan's administration and that has all the earmarks of gross miscalculation. It was the administration's decision in May 1981 to propose to Congress a drastic reduction in Social Security

Another potential candidate for groupthink analysis? President Ronald Reagan and his group of key economic advisers at the White House—on his right, Murray Weidenbaum, Chairman of the Council of Economic Advisers, and on his left, Secretary of Treasury Donald T. Regan and Budget Director David Stockman. In May 1981, Reagan and his advisers decided to present a proposal that Congress should make drastic cuts in Social Security benefits. The proposal evoked a "firestorm" of protest and was overwhelmingly defeated by a unanimous vote in the Senate. This decision has been described by political commentators as a serious blunder that resulted from overconfidence, insufficient concern about reactions in Congress, and failure to consider the full range of consequences.

benefits, which would affect everyone who entered the system after January 1, 1982. The proposal included substantial cuts in benefits for the disabled, for people who retire before the age of sixty-five, for retired federal workers, and for surviving spouses of retirees.

The financial problem facing the administration was a serious one. "No one disputes that something has to be done; without Congressional action, the old-age trust fund could be exhausted by fall of next year [1982]." But the drastic solution proposed by the Reagan administration, which was presented without adequately preparing the Congress and the public, evoked a "firestorm" of protest that was followed by a "stunning" defeat (96–0) in the Senate. Even Republicans admitted it was a "blunder" to confront the nation suddenly with such a proposal. Months later, Republican Congressmen were still worried that President Reagan's proposals to cut Social Security benefits drastically could have an adverse effect on the congressional elections in 1982, even though the President had responded to political pressures by not pushing for those proposals. Public opinion polls indicated that President Reagan's "once solid grip on public support appears to be loosening." A *New York Times*—CBS News Poll in September 1981 attributed the "slippage" (a 6 percent decline in approval of Reagan's handling of the presidency) partly to "unhappiness over Mr. Reagan's handling of Social Security."

Essential facts about how the decision was arrived at are not yet available but if the stories and analyses in the *New York Times, Washington Post, Time,* and *Newsweek* turn out to be at least roughly correct, the Social Security "blunder" could be regarded as a minor political fiasco resulting from, as Hugh Sidey put it, a "premature and ill-considered" plan.

A *Washington Post* Service news story by Art Pine on May 25, 1981 presented a relatively favorable view by suggesting that perhaps in the long run the "Social Security flap" might benefit Reagan by allowing him "to get much larger cuts in Social Security than anyone believed," but asserted that "it is easy to recite the negatives." Pine's recitation of those negatives is representative of the way in which the "ill-considered" decision has been described in the press:

> Ronald Reagan plainly made the first serious political *blunder* of his presidency in proposing large cuts in Social Security. . . .
>
> The White House, fresh from its budget victories, was *too confident.* The plan was put together *too hastily.* Strategists were too preoccupied with assuaging the financial markets, *too little concerned* with likely reaction in Congress. Mr. Reagan lost momentum; the Democrats were able to regroup. . . .
>
> As Murray L. Weidenbaum, Mr. Reagan's chief economist, conceded, "Hindsight tells us that we would have been better advised to spend more time discussing our views" with Congress.
>
> How did an administration that was credited with being so politically savvy get into this bind?
>
> The short answer—obtained from a series of interviews with White House officials and other strategists—is that even savvy administrations can

"Now let's hear it for good old Al, whose idea this Group Think was in the first place."

get into trouble, particularly when they are so caught up in other issues they *fail to look at their proposals realistically.*

In addition to political blunders of this kind committed by policy-makers in the White House, the sample of potential candidates for groupthink analysis could also include instances of national and local governmental decisions made by executive groups below the top level—comparable to the decisions of Admiral Kimmel's naval group in Hawaii in 1941. Serious miscalculations made by business firms and public welfare institutions might also be examined in order to investigate groupthink tendencies in organizations outside of governmental bureaucracies.

Only in America?

Is groupthink essentially an American phenomenon? American public administrators and corporation executives are well known for their peculiar eagerness to invest time and money in brainstorming groups, T-groups, executive training workshops in group relations, and the like. Does something unique in the national character incline American executives to rely excessively on group support? If so, perhaps groupthink tendencies are to be found among policy-makers only in America. Is there reason to believe that groupthink is not limited to just one country?

Actually, it is simply a matter of happenstance that all the examples of groupthink presented so far have involved American political and military leaders. If I had been more familiar with European, Asian, and African history, or if I had first consulted specialists other than American political scientists, I might have selected non-American decisions that perhaps would reveal the symptoms of groupthink. From recent discussions with specialists in European history, I have the strong impression that I could find excellent candidates for an analysis of groupthink tendencies in many times and places—in ancient Rome and the city-states of Renaissance Italy, as well as in the capitals of post-Renaissance Europe—if records of decision-making meetings, memoirs, diaries, and other evidence of the deliberations and interactions of participants are available.

Studies of national differences might some day show that executives in America are more inclined than those elsewhere to rely on group judgments and to indulge in groupthink. In a large series of policy decisions by government committees in America, groupthink tendencies might be sufficiently strong to have a noticeably adverse effect on the quality of decision-making in, let us say, one out of every three decisions on the average; whereas in European countries the average rate might be just half as great, about one out of six. Still, such a relatively low rate for Europe would be far from negligible and would be a matter of grave concern whenever a policy decision affected the lives of millions of people. Of course, we are a long way from being able to make reliable quantitative estimates. So, for the present, we shall have to be satisfied with qualitative evidence that furnishes answers to a simpler question: Can we point to a European fiasco that makes it plausible to assume that policy-making committees in nations other than the United States at least occasionally suffer from the symptoms of groupthink?

Candidates for a casebook of European fiascoes

In accounts of how the major powers of Europe in 1914 stumbled into the first world war, I recognized some familiar signs of group processes at work and noted several excellent candidates for case studies that might prove to be prime examples of groupthink. For example, in 1914 the French military high command ignored repeated warnings that Germany had adopted the Schlieffen Plan, which called for a rapid assault through Belgium and then southward to Paris in order to outflank France's defenses in the west. With high esprit de corps, French government officials and military leaders supported each other in ignoring the danger of being outflanked. Their reliance on simplistic slogans about French élan and shared illusions about France's invulnerability bolstered their decision to adopt an unrealistic military plan to launch a frontal assault against Germany's most heavily fortified frontiers in the west. They apparently continued to ignore all warnings about France's vulnerability until their illusions were shattered when the Germans broke through France's weakly fortified Belgian frontier in the first few weeks of the war and approached the gates of Paris.

In historical analyses of the origins of World War II, another candidate for a casebook of European fiascoes appears, and it might even be a more instructive example of groupthink than any of the others: The British government's attempt to appease Nazi Germany during 1938 and early 1939, which has been called "the most discreditable episode in modern English history." The attempt was carried out by an anti-war group of British policy-makers—Neville Chamberlain's "inner circle"—whose unrealistic policy of appeasing the unappeasable Nazis contributed unintentionally to the outbreak of the second world war. Authoritative accounts of Britain's appeasement policy contain suggestive indications that the groupthink hypothesis may apply even when the intent of a group's decision is to avoid war, rather than moving toward war as in all the examples of groupthink I have discussed so far.

Popular accounts of the events leading up to World War II present Chamberlain as a lone old man with an umbrella who imposed his own will upon the British government. But those who knew him well and those who have studied his personal diary, his correspondence, and his political actions have come to the conclusion that his decisions were constantly influenced by his inner circle of close associates—Sir Horace Wilson, the Prime Minister's closest adviser on foreign affairs; Sir John Simon, Chancellor of the Exchequer; Sir Samuel Hoare, Home Secretary; Viscount Halifax, who became Foreign Secretary in February 1938 (after Anthony Eden resigned in protest against the British government's acquiescence to Mussolini's conquests); and Sir Neville Henderson, Britain's ambassador to Germany.

William R. Rock, in a well-documented study of the political consequences of the inner circle's appeasement policy, asserts that the gap between good intentions and unjustifiable practices was enormous. Although starting out as a high-minded attempt to redress justifiable grievances, Rock says, the British government's policy of appeasement degenerated into passive "surrender to aggressive and unscrupulous powers, mainly from motives of fear, indolence, or simple indifference. Invariably the concessions were made at the expense of some weaker nation."

All the members of the inner circle supported Chamberlain's view of his special mission to save Europe from war. They pressured him to avoid creating a collective-security alliance with Russia, Czechoslovakia, and other anti-Nazi countries. Time and again, they urged him to give in to Hitler's demands for territory from neighboring countries in exchange for nothing more than promises that he would make no further demands. Indeed, it was one of Chamberlain's closest associates in the inner circle, Sir Horace Wilson, who suggested to him the plan of unilaterally resolving the Czechoslovak crisis in September 1938 by flying to Germany for a summit conference with Hitler without consulting any of England's military allies. Despite his initial doubts about the plan, the Prime Minister by-passed all the experts in the Foreign Office and elsewhere in the government, consulting only his inner circle before he publicly announced his arrangements for a personal conference with Hitler. Chamberlain and his fellow appeasers were gratified to receive widespread approval of the announcement from the nation's press. They did not take account of the fact that "much of the initial support from the press was based on the belief that the visit would provide an opportunity for Chamberlain to impress upon Hitler Britain's determination to stand firm against German demands."

Commenting on the amazing inflexibility displayed by the members of the inner circle in pursuit of their fallacious policy, as they allowed Nazi Germany to make one bloodless conquest after another during the period from 1937 to 1939, Rock describes a historical puzzle:

> the historian is left to wonder how any government could have deliberately closed its eyes and those of the nation to so clear and imminent a peril. The magnitude of German preparations for war, the ruthless speed with which they were pushed ahead, and the vast scope of German ambitions were all well known to those in positions of leadership. They seemed to leave the government largely unmoved.

The groupthink syndrome may provide a large part of the solution to this puzzle. There are many indications that the group developed a shared illusion

Members of Neville Chamberlain's War Cabinet with the ministers who formed his "inner circle" sitting in the front row. Seated, left to right, are: Viscount Halifax, the Foreign Secretary; Sir John Simon, the Chancellor of the Exchequer; Neville Chamberlain, the Prime Minister; and Sir Samuel Hoare, Home Secretary. Also seated, on the far right, is Lord Chatfield, Minister for the Coordination of Defence. Standing, left to right, are: Sir John Anderson, Minister for Home Security; Lord Hankey, Minister without portfolio; Leslie Hoare Belisha, War Minister; Winston Churchill, First Lord of the Admiralty; Sir Kingsley Wood, Air Minister; Anthony Eden, Dominions Minister; and Sir Edward Bridges, permanent secretary and secretary of the War Cabinet. Two other members of Chamberlain's inner circle were not members of the Cabinet: Sir Horace Wilson, permanent secretary (in the Civil Service) and the Prime Minister's closest adviser on foreign affairs, and Sir Neville Henderson, Britain's ambassador to Germany.

of invulnerability. Most historians and political analysts who have discussed the gross miscalculations of Chamberlain and his close advisers have emphasized their overoptimism and their unresponsiveness to impressive warnings from inside and outside their government. Chamberlain, in his private letters and diary, repeatedly mentioned his supreme confidence that the appeasement policy would preserve England from the dangers of war. On rare occasions when he expressed his doubts, he would dismiss them by mentioning the reassurances he had received from one or another of his inner circle.[2]

The appeasers' complacency appears to have been based on their assumption that Britain could assert itself as the arbiter of Europe and, if forced to fight a war, would certainly be successful. The members of the inner circle acknowledged and sometimes for propaganda purposes exaggerated the military weakness of Britain, but they apparently were convinced of their capacity to win diplomatic victories through their political astuteness and moral influence. They had no interest in information that might challenge the soundness of their assumptions. They encouraged Chamberlain to by-pass the Foreign Office and to ignore government experts who were aware of the risks of giving in to Hitler's demands. "As early as January, 1938," according to Rock, "Chamberlain had branded the Foreign Office 'not sincere' in its approach to the dictators, and all its expert knowledge was cast aside because the knowledge seemed in conflict with hope." Every political or military analyst in the government who called attention to defects in the appeasers' plans was labeled by the inner circle as a biased anti-Nazi who could not be trusted.

After the war, captured German documents showed that the alternative policy of presenting a united military front to guarantee the independence of each country threatened by Hitler would have met with strong support from the German generals in command of the German army, many of whom were strongly opposed to risking war against the armies of England, France, and Czechoslovakia. The combined military strength of these armies, they realized, was far greater than that of Germany. We might think that if only Chamberlain's group had known about internal German opposition to Hitler's war moves, the members would at least have debated the pros and cons of a modified policy combining concessions with a firm deterrent, in order to achieve their goal of preventing the outbreak of world war. The fact is that Chamberlain and leading members of the group were informed more than once about Hitler's war plans and the German generals' opposition to it. There is documentary evidence that the Germany generals sent at least three separate messages to the British government urging a firm stand against Hitler. But the members of the inner circle who received the information were content to rely on what their colleague Neville Henderson told them about the situation in Berlin. Acting as a mindguard, Henderson repeatedly advised the others to ignore all the inside information they were receiving from emissaries of the German general staff as untrustworthy and irrelevant.

Despite overwhelming evidence to the contrary, all members of the inner circle thought Hitler a sincere nationalist who could be won over to the cause of keeping the peaceful status quo in Europe—if he were properly appeased. For them, the real villains were the Communists and all those who stood in the way of appeasement, including Winston Churchill and other politicians at home who were willing to risk war in order to oppose the Nazis' demands. Throughout the Czechoslovak crisis, the Czechs were castigated for threatening the peace because they were refusing to accept the concessions that the British policy-makers were prepared to give in order to appease Hitler. "The Czechs," Henderson wrote to a fellow appeaser, "are incorrigibly pigheaded people." "It is morally unjust," he admonished in another letter, "to compel this solid Teuton minority [the German Sudetens] to remain subjected to a Slav central government at Prague." "The moment has come," he concluded in yet another letter, "for Prague to get a real twist of the screw."

Whether or not all members of the inner circle shared Henderson's extreme views of the leaders of the Czechoslovak government, all agreed to exclude them from the negotiations with Hitler and to "twist the screw" to get them to accept the harsh terms of the Munich agreement. Five weeks before the Munich agreement, Horace Wilson had assured a member of the German embassy, according to a document found in the files of the former Nazi ambassador to Britain, that "if we two, Great Britain and Germany, can come to agreement regarding the settlement of the Czech problem, we shall simply brush aside the resistance that France or Czechoslovakia herself may offer to the decision." That is precisely what Wilson and his associates in the inner circle succeeded in doing.

Many historians and political scientists try to explain the gross miscalculations made by Chamberlain and his fellow appeasers in terms of their personality traits. Trevor-Roper, for example, highlights Chamberlain's personality defects—his vanity, his self-confidence in being able to triumph over any opponent, his capacity for self-deception, and his inability to tolerate dissent. Gilbert, in *The Roots of Appeasement,* ascribes similar negative attributes to Chamberlain and refers to the chronic indecisiveness, muddle-headedness, and other personal defects of his principal associates.

The groupthink hypothesis does not necessarily contradict this type of explanation. But instead of placing all the blame on the policy-makers' personal deficiencies, the groupthink hypothesis adds that these defects are augmented when a leader participates in a cohesive decision-making group in which loyalty to group norms takes precedence over independent, critical judgment. Chamberlain may have been chronically self-confident and obstinate; he may have enjoyed the opportunity to display his capacity to out-debate his critics in Parliament and to win points in the political game. But he was, nevertheless, quite amenable to influence on occasions when members of his ingroup raised objections and urged him to change his plans. The groupthink hypothesis highlights the importance of the social support received from close associates. Such support bolsters any personality traits that incline a leader to overlook the unfavorable consequences of his pet plans and of his preferred ways of doing things. The case material bearing on Chamberlain and the

In Munich, September 1938, Chancellor Hitler and Prime Minister Chamberlain shake hands after concluding the "Peace of Munich." Next to Chamberlain is Sir Neville Henderson, Britain's ambassador to Germany.

members of his inner circle suggests that a detailed analysis of all available historical records will show that their policy decisions were just as badly impaired by groupthink tendencies as those made by policy-making groups in the American government. Only one such case is required to indicate that America has no monopoly on groupthink.

The "only-in-America" question could be pursued further in an examination of a substantial number of other ill-considered decisions made by various European and other foreign governments, including some from earlier centuries. Among the fiascoes of recent decades to be considered would be the Nasser government's provocations in 1967 that led to the outbreak of the six-day Israeli-Arab War, the Pakistan government's provocations in 1971 that led to the outbreak of the thirteen-day Indian-Pakistani War, and the Israeli government's failure to be prepared for the Egyptian invasion at the outset of the devastating Yom Kippur War in 1973.

Before looking into any such decisions for symptoms of groupthink, we first must check the facts in detail to make sure that each decision in the sample was a group product and not simply based on the judgment of one powerful leader who induced the others to go along with him regardless of whether they thought his decision was good, bad, or indifferent. This consideration has kept me from nominating as candidates a number of fiascoes caused by totalitarian governments—Mussolini's decision to enter the war in 1940 when Italy was completely unprepared, Stalin's failure to anticipate a German invasion while implementing the Nazi-Soviet pact in 1941, Hitler's fatal decision to invade Russia in 1941—although it is conceivable that in some of these decisions the dictator's advisers participated as genuine policy-makers, not merely as sycophants.

Groupthink versus other causes of miscalculation

When carrying out an analysis of any defective policy decision—including the Watergate cover-up and each of the other examples that I have mentioned as candidates in this chapter—one has to examine the available evidence carefully in order to answer a series of key questions before drawing any conclusion as to whether the groupthink syndrome provides at least part of the explanation for whatever errors were made. Obviously, one cannot assume that groupthink is the cause of practically all policy miscalculations and fiascoes. Anyone who relies on that naive assumption in preparing a case study would be carrying out a worthless exercise in unadulterated hindsight. A groupthink analysis of the Watergate cover-up or any other policy that has ended up as a fiasco could be discarded on the basis of the following devastating criticism: Knowing in advance how bad the outcome was, the author simply assumed that it must be because the policy-makers did a poor job; he also assumed that any poorly made decision (if more than one person was involved) must have been due to groupthink. So the author searched selectively for anecdotes that could be construed as illustrating the symptoms of groupthink. And behold!—he detected groupthink as the cause of the fiasco.

There is, however, a genuine problem of hindsight in analyzing case studies. Research by Baruch Fischhoff and others shows that "people consistently overestimate the predictability of past events once they know how they turned out." When one looks at fiascoes of the past, as Dostoyevsky pithily put it, "everything seems stupid when it fails." That is why I believe that one must examine all the available evidence bearing on each fiasco to see if it really was the product of stupidity, and if so, whether groupthink contributed to it.

In order to minimize psychological tendencies to indulge in hindsight and to find what one is looking for in case study material, I propose that the investigator should go through the somewhat tedious process of structuring the inquiry. It requires examining the facts carefully in order to answer the following series of four key questions before concluding that groupthink was a contributory cause of any fiasco:

1. Who made the policy decisions? Was it essentially the leader alone or did *group* members participate to a significant degree? If the members participated, were they in a *cohesive* group?
2. To what extent was the policy a result of *defective decision-making procedures* on the part of those who were responsible?
3. Can *symptoms of groupthink* be discerned in the group's deliberations? (Do the prime symptoms pervade the planning discussions?)
4. Were the *conditions* that foster the groupthink syndrome present?

There is also another question, which is intended to see if something new can be learned: If the answers to the four questions above are positive, can any leads be detected that suggest *new hypotheses* concerning the *conditions* that promote groupthink?

In examining case material for the purpose of answering the key questions, it is essential to seek evidence enabling one to make discriminations that separate facts from myths about how decisions are actually made. In America, according to traditional political doctrine, the President has sole responsibility for every decision authorized by the executive branch. This doctrine pertains to the accountability of the President, but it is often misunderstood as describing who actually made the decision. The doctrine places responsibility on President Eisenhower for the erroneous decision to send U-2 spy planes over the Soviet Union even though he was not even informed about them by the Pentagon until after he had publicly denied that the United States had launched any such flights. President Truman, according to the doctrine, had sole responsibility for the Korean War decisions even though he was highly responsive to his advisers' recommendations and on at least one important decision was induced to change his mind completely. (It will be recalled that Truman had wanted to accept Chiang Kai-shek's offer to send Chinese Nationalist troops to Korea but was talked out of it by members of his inner circle.) John F. Kennedy reinforced the traditional doctrine by publicly assuming full responsibility for the Bay of Pigs fiasco. Nevertheless, his advisers knew that they shared the responsibility, and some of them acknowledged feeling personally humiliated. The known facts about how these decisions were arrived at certainly do not correspond to the myth stemming from the traditional doctrine of accountability.

The reverse situation must also be expected, perhaps even more often: The myth that is likely to be promoted by a leader and his followers is that an entire group participated in arriving at a decision, whereas, in fact, the choice was made only by the leader. The problem of discerning whether advisers participated as policy-makers arises in connection with the major decisions made by any government, business firm, educational institution, or any other large organization, whenever a leader has nominal responsibility for the organization's policies. Only decisions in which the consensus of a stable in-group plays a crucial role in determining the chosen policy are relevant to investigations of the groupthink hypothesis. Thus the list of potential candidates presented earlier in this chapter will have to be cut by eliminating those that cannot properly be classified as group decisions.

The second and third key questions require most of the work that goes into the search for and appraisal of the available evidence used in case study reports like those presented in Chapters 2 through 7. Throughout this book, I repeatedly emphasize (and here I am doing it again) that *just because a policy turns out to have a bad outcome does not enable us to conclude that the group responsible for working out that policy did a poor job*. A disastrous outcome can be the result of unforeseeable sabotage, poor implementation by people outside the decision-making group, or unexpected accidents beyond the control of the policy-makers, some of which have to be chalked up to just plain bad luck. There is also such a thing as good luck whereby poorly made decisions end up being undeservedly successful. Like many other social scientists, however, I assume that the more defects there are in making a decision (as specified by the seven criteria listed earlier in this chapter), the greater the chances that unanticipated setbacks will occur and that the long-term outcome will fail to meet the decision-makers' objectives.

Even when the members of a decision-making group select a defective course of action as a result of their own miscalculations, the main cause of their errors may prove to be misinformation from seemingly trustworthy experts, bolstered by seemingly sound supportive evidence from other sources of intelligence, which could lead even the most vigilant policy-makers to draw the wrong conclusions. Unfavorable outcomes can result from such errors, even though the decision-makers have made a fairly careful information search. In such instances, the miscalculations are not attributable to defective decision-making procedures and therefore are not candidates for an explanation in terms of groupthink. Nor are they candidates for explanation in terms of any other psychological causes involving emotional reactions, such as guilt, anger, or anxiety, which can reduce the cognitive efficiency of members of a decision-making group.

There are, in addition, as Leon Mann and I point out in our book *Decision Making*,

> [various] flaws and limitations in human information processing, such as the propensity of decision makers to be distracted by irrelevant aspects of the alternatives, which leads to loose predictions about outcomes (Abelson, 1976); the tendency of decision makers to be swayed by the form in which information about risks is packaged and presented (Slovic et al., 1976); their reliance on faulty categories and stereotypes, which leads to erroneous decisions relating to social groups and ethnic minorities (Hamilton, 1976); and their illusion of control, which makes for overoptimistic estimates of outcomes that are a matter of chance or luck (Langer, 1975).
>
> Tversky and Kahnemann (1974) describe various other illusions, some notorious and others not yet well known, that arise from intuitive assessments of probabilities that may incline all but the most statistically sophisticated of decision makers to make biased miscalculations in using evidence about the consequences of alternative courses of action.

All sorts of people, including experts trained in statistics, make mistakes in drawing inferences from the information available to them when they are making vital decisions—"overestimating the likelihood of events that can be easily and vividly imagined, giving too much weight to information about representativeness, ignoring information about base rates, relying too much on evidence from small samples, and failing to discount evidence from biased samples." Even without all these sources of miscalculation, the mere fact that a huge overload of complicated information has to be processed in order to arrive at an optimal choice is sufficient to induce competent and highly efficient decision-makers to resort to simple decision rules that fail to take account of the full complexity of the issues at hand. Then, too, there are ego-defensive tendencies and all sorts of self-serving biases that incline a person to lapse into wishful thinking rather than expending the effort to obtain the best available realistic information and to evaluate it critically.

Most of the sources of error I have just mentioned enter into a kind of "feedback loop" with groupthink. Informational overload, for example, contributes to groupthink tendencies which, in turn, greatly aggravate the detrimental effects of the overload on the mental efficiency of decision-makers. But the main point is that *blunders have all sorts of causes*—some, like informational overload, being magnified by groupthink; others, like sheer incompetence or ignorance, having nothing at all to do with groupthink. When one is analyzing any ill-conceived decision to find out whether the groupthink syndrome was a probable cause, it is essential to examine the evidence carefully to see if any alternative causal sequence, involving some other known sources of error, could account adequately for the decision-makers' failure.

Now let us return for a moment to the unanswered question: How widespread is groupthink? Although nongroupthink sources of error may account for the majority of fiascoes that deserve to be fiascoes, I expect that investigations of a wide variety of group decisions on vital issues will probably show that clear-cut symptoms of groupthink are present in at least a substantial percentage of all miscalculated executive decisions—governmental and nongovernmental, American and foreign. Often, the groupthink syndrome is likely to be only a contributing cause that augments the influence of other sources of error, such as overestimating the probability of the threats that are most vividly presented and other such faulty inferences about possible outcomes. The groupthink syndrome, however, can sometimes turn out to be diagnosed as one of the *primary* causes, as we shall see in the case study of the Watergate cover-up in the next chapter. That diagnosis is made when there are numerous indications that groupthink played a crucial role, in the sense that if the group members had been less intent upon seeking for concurrence within the group they would have been able to correct their initial errors of judgment, curtail collective wishful thinking, and arrive at a much sounder decision.

9

The Watergate Cover-up: How Clever Manipulators Can Get Caught in an Avoidable Quagmire

Unique features of this case study

The case study presented in this chapter differs from those presented in the earlier chapters in one fundamental respect. All the preceding case studies were prepared while I was developing the theory of groupthink, which was briefly summarized in the preceding chapter. After having developed the theory, I realized that in order to determine whether the groupthink hypothesis can be applied to any given fiasco, several kinds of questions have to be answered. It does not suffice merely to see whether the symptoms of groupthink can be detected. It is necessary to find out whether the antecedent conditions and the expected consequences are also present. Therefore, in this case study of the Watergate cover-up, unlike the earlier case studies, I systematically consider each of the key questions derived from the theoretical analysis.

Fortunately, objective evidence is available of what was actually said when Nixon and his White House aides were planning each phase of the cover-up. In contrast to all the other case studies of groupthink presented earlier, this one offers us an embarrassment of riches. This case study is unique in that we have verbatim transcripts of the crucial meetings in which the major policy issues were discussed and settled.

In addition to the transcripts of Nixon's tapes, a massive collection exists of sworn testimony from the principals, all of whom except Nixon were required to answer probing questions under oath in congressional inquiries and in court trials for perjury or other criminal offenses arising from the Watergate cover-up. Three of the main participants (Nixon, Haldeman, and Dean) have published their memoirs, with their memories refreshed and their self-justification motivations curbed to a considerable extent by the publicly available transcripts of what they actually said to each other. On top of all that, a whole battalion of investigative reporters have printed interviews with practically everyone having anything to do with the Watergate cover-up.

It is useful to repeat the five key questions at this point because they provide the basic outline for the case study presented in this chapter:

1. Who made the policy decision? Was it essentially the leader alone or did *group* members participate to a significant degree? If the members participated, were they in a *cohesive* group?
2. To what extent was the policy a result of *defective decision-making procedures* on the part of those who were responsible?
3. Can *symptoms of groupthink* be discerned in the group's deliberations?
4. Were the previously observed *conditions* that foster the groupthink syndrome present?
5. If the answers to the four questions above are positive, can any leads be detected that suggest new hypotheses concerning the conditions that promote groupthink?

In each of the earlier case studies of groupthink (Chapters 2–5), I have answered the first three of these questions, but in a rather unsystematic way. Now I propose to use all five questions as a guide for the successive steps to be carried out systematically in any case study, whenever there is any reason to suspect that the groupthink hypothesis might help to explain why decision-makers have made avoidable errors. The sequence of the questions is intended to enable investigators to identify unpromising candidates as early in an inquiry as possible, so as to avoid wasting time on the wrong track. In order to answer the questions in the appropriate sequence, it is unfortunately necessary to be repetitious. The same crucial meetings and sometimes the same quoted statements in the transcripts have to be reexamined from different standpoints so as to determine first, who was responsible for the cover-up decisions; next, what, if anything, was wrong with the way the decisions were arrived at; then, whether there were manifestations of groupthink that help to explain any errors; and finally, whether the antecedent conditions conducive to groupthink can be detected.

The decision to authorize the Watergate burglary

The first two of the key questions are preliminary in the sense that the answers are needed in order to determine whether any given fiasco is a *likely candidate* for a groupthink analysis. Before investing time and effort to see if the symptoms of groupthink are present, it is prudent to ascertain first whether the context or circumstances are such that concurrence-seeking by a cohesive group might be one of the factors that could help to account for avoidable errors made by capable decision-makers.

Let us take a quick look from this standpoint at the ill-fated decision made by one or more Republican leaders to authorize a team of burglars to break into the Watergate building in order to plant electronic eavesdropping devices in the offices of the Democratic party's national headquarters.

(This was the crime that President Nixon and his aides subsequently tried to cover up.) When we start with the first key question, we soon find that the answer emerging from the somewhat ambiguous evidence does *not* make the decision to authorize the break-in seem a likely candidate for an explanation in terms of groupthink.

Congressional inquiries revealed that three meetings were held (two in Attorney General John Mitchell's office in Washington, one in Key Biscayne, Florida) to discuss proposed plans for illegal surveillance of the Democratic party concocted by G. Gordon Liddy, an unscrupulous attorney who has been characterized by a knowledgeable political correspondent as a "gun loving . . . man of violence . . . [with a] warped sense of patriotism." The proposed plans, according to John Dean, the President's Counsel in the Nixon White House, included not only "bugging" but also "black bag operations, kidnapping, providing prostitutes to weaken the opposition . . . [and] mugging." The meetings were attended by representatives of rival factions within the Nixon administration—John Mitchell, Gordon Liddy, John Dean, Jeb Magruder, and Fred LaRue. Only two of these men were present at all three meetings. Certain of them did not trust each other and they definitely did not constitute a cohesive group. Magruder testified under oath that he and LaRue attended the meeting in Florida where Mitchell, overloaded by the demands of his new role as Chairman of the Committee to Re-elect the President, hastily and unenthusiastically gave his approval after having gone over with them about thirty other agenda items.[1]

Execution of the Watergate break-in by a team of ex-CIA agents organized by Howard Hunt and Gordon Liddy was so badly bungled that there is some basis for a popular view which holds that deliberate sabotage on the part of one or more of the burglars (at least one of whom has admitted to being an active CIA agent at the time of the break-in) is the most plausible explanation for the series of out-of-the-ordinary errors leading to the prompt capture of all the Watergate burglars in the very act of committing the crime. Their incredible ineptness also allowed the Washington, D.C., police to obtain evidence leading to the arrest of Howard Hunt and Gordon Liddy, the organizers of the break-in, who had not been caught at the scene of the crime. Then there were the tell-tale sequentially numbered one-hundred-dollar bills found on the burglars. These bills enabled the FBI in a short time to trace the funds to the Committee to Re-elect the President. With implementation like that from friends, you don't need poor decision-making for an enemy.

So the probable causes for errors made in the Watergate *break-in* might lie in such factors as distraction on the part of a single policy-maker responsible for approving a risky plan prepared by an irresponsible underground agent, and defective implementation by underlings who intentionally or unintentionally sabotaged the plan. There is no reason therefore to look into groupthink or any other aspect of group dynamics in an inquiry that attempts to understand how the Watergate *burglary* fiasco happened.

But the Watergate *cover-up* by the White House that started on June 17,

1972, the day the burglars were arrested, is a completely different story. Although Nixon and his chief White House aides, Bob Haldeman and John Ehrlichman, have persistently denied any responsibility at all for the Watergate break-in, all three admit that they were not innocent bystanders insofar as the cover-up was concerned.

Explanations of how the cover-up fiasco came about

Of the millions of words published about Watergate, only a tiny percentage have addressed the fundamental psychological question: How could a group of clever, politically astute men who had reached the pinnacle of power in the White House make so many errors of judgment and fail to foresee the potentially disastrous consequences of their illegal cover-up actions? All the principals in the Watergate cover-up have acknowledged that they made a series of blundering decisions. For example, H. R. (Bob) Haldeman, President Nixon's Chief of Staff, at the beginning of his book on Watergate, says: ". . . all of us at the White House involved in Watergate did a lot of things wrong. Some criminal, some harmless, some willful, some accidental, some shrewdly calculated, some stupidly blundered, but each wrong." Later in the book, he adds: ". . . *failure to face the irrefutable facts,* even when it was absolutely clear that they were irrefutable, was one of our fatal flaws in handling Watergate at every stage."

John Ehrlichman, a top White House aide who was President Nixon's chief adviser on domestic affairs, also admitted that they made erroneous decisions. During and after the trial in which he was found guilty of criminal offenses, his defense was that "things were compartmentalized" in the White House, and he really did not know much about what was going on in connection with the cover-up. Nevertheless, he had this to say about his personal mistakes: "One necessarily regrets not having said the word that would have deflected the course of history. The situation was probably festooned with landmarks I didn't see."

Richard Nixon himself, although continuing to deny some of the irrefutable facts in order to disclaim his illegal acts as President, admitted after leaving the White House in disgrace that he "screwed up terribly," that he "botched up" the handling of Watergate and "made many bad judgments." "I let the American people down," he concluded, "and I have to carry that burden with me for the rest of my life."

The history of the cover-up is a history of belated admissions. It ended in August 1974 when Nixon finally admitted that he had known about the complicity of White House officials within the first week after the Watergate burglary in June 1972—an admission wrung from him only after he was required by a unanimous Supreme Court decision to release a "smoking gun"

President Richard M. Nixon announcing his resignation from
the presidency on August 8, 1974. This occurred three days
after Nixon was forced to release the incriminating "smoking
gun" tape that established his guilt in the Watergate cover-up.
He knew that the House of Representatives was on the verge
of impeaching him and that the Senate in all probability would
convict him.

tape that contained unequivocal evidence of his guilt. Immediately after that final admission, he resigned rather than face the near-certain prospect of impeachment by the House of Representatives and conviction by the Senate.

For months after Nixon's resignation, the press all over the world was filled with speculative comments that tried to explain why the President allowed himself to become involved in a series of ill-conceived obstructions of justice and why he failed to realize until it was too late that he would be unable to withhold the incriminating evidence in his White House tapes. Among the most thoughtful commentaries were those in a special Watergate issue of *Harper's,* published in October 1974. The editors asked leading historians, social scientists, and political commentators to explain why Nixon misperceived the facts, misjudged the options open to him, and risked fatal mistakes. Among the ten contributors were Senator Eugene J. McCarthy, General Matthew B. Ridgway, Arthur M. Schlesinger, Jr., and Theodore C. Sorensen.[2] There is little agreement in the explanations offered in the ten short essays, but collectively they provide a fairly good survey of conventional wisdom about the lessons of Watergate.

Among the main factors singled out are Nixon's personal shortcomings—his defective ethical standards, his lack of commitment to accountability, his preference for seclusiveness, furtiveness, and secrecy, his isolation from all voices except those of sycophants. Some general features of the social milieu are also mentioned, such as the cumbersome governmental bureaucracy that prevents cogent information from reaching the President, the deterioration in the values of the American people which fosters in their leaders misuse of high office, and the inevitable corruption that comes from possessing enormous political power, whether in America or anywhere else, and from being the nation's number one celebrity.

In my opinion, there is some truth in all but one of these ideas (his top aides were not sycophants, as will soon be seen). Many factors undoubtedly contribute to the explanation of Nixon's grossly deficient handling of the moral and political problems collectively referred to as Watergate. What is most striking to me, however, is that not one of the ten essays mentions anything at all about group dynamics, except for the one incidental (and I think erroneous) allusion to sycophants, implying that Nixon was surrounded by yes-men.

During the many years that have elapsed since the scandal erupted, I have continued to be a Watergate buff, but I have found very few references in the mass media to anything approximating the groupthink concept in the explanations put forward to account for Nixon's fatal mistakes.[3] I surmise, therefore, that the groupthink hypothesis, with its emphasis on situational conditions that foster concurrence-seeking even among hard-headed presidential advisers, is not at present part of conventional wisdom in explaining major fiascoes.

The groupthink hypothesis has not been completely neglected, however, by social psychologists. Three psychological studies have been based on analyses of some of the available documents. One of them, by Bertram H. Raven, was published in a professional journal and reprinted in a social psychology textbook. The other two—one by Duane Green and Edward Conolley and the other by William Wong-McCarthy—have not as yet been published. All three studies note that there were clear-cut symptoms of groupthink in the way Nixon and his inner circle handled the Watergate cover-up. In this chapter, I draw upon their work as well as my own detailed analyses of the primary documents. If the groupthink hypothesis can help to explain Nixon's disastrous course of action, it could provide a new perspective for preventing Watergate-like fiascoes in government, private industry, and public welfare organizations.

Chronology: Highlights of the Watergate cover-up

In order to keep in mind the sequence of major events that form the context for various meetings in the White House discussed in the sections that follow, it may be helpful to consult the following chronology:

1972

June 17:   *Washington, D.C., police arrest James McCord, the security officer of the Committee to Re-elect the President, and four other burglars who have broken into the Democratic National Committee's offices in the Watergate building in order to plant electronic eavesdropping equipment.*

June 17:   *FBI agents find in the possession of the burglars a check from Howard Hunt and an address book containing Hunt's initials next to his telephone number at the White House.*

June 20:   *John Dean, the President's Counsel, opens Hunt's safe to prevent FBI agents from confiscating evidence of his participation in the Watergate break-in and in other illegal activities carried out by the White House "plumbers." Dean, according to his subsequent testimony, is told by John Ehrlichman, the President's chief adviser on domestic affairs, to "deep six" a briefcase filled with incriminating evidence.*

June 20:   *In a conversation with President Nixon, Charles Colson, a high-level White House aide, recommends that the Watergate "caper" should be attributed to the burglars operating on their own and that the charges that higher-ups in the administration are involved should be ignored. The President agrees and says, "The hell with it . . . I just stonewall it."*

June 23:   *President Nixon orders his Chief of Staff H. R. (Bob) Haldeman to ask the CIA to block the FBI investigation, which is starting to* trace funds in the possession of the Watergate burglars to the Committee to Re-elect the President.

June 23:   President Nixon's two chief aides, Ehrlichman and Haldeman, meet with CIA Director Richard Helms and CIA Deputy Director Vernon Walters to convey the "President's wish."

June 23:   Herbert Kalmbach, the President's personal lawyer, responds to requests by Dean and Ehrlichman by obtaining funds from the Finance Committee to Re-elect the President to distribute to the Watergate burglars and their lawyers. (The initial payment was $75,000, a small fraction of the total of over $400,000 that eventually was paid to them.)

June 28:   Mitchell announces that he has fired Gordon Liddy for refusing to cooperate with FBI investigators. From this point on, for the next few months, White House spokesmen assert that Liddy and Hunt engineered the Watergate break-in entirely on their own, in an excess of zeal, without authorization by any higher officials.

Aug. 29:   Nixon states at a news conference that "no one in this Administration, currently employed, was involved in this very bizarre incident." He attributes this conclusion to Dean's thorough investigation (which, according to Dean's subsequent testimony, was never made).

Sept. 15:   Indictments by the Watergate Grand Jury are announced; they are limited to Liddy, Hunt, and the five men arrested inside the Watergate building.

Sept. 15:   At a meeting in the White House, Nixon praises Dean for his skillful handling of potential leaks that might have implicated former Attorney General John Mitchell and other higher-ups.

Oct. 10:   The Washington Post publishes a startling news story by Carl Bernstein and Bob Woodward, relying partly on disclosures by "Deep Throat." It states that the FBI has traced the Watergate break-in to a campaign of political spying and sabotage carried out by the Committee to Re-elect the President under the direction of officials in the White House.

Nov. 7:   Nixon is reelected by a landslide (61 percent of the vote). "Watergate is all but forgotten."

1973

Feb. 2:   Judge John Sirica, who presided at the trial of Liddy, Hunt, McCord, and the four other Watergate defendants, announces that he is not satisfied that the full story has been disclosed.

Feb. 7:   Taking into account Judge Sirica's statement and a series of news items reporting alleged evidence that implicates White

House aides in the Watergate cover-up and other improprieties, the Senate votes unanimously to set up a select committee to investigate the allegations.

Feb. 28:   L. Patrick Gray, at the Senate Judiciary Committee hearings to confirm his appointment as FBI Director, admits that he gave John Dean and others at the White House access to FBI reports on the Watergate investigation. He also reveals that there is evidence that Dwight Chapin and Herbert Kalmbach, associated with the White House, were involved in illegal activities.

Mar. 13:   The Senate Judiciary Committee votes unanimously to demand that Dean appear before them as a witness in the Gray hearings. The Committee rejects the claim of executive privilege made by Nixon the preceding day, which stated that the manner in which the President and members of his staff exercise the executive powers of the presidency "is not subject to questioning by another branch of the government."

Mar. 21:   Dean's "cancer within the presidency" session with Nixon: Dean tells the President that Haldeman, Ehrlichman, and Dean could be sent to jail for obstructing justice. When discussing Hunt's most recent "blackmail" demands for huge sums of money, Nixon says, "For Christ's sake get it!"

Mar. 22:   Gray, at his confirmation hearings, states that Dean "probably lied" by telling FBI agents that Hunt was not connected with the White House.

Mar. 23:   Judge Sirica reads the court a letter from McCord charging that he and the other Watergate defendants were under pressure to remain silent and that perjury was committed at their trial.

Mar. 28:   In line with the long-standing "stonewall" policy, Ehrlichman informs Attorney General Richard Kleindienst that no one at the White House knew anything about the Watergate break-in beforehand.

Apr. 8:   Dean begins cooperating with the Watergate prosecutors in the Department of Justice. In his many meetings with them in the weeks that follow, he implicates Haldeman and Ehrlichman as well as himself in obstructions of justice.

Apr. 13:   Magruder, who was second-in-command of the Committee to Re-elect the President at the time of the break-in, admits to Watergate prosecutors that he committed perjury at the trial of the Watergate defendants.

Apr. 15:   Dean reveals to the Watergate prosecutors that in 1971 the White House "plumbers," Liddy and Hunt, had illegally broken into the office of Daniel Ellsberg's psychiatrist.

Apr. 15:   The Watergate prosecutors inform Nixon that Haldeman, Ehr-
              lichman, Dean, and others on the White House staff are im-
              plicated in the cover-up. Department of Justice officials urge
              Nixon to fire them.

Apr. 30:   President Nixon announces the resignations of Haldeman and
              Ehrlichman—"two of the finest public servants it has been my
              privilege to know." He also announces the resignations of Dean
              and Attorney General Kleindienst.

May 22:   In response to damaging new revelations starting to emerge at
              the Senate Watergate Committee hearings chaired by Senator
              Sam Ervin, President Nixon publicly admits for the first time
              that some officials in the White House had engaged in a cover-
              up. But he claims that he did not participate in it. He asserts that
              in June 1972 he limited the Watergate investigations only to pro-
              tect "national security." The President revokes the extreme
              position he had taken on executive privilege on March 12,
              thereby allowing his aides to give testimony under oath about
              Watergate and related issues.

June 25–29:   Dean testifies at the televised Senate Watergate Committee
              hearings that Nixon knew about the cover-up by September 15,
              1972, and encouraged it.

July 16:   Alexander Butterfield, a White House aide, informs the Senate
              Watergate Committee that President Nixon made secret tape
              recordings of his conversations.

July 23:   Nixon rejects requests from Special Prosecutor Archibald Cox
              and from Senator Ervin's committee for various tape recordings
              of his Watergate conversations made during the preceding thir-
              teen months.

Oct. 20:   Special Prosecutor Cox rejects President Nixon's compromise
              offer to provide summaries of the tapes, which would be verified
              by Senator John Stennis, instead of turning over the actual sub-
              poenaed tapes.

Oct. 20:   The "Saturday night massacre": President Nixon fires Cox. At-
              torney General Elliot Richardson resigns in protest and so does
              Deputy Attorney General William D. Ruckelshaus, the man
              next in line of authority at the Department of Justice.

Oct. 21–23:   "A fire storm" of protest sweeps through Congress and the na-
              tion's press, culminating in strong demands for the President's
              resignation or impeachment.

Nov. 21:   White House Special Counsel J. Fred Buzhardt informs Judge
              Sirica of an inexplicable gap of 18½ minutes in the tape of a
              crucial conversation between the President and Haldeman on
              June 20, 1972.

1974

Mar. 1:   *On grounds of obstructing justice, the Watergate Grand Jury in-*
                  dicts Haldeman, Ehrlichman, Colson, Mitchell, and three other
                  former officials appointed by Nixon.

Apr. 30:   *The White House releases edited versions of some of the many*
                  tapes subpoenaed by Special Prosecutor Leon Jaworski and by
                  the Judiciary Committee of the House of Representatives,
                  which is about to begin its inquiry into Nixon's misconduct in
                  office. The text of the 1,254 pages of edited White House con-
                  versations is widely interpreted in the press as bearing out
                  Dean's charge that the President knew about the cover-up
                  before March 21, 1973, and that he told his aides to pay Hunt a
                  large sum of money to keep him from talking.

July 24:   *The Supreme Court unanimously rules that the President must*
                  turn over all the tapes subpoenaed by Special Prosecutor Jawor-
                  ski.

Aug. 5:   *Nixon admits that starting in late June 1972, he participated in*
                  the cover-up. A five-minute portion of the newly released tape
                  of June 23, which reveals that Nixon told Haldeman to use the
                  CIA to block the FBI investigation, is regarded by practically all
                  Congressmen and all news commentators as the "smoking gun"
                  that establishes Nixon's guilt.

Aug. 8:   *Knowing that the House of Representatives is about to impeach*
                  him and that the Senate will in all probability convict him, Nixon
                  announces his resignation of the presidency effective the next
                  day.

Did Nixon's aides fully participate with him
in making the cover-up decisions
or were they merely yes-men?

Anyone who carefully examines the transcripts of the Watergate tapes
and the other public documents, it seems to me, will find that during the
period starting with the first news story of the Watergate burglary in June
1972 until the end of March 1973, the cover-up was the product of decisions
made collaboratively by President Nixon with his chief aides—H. R.
Haldeman (Chief of Staff), John Ehrlichman (Assistant to the President for
Domestic Affairs), and John Dean (the President's Counsel). During the first
few weeks, Charles Colson (Special Counsel to the President) and, to a much
lesser extent, John Mitchell (ex–Attorney General and chairman of the Committee to Re-elect the President) also occasionally participated. Toward the
end of March 1973, as the cover-up began to unravel, John Dean became
disaffected. In the words of Haldeman, "Dean shifted roles from one of the

President Richard M. Nixon conferring with his Chief of Staff
H. R. (Bob) Haldeman, who was also his chief co-
conspirator. They were the leading participants in the White
House group that planned the Watergate cover-up; the group
included John Ehrlichman, John Dean, and Charles Colson.
Nixon and Haldeman were responsible for making and preserving the notorious White House tapes during 1972 and 1973,
which contained incriminating evidence that led to
Haldeman's jail sentence and Nixon's forced resignation.

protectors of the President to the protector of himself—a shift of enormous historical consequence." During the next few weeks, the inner circle disintegrated as the press revealed one "bombshell" after another. On April 29, 1973, Nixon personally decided to fire Haldeman and Ehrlichman in a futile effort to be, like Dean, his own protector.

After that, Nixon appointed a new set of White House aides—Alexander Haig, Melvin Laird, Leonard Garment, and J. Fred Buzhardt—who felt no personal loyalty to Nixon and were wary of one another. From then on, the decision-making process concerning problems arising from the mounting Watergate crisis apparently involved patterns different from those characterizing the first nine months of the cover-up, with which we are concerned in this case study. Consider, for example, the notorious "Saturday night massacre" on October 20, 1973, when Nixon decided to fire Special Prosecutor Archibald Cox, even though he knew that Attorney General Elliot Richardson would resign in a way that would be extremely damaging to his already weakened administration. That decision may well have been made by Nixon essentially on his own. By provoking Cox's defiance and withholding essential information from everyone on his staff, Nixon may have obtained the advice he wanted to hear when he went through the motions of seeking the counsel of the men around him in the White House. At that particular time, the President was beset by simultaneous crises created by the dangerous escalation of the Yom Kippur War in the Near East, which threatened a United States–Soviet armed confrontation, and the subpoenas for the White House tapes at home, which threatened his impeachment. He was very agitated and getting little sleep. Nixon may have made his ill-conceived decision to fire Cox in a distraught panic-like state of hypervigilance, which is at the opposite pole from the manifestly calm state of overoptimism that characterizes a leader who is a victim of groupthink. (Hypervigilance leads to even worse errors in decision-making than groupthink does.)

Going back now to the last half of 1972, the transcripts of Nixon's White House meetings and telephone calls during the formative period of the cover-up show that his aides, Haldeman, Ehrlichman, Dean, and Colson, were far from passive yes-men. The *Congressional Quarterly* in June 1974 published a special commentary on the presidential transcripts which states that "Haldeman and Ehrlichman . . . appear in the transcripts as acting as Nixon's peers, rather than subordinates, often telling him what to do rather than suggesting." *Newsweek*'s review of the published presidential transcripts in May 1974 also emphasizes that the image of Nixon as a domineering leader is not supported by the evidence. "Behind the closed door of his office, he seems . . . a waffling executive, a President who instead of presiding at these critical discussions, defers continuously to his subordinates . . . [In] many conversations the President seems . . . a bystander, almost a yes-man, letting others take the lead."

It is also apparent that Nixon frequently delegated responsibility to his aides, allowing them to use their own judgment to carry out the so-called containment policy (their term for the cover-up) in whatever ways they saw fit.[4] Haldeman, Ehrlichman, and Dean frequently initiated new cover-up activities and then discussed with Nixon how best to continue doing what they had already started. They encouraged Nixon to make changes in his own plans for dealing with the Watergate scandal. At every stage, they guided his strategies as each new problem arose. For example, on June 23, 1972, Haldeman tells Nixon that because the FBI investigation of ramifications of the Watergate break-in is not under control, "we" should put an end to it by getting the CIA to intervene. Haldeman says, "the only way to solve this, and we're beautifully set up to do it . . . is for us to have Walters [the Deputy Director of the CIA] call Pat Gray [the Acting Director of the FBI] and just say 'stay the hell out of this—this is, ah, business here we don't want you to go any further on it.' " Nixon agrees to Haldeman's plan and adds a few finishing touches to make it more effective. It was the tape recording of this conversation that became in the eyes of practically all members of Congress the "smoking gun" that established Nixon's guilt on the impeachable charge of misusing the CIA and the FBI to serve his personal political interests.

Similar examples can be cited of Nixon working collaboratively on cover-up plans with other members of the in-group. Nixon did not hesitate to tell the men in his inner circle what he thought ought to be done and how it should be done, but on numerous occasions he promptly withdrew his suggestions in the face of objections from one or another of his key aides. From numerous examples in the transcripts, it seems highly probable that Nixon was repeatedly influenced by the suggestions and objections made by his key aides, with whom he continually consulted. *The cover-up policy decisions certainly were not made by the President alone and his key aides certainly were not mere yes-men.*

Was the decision-making group cohesive?

This is a complicated question to answer. If we look at Nixon's entire set of advisers, inside and outside the White House, it is apparent that they did *not* form a cohesive group. Bertram H. Raven, who made a close study of the Nixon administration, concluded that there were "at least two major contending factions, with a number of individuals within each faction contending for power and disliking one another." In speaking about the power struggles and mutual dislikes that made for disharmony, Raven is referring particularly to the long-standing antagonisms between Mitchell and Haldeman and their respective followers. Raven prepared a sociometric diagram (shown in Figure 9–1) to represent the social relationships among twelve men on whom Nixon relied heavily on domestic political issues. The chart shows which men were

FIGURE 9–1. SOCIOMETRIC DIAGRAM OF NIXON AND HIS MEN

Note: President Nixon had positive relationships with nearly everyone on the chart. Only the most significant of these are illustrated.

Adapted from Bertram H. Raven, "The Nixon Group," Journal of Social Issues, *1974, 30, 297–320, Plenum Publishing Corporation.*

friendly coworkers and which ones were unfriendly rivals. At the center of the diagram is the friendly White House trio, Nixon, Haldeman, and Ehrlichman. It was this compatible triumvirate together with two of their assistants—Dean and Colson—that made up the decision-making group primarily responsible for Watergate cover-up policy.

John Dean is represented in Raven's diagram as having, like all of the others, a positive relationship with the President. But Dean is shown as having negative relationships with Haldeman and Ehrlichman. This does not seem to me to be accurate for the nine-month period with which we are concerned—from the end of June 1972 to the end of March 1973. It is true that when Dean first came to the White House, he was regarded with suspicion by Nixon's two chief aides because he had been a member of Mitchell's rival clique in the Justice Department. But during the first few months on the job, Dean made such a favorable impression that Haldeman and Ehrlichman gave him more and more responsibility and, in effect, admitted him as at least a peripheral member of the core team.

On September 15, 1972, Haldeman strongly encouraged Nixon to rely on Dean because of his skillful handling of numerous problems arising from the Watergate scandal. "John is one of the quiet guys that gets a lot done," Haldeman told Nixon. "He turned out to be tougher than I thought he would. . . ." In the lexicon of Nixon's in-group, this is, of course, very high praise. Even after Dean became a renegade and exposed all the "White House horrors," Haldeman admitted, as I mentioned earlier, that before he "shifted roles," Dean had been "one of the protectors of the President."

Nixon was highly responsive to Haldeman's endorsement of Dean. In his diary on September 15, 1972, Nixon wrote glowingly about Dean. He said he "was enormously impressed with him" and that he told Haldeman that Dean "had the kind of steel and really *mean* instinct that we needed." For Nixon this was perhaps the most praiseworthy thing that could be said about a new recruit to his team. Dean continued to be highly regarded as having the right stuff by his superiors during the next six months.

In February 1973, Nixon, Haldeman, and Ehrlichman agreed that Dean should have more direct contact with the President. Initially this was for the sake of the record, to cover up the cover-up: It would enable Dean to refuse to answer questions in all the forthcoming inquiries on the grounds that he had an attorney-client relationship with the President. Dean did so well in his new role and was so highly trusted that he was able to capitalize on the opportunity to achieve much higher status. Nixon reports that "Ehrlichman and I decided that instead of working through Haldeman, I would work directly with John Dean." Thereafter, with Haldeman's full approval, Dean not only had frequent face-to-face sessions with Nixon but also attended many of the President's meetings with Haldeman and Ehrlichman. Even after Dean began to deviate from the group norms by urging that the cover-up policy be replaced by open admission of White House complicity, Nixon continued for a time to have strong positive feelings toward him as a valuable member of his team. On

March 25, 1973, Nixon wrote in his diary that it was a "hard day" (because James McCord, one of the convicted White House burglars, had accused Dean and other officials of having known in advance of the Watergate break-in plan), and he added, "Dean . . . is really the one who deserves the most consideration because he was always acting as a counsel, giving his best advice."

When he discussed Watergate matters with Nixon, Haldeman, and Ehrlichman, John Dean participated in the informal social atmosphere that had long characterized the meetings of the friendly triumvirate. In the expurgated edition of presidential transcripts sent to the House Judiciary Committee by the White House in 1974, Dean's quoted statements contained his full share of expletives that had to be deleted. This, too, is a sign of the change in Dean's status as a member of the in-group.

Dean felt that his successful "firefighting" enabled him "at last [to] make the first team," and he cherished the "ego-boosting badges of intimacy" with the President. He reports that although he continued to be fond of his first boss, John Mitchell, he transferred his loyalty to the Nixon-Haldeman team to such an extent that he would not tell Mitchell what was going on in the White House. When Haldeman and Ehrlichman took the position in late June 1972 that Mitchell, their old rival, should be removed from his post, Dean supported them. A central theme of Dean's book about his role in Watergate, *Blind Ambition,* is that he valued his membership in the top White House group to such an extent that he was willing to suppress his misgivings and do whatever was expected of him, regardless of whether it violated the ethical and legal standards to which he was supposed to be committed. "I became possessed," he says, "of the toughness I imagined generals display when called upon to sacrifice divisions and battalions for the overall effort."

The first time Dean met with Nixon and Haldeman, in September 1972, he was surprised that they behaved like old cronies, making no attempt to create the atmosphere of dignified decorum he had expected in the Oval Office.

> I was not prepared for what I found. Haldeman was slumped in a chair in front of the President's desk, his yellow pad dangling from his hand rather than poised as usual for note taking. The President was reclining in his swivel chair at what seemed a precarious angle, his feet propped up on his desk to leave the Presidential heel marks. From his nearly supine position, the President looked at me through the V his shoes formed. I paused at the door, feeling like an intruder, and waited for Haldeman and the President to snap back into form. But they didn't, and I walked hesitantly to a chair. I wouldn't have been much more surprised by the atmosphere if the two of them had been wearing dresses. I was flattered to be so collegially received.

Dean's subsequent participation in the relaxed, friendly interchanges among the "first team" is manifested not only by his joining the others in using vulgarisms in his speech but also by his readiness, from time to time, to express openly his personal feelings about ongoing events. That he felt free to do so is illustrated by what he said in a meeting in Nixon's office on March 22, 1973, when the group was considering what to do about a new "bombshell." Patrick Gray, the acting head of the FBI who was expected to be "one hundred percent loyal" to Nixon, had just testified at his Senate confirmation hearings that John Dean had "probably lied" to the FBI. Haldeman made a sarcastic comment to Nixon about Gray having become the "symbol of wisdom" because "he accused your counsel of being a liar." Ehrlichman commented that Gray would be "dead" so far as his confirmation on the floor of Congress was concerned. Dean, who was "furious at Gray" when he learned the bad news, picked up on Ehrlichman's imagery to express his personal emotional reactions to Gray's accusations against him. "He may be dead," Dean stated, "cause I may shoot him." The others responded with loud laughter. In making his not-so-funny joke about executing Gray, Dean may have been resonating to the vivid image of a traitor's execution conveyed in a telephone call he had received earlier, when Ehrlichman made the most memorable remark in the entire Watergate saga.

> **Ehrlichman:** Hi, just had a call from your favorite witness.
> **Dean:** Which is?
> **Ehrlichman:** Patrick J. Gray.
> **Dean:** Oh really?
> **Ehrlichman:** And he says to make sure that old John Dean stays very, very firm on his story . . .
> **Dean:** Yes, he's really hanging tough. You ought to read the transcript. He makes me gag.
> **Ehrlichman:** Let him hang there . . . Let him twist slowly, slowly in the wind.

The strong positive relationships of Haldeman to Nixon and Ehrlichman, represented in Figure 9–1, had been established long before the Watergate cover-up began. They had been working together in the White House for almost four years, but they had developed close ties years earlier. When Nixon entered the White House, Haldeman had long been one of his closest advisers—"closer than anyone else professionally," Haldeman says, and he accepts Alex Butterfield's characterization of himself as "an extension of Nixon, his alter ego."

Ehrlichman, an intimate personal friend of Haldeman since their college days, was highly regarded by Nixon, who appreciated his unswerving loyalty and constant protectiveness. Nixon relied heavily on Ehrlichman as his main adviser on domestic affairs.

In light of the various indications I have summarized, it seems fairly safe to conclude that the core of the White House decision-making group—Nixon, Haldeman, and Ehrlichman—was a highly cohesive trio, with a strong sense of mutual loyalty and high esprit de corps. Although Haldeman and Ehrlichman occasionally were abrasive in their dealings with Dean and Colson, the two junior members of the decision-making group were treated, by and large, as loyal and valuable members of the team during the formative period of the Watergate cover-up. In general, one finds hardly any signs at all in the transcripts of recriminations, bickering, or clashes of any kind among the five men on the White House team who engineered the cover-up. There are no signs of internal warfare within this group until April 1973, when the cover-up was unraveling and John Dean defected from the group. Up to that time, the expletives that were deleted in the laundered version of the transcripts were shared expressions of frustration or antagonism directed against political enemies, never against anyone else within the group. The transcripts of the meetings are filled with friendly chatter, joking, and shared sentiments about a variety of topics irrelevant to the business at hand—just what one would expect in a cohesive team whose members share the same basic values and goals.

Did defective decision-making play a major role in causing the fiasco?

As in the analysis of each of the fiascoes presented in earlier chapters, an essential step is to ascertain whether the failure of the in-group's policy was at least partly attributable to errors in decision-making rather than to other causes, such as unforeseeable accidents. In the case of the Watergate cover-up policy, practically all knowledgeable commentators, as well as the participants themselves, agree that Nixon and his in-group did a very poor job of decision-making. Nixon himself has acknowledged that the so-called containment policy was not carefully thought out. "I have sometimes wondered whether, if we had only spent more time on the problem at the outset, we might have handled it less stupidly."

Haldeman, too, does not try to place the blame anywhere except on the "foolish" way he and the others made their decisions.

> The cover-up collapsed because it was doomed from the start . . . too many people knew too much. Too many foolish risks were taken. Too little judgment was used at every stage to evaluate the potential risk vs. the gains. . . .
>
> * * *
>
> . . . It was not planned ahead . . . it just grew one step at a time as people, believing they were acting in the best interests of the President, took steps to meet each problem as it arose. My most profound personal remorse today comes from the realization that my errors contributed to that growth.

Examination of the transcripts of the White House meetings bears out Haldeman's statements about the haphazard way the crucial decisions were arrived at. Alternatives to the cover-up policy were hardly considered at all during the first eight months following the Watergate break-in. Then, during the months when their containment policy was not succeeding very well because of new disclosures almost daily in the press, various modifications and alternatives were introduced in the group meetings but were discussed very superficially—for example, to arrange for a new grand jury or to set up a presidential investigation commission where John Dean and other aides would give testimony acknowledging some of their complicity. But none of the alternatives was examined carefully in terms of pros and cons.

Numerous examples could be cited for each of the seven criteria of defective decision-making listed near the end of Chapter 1. Some typical examples will be presented shortly when I illustrate the main symptoms of groupthink that interfered with effective decision-making. Of the seven types of defects, the one that recurs most frequently throughout the meetings is the group's failure to evaluate the long-range consequences of the illegal cover-up actions. Almost as prominent was their failure to work out contingency plans to deal with foreseeable risks that might materialize. The image that many supposedly sophisticated people had of the efficient way plans were made in the White House, as economist Murray N. Rothbard points out, was shattered by the Nixon transcripts.

> Orthodox political scientists . . . maintain that while private citizens are wrapped up in grubby, short-range concerns, the rulers of government, up there on Mount Olympus, can and do plan wisely for the distant future. There is no clearer conclusion from the Nixon transcripts than the almost incredibly short-range vision of the top executive bureaucracy. They are interested, not just in the next election, but in the next six o'clock news on television.

Only by reading extensively in the transcripts of the meetings can one appreciate the extent to which the cover-up fiasco was the product of defective decision-making by the White House group. In the words of an editor of one of the nation's leading magazines of informed political commentary, the cover-up clearly appears to have been "an entirely avoidable quagmire."

We have now reached the crucial step in our inquiry to determine whether the groupthink hypothesis can provide at least part of the explanation for Nixon's White House group allowing itself to sink into a quagmire. Why did the members make so many mistakes for such a long period of time? Why did they fail to prepare for the obvious troubles to be expected from the risky cover-up policy to which they carelessly committed and recommitted themselves? Why did they continue to make biased appraisals of unwelcome warnings informing them they were not going to be able to get away with it?

Can symptoms of groupthink be discerned?

Only after one has concluded that a fiasco was probably a product of defective decision-making by a cohesive group does it become worthwhile to try to find out whether groupthink is one of the major causes. In order to pursue further the hypothesis that groupthink was a probable cause of the gross errors made by the group responsible for the Watergate cover-up, we must now consider whether the available records of the group's deliberations contain clear-cut indications that concurrence-seeking tendencies were operating during the meetings at which the defective group decisions were made. At the same time, we need to see if it is warranted to preclude alternative explanations, especially those antithetical to the groupthink hypothesis. Antithetical causes include psychological states that are incompatible with the manifestly placid group atmosphere that characterizes groupthink—such as a distraught panic-like state of hypervigilance among group members in response to threatening events, which greatly reduces their cognitive efficiency.

The few social psychologists who have reported on their examination of pertinent evidence concerning the Watergate cover-up have concluded that symptoms of groupthink can clearly be discerned in the deliberations of the White House group. In a preliminary review of newspaper accounts, before the presidential transcripts and other records became available, Duane Green and Edward Conolley presented numerous examples of a shared illusion of invulnerability, collective rationalizations, and other characteristic symptoms. A more complete study was later made by Bertram H. Raven, using the transcripts of Nixon's tapes, the testimony given in the hearings conducted by the Senate and the House of Representatives, and other available sources. Raven concluded that "the groupthink phenomenon described by Janis . . . was evident in the Nixon group."[5]

William Wong-McCarthy has carried out the most detailed analysis of the unedited White House tapes transcribed from Nixon's secret recordings by the House Judiciary Committee and the Watergate trial prosecutors. As in the other two studies, he finds numerous signs of groupthink during the period when the White House in-group was carrying out the cover-up. Wong-McCarthy's textual analysis, which is documented by a large number of quotations from the verbatim transcripts of the White House meetings, concludes that groupthink prevented Nixon, Haldeman, and Ehrlichman from making objectively reasonable decisions in their handling of the Watergate affair.

In a separate study, Wong-McCarthy carried out a systematic content analysis that provides relevant quantitative data bearing on concurrence in the meetings in the White House of Nixon with his chief aides, Haldeman, Ehrlichman, and Dean. For the purpose of obtaining a measure of the degree of concurrence at each meeting, Wong-McCarthy devised a way of coding every expression of agreement or disagreement by any member of the group in response to any relevant statement, whether a diagnostic or prognostic speculation or a pragmatic proposal for action, made by any other member. According to his coding scheme, agreement could be expressed by making explicit assertions, such as "that's right," or by elaborating in a positive way on what was being proposed by the preceding speaker. He counted the number of agreements and disagreements in all the statements that pertained to the interests of the White House in-group (which usually made some reference to what is happening to *us*, what *we* should do, or *our* plans).

Wong-McCarthy's measure of concurrence consisted of an overall percentage of agreement which can be applied to any single meeting or to any series of meetings. It was used by Wong-McCarthy to compare the amount of concurrence in meetings that took place during two successive months during which the major change took place from group solidarity to disintegration. The period from the last week in February 1973 to the beginning of the last week in March 1973 was characterized by concerted cover-up actions by the cohesive White House group to deal with growing threats of exposure, particularly arising from the U.S. Senate's unanimous vote to empower a panel (the Ervin Committee) to investigate Watergate. In contrast, the following month was the period when John Dean defected, and as Lukas puts it in his book on Watergate, "the Nixon 'team' which had held together so well for months was falling apart, day by day." By mid-April 1973, Nixon was telling Haldeman and Ehrlichman that they might have to leave in order to preserve the "presidency" and they were objecting on the grounds that this action would be widely interpreted as confirming their guilt—and besides, Nixon would need their help to avoid being impeached. As expected, during the earlier month when the members were functioning as a cohesive group, *scores were relatively high on the measure of concurrence, which is presumed to be indicative of groupthink.* During the following month, when they were no longer a cohesive group, scores on concurrence fell sharply.[6]

In my own reading of the transcripts of the meetings from June 1972 to March 1973, I find, as Wong-McCarthy's content analysis indicates, *relatively few instances of disagreement and very little debate about what is the best thing to do.* After a suggestion is made by anyone in the group, the others most often accept it immediately and start building on it. If a plan of action suggested by Nixon elicits an expression of doubt from one of his aides, he often withdraws his suggestion immediately without even finding out what the objections might be. Similarly, each of the aides frequently withdraws his suggestions if Nixon or anyone else in the group is hesitant about accepting it. In this way, expressions of divergent points of view tend to be quickly passed over, creating a homogenized atmosphere of apparent unanimity, with disagreements kept to a minimum. Very seldom is there any hard-headed debating, one member of the group favoring one position, another an opposing position. When the group is discussing an unusually difficult problem, such as what to do about McCord's charges that government officials engaged in perjury at the trial of the Watergate burglars, one suggestion after another is withdrawn, leaving everything completely up in the air. This type of indecisiveness increases during the month of March 1973, as more and more revelations in the press pose challenges to the group's defective cover-up policy. By early April 1973, disagreements are being openly voiced and the atmosphere of apparent unanimity can no longer be maintained.

Turning now to the specific symptoms of groupthink, I draw upon the work of Green and Conolley, Raven, and Wong-McCarthy, as well as my own detailed analysis of the unedited transcripts.

Did a shared illusion of invulnerability pervade the group's deliberations?

The prime symptom of groupthink—a shared sense of invulnerability of the group—can be manifested by members in at least two different ways: by expressing *overoptimistic views* about the group's power or their leader's power to control events whenever troubles arise; and by *ignoring warnings* that call attention to the dangers of continuing the current course of action. Both of these signs of a shared sense of invulnerability are constantly present through the period from late June 1972 when the cover-up began until near the end of March 1973. Even when the group was disintegrating as a result of the "bombshells" that shattered their defenses, the members appear to have been striving to regain a sense of invulnerability by giving grossly overoptimistic reassurances to each other.

At the outset, when the troublesome news came in about White House personnel being linked with the Watergate break-in, the members of Nixon's in-group felt confident that the enormous power of the White House could eliminate any difficulties. Haldeman says that this was his attitude.

> Whatever the problems, if any, I felt I could handle them . . . And if I somehow slipped, the most astute politician in the nation, Richard Nixon, would step into the breach. At that point I believed Nixon could accomplish anything . . . Nothing could hurt him now.

For many months, Haldeman reports, he continued to be *"confident that . . . any* political attempt to tie it [Watergate] to the White House would fail." He felt that he could safely leave it to "other staffers such as Dean." It never occurred to him that as a result of the cover-up he could be sent to jail or that Nixon could be impeached. Like Nixon, Ehrlichman, Dean, and Colson, he grossly underestimated the danger that the cover-up might be exposed by a disgruntled Watergate defendant, by one of the many secretaries who had wind of what was going on, or by assiduous investigators in the Department of Justice. During the fall of 1972, the only concern of the White House group was the possibility that the Watergate burglary could result in bad publicity that might cost Nixon some votes in the election. Even with regard to this very limited threat, they felt secure about being able to counteract it by means of their enormous public relations capabilities.

Here is the way Theodore H. White describes the group's sense of invulnerability to the consequences of the cover-up:

> There is an unreality to the summer cover-up—as if a handful of men with nominal authority could outwit the vast outside reality of the American system: the offices of the prosecutors, the hidden loyal underground of civil servants, the remorseless grinding responsibility of courts, the curiosity and appetite of the press. It was as if, *intoxicated by the power of the White House,* they truly believed that they could circumvent what it had taken 200 years of American civilization to build. They could not imagine that to use the powers of office to erase the [small] crime would wipe out all that Nixon had really accomplished.

As a new junior member of the team, Dean felt much less confident than his superiors about handling the worrisome problems of the cover-up, especially as he came to realize that more and more hush money would have to be paid to the Watergate defendants. Nevertheless, for many months, according to his memoirs, he shared the attitude of Haldeman and the others about the omnipotence and omniscience of their leader: Dean says that he had "faith that the President could overcome the Watergate scandal by infinite power and wisdom."

As he encountered more and more difficulties raising hush money and trying to induce officials with inside information to commit perjury at grand jury hearings, court trials, and congressional hearings, Dean came to rely on the buoyant optimism expressed by fellow members of Nixon's in-group when Watergate matters were discussed. At his first meeting with Nixon and Haldeman, on September 15, 1972, Dean was told by Nixon that he was doing a good job keeping the Watergate charges confined to the burglars, all of whom had either remained silent or had explicitly testified in court that no higher-ups were involved. Nixon said, "the way you, you've handled it, it seems to me, has been very skillful, because you—putting your finger in the dikes every time that leaks have sprung here and sprung there." Nixon, sounding as if all their troubles would soon be over, talked about how after the election they would get their revenge against their political enemies who were responsible for the bad publicity about Watergate. Nixon told Dean, "I wouldn't want to be on the other side right now, would you?" Dean, eagerly compliant and deferential, emphatically agreed, "No, no!"

At that time Nixon himself believed in his invulnerability as President. Despite knowing that Mitchell, Colson, Dean, and others on his team were deeply implicated in the Watergate cover-up, he thought that there was nothing to worry about except a bit of bad publicity that would have to be refuted. "I felt sure," he said in retrospect, "that it was just a public relations problem that only needed a public relations solution."

The "stroking" session of September 15, 1972, apparently had the intended effect on Dean. Starting with that meeting, Dean felt the contagious effect of the optimism exuded by the leader and by the second in command. "As would be the pattern," Dean asserts, "I felt at my toughest and most hopeful after receiving a boost from Haldeman or the President himself. Away from them, however, disturbing events cropped up that fed my doubts about the ultimate success of the cover-up." At times, Dean says, disturbing events "deflated my confidence, but Haldeman usually pumped me back up . . . That fall Bob had become very friendly and increasingly open." For several months, according to Dean's account, he looked forward to meetings with Nixon, Haldeman, and Ehrlichman, because "they offered me confidence." Later on, when he realized that the cover-up was failing, he "began to lose faith" in the omnipotence of the President and sought refuge in heavy drinking at home each night. But up until then he was helped to keep up an "optimistic front," while doing his best to maintain the cover-up, by his firm belief in the President's unlimited power.

Dean's reactions give us some clues to how the members of the in-group were dealing with obvious dangers that could not be denied. Despite his mounting misgivings, Dean apparently was caught up in the group atmosphere of high optimism, sufficiently so that time and again he conveyed a rosy picture to the others. On February 28, 1973, for example, Nixon raised a few questions about the Ervin Committee investigation and then expressed the grossly overoptimistic view that public interest in the whole thing would fall off after only one week. As the discussion continued to touch lightly upon one potential danger spot after another, Dean was completely reassuring. He said that the public was already bored with Watergate publicity; the congressional staff was inadequate; Colson's threat of a libel suit was having a sobering effect on the press; Kalmbach would be a "tough" witness who "is hunkered down . . . so I am not worried about Herb at all"; no one of importance in the Nixon administration would be hurt by the Senate Committee, "they may even paint themselves as being partisans and off base." After minimizing all the threatening developments, Dean concluded, "we have made it this far and I am convinced we are going to make it the whole road and put this thing in, in, in, uh, the funny pages of the history books rather than anything serious."

By three weeks later, Dean had become convinced that the cover-up was breaking down so rapidly that he and all of Nixon's other key aides would end up being convicted as criminals and sent to prison with long sentences unless some drastic new actions were taken. In his "cancer within the presidency" meeting with Nixon on March 21, 1973, he urged a full-disclosure plan that would cut their losses. No longer minimizing the negative consequences of the cover-up policy, he called Nixon's attention to some dire threats: One of the Watergate defendants (Hunt) was blackmailing the White House, and Haldeman, Ehrlichman, and Dean could be sent to jail for obstructing justice. But Nixon seemed to be already aware of this unpleasant information, and when he raised skeptical questions, Dean reverted to his habitual compliant response, "to snap to my usual optimism for his benefit." When answering Nixon's questions, Dean at first pulled no punches in describing Haldeman's role in making hush money available to the Watergate burglars and Colson's assurances of presidential clemency to Hunt. "They are," Dean told Nixon, "the very sort of thing that the Senate is going to be looking most for." But then he added a grossly overoptimistic statement that completely undercut his position. "I don't think they can find them, frankly."

Later in the conversation when Nixon indicated that Hunt should be paid off "damn soon . . . to keep the cap on the bottle," Dean for the moment abandoned his position entirely. "That's right. That's right," he answered. At that moment, according to his memoirs, Dean thought to himself, "Maybe he *is* right . . . After all, he is an old pro at this sort of thing." If Dean is remembering correctly the thoughts he had during this meeting, he was reacting in a way that is characteristic of a loyal group member: Once again, he was bringing his private thinking in line with what the leader wanted. When Nixon later asked, "What are *your* feelings about the options?" Dean gave a much watered-down version of the dissenting position he had intended to present forcefully, alluding merely to "soft spots" that made him feel "not confident that we can ride through this." As he was saying this, Dean informs us in his memoirs, he was feeling guilty, wondering if he was being disloyal, as well as feeling worried about losing the leader's approval.

Toward the end of the session, Haldeman joined them and was briefed on the impressive warnings Dean had been giving Nixon about the cancer that should be excised. Haldeman gave some support to Dean's position and told the President that "John's point is exactly right, that the erosion here now is going to you [Nixon], and that is the thing that we've got to turn off, at whatever the cost." Nevertheless, at a meeting later that same day, Dean and Haldeman, in effect, dropped the full-disclosure alternative they were proposing. Nixon gave Dean the opportunity to repeat his warnings about various ways that the cover-up might soon be revealed. But with a strong push from Ehrlichman, the conversation soon turned to the same old public relations tactics the group had been using to deal with all such threats.

In his memoirs, Nixon says that he was quite unperturbed by the crucial meeting with Dean on March 21, 1973, which, as he points out, "was later to be seen as a disastrous turning point in my presidency":

> I left the meeting only troubled by the new dimensions of what he [Dean] had described rather than galvanized into action by the urgency and peril of our situation . . . more disturbed than shocked; more anxious than alarmed. The practical effect of my failure to grasp the full import of what I had been told was that I doggedly persisted in the same course I was on before the conversation. I continued to concentrate on the question of who was vulnerable because of prior knowledge of the break-in and to look for some way to change our public relations posture so that the White House did not look so defensive.

If Nixon really felt somewhat anxious, it was about others, not himself, according to the diary entry he made when he was alone at the end of that fateful day. The entry starts off with the bland sentence, "As far as the day was concerned it was relatively *uneventful* except for the talk with Dean." The rest of the entry is devoted mostly to describing Dean's feelings of depression, speculating about what might be causing Dean to feel so upset, and expressing feelings of sympathy for Dean and his other aides. Not a word of concern about his own vulnerability. Perhaps he is displacing his own anxiety onto the messenger who brought him bad news. In any case, the next day he again is striving to maintain that he and his in-group are invulnerable, and Haldeman joins him in this effort. In their morning conversation on March 22, 1973, Haldeman no longer deviates from the norm of maintaining an optimistic outlook, both men apparently relying once again upon the great power of the President to eliminate charges of illegalities. The two agree that Dean really has no need to worry about being charged with obstructing justice, nor does Haldeman, who had authorized the payments from the $350,000 slush fund he controlled. All the money they gave to the Watergate defendants could be explained away as having been donated "out of compassion," and besides, Dean (and Haldeman) did not personally handle the payments.

At one point, however, Haldeman makes a revealing slip of speech as he is attempting to add yet another reassuring thought: "Again, Dean looks at the, what might be the worst. *It may not be the worst.*" This bit of inadvertent pessimism is immediately followed by much laughter, and then Haldeman smoothes it over with the philosophical remark, "In fact what usually happens is something beyond what you thought was the worst." Right after that, the conversation includes direct acknowledgements of current threats as Nixon speaks about putting the wagons up around the White House by sacrificing expendable supporters outside the White House: "Who do you let down the tube? Do you let Magruder down?" Haldeman implies that his answer is yes by asserting that there really is no White House cover-up, the only cover-up has been to protect Magruder and others in the Committee to Re-elect the President. Now, he says, they can and should be "totally cut off" from the White House. Returning to a completely optimistic stance, he flatly states, "The White House has no guilt in the Watergate thing," and Nixon agrees.

Later in the conversation, Haldeman proposes that Mitchell will also have to be let down the tube rather than being allowed to continue "to hide under the blanket of the White House." In arguing that this sacrifice is necessary, Haldeman urges Nixon to give priority to protecting members of the White House group. "He's awfully close to you . . . [but] he's not as close to you as Erhlichman . . . Dean and Haldeman now. . . ." Haldeman sweetens the distasteful medicine with the usual bits of optimism: "Mitchell will find a way out . . . They may not be able to convict [Magruder] . . . Then Magruder indicted and winning, uh, acquittal may be a pretty good route for us to go."

There is a defensive quality to their mutual reassurances during this conversation, as Haldeman and Nixon vacillate between jointly acknowledging realistic threats and trying to deny them. Although they agree that they may now need the advice of an expert in criminal law, they end up working out together a reassuring view of controlling the dangers if any one of "us" is called to testify:

Haldeman: . . . we're under rules of evidence and, and . . .
Nixon: Right.
Haldeman: . . . oh, and germaneness.
Nixon: You've got lawyers who object, you can go to relevancy there.
Haldeman: Yeah, and they can only . . .
Nixon: Go to relevancy, that's no problem there.
Haldeman: So they can't go fishing. . . .

When the two are together again at a meeting with Dean, Ehrlichman, and Mitchell held later that same day (March 22, 1973), they concur on a proposal that Ehrlichman has been pushing for some time—to have Dean prepare a report that will put a new coat of whitewash on the White House. In their conversation, they keep reverting to the same old optimistic refrain—the only real problem facing them is to counteract the bad publicity they are getting. "What we're fighting," Nixon solemnly states, "is a public relations battle." It would be one of the last times that he or any of the other members of the group could deny the real danger of being convicted for their criminal actions. Less than a week later, Dean would decide to fight an entirely different kind of battle in order, as his lawyer put it in their first private conversation, to save his "own ass."

The failure of Nixon, Haldeman, and Ehrlichman to revise their unsuccessful cover-up policy in response to Dean's clear-cut warning about their vulnerability proved to be a fatal error. On top of all the other dangers they were neglecting, Nixon and his two chief aides overlooked the potential damage that Dean could cause them if he defected. The trio's misplaced belief in their power to counteract all the dangers evidently led them to feel sufficiently confident to allow the cancer Dean warned them about to grow even larger by giving additional blackmail payments to Hunt and by asking Dean to prepare a report containing falsehoods that would unavoidably put him under pressure to commit perjury on behalf of the White House. Dean knew all about the group's readiness to deal with each crisis by selecting a fall guy to go down the tubes. Because of the way he was being treated, he began to feel that he was being set up to be the next one. The trio's gross mishandling of Dean's deviant stance, which I shall describe in more detail shortly, was evidently based on overconfidence in their power to control him as well as to contain the threats he was so concerned about. Their overoptimistic expectations of invulnerability were rudely shaken when Dean, having lost faith in the leader and the group, told the Watergate prosecutors everything he knew about the illegal actions authorized by the men in the White House. This was the first giant step toward the ruination of Nixon, Haldeman, and Ehrlichman. But the documentary evidence I have just reviewed indicates that from the time of the Watergate burglary in June 1972 until the end of March 1973, *Nixon and his in-group of White House aides who participated in the cover-up repeatedly showed clear-cut signs of a shared illusion of invulnerability throughout their discussions about cover-up activities.*

Are there signs that potential disagreements were being suppressed?

In the White House discussions during the last ten days of March 1973 provoked by Dean's last-ditch attempt to sound the alarm about the growing cancer, other manifestations of groupthink can be discerned in addition to the denials and mutual reassurances that appear to be efforts to reinstate a sense of invulnerability. We have just seen that there was something illusory about the apparent unanimity of the group in arriving at their decision to continue their public relations battle, despite the imminent danger that members of the White House team, if not the President himself, would soon be charged with criminal liability. Dean often and Haldeman occasionally must have been engaging in *self-censorship*. They avoided presenting fully their misgivings and objections in the face of strong pressures, for example, when they agreed with the President and Ehrlichman to continue the unsuccessful public relations strategy by preparing yet another whitewashing report.

There are also other indications that the apparent unanimity of the group was an illusion. In his memoirs, Nixon has this to say in retrospect about the crucial meetings that took place on March 21, 1973: "Looking back on it now, I can see that we were all operating from different bases of knowledge and with different perceptions of our own vulnerabilities." As examples he cites Haldeman's primary concern, rarely mentioned out loud, about being accused of prior knowledge of the Watergate break-in, in contrast to Dean's overriding fear of being held criminally responsible for the payments made to keep the burglars silent. "These differing perceptions and the chasms they created in our overall understanding," Nixon asserts, "are apparent now. At the time, however, the problem only seemed very complicated, and our strategy sessions were just frustrating and inefficient minuets around the problem."

Although Nixon's account of such matters might not be trustworthy, his characterization of the sessions as dancing around the serious issues appears to be quite correct when one studies transcripts of the meetings. The participants were highly inconsistent, blowing both hot and cold in what they said about dealing with the lurking dangers, which suggests that they were not revealing their own major concerns. The vacillations fit with an interpretation that posits suppression on the part of individual members—suppression of misgivings that might make them out of step with the others, that might violate the norms being set by the leader, disturb the sense of collective strength, and disrupt the harmonious group atmosphere by provoking open disagreements. Dampening the potential sources of disharmony in order to maintain a collective illusion of unanimity is, of course, an outstanding feature of groupthink.

Are there manifestations of collective rationalizations?

Of the various symptoms of groupthink, the most frequent in the transcripts of the White House meetings appears to be the collective rationalizations developed by the members to buttress their overconfidence about their chances of successfully covering up the cover-up. A typical example has just been cited in the conversation of Haldeman and Nixon on March 22, 1973, when they agreed that the payments of hush money to the Watergate burglars was perfectly legal, which they apparently believed at the time.

One of the most persistent rationalizations, repeatedly put forth by the leader and shared by members of the group, was that the charges of mis-behavior against them in the press had nothing to do with their own culpability but were merely part of "the public relations war" instigated by their political enemies. The way in which this type of rationalization was used is well illustrated by a conversation between Nixon and Dean on March 13, 1973, when they were talking about news stories that correctly accused the White House of having hired Donald Segretti to carry out his dirty tricks in the recent election campaign. "Shit," Nixon said, "it's not sinister. None of it is," and Dean responded, "It's quite humorous as a matter of fact." Then Nixon enunciated a classic version of the rationalization that the whole thing was merely a weak and contemptible propaganda attack against their strong and upright group: "the last gasp . . . of our partisan opponents. They've just got to have something to squeal about." Dean reinforced Nixon's wishful explanation by adding, "the *only* thing they have to squeal on."

This type of explanation for current troubles seems to have been genuinely believed by Nixon and others in the group, in contrast to the numerous false statements they deliberately made up to deny or excuse their misdeeds in press releases and public speeches. Time and again when the propaganda machinations of their political opponents are mentioned as the source of whatever accusations are currently causing them trouble, they act as if they really believe they have explained why they are in trouble; they stop discussing any alternative ways of handling the problem and revert to their business-as-usual public relations approach, expanding the cover-up by issuing more false statements.

The most obvious examples of shared rationalizations that supported their recommitment to the same old course of action with accompanying feelings of unwarranted optimism have to do with Nixon's incriminating tapes which, as Haldeman said, "destroyed him." Leon Jaworski, the government Special Prosecutor who headed the final stages of the legal investigation of charges against Nixon and his aides, stated as his considered opinion that if Nixon had destroyed his tapes before they were subpoenaed, he could have weathered the storm of criticism and finished his term in office. Why didn't Nixon destroy them before they began to destroy him?

Jaworski's answer agrees with the answer given by others who have carefully studied the records.

> Nixon did not destroy the tapes because it never occurred to him that legal action might force him to surrender them. During 1972, and perhaps during the early part of 1973, he thought the tapes possessed extraordinary monetary value. . . . I am confident that he felt secure in his claim of executive privilege. And when that claim was jeopardized by the actions of the Special Prosecutor's office, it was too late.

It was assumed by Nixon and Haldeman from the outset—and later by Ehrlichman when he learned that Nixon's meeting with Dean on March 21, 1973 had been recorded—that the tapes would always be fully under Nixon's control. Under no conceivable circumstances, they believed, could the tapes ever be used as evidence in public trials or congressional investigations. The three men were able to maintain this wishful belief because they never sought any legal information or advice until the issue had already become a public controversy.

Nixon must have been at least vaguely aware of the potential danger because he once suggested to Haldeman, about three months before the existence of the tapes was revealed at the Senate Watergate Committee hearings in July 1973, that they should be destroyed. But Haldeman said he thought the tapes should be kept, and without any further discussion, Nixon agreed. He never again raised the issue with Haldeman. Their main rationalization, which enabled them to discount the danger of preserving the incriminating evidence, was that the tapes could be a great asset to Nixon and not to his opponents. In mid-April 1973, when Dean began to inform the Watergate prosecutors in the Department of Justice about his conversations in the President's office, Nixon and Haldeman, according to Haldeman's account, believed that "the President might be able to use the tapes to trip him up."

About ten days later, Nixon and his two chief aides agreed that the time had come to use their great secret asset. Ehrlichman recommended to Nixon that he or Haldeman should listen to the tapes to find out exactly what was said during the session of March 21, 1973, which Dean had singled out in his damaging testimony. Haldeman strongly backed the idea. Nixon accepted their recommendation and asked Haldeman to listen to the tape in question in order to prepare the best possible defense. Always prompt, efficient, and loyal, Haldeman on that very same day carried out the assignment all too well, much to his subsequent sorrow. (He was convicted of perjury and sent to jail for his testimony before the Senate Committee about what he claimed to have heard on that tape.) Haldeman's conclusion was that the tapes did not support Dean's charges (perhaps partly because Dean has misremembered the dates of the conversations and some of the important details).[7] That same evening Nixon talked again about their great asset in a telephone call to Haldeman. "I always wondered about that taping equipment," Nixon said, "but *I'm damn glad we have it, aren't you?*" Haldeman agreed that yes indeed the tapes were helpful.

The various examples just cited of the way Nixon and his top aides justified their illegal actions and dismissed the danger of their misdeeds being exposed by the incriminating tapes are typical of the *collective rationalizations* frequently manifested in the unedited transcripts of the tapes. *This is another prominent symptom of groupthink that pervaded the group's deliberations.*

Are there signs of a shared belief in the inherent morality of the group?

In the White House conversations bearing on the cover-up, there is no direct evidence that Nixon and his key aides shared a belief in the inherent morality of the group. The group practically never talked about the ethical or moral aspects of the obstructions of justice and misuses of presidential power they were planning to carry out, or had already carried out, except in the context of preparing arguments for public relations purposes. Their only concern in each instance appears to have been whether they could get away with it. Consequently, the only warranted answer to the question above is no, this particular symptom of groupthink was *not* observed.[8]

Did the group rely on crude stereotypes?

The transcripts are filled with epithets and derogatory comments about opponents, which bespeak the members' continual use of negative stereotypes to characterize those who opposed any of the group's goals. There is no question that this symptom of groupthink constantly appears in their conversations. In the White House conversations that contain manifestations of the illusion of invulnerability and collective rationalizations, there are numerous examples of the crude stereotypes the group used when talking about the Democrats, the press, the government prosecutors, and even their own supporters who dared to urge fuller disclosures. A few of the typical examples might suffice to indicate the way in which Nixon and his chief aides relied upon crude stereotypes similar to those repeatedly encountered in all the preceding case studies of groupthink.

When perturbed on March 13, 1973, about newspapers and magazines that were talking about a "crisis in the confidence of the presidency" as a result of new Watergate disclosures, Nixon, in a conversation with Dean, dismissed the whole thing with a stereotype of the oppositional press: "It'll be mainly a crisis," he said, "among the upper intellectual types, the ass holes . . . Average people won't think it is much of a crisis unless it affects them."

When discussing how to deal with the recently established Senate Watergate Committee during that same period, Dean took the lead in labeling it a conspiracy by their political enemies and asserting that Senator Ervin, the chairman, and Sam Dash, the chief counsel for the Committee, were mere puppets of Edward Kennedy. Nixon agreed. "Yeah. I guess the Kennedy crowd is just laying in the bushes waiting to make their move." And they worked out plans for dealing with the Committee accordingly. In using such stereotypes, Nixon and his aides appear to be attributing the criticisms leveled against them by the press and the demands for congressional investigations entirely to the machinations of their enemies, and not at all to their own misjudgments or misdeeds.

Stereotypes were also used by the White House group to characterize those supporters who became dissidents by violating their group's norms. This is well illustrated by the transformation in the way the White House trio talked about Dean after it became known that he was revealing the truth about the cover-up to the Watergate prosecutors. By late April 1973, Dean was no longer a fair-haired boy being groomed for a top position in the government, but was being referred to as weak and despicable. In an emergency meeting of the White House trio on Sunday evening, April 15, 1973—the day Nixon was informed by Attorney General Kleindienst and the chief Watergate prosecutor, Henry Petersen, that Dean had given information to the Department of Justice implicating his key aides in the cover-up—Dean was immediately characterized as a sneaky traitor by Ehrlichman. He argued that Dean should be kicked out as soon as possible because "You certainly can't risk his bouncing around here, playing his little game, tip-toeing through the files gathering ammunition."

The afternoon of April 25 was one of many times when Nixon expressed an obsessional idea about Dean's treachery, which was plaguing him: "I just wonder if the son-of-a-bitch had a recorder on him" (referring to the crucial meeting on March 21). Haldeman, however, said, "it's almost inconceivable," and argued that Dean was undoubtedly sincere at the time when he warned Nixon about problems that needed to be solved in a different way. That same evening Nixon again characterized Dean in derogatory, stereotyped terms. He referred to Dean's latest disclosure of the White House role in the illegal break-in of the office of Ellsberg's psychiatrist as "basically a little *blackmail* by him." This time Haldeman expressed his agreement. Haldeman did not do so, however, when Nixon went on to say: "I think he's out to save himself . . . he's . . . a desperate man he may wanna bring the President down too, but in this case then, Bob, there's no, no other choice, it's to, to fight like hell. Ah, this is ah, this is an *evil* man, you know. He knows that this [containment] was a legitimate thing [for us] to be doing, he was deeply in it." Later in the conversation, Nixon says that Dean has to be cleverly manipulated in order to prevent him from revealing his most dangerous information. It is necessary, he says, "to handle it in such a way that he doesn't become, uh, [a] totally implacable enemy . . . I, at least, have treated him decently. Ah, in fact, more decently than he deserves." But, of course, Nixon mishandled the "evil man" so badly in his efforts to "fight like hell" that Dean soon did, in fact, become totally implacable, revealing all he knew about Nixon's illegal actions as well as his aides'.

Although at that time Haldeman did not fully share Nixon's and Ehrlichman's extreme stereotype of Dean, he subsequently appears to have taken over their view that Dean's motives were despicable. In his memoirs, Haldeman says that Dean "in desperation . . . implicated the President," that he revealed the full truth about the cover-up only because he "panicked" when he realized that he was failing to obtain immunity from prosecution, and foolishly allowed himself to be "shafted" by the Watergate prosecutors.

In keeping with the derogatory labels of Dean as a despicable person engaging in "blackmail," the embattled trio failed to reflect about other ways of interpreting the significance of Dean's deviant action. The evidence from the transcripts of their conversations indicates that Nixon, Haldeman, and Ehrlichman did not consider the possibility that Dean, having lost all hope of convincing them to end the cover-up policy, was now taking steps to do what he sincerely thought was needed to expiate his guilt or to avoid a long prison sentence, or both. This train of thought might have led them to reconsider their own vulnerabilities and to entertain the painful idea that the road Dean decided to take might be worth examining as an alternative for each of them to follow before it became too late. When members of a group resort to extremely negative stereotypes to account for the nonconformist actions of a dissident, it may help them to preserve morale, but it keeps them from deliberating on the likelihood that the best thing for the rest of the group might be to stop clinging to the old policy in the face of new objective threats that have already proved to be powerful enough to induce at least one of their close associates to become nonconformist. This brings us to still other characteristic symptoms of groupthink.

Did the group put pressure on dissenters and display related symptoms of groupthink?

Studies of cohesive policy-making groups indicate that charges of disloyalty and other derogatory epithets that impugn the deviant's motives do not invariably occur when a member is getting out of line by advocating a policy that differs from the one favored by the leader and the rest of the members. One of the dysfunctional features of a groupthink-dominated group is that anyone who expresses doubts about the wisdom of a current policy is put under pressure to suppress misgivings. Then, if he does not comply, the dissenter is no longer treated as a member in good standing and may even be condemned as a traitor.

In the conversations of the White House trio during late March and early April 1973, some of which I have already quoted, it is not difficult to discern in what they were saying to and about Dean the dysfunctional treatment I have just described. Nixon put pressure on Dean as early as March 17, 1973, to avoid making any plans to deal with the threat of criminal charges against him. Nixon said others may be "potentially subject to criminal liability . . . you're not." He emphasized that "*you* have no problem."

About a month later, when Nixon was almost ready to fire Dean, he tried to act in accordance with his resolution to keep the dissident from becoming an implacable enemy by setting up another "stroking" session. In that session the President acted as though he were listening sympathetically to Dean's account of why he had decided to tell the truth to the Watergate prosecutors about Haldeman's and Ehrlichman's involvement in the cover-up. Dean's explanation included an explicit reference to the strong pressure exerted on him by others in the Nixon group to abandon the pro-disclosure position he had been urging them to adopt: "I said the containment theory is not working anymore so you might as well forget it . . . Finally, I started coming in to see you . . . *Then I was told by all . . . that I'd be talking surrender,* I'm not talking surrender, I'm talking realistically."

Long before he began to express doubts openly about the containment policy, probably as early as November 1972, Dean had started to worry about the likelihood that he and others in the group would be caught, tried, and convicted for obstructing justice. But except for a few brief conversations with Haldeman, he generally did not talk about those worries with others in the White House group until March 1973. His failure over a period of several months to discuss in detail his realistic worries with Nixon and the others at the White House meetings illustrates another symptom of groupthink that I have already mentioned as contributing to the illusion of unanimity—*self-censorship of ideas that go counter to the group's norms.*

Dean was not the only member of the group to engage in this type of self-censorship. Ehrlichman, as an attorney, realized that the Congressmen and editorial writers who were demanding Nixon's impeachment in March and early April of 1973 were not mouthing empty propaganda phrases. But neither he nor Haldeman mentioned a word to the President about this real threat until one day when Nixon shocked the two of them with the unexpected information that both might be forced to leave the government, which destroyed the cohesiveness of the trio. (Up until then Ehrlichman was completely optimistic that "he would weather the storm and stay," and Haldeman, although somewhat less optimistic during those oppressive weeks, did not think he would be asked to resign and expected "to be found innocent" when his case was investigated.) Haldeman's report of the dramatic scene includes exact quotations from the transcript of the meeting on April 22, 1973.

> The President said that he had talked to the prosecutors again and they believed that "for the sake of the Presidency, uh, uh, you should step out . . ."
> And then Ehrlichman nailed him with a right cross. "Now let me just spin something out for you . . . I think it's entirely conceivable that if Dean is totally out of control, and if matters are not handled adroitly, that you could get a resolution of impeachment."
> The President looked absolutely stunned. This was the first time the grim word impeachment had ever entered our conversations. Ehrlichman pounded ahead . . . "On the ground that you've committed a crime . . . and that there is no other legal process available to the United States people other than impeachment. . . ."
> I can say that Nixon never recovered from this statement. Everything he did and said during the last days we were with him harked back to Ehrlichman's prophetic remark about impeachment. He would refer to it over and over again. The unthinkable had been uttered.

Suppose that five or six weeks before saying it in the heat of anger, Ehrlichman had spoken about the threat of impeachment with Nixon in the same way as he had often raised other touchy issues with the President—dispassionately, empathically, and deferentially. It seems quite conceivable that Nixon might then have been much less stunned and much more willing to examine objectively an alternative course of action in line with what Dean had been suggesting on March 21, 1972, which at that time was also temporarily supported by Haldeman—to discontinue the cover-up by openly revealing the gist of the truth along with plausible explanations that might have enabled Nixon and his men to survive in office despite public censure. By abstaining from any mention of the impeachment threat, Ehrlichman and Haldeman appear to have been functioning as *mindguards;* they were protecting the leader from distressing ideas he would not welcome, which might impair their relationship to the leader and lead to dissension within the group.

In summary, there are clear-cut indications that the White House group responsible for the cover-up policy engaged in *mindguarding* as well as *self-censorship* of ideas that were not in line with the group's norms. They also put *direct pressure* on one of the members when he no longer engaged in self-censorship and became a dissenter. We have seen that in addition to these three symptoms of groupthink there is considerable evidence in the unedited transcripts of a *shared illusion of invulnerability, collective rationalizations,* and *stereotypes of out-groups.* Some suggestive evidence of an *illusion of unanimity* was also observed. But since moral issues were never discussed except in the context of preparing excuses for public relations purposes, there was no clear-cut evidence of a shared belief in the inherent morality of the group. In short, seven of the eight symptoms that make up the groupthink syndrome were observed in the recorded deliberations of Nixon's White House group. It appears likely, therefore, that the groupthink syndrome is a probable cause of the defective decision-making that characterized the group's cover-up policy.

Were conditions present that foster groupthink?

One of the essential conditions that makes for groupthink was discussed in detail earlier in this chapter—namely, the cohesiveness of the decision-making group. We have seen that the evidence indicates that before and during the planning of the Watergate cover-up the central trio, Nixon, Haldeman, and Ehrlichman, felt closely bound together by mutual ties and commitment to common goals, which made for a keen sense of loyalty to each other and adherence to a shared set of norms. Dean and Colson, who were junior members of the in-group when the series of cover-up decisions were made, had similar feelings of loyalty to the White House group. They, too, participated in the esprit de corps of the "first team" and conformed to the norms set by their leader. The conclusion that follows from the documentary evidence I cited earlier is that *the group responsible for the cover-up policy for nine months following the Watergate break-in was at least moderately, if not highly, cohesive.*

Group cohesiveness, however, appears to be only a necessary but not a sufficient condition of groupthink. On the basis of the comparative case studies presented earlier in this book and other evidence from prior research on group dynamics, I postulate that groupthink tendencies are not likely to become strong enough to lower the quality of a group's decision-making activities unless certain other conditions are also present in addition to cohesiveness. Those additional conditions involve factors that are conducive to collective uncritical thinking by allowing the pressures toward uniformity within a cohesive group to become dominant when the members are grappling with the problems of policy-making.

Three such factors have clearly emerged in the preceding case studies of groupthink decisions. One is *insulation* of the members of the group from outside sources of information, which could correct their uniform sectarian approach to the problems by introducing impressive new information that might generate critical examination of their initial assumptions and debate about alternatives. A second factor is *absence of norms requiring methodical procedures* for instituting information search and objective appraisals of the consequences of the main alternatives open to them. Long-standing norms within the organization that foster methodical procedures of search and appraisal could overcome the members' readiness to concur without dissent on whatever proposal the leader or the majority initially favors before they examine the full range of issues involved. A third factor is *lack of a tradition of impartial leadership* within the organization. As a result of this structural fault, the leader is unconstrained in pushing for his own pet solutions to whatever problems the group discusses and does not discourage the members from mindlessly concurring on whatever course of action the leader happens to prefer.

The questions to which we now turn pertain to those three administrative or structural conditions. Can one reasonably say in light of the available evidence that any of the three structural antecedent conditions that promote groupthink in a cohesive group were present and were exerting their expected influence on the deliberations of Nixon and his closest aides?

The first question is whether the group was insulated. In a summary of pertinent observations, Bertram H. Raven concludes that starting long before Watergate, Nixon and his in-group were insulated from contrary opinions from the outside.

> . . . there is ample evidence of insulation . . . Herbert Klein (1974) describes in some detail how the president was gradually isolated from "outsiders" with contrary opinions . . . The cabinet officers and other high officials were denied access. Republican and Democratic leaders of Congress were also barred. Even press conferences were severely limited. Anyone who wished to see the president . . . had first to present an exact agenda to Haldeman for his approval, and they were admonished not to deviate from that agenda (Mollenhoff, 1974). The insulation was in part required by the needs of the office, in part dictated by the president's personality and desire for only limited contact with others, in part a response to an obsessive concern with security. In trying to keep information from getting out, the so-called Berlin Wall [formed by Haldeman and other aides with Germanic names] also restricted the possibilities of contrary information getting in, not only to the president but also to the other members of the Nixon group.

What about norms requiring methodical procedures? According to Haldeman, Nixon on one occasion conducted a session in a highly systematic way, using a prepared list of questions and problems to be faced, in "disciplined, lawyer-like fashion." But there are no signs that this intellectually disciplined approach or any other methodical procedure was the norm when the group discussed policy issues. On the contrary, there are no indications of any such standard operating procedures in the transcripts of the White House group. One finds that in practically every meeting with members of his in-group, Nixon encourages a free-floating conversation, and the members of the group go right along with that completely unstructured approach.

Commenting on the planning meetings of Nixon with Haldeman and Ehrlichman held in mid-April 1973, Theodore H. White says that "the transcripts . . . make no sense if one seeks the working of sequential minds." And speaking more generally about that month of crisis, White portrays the trio's chaotic planning sessions in these terms:

> The transcripts, read them how one will, make all coherence impossible. The taped conversations slither about, intertwine, shift gear and thought in mid-sentence; they serpentine in and out of the President's conscience, his loyalty to his loyalists, his responsibilities, his vulnerability, their vulnerability, the principle of executive privilege, the political dimensions of the Ervin hearings.
>
> The single thread that runs through them, if any thread can be found at all, is the thread of non-comprehension and his assumption of his own innocence.

During the preceding months, the transcripts are not as incoherent but there is almost as much slithering about. In haphazard fashion throughout February and March 1973, the group comes back time and again to the same unresolved problems they had superficially been discussing earlier, without any attempt to organize their planning. When one member starts to lay out a plan, it is either uncritically accepted or derailed by someone else who switches to a different issue. In the recorded deliberations bearing on the cover-up policy, neither Nixon nor anyone else in the group structured the conversation so that the main alternatives would be examined. No one ever refers to the desirability of using methodical decision-making procedures.

So far as a tradition of impartial leadership is concerned, there is no sign of it at all in the Nixon White House. In the transcripts Nixon time and again let everyone in the group know which policy he favored, and he did not encourage open inquiry. He certainly did *not* show any awareness of the type of norms and traditions adopted by President Kennedy after the Bay of Pigs fiasco to abstain from using his power as head man to induce the group to approve his preferences without examining objectively the relative advantages of alternatives.

Directive leadership carried to an extreme, of course, becomes equivalent to one-man rule, in which case the leader's so-called advisers are nothing more than yes-men. Earlier in this chapter, however, the one-man-rule hypothesis, as an alternative to the groupthink hypothesis, was found to be wanting in light of a great deal of documentary evidence. We have seen that Nixon was highly responsive to proposals and objections from members of his in-group, especially from Haldeman and Ehrlichman, who often took the lead in telling him what should be done. When we put this evidence together with the evidence I am about to discuss concerning the norms set by Nixon, his directive leadership emerges as being somewhat circumscribed but nevertheless sufficiently potent to discourage open discussion of alternatives, thereby promoting concurrence-seeking.

Nixon was somewhat directive in that he established the direction for the handling of the Watergate break-in right from the beginning. When he learned about the first emergency steps his aides had taken in the cover-up, Nixon promptly approved of what they had done and, in discussions with them, made it clear that he wanted them to take whatever additional steps might be necessary to avoid bad publicity that could affect his reelection campaign. According to Haldeman, "the pattern had been set" by the President within three days after the burglars were arrested. Haldeman claims to have notes of a telephone conversation on June 20, 1972, in which Nixon allegedly initiated the idea of raising funds for the Watergate defendants. Haldeman says that he immediately accepted Nixon's cover-up approach, and when Dean subsequently asked him if he could ask Nixon's personal lawyer, Kalmbach, to raise money for the defendants, "it never occurred to me to question the basic concept." Thereafter, Haldeman had no hesitation about proposing and initiating further steps in the cover-up, such as suggesting to Nixon that the CIA could be used to induce the FBI to curtail the Watergate investigation on the alleged grounds of protecting national security. Haldeman consistently presented himself as participating in the cover-up as a loyal member of the White House team who sincerely believed that he and the others were doing the right thing, "with no personal motivation other than the presumed wish of the President and the protection of the reelection campaign."

Even though we do not know how much Haldeman's account has to be discounted as a self-serving attempt to minimize his own role in the illegal cover-up activities, we have corroborative evidence from other sources concerning Nixon's stance.

The pattern that Haldeman says was set by Nixon was also apparent during an earlier period, before Watergate, when other illegal actions were discussed. Ehrlichman writes, "when I told Nixon in 1972 what I knew of that [earlier] break-in [of the office of Ellsberg's psychiatrist], he instantly voiced his approval of it."

In his memoirs, Nixon admits that he took a cynical view of the Watergate break-in from the start, ignoring all the moral and legal aspects of the crime committed to serve his political ends.

My reaction to the Watergate break-in was completely pragmatic. If it was also cynical, it was a cynicism born of experience. I had been in politics too long, and seen everything from dirty tricks to vote fraud. I could not muster much moral outrage over a political bugging. . . .

In fact, my confidence in the CRP was undermined more by the stupidity of the DNC bugging attempt than by its illegality.

A few days after the Watergate break-in, when Haldeman told Nixon that he and Ehrlichman thought John Mitchell might be involved, especially because he was giving such evasive answers to their inquiries, Nixon made it clear that he did not want any more questions asked of Mitchell and the matter should not be pursued. Nixon acknowledges that for ten months he suspected that Mitchell was guilty, but he avoided asking Mitchell for the inside story because he had "a desire not to know the truth in case it turned out to be unpleasant."

Nixon's desire not to know was probably not just a simple matter of avoiding the unpleasant feelings engendered by finding out that a friend and loyal political supporter had committed a crime. It appears to have been part of a more general norm to protect the President from legal responsibility for misdeeds. In a study of recent American politics, Blanchard describes the "deniability" norm set by Nixon long before the time of the Watergate break-in:

The president, as John Dean remarked, must have "deniability." He must be at least one step away from all questionable orders so that his name cannot be connected with anything illegal or unethical. This preservation of deniability was already a common practice in the Nixon White House at the time John Dean first accepted his position.

The president deliberately designed a system of decision-making in which his wishes could be carried out without his being "aware" of the details.

Dean referred explicitly to this norm in a meeting with Nixon on April 16, 1973, when he was explaining why he had not given Nixon certain details about White House crimes earlier. "I, I have tried, uh, all along to make sure that anything I passed to you myself didn't cause you any personal problems."

In addition to wanting to maintain deniability, Nixon also wanted to be able to say, without contradiction, something more positive—that he had been assured by his trusted aides that nobody in the White House was involved in Watergate—while he himself was covertly encouraging them to carry out the cover-up. Here is Blanchard's summary of the evidence in the transcripts:

. . . the president's conversations leave no doubt that he was involved in the cover-up, once the arrests were made [in June 1972]. . . .

It is clear from Mr. Nixon's conversations with Dean, Haldeman and Ehrlichman that he *did not want to know* if illegal acts had taken place with the involvement of White House staff, that he *wanted* to be told that White

House staff were not involved. Without saying it in so many words, he invited others to tell him that he and his staff were not involved with the dirty details of Watergate. . . .

The circumscribed type of directive leadership just described has the effect of inhibiting open discussion of alternative courses of action, partly because the members feel that they should not examine in the leader's presence all the detailed ramifications of a shady course of action that is under consideration. Worse yet, each member would have little hope of getting others to support a change in policy that would displease the great man, once he has indicated the direction in which he wants them to go, even though they are not yes-men and expect that the leader would be responsive to their suggestions. When the members feel that way, they are especially likely to react to any crisis—like the ones faced by the embattled White House team when the "bombshells" started dropping in February and March 1973—by inhibiting their disagreements with whatever course of action is favored by the leader. This inhibition is strongest in circumstances in which each member is relying heavily on the group for psychological support and the leader is not being impartial. It tends to increase greatly the likelihood that the symptoms of groupthink will appear.

From what I have just said, it is apparent that one of the main inferences derived from the case studies in the preceding chapters is also suggested by the present case study. The inference is that when the decision-makers form a cohesive group and some of the other conditions are present that make for groupthink tendencies, the degree to which those tendencies will interfere with effective information search and appraisal of alternatives depends to a considerable extent on whether the leader is pushing for the position he initially prefers instead of pushing for open inquiry and critical thinking. I shall return to this fundamental inference in the final chapter in order to explore its implications for preventing groupthink.

Are there suggestive new leads?

One last question remains to be considered now that all the other key questions used as guidelines for this structured case study have been answered in the affirmative: Are there any new suggestive leads that can be extracted from the case study of the Watergate cover-up concerning the conditions that promote groupthink? In other words, does this case study make salient any additional factors that may have contributed to the predominance of concurrence-seeking in the crucial cover-up decisions made by the cohesive White House group? What I have in mind are factors that may not have been noticeable in the earlier case studies but that might nevertheless have been exerting some influence, perhaps in more obscure ways, in other instances of groupthink.

One such lead stands out very clearly in the case of Nixon's in-group. It has to do with the common political background and ideology of the core members. Theodore H. White emphasizes that their thinking and planning was heavily influenced by the style of politics in which Nixon, Haldeman, and Ehrlichman were bred. From their "hardball" political training, they were convinced long before coming to the White House that a successful campaign requires attacking an enemy, that dirty tricks can be useful, and that "PR—public relations was the name of the game." Colson, before his entry into the White House, was schooled in a very similar kind of "hardball" politics. Dean, as a "white collar striver" and "conniver," was sufficiently receptive to the political ideology that pervaded the White House to have become an avid "hardball" politico very quickly, while still awaiting his big chance to make the first team.

In September 1981, a newly disclosed tape recording revealed for the first time the extreme forms of violence that members of the Nixon team were willing to consider as appropriate means for dealing with fellow Americans who opposed their policies. If that presidential tape, dated May 5, 1971, is authentic, the conversation included the following items: Haldeman spoke approvingly to Nixon about dirty tricks that Colson was carrying out against the Democrats. He mentioned that Colson was now planning to stir up trouble "through hard hats and Legionnaires" by using his ties with labor organizations and other groups. The President, annoyed about the anti–Vietnam War protests then going on in Washington, suggested that "thugs" from the Teamster's Union might be used immediately to "go in and knock their heads off." Haldeman strongly agreed. "Sure," Haldeman said. "Murderers . . . it's the regular strike-buster types." He added, "then they're gonna beat the [obscenity] out of some of these people. And . . . hope they really hurt'em. You know . . . smash some noses."[9]

When a cohesive group is composed of persons who share a common background and ideology, one of the deterrents that prevent groupthink is absent. That is, disparities in background and values among the members of a cohesive group reduce the chances that the members will give in to the social pressures that make for concurrence-seeking and premature consensus. Such disparities, especially when they involve ongoing loyalties to diverse outside reference groups, can be a deterrent to a mindless consensus to engage in unethical or criminal actions, because even when the group is highly cohesive, the chances are greater that a few of the individualistic members will be appalled when the majority favor a plan that cavalierly ignores what the minority regard as proper standards of conduct. If only one ethically sensitive individual within the group were to feel strongly enough about it, he or she might induce the less sensitive members of the majority to reconsider.

There is another much less obvious lead that can also be inferred from the case study of the Watergate cover-up. Symptoms of groupthink appear to have increased in February and March of 1973, which was the early part of the period of mounting crisis. But then, as the nature of the crisis began to change during late March 1973, manifestations of groupthink diminished; finally, during the following month, the group disintegrated. The earlier crisis phase during which groupthink increased appears to differ from the later phases in that the members, despite being in a state of high stress generated by the patent failures of their policy of containment, still retained confidence in their leader. They apparently were still counting on him to point the way to solving the dilemma without any of them suffering serious losses, such as being fired or sent to jail. These observations suggest that to the factors promoting groupthink in a cohesive group we should add *the combination of high stress from external threats with low hope of finding a better solution than the one favored by the leader.*

In order to evaluate the plausibility of this suggestive hypothesis, it is necessary to look into examples of group reactions to crises in some detail, drawing on case material not only from the study of the Watergate cover-up but from the preceding case studies as well. It is also essential to consider how well the hypothesis fits in with other observations bearing on the determinants of groupthink, including those from prior research in the field of group dynamics that tell us something about how cohesive groups react to crises. Accordingly, further discussion of this new lead is postponed until the next chapter, where the theoretical implications of all the case studies are examined.

Conclusion

As is true of all major fiascoes, this one can be said to be the result of a confluence of a number of different causes. Early in this chapter, I listed the causal factors most frequently mentioned in the popular press, most of which pertain to Nixon's personal characteristics—his cynicism, suspiciousness, secretiveness, and other personality weaknesses. Social scientists and political commentators have emphasized additional contributing factors, such as those pertaining to the subcultural background and ideology of Nixon and the men who surrounded him, which made it easy for them to lie, cheat, manipulate others and resort to shady practices in violation of the standards expected of officials in the White House. To this set of antecedent causes, the documentary evidence presented in this chapter adds another major causal factor—groupthink—which helps to account for the gross errors made collectively by the in-group that authorized the Watergate cover-up.[10] Documentary evidence was cited indicating that most of the symptoms included in the groupthink syndrome were manifested in the unedited transcripts of the group's deliberations. Scattered throughout this case study are indications suggesting that groupthink augmented the influence of other contributing factors—most notably the "dark side" of Nixon's personality, which inclined him to be deeply suspicious of political opponents, and the values he and his aides lived by, which inclined all of them to be relatively unconstrained about the use of lawless actions. Nixon's personality and the political habits and ideology he shared with his key aides would be sufficient to account for their readiness to engage in all sorts of crafty improprieties. But without the added pervasive influence of groupthink, it seems improbable that those wily men would have compounded all the avoidable stupidities of the Watergate cover-up to bring about their own undoing.

10

Generalizations: Who Succumbs, When, and Why

A working assumption about who is susceptible

Who is susceptible to groupthink pertains not only to the nationality of the policy-makers, which I have already discussed (Chapter 8), but also to their personality predispositions. Some chief executives, for example, probably become more dependent than others on an inner circle of advisers and set up group norms that encourage unanimity. Psychological studies have shown marked individual differences in responsiveness to social pressure. Some individuals consistently yield to the views of the majority, and others consistently adhere to their own independent judgments. Personality research suggests that conformity tendencies may be strongest in persons who are most fearful of disapproval and rejection. People with strong affiliative needs prefer their work colleagues to be good friends, even if those friends are not very competent. Such people give priority to preserving friendly relationships, at the expense of achieving success in the group's work tasks.

Most of the systematic research from which these findings are derived, however, has dealt with superficial conformity in groups made up of strangers who meet together once and do not expect to see one another again. To understand the predispositions conducive to groupthink, we need studies of groups that meet together for many weeks and work on decisions to which each member will be committed. Such studies are also essential to find out whether other characteristics of group members in addition to personality factors give rise to individual differences in susceptibility to groupthink—for example, social class, ethnic origin, occupational training, and prior experience in group decision-making.

Groups of individuals showing a preponderance of certain personality and social attributes may prove to be the ones that succumb most readily to groupthink. But persons with the most detrimental of these attributes would seldom survive the career struggles required to reach high executive positions. Nevertheless, my own observations of the way successful as well as unsuccessful executives react when they become involved in two-week workshops in group relations training suggest that none is immune to groupthink. Even individuals who are generally high in self-esteem and low in dependency and submissiveness are quite capable of being caught up from time to time in the group madness that produces the symptoms of groupthink. In certain powerful circumstances that make for groupthink, probably every member of every policy-making group, no matter whether strongly or mildly predisposed, is susceptible. I propose to adopt the general working assumption that all policy-makers are vulnerable whenever circumstances promote concurrence-seeking. This assumption leads me to expect that if the series of decisions made by any single policy-making group (in the government, industry, medicine, law, education, or any field) is examined carefully over a period of several years, a sizable percentage of that group's decision errors will prove to be at least partly attributable to groupthink tendencies, if the group is moderately or highly cohesive. This is what I mean in tentatively suggesting that every executive who participates in group decisions is potentially susceptible to groupthink.

Irrespective of the personality characteristics and other predispositions of the members who make up the policy-making group, the groupthink syndrome is expected to emerge whenever the situational conditions that are conducive to it are present. This chapter is devoted mainly to discussing generalizations about those conditions in sufficient detail so that the determinants of groupthink can be more fully comprehended and their implications for preventing groupthink (outlined in Chapter 11) can be readily grasped.

Overview of the theoretical model

As we examine each of the antecedent conditions, it will be useful to keep in mind an overview of the theoretical model of groupthink. Figure 10–1 provides an overview by summarizing the antecedent conditions (boxes A, B–1, and B–2) and the symptoms that make up the groupthink syndrome (box C). It also shows the observable consequences with regard to the poor quality of the group's decision-making procedures (box D), and the probable unsuccessful outcome of their decisions (box E).[1] All the components of the theory that were briefly discussed in Chapter 8 are included in this figure. In addition, the figure contains two additional components inferred from the Watergate case study (item 4 in box B–1 and item 1 in box B–2). It also contains a new set of components, inferred from a theory of self-esteem dynamics, which will be discussed for the first time at the end of this chapter (items 2a, b, and c in box B–2).

According to the theoretical analysis represented in Figure 10–1, the provocative situational context factors (box B–2), like the structural faults of the organization (box B–1) and the degree of cohesiveness (box A), are antecedent

FIGURE 10–1. THEORETICAL ANALYSIS OF GROUPTHINK

ANTECEDENT CONDITIONS

OBSERVABLE CONSEQUENCES

A
Decision-Makers Constitute a Cohesive Group

+

B-1
Structural Faults of the Organization
1. Insulation of the Group
2. Lack of Tradition of Impartial Leadership
3. Lack of Norms Requiring Methodical Procedures
4. Homogeneity of Members' Social Background and Ideology

Etc.

+

B-2
Provocative Situational Context
1. High Stress from External Threats with Low Hope of a Better Solution than the Leader's
2. Low Self-Esteem Temporarily Induced by:
   a. Recent Failures that Make Members' Inadequacies Salient
   b. Excessive Difficulties on Current Decision-Making Tasks that Lower Each Member's Sense of Self-Efficacy
   c. Moral Dilemmas: Apparent Lack of Feasible Alternatives Except Ones that Violate Ethical Standards

Etc.

⟹

Concurrence-Seeking (Groupthink) Tendency

⟹

C
Symptoms of Groupthink
Type I. Overestimation of the Group
1. Illusion of Invulnerability
2. Belief in Inherent Morality of the Group
Type II. Closed-Mindedness
3. Collective Rationalizations
4. Stereotypes of Out-Groups
Type III. Pressures Toward Uniformity
5. Self-Censorship
6. Illusion of Unanimity
7. Direct Pressure on Dissenters
8. Self-Appointed Mindguards

⟹

D
Symptoms of Defective Decision-Making
1. Incomplete Survey of Alternatives
2. Incomplete Survey of Objectives
3. Failure to Examine Risks of Preferred Choice
4. Failure to Reappraise Initially Rejected Alternatives
5. Poor Information Search
6. Selective Bias in Processing Information at Hand
7. Failure to Work Out Contingency Plans

⟹

E
Low Probability of Successful Outcome

Based on Janis, I. L., Mann, L., Decision Making, Copyright © 1977 by The Free Press, A Division of Macmillan Publishing Co., Inc.

conditions that determine the probability that the symptoms of groupthink (box C) will occur to such an extent as to give rise to defective decision-making (box D). The set of antecedent conditions shown in the first column is to be interpreted in the following way: When a group is moderately or highly cohesive (box A), *the more of the antecedent conditions listed in boxes B–1 and B–2 that are present, the greater the chances of defective decision-making as a result of the groupthink syndrome.* In research designed to test this generalization, of course, it will be necessary to assess the antecedent conditions *prior* to the time when the group starts its deliberations about whether to adopt a new policy—for example, just after the members of the group have been briefed on the nature of the policy problem, but before they have an opportunity to display any symptoms of groupthink or any symptoms of defective decision-making on that particular policy choice.

Are cohesive groups doomed to be victims?

Cohesiveness of the policy-making group (box A in Figure 10–1) is a major antecedent condition that has been emphasized throughout this book. In the very first chapter I stated as the central theme the following generalization: The more amiability and esprit de corps among the members of an ingroup of policy-makers, the greater is the danger that independent critical thinking will be replaced by groupthink, which is likely to result in irrational and dehumanizing actions directed at out-groups. Yet when we recall the case studies of the Cuban missile crisis and the Marshall Plan, we surmise that some caveats about applying this generalization are in order. A high degree of "amiability and esprit de corps among the members" are manifestations of the high degree to which the members value their membership in the group and want to continue to be affiliated—that is, group cohesiveness. But, as I have stated in earlier chapters, group cohesiveness does not invariably lead to symptoms of groupthink. It is a necessary condition, but it is not a sufficient condition. Taking this into account, I have introduced an explicit proviso in the wording of the generalization, asserting that the greater the cohesiveness of the group, "the greater is the danger" of a groupthink type of decision. Dangers do not always materialize and can sometimes be prevented by precautionary measures. Structural features of the group and situational context factors (represented by boxes B–1 and B–2 in Figure 10–1) play a crucial role in determining whether a moderately or highly cohesive group will develop symptoms of groupthink. It follows that the positive relationship between cohesiveness and groupthink cannot be regarded as an iron law of executive behavior that dooms the members of every cohesive group to become victims of groupthink every time they make a collective decision. Rather, we should expect high cohesiveness to be conducive to groupthink only when certain additional determining conditions are present but not under other conditions, such as when special precautions are taken to set up norms for vigilant search and appraisal that counteract collective uncritical thinking and premature consensus.

When appropriate precautions are taken, a group that has become moderately or highly cohesive probably can do a much better job on its decision-making tasks than if it had remained noncohesive. Compliance out of fear of recrimination is likely to be strongest when there is little or no sense of solidarity among the group members. In order to overcome this fear, each participant in the group's deliberations needs to have a great deal of confidence that he is a member in good standing and that the others will continue to value his role in the group, whether or not he argues with them about the issue under discussion. Social psychological studies indicate that as a member of a group is made to feel more accepted by the others—a feature that is usually associated with increased group cohesiveness—he acquires greater freedom to say what he really thinks. Dittes and Kelley, for example, discovered in a social psychological experiment that when individuals in a group were given information indicating that they were highly accepted by their fellow members, they became more willing to express opinions that deviated from the group consensus. Members who were made to feel that they were not accepted by their colleagues became subdued. After being informed about the low acceptance ratings, they participated in the group discussions only half as often as they had before. When they did speak, they showed much more conformity with the group consensus than the other participants did. However, these conformists had developed an attitude of inner detachment from the group. This was revealed in their answers to questions that elicited their private views, which showed little conformity to the group's norms and low valuation of membership in the group. Their superficial conformity appears to have been motivated by a fear of being humiliated by being expelled from the group altogether.

The unaccepted members in the Dittes and Kelley study probably reacted the way most people do in a group of high-status people who are strangers, before cohesiveness and feelings of security have developed. The highly accepted members probably reacted like members of cohesive groups who feel secure about their status as members. In the Dittes and Kelley study, the accepted members were more responsive than unaccepted members to new information that contradicted the group's earlier assumptions and more freely expressed opinions differing from the group consensus. This pattern of relatively independent thinking is probably characteristic of group members who have developed a relationship of mutual acceptance in which each person assumes that the others in the group want to know what he really thinks and will want him to continue as a member regardless of what he says.

When a group has a low degree of cohesiveness, there are, of course, sources of error in decision-making in addition to deliberate conformity out of fear of recrimination. One that is especially likely to plague a noncohesive group of politicians or administrators is a win-lose fighting stance, which inclines each participant to fight hard for his own point of view (or the point of view of his organization), without much regard for the real issues at stake.

When unlike-minded people who are political opponents are forced to meet together in a group, they can be expected to behave like couples in olden times who were forced to live together by a shotgun marriage. The incompatible members of a shotgun committee often indulge in painfully repetitious debates, frequently punctuated with invective, mutual ridicule, and maneuvers of one-upmanship in a continuous struggle for power that is not at all conducive to decisions of high quality. This is another reason for expecting that policy-making groups lacking amiability and esprit de corps, even though spared the unfavorable symptoms of groupthink, will sometimes show more symptoms of defective decision-making and produce worse fiascoes than groups that are moderately or highly cohesive. When we consider the two major sources of error that beset noncohesive groups—deliberate conformity out of fear of recrimination and a win-lose fighting stance—we see that cohesive groups can have great advantages if groupthink tendencies can be kept from becoming dominant.

As the members of a decision-making group develop bonds of friendship and esprit de corps, they become less competitive and begin to trust each other to tolerate disagreements. They are less likely to use deceitful arguments or to play safe by dancing around the issues with vapid or conventional comments. We expect that the more cohesive a group becomes, the less the members will deliberately censor what they say because of fear of being socially punished for antagonizing the leader or any of their fellow members. But the outcome is complicated because the more cohesive a group becomes, the more each member is likely to censor what he or she thinks because of the newly acquired motivation to preserve the unity of the group and to adhere to its norms. Thus, although the members of a highly cohesive group feel much freer to deviate from the majority, their desire for genuine concurrence on all important issues—to match their opinions with each other and to conduct themselves in accordance with each other's wishes—often inclines them not to use this freedom. In a cohesive group of policy-makers the danger is not that each individual will fail to reveal his strong objections to a proposal favored by the majority but that he will think the proposal is a good one, without attempting to carry out a critical scrutiny that could lead him to see that there are grounds for strong objections. When groupthink dominates, suppression of deviant thoughts takes the form of each person's deciding that his misgivings are not relevant, that the benefit of any doubt should be given to the group consensus. A member of a cohesive group will rarely be subjected to direct group pressures from the majority because he or she will rarely take a position that threatens the unity of the group.

Prior research on group dynamics indicates that at least three different types of social rewards tend to increase group cohesiveness—friendship, prestige, and enhanced competence. Concurrence-seeking tendencies probably are stronger when high cohesiveness is based primarily on the rewards of being in a pleasant "clubby" atmosphere or of gaining prestige from being a member of an elite group than when it is based primarily on the opportunity to function competently on work tasks with effective co-workers. In a cohesive policy-making group of the latter type, careful appraisal of policy alternatives is likely to become a group norm to which the members conscientiously adhere; this helps to counteract groupthink. But even when the basis of high cohesiveness is enhancement of task-oriented values in a well-functioning group whose members trust each other sufficiently to tolerate disagreements, there is still the danger that groupthink will become a dominant tendency. Each member develops a strong motivation to preserve the rewards of group solidarity, an inner compulsion to avoid creating disunity, which inclines him or her to believe in the soundness of the proposals promoted by the leader or by a majority of the group's members.

A cohesive group that on one occasion suffers from groupthink is capable on other occasions of gaining the advantages of high morale and free expression of dissent, depending on whether special conditions that promote groupthink are present. The duality of cohesiveness may explain some of the inconsistencies in research results on group effectiveness. For example, Marvin Shaw in his textbook, *Group Dynamics,* presents as a plausible hypothesis the proposition, "High-cohesive groups are more effective than low-cohesive groups in achieving their respective goals," but he acknowledges that the evidence "is not altogether consistent." A major source of inconsistency may be attributed to concurrence-seeking tendencies: Sometimes the groupthink syndrome occurs in highly cohesive groups when the members are working on certain kinds of decision-making tasks, which reduces their effectiveness; when working on other kinds of decision-making tasks (and also on a variety of other tasks that do not involve decision-making) the members of highly cohesive groups show increased effectiveness. This is how I interpret the difference between the ineffective Bay of Pigs decision and the effective Cuban missile crisis decision made by nearly identical cohesive groups of policy-makers headed by the same leader.

For most groups, optimal functioning in decision-making tasks may prove to be at a moderate level of cohesiveness, avoiding the disadvantages of conformity out of fear of recrimination when cohesiveness is low and the disadvantages of strong concurrence-seeking tendencies when cohesiveness is high. If, however, the latter disadvantages can be held to a minimum by administrative practices that prevent groupthink tendencies from becoming dominant, then the optimal level of cohesiveness for effective decision-making could prove to be much higher.[2]

Additional hypotheses about when groupthink occurs: Structural faults of the organization

When groupthink is most likely to occur pertains to structural features and situational circumstances of the group or organization that make it easy for the symptoms to become dominant. In addition to group cohesiveness, three other antecedent conditions were suggested in Chapter 8 on the basis of the preceding case studies. These hypotheses assert that the chances of the decision-making process being pervaded by symptoms of groupthink are increased when each of the following structural faults of the organization is present prior to and at the outset of the group's deliberations on a policy decision, even when the leader does not want the members to be yes-men and the individual members try to resist conforming: (1) the cohesive decision-making group is insulated from the judgments of qualified associates within the organization who, as "outsiders," are not permitted to know about the new policies under discussion until after a final decision has been made; (2) from the outset of the cohesive group's deliberations, the leader does not feel constrained by any organizational tradition to avoid pushing for his own preferred policies and, instead, to encourage open, unbiased inquiry into the available alternatives; (3) the organization to which the cohesive decision-making group is responsible does not have previously established norms requiring the members to adopt methodical procedures of information search and appraisal (such as filling out a balance sheet of pros and cons for each available option). It seems plausible to assume that these three structural features of the organization encourage groupthink in a cohesive policy-making group partly because each of them increases the chances that, early in their deliberations, before all the feasible alternatives have been surveyed and carefully evaluated, the members of the cohesive group will develop the impression that there is an existing or emerging *group norm* in favor of one particular course of action (or inaction) to which all the members are expected to conform. Perhaps it would be more precise to say that each of these antecedent conditions represents the *absence* of a potential source of organizational *constraint* that could help to prevent the members of a cohesive policy-making group from developing a norm of indulging in uncritical conformity.

> When the cohesiveness of a group increases from a low to a moderate or high level, each member becomes more psychologically dependent on the group and displays greater readiness to adhere to the group's norms. If the group is insulated in such a way that the members have little or no opportunity to discuss certain policy issues outside the group, they can be expected to show an increased tendency to rely upon the judgments of the group on those issues as norms. The . . . lack of methodical procedures for search and appraisal affords an unbridled license to conformity tendencies within the group, because of the absence of procedural safeguards against cursory and biased treatment of policy issues. The . . . [lack of a tradition of impartial leadership] increases the likelihood that the leader will use his power, subtly or blatantly, to induce the members to conform with his decisions. When a directive leader announces his preference on a policy issue—whether it be to postpone making any decision, to pass the buck to another group in the organization, or to select one particular alternative as the best policy—the members of a cohesive group will tend to accept his choice somewhat uncritically, as though it were equivalent to a group norm.

Another hypothesis that specifies a different type of structural fault of the organization was introduced at the end of the case study of the Watergate cover-up (Chapter 9). It pertains to the homogeneity factor: Lack of disparity in social background and ideology among the members of a cohesive group makes it easier for them to concur on whatever proposals are put forth by the leader to deal with the policy problems they are confronting. This structural fault decreases the likelihood of disparate views being presented and productively debated within the group. When there is a moderate (but not extreme) degree of heterogeneity in social background and ideology among the members, they are more likely to engage in *constructive multiple advocacy,* which means that the group will devote their deliberations to exploring the pros and cons of two or more alternatives, rather than focusing on just one available option and gravitating toward a premature consensus. As proposed by Alexander George, a system of multiple advocacy—which involves selecting the members for each policy-making group to represent divergent positions within the organization and giving each of them full opportunity to develop his or her case—might go a long way toward reducing the chances of groupthink, even when all three of the other structural faults are present. Although adopting the system of multiple advocacy might tend to lower, on the average, the degree of cohesiveness of policy-making groups, it should be possible to set up appropriate circumstances for such groups to develop sufficient cohesiveness to gain the full advantages of a moderate level.

The role of stress as a provocative situational factor

One of the hypotheses extracted from the Watergate case study (at the end of Chapter 9) deals with a combination of two situational context factors: Groupthink tendencies are increased when the situational context at the time the group starts its deliberations is such that the members are undergoing *high stress* from external threats of losses to be expected from whatever alternative is chosen and have *low hope* of finding a better solution than the one favored by the leader. The influence of the two factors has been elaborated as follows:

> [This pair] specifies the prime conditions that foster defensive avoidance. After a leader lets it be known that he favors a particular policy alternative, the members are in the common predicament of having little hope of finding a better solution (because advocating a different alternative will evoke the disapproval of the most esteemed person in the group and of all those who uncritically support him). They will be motivated to reduce the high stress of their decisional conflict by collectively bolstering the choice made by the leader.

This two-factor hypothesis is complicated and requires more extended discussion. For one thing, it is immediately apparent as one goes over the entire set of case studies in this book that high stress alone is certainly not a necessary or sufficient condition for groupthink. The Kennedy administration's Cuban missile decision, worked out during an unprecedented crisis posing the grave danger of imminent nuclear war, occurred under the most stressful conditions of all, and yet groupthink tendencies were kept to a minimum. Some of the groupthink-dominated decisions were made under conditions of relatively low stress from external threats—for example, the decisions to ignore the danger of an enemy attack on Pearl Harbor by Admiral Kimmel and his cohesive in-group during the summer and early fall of 1941 (before the war warnings of late November started to arrive). The Bay of Pigs decision was not made at a time of crisis and the level of stress from external threats was not very high most of the time, although the participants may have been functioning at a moderately high level of stress during some of the meetings because President Kennedy and his advisers were in a state of conflict about the CIA invasion plan. They did not want to create an international incident by having the United States openly invade Cuba, but at the same time, they wanted to avoid being labeled soft on communism and also to avoid antagonizing the top leadership of the CIA, which was sponsoring the plan.

The case study of the Vietnam War escalation decisions suggests that when the level of stress from external threats increases, it can sometimes lead to a decrease in groupthink and a corresponding increase in critical thinking among the members of a policy-making group. McNamara responded to the growing conflict about continuing the Vietnam War (when political opposition within the United States became so strong that he and other top officials could no longer give public speeches without being picketed and heckled) by becoming more rather than less vigilant—he instituted a thorough information search, including an analysis of available data on the military effectiveness of air attacks and ground operations in Vietnam. After examining the evidence carefully, McNamara came to the conclusion that the escalation policy to which he and the other members of the Tuesday Lunch Group were committed was failing as a military enterprise, in addition to creating political turmoil at home. In a much higher state of stress than ever before, he introduced arguments against the war policy within the group. Once he became a dissenter, he was promptly removed from his powerful position as Secretary of Defense. His replacement, Clark Clifford, exposed to the same evidence in classified Defense Department documents, soon became convinced that McNamara was right. He strongly reinforced the influential arguments that McNamara had started to present to the members of the Tuesday Lunch Group, and convinced enough of them so that the die-hard leader of the group, President Johnson, was forced to abandon his hawkish policy. In this case, the increase in the level of stress generated by the heightening of the conflict about the war policy led to an improvement in the problem-solving activity of some of the members. It also led to the group becoming much less cohesive.

Something similar happened as the level of stress increased during the period when President Nixon and his in-group were being exposed to the "bombshell" revelations that eventuated in John Dean's defection. It is worthwhile to reexamine this case study because it illustrates the way in which the level of stress can interact with other factors as a determinant of increases as well as decreases in groupthink tendencies.

When we look over the nine-month period from late June 1972 to late March 1973, we can see that the concurrence-seeking tendency was dominant whether the level of stress was low, medium, or high, provided only that the members had little hope of finding a better solution to the problems generated by the Watergate break-in than the "stonewalling" policy favored by the leader. In the first months of the cover-up, up to about the end of December 1972, the level of stress seems to have been quite low. The members of the White House group believed that the only risks posed by their Watergate-related decisions were limited to bad publicity. Thinking that very little was at stake, they were able to concur very rapidly on whatever course of action seemed expedient for the short run, without bothering to consider the long-range consequences. The crucial "smoking gun" conversation during the meeting of June 21, 1972—when Haldeman suggested using the CIA to curtail the FBI's investigation of the source of the money supplied to the Watergate burglars and Nixon agreed to it—lasted *less than five minutes*. Here we have a prime example of premature closure linked with complacent concurrence under conditions of *low* stress from external threats. In those few minutes, the two leading members of the White House team set into motion an illegal policy that entailed two criminal offenses that were grounds for impeachment—misusing governmental agencies and obstructing justice. They were not stimulated to give any further thought to what they were about to do by Ehrlichman when he was informed of the dangerous decision. Ehrlichman was asked to help implement it by meeting with top officials of the CIA, which he calmly proceeded to do without raising any thought-provoking questions about the legality, propriety, or long-term expediency of the cover-up action, even though he was an attorney and was expected to function as the President's main counselor on domestic affairs.

There was no complacency a few months later, during February and March of 1973, when the members of the White House group were undergoing mounting stress as more and more cracks appeared in the flimsy defenses they were trying to erect. Now the members were under *high* stress as they faced the extremely worrisome conflict posed by the increasingly enormous dangers of having bits and pieces of the cover-up exposed if they tried to continue the stonewalling policy and what seemed to be the even greater dangers to be expected if they were to disclose their own misdeeds. As Nixon put it when he and his top aides were briefly considering the possibility of having Dean or Mitchell reveal some of the truth about the cover-up: "What the hell is he going to disclose that isn't going to blow something?" During this stressful period they spent much more time talking about what to do, but their rambling conversations invariably ended up reaffirming and extending the cover-up policy. These long conversations could be characterized as displaying collective uncritical thinking: After each "bombshell," the group members decided to continue the policy without having examined the ramifications of their decision, especially the potentially dangerous legal and political consequences that were growing increasingly ominous because a number of new official investigations were about to call in many knowledgeable witnesses to give testimony under oath.

The simple idea that "we could be sent to jail" was never mentioned until Dean started talking about it after he consulted his law books and became convinced that it was already too late to prevent it from happening. The very word *impeachment* was carefully kept out of all their conversations until well after it, too, had already become an imminent danger. In their meetings during the early part of 1973, the members of Nixon's in-group recommitted themselves time and again to the same old cover-up policy while displaying, more than ever before, the most florid symptoms of groupthink.

Apparently under conditions of high stress the members had become highly dependent on the group for social support—to maintain their morale as well as to protect them from criminal liability through their affiliation with the presidency. Nevertheless, it was under the same conditions of high stress that John Dean, badly shaken to the point where he was resorting to alcohol every night, gradually became disillusioned with the leader and began urging a change in policy. Finally Dean ended up being unwilling to conform with the group's norms. His disaffiliation soon led to internal conflicts within the group, with each member taking an every-man-for-himself stance that destroyed the group's cohesiveness. All this came about when Dean *lost hope* that the group would be able to protect him. His loss of hope was accompanied by increased vigilance: He realized, once he looked carefully into his law books, that the President did not have the power to keep the legal system from indicting and convicting him as a criminal. He also noticed various signs suggesting that the President was getting ready to make him the next scapegoat in an effort to protect himself.

Ehrlichman, too, went through a terminal phase of disillusionment and transformation of a similar kind under conditions of increased stress when his name appeared on front page headlines as the instigator of illegal activities and his removal from office was being demanded by Department of Justice officials. He too reached the point where he was no longer willing to adhere to the norms set by the leader; it was then that he talked so uninhibitedly about impeachment that Nixon was stunned. At that point, Ehrlichman, like Dean, believed that the leader was getting ready to unload him "down the tubes" to save himself. From then on, group cohesiveness plummeted to a very low level. But until the time of their disillusionment, Dean and Ehrlichman apparently went right along with Nixon and Haldeman, participating wholeheartedly not only in the cover-up policy but also in all those forms of conformity behavior and illusory thinking that enter into the groupthink syndrome.

I surmise that circumstances of high stress from external threats, which generally make for high reliance on the group for social support, will result in an increase in concurrence-seeking only when the members still retain their faith in the leader's wisdom and trustworthiness and therefore have little hope of finding a way out of the dilemma better than the leader's. Conversely, concurrence-seeking will markedly decrease during a crisis if the leader is no longer seen to be sufficiently wise or trustworthy to be relied upon, since the members no longer will pin their hopes on his or her solutions. Under those conditions, group cohesiveness is drastically decreased. With a necessary antecedent condition no longer present, the members are unlikely to display symptoms of groupthink, even though their heightened level of stress increases their need for affiliation and social support, which would motivate them to conform more than ever if their reliance on the leader were not impaired.

If my assumptions are correct, we should find that the symptoms of groupthink are most pronounced when the two factors specified by the hypothesis are present—high stress from external threats together with low hope of finding a better solution than the one favored by the leader. But it follows from the two-factor hypothesis that high stress will not necessarily augment concurrence-seeking. The chances of groupthink developing during a crisis period of high stress will be markedly reduced *if the leader conducts the policy deliberations in a relatively impartial way, so as to set the norm for open discussion of a wide range of alternatives,* even though the members temporarily may be more dependent on the leader than during periods of low stress. This is essentially what President Kennedy did during the Cuban missile crisis and what he failed to do when the conflictful issues posed by the Bay of Pigs plan were under discussion.

Rudiments of an explanatory theory

The problem of *why* groupthink occurs is more difficult to investigate than the problem of *who* is vulnerable and *when*. But *why* is the heart of the matter if we want to explain the observed phenomena of concurrence-seeking. An adequate explanation would specify the main incentives for engaging in the types of behavior that constitute the groupthink syndrome. It would account for the known conditions that promote concurrence-seeking tendencies and would enable us to predict the effects of conditions that we do not yet know about.

The search for an explanation forces us to tread through a morass of complicated theoretical issues in still largely uncharted areas of human motivation. For many years, psychologists have been trying to formulate general psychological principles that would apply to all the observed phenomena of group dynamics, but no well-established theory is generally accepted by behavioral scientists. However, promising leads extracted from recent social psychological research may point the way to an explanation of the groupthink syndrome.

The central explanatory concept I have in mind involves viewing concurrence-seeking as a form of striving for mutual support based on a powerful motivation in all group members to cope with the external or internal stresses of decision-making. When the source of stress is an *external* threat, such as being defeated in a struggle with a rival group or being caught and punished for illegal actions, the concurrence-seeking tendency, as we have just seen, is expected to increase, provided that the members have little hope of finding a better way to deal with the impending dangers than the solution favored by the leader. Under conditions of high external stress, the main incentive for the members to rely on the leader's wisdom and to try to maintain group harmony is their motivation to relieve the anxieties generated by the salient external threats.

Even when the members are not particularly concerned about risks of material losses for themselves or their organization, so that the level of external stress is low, they may nevertheless be subjected to *internal* sources of stress, which cannot be handled in quite the same way. This source of stress (represented in Figure 10–1 by items 2a, b, and c in box B–2) involves a temporary lowering of self-esteem as a result of situational provocations. The most frequent provocations are (1) recent failures, such as an unanticipated poor outcome resulting from a prior decision for which the members of the policy-making group feel responsible, which makes the members keenly aware of their personal inadequacies; (2) a current complicated and perplexing choice requiring the members of the policy-making group to carry out extremely difficult decision-making tasks that they perceive as being beyond their level of competence, which lowers each member's sense of self-efficacy; and (3) a moral dilemma posed by the necessity to make a vital decision when the members of the policy-making group perceive a lack of any feasible alternatives except ones that violate their ethical standards of conduct. The third type of provocation will occur most frequently, of course, when the policy-makers have been selected for their top-level positions not only for their competence and practical wisdom but also as standard bearers of humanitarian and ethical values. Such policy-makers are more likely than others to be confronted with moral dilemmas that generate an intense conflict between humanitarian or ethical values on the one hand and the utilitarian demands of national or organizational goals, practical politics, and economics on the other. The participants may try to reassure themselves with the platitudinous thought that "you can't make an omelet without breaking some eggs." Nevertheless, each time they realize they are sacrificing moral values in order to arrive at a viable policy, they will be burdened with anticipatory feelings of shame, guilt, and related feelings of self-depreciation, which lower their self-esteem. Even those policy-makers who pride themselves on their capacity to play the game of "hardball" politics without any qualms may have to contend from time to time with anticipatory shame or guilt arising from "super-ego" conflicts of which they are not fully aware. The point is that no one is likely to be exempt from undergoing a temporary lowering of self-esteem occasionally

as a result of being exposed to any one of the three types of situational provocations. For all such sources of internal stress, participating in a unanimous
consensus along with the respected fellow members of a congenial group will
bolster the decision-maker's self-esteem.

Some individuals are extraordinarily self-confident practically all the
time and may seldom need the support of a cohesive group when their decisions are subject to social criticism and self-disapproval. For example, the
spirited symphony orchestra conductor Sir Thomas Beecham once said, "I
have made just one mistake in my entire life and that was one time when I
thought I was wrong but actually I was right." Very few people who are required to put it on the line as decision-makers are able to maintain such an
unassailable sense of self-assurance.

Psychological functions of the eight symptoms

Concurrence-seeking and the various symptoms of groupthink to which
it gives rise might be best understood as a mutual effort among the members
of a group to maintain emotional equanimity in the face of external and internal sources of stress arising when they share responsibility for making vital
decisions that pose threats of failure, social disapproval, and self-
disapproval. The eight symptoms of groupthink form a coherent pattern if
viewed in the context of this explanatory hypothesis. The symptoms may
function in somewhat different ways to produce the same result.

A shared illusion of invulnerability and shared rationalizations can
alleviate incipient fears of failure and prevent unnerving feelings of personal
inadequacy, especially during a crisis. Even during noncrisis periods,
whenever the members foresee great gains from taking a dangerous, a socially
disapproved, or an unethical course of action, they may be seeking some way
of disregarding the disturbing threats and welcome the optimistic views of the
members who argue for the attractive but risky course of action.[3] At such
times, as well as during distressing crises, if the threat of failure is salient, the
members are likely to convey to each other the attitude that "we needn't
worry, everything will go our way." By pooling their intellectual resources to
develop rationalizations, the members build up each other's confidence and
feel reassured about unfamiliar risks, which, if taken seriously, would be
dealt with by applying standard operating procedures to obtain additional information and to carry out careful planning.

The members' firm belief in the inherent morality of their group and their
use of undifferentiated negative stereotypes of opponents would enable them
to minimize decision conflicts between ethical values and expediency,
especially when they are inclined to resort to violence. The shared belief that
"we are a good and wise group" inclines them to use group concurrence as a
major criterion to judge the morality as well as the efficacy of any policy

under discussion. "Since our group's objectives are good," the members feel, "any means we decide to use must be good." This shared assumption helps the members avoid feelings of shame or guilt about decisions that may violate their personal code of ethical behavior. Shared negative stereotypes that feature the evil nature of the enemy would enhance their sense of moral righteousness as well as their pride in the lofty mission of the in-group. Shared stereotypes that feature the weakness of the enemy would alleviate their incipient fears of being defeated.

Every cohesive group that is required to make policy decisions tends to develop a set of policy doctrines, derived from the members' subculture, that provides the members with a cognitive map for conceptualizing the intentions and reactions of opponents, allies, and neutrals. But to be effective decision-makers, the members need to exercise a certain flexibility in the use of those doctrines in order to take account of new information and their own feelings of empathy. They can then evolve sophisticated concepts that enable them to weigh the prospects for negotiations in the light of fresh evidence about their opponents' current objectives and strategies. During a confrontation involving the threat of open hostilities, the loss of flexibility is the price a cohesive group pays to gain the greater sense of confidence and moral righteousness from sharing an image of the enemy as weak, intractable, and deserving of punishment. Stereotypes that dehumanize out-groups alleviate guilt by legitimizing destructive and inhumane acts against them. As Donald Campbell says, "The out-group's opprobrious characteristics seem [to the in-grouper] to fully justify the hostility and rejection he shows toward it." Focusing hostility on out-groups probably also serves the psychological function of displacing aggression away from the in-group, thereby reducing stress arising from latent jealousies and antagonisms within the group.

When most members fall back upon the familiar forms of social pressure directed against a member who questions the group's wisdom or morality, they are in effect protecting psychological defenses that help them to keep anxiety, shame, and guilt to a minimum. If subtle pressures fail, stronger efforts are made to limit the extent of his deviation, to make him a domesticated dissenter. We have seen this clearly in the case of President Johnson's in-group when one or two of the members disagreed with the majority's position that air attacks against North Vietnam should be increased. A doubter who accepts the role is no longer a problem because his objections are confined to issues that do not threaten to shake the confidence of the group members in the reasonableness and righteousness of their collective judgments. At the same time, the doubter's tamed presentation of an opposing viewpoint permits the others to think that their group is strong-minded enough to tolerate dissent. If the domestication efforts do not succeed, the dissenter is ultimately ostracized, so that the relatively tranquil emotional atmosphere of a homogeneous group is restored.

When a member is dependent on the group for bolstering his feelings of confidence and self-esteem, he tends to exercise self-censorship over his misgivings. The greater the dependence, the stronger will be the motivation to adhere to the group's norms. One of the norms that is likely to become dominant under conditions of high external or internal stress involves living up to a mutual nonaggression pact. Each individual in the group feels himself to be under an injunction to avoid making penetrating criticisms that might bring on a clash with fellow members and destroy the unity of the group. Adhering to this norm promotes a sense of collective strength and also eliminates the threat of damage to each member's self-esteem from hearing his or her own judgments on vital issues criticized by respected associates. We have seen how much painful emotion was generated in Kennan's group of critical thinkers working on the Marshall Plan and in Kennedy's Executive Committee debating alternative ways to get rid of the Soviet missiles in Cuba. In contrast, the emotional state of those who participated in the groupthink-dominated deliberations that led to fiascoes was relatively placid. When the mutual nonagression pact and other related norms for preserving the unity of the group are internalized, each member avoids interfering with an emerging consensus by assuring himself that the opposing arguments he had in mind must be erroneous or that his misgivings are too unimportant to be worth mentioning.

The various devices to enhance confidence and self-esteem require an illusion of unanimity about all important judgments. Without it, the sense of group unity would be lost, gnawing doubts would start to grow, confidence in the group's problem-solving capacity would shrink, and soon the full emotional impact of all the internal and external sources of stress generated by making a difficult decision would be aroused. Preserving the sense of unity can do more than keep anxiety, shame, and guilt to a minimum; it can induce pleasant feelings of elation. Members of a group sometimes enjoy an exhilarating sense of omnipotence from participating in a crisis decision with a group that displays solidarity against an evil enemy and complete unanimity about everything that needs to be done.[4]

Self-appointed mindguards help to preserve the shared sense of complacency by making sure that the leader and other members are not exposed to information that might challenge their self-confidence. If the mindguard were to transmit the potentially distressing information, he and the others might become discouraged by the apparent defects in their cherished policy and find themselves impelled to initiate a painful reevaluation in an unpleasant state of emotional tension.

The explanatory hypothesis about why groupthink occurs gives preeminence to the provocative situational factors in Figure 10–1 (box B–2). According to this hypothesis, the crucial incentives that induce the groupthink syndrome occur when members of a cohesive group are confronted by a situation that evokes either (1) a high level of stress from external threats combined with low hope of a better solution than the one favored by the leader or (2) a marked lowering of self-esteem (constituting an *internal* source of stress) induced by recent failures, excessive difficulties on current decision-making tasks, or moral dilemmas.[5]

Until the explanation of groupthink in terms of mutual support to cope with external or internal sources of stress and all the various antecedent factors shown in Figure 10–1 are substantially confirmed by systematic research, it is risky to make huge inferential leaps from theory to the practical sphere of prevention.[6] Ultimately, a well-substantiated theoretical analysis should have valuable practical applications to the formulation of effective prescriptions. As Kurt Lewin pointed out, "Nothing is so practical as a good theory." But until we know we have a good theory—one that is well supported by controlled experiments and systematic correlational research, as well as by case studies—we must recognize that any prescriptions we draw up are speculative inferences based on what little we know, or think we know, about when and why groupthink occurs. Still, we should not be inhibited from drawing tentative inferences in order to call attention to potentially useful means of prevention—as long as we label them as presumptions, or, to use Michael Scriven's term, "significant possibilities":

> We can . . . answer the question, what do we learn from history, without having to produce absurd or trivial laws, or bare particulars about the past, or murmur mysteriously about deepening our understanding of man. What we most importantly learn from history is a range of possibilities—not of probabilities, not of certainties. And of course these are not mere possibilities, of the kind that one has in mind when one says, Oh, anything is possible! They are significant possibilities, ones that have shaken empires or cabinets before and may do so again for all that we know to the contrary. They are thus most deserving of our respect, and with our knowledge of them we can plan more rationally for the future. If we wish to make a certain outcome more likely, then we can try to bring about those conditions which on previous occasions, not demonstrably irrelevant to the present case, [apparently] did bring about that outcome. If we wish to prevent an outcome, what we can do is to make it less likely; we try to eliminate those circumstances which [seem to] have in the relevant past brought about this result or repeat those circumstances that [seem to] have previously frustrated it.

Perhaps the worst consequences can be prevented if we take steps to avoid the circumstances in which groupthink seems to flourish.

11

Preventing Groupthink

A pretzel-shaped question

One obvious way to prevent groupthink is simply to make one person responsible for every important decision, eliminating all the problems of group dynamics from the outset. But clearly this solution would be self-defeating. Only the most authoritarian of leaders fails to recognize the peril in relying solely on his own deliberations.

For constructive thinking to go on, a group must have a fairly high degree of like-mindedness about basic values and mutual respect. The members must forgo trying to score points in a power struggle or to obtain ego gratification by deflating rivals. These basic conditions are not likely to be created until the policy-making group becomes at least moderately cohesive. But then the quality of the group's deliberations may deteriorate as a result of the concurrence-seeking tendency that gives rise to the symptoms of groupthink. Consequently, the problem of preventing costly miscalculations and lapses from sound thinking in decision-making bodies is complicated: How can policy-makers benefit from the cohesiveness of their group without suffering serious losses from groupthink? This sort of intricate psychological issue has been called a pretzel-shaped question and it may require pretzel-shaped answers.

Therefore, what?

The difficulties of making inferential leaps from generalizations about the conditions that foster groupthink to concrete proposals for preventive action are essentially the same for our pretzel-shaped problem as for any other complicated social problem, such as environmental pollution. F. Kenneth Hare has pointed out that although life scientists have accumulated considerable knowledge about the causes and consequences of air pollution and other forms of environmental contamination, the scientists with the greatest expertise do not have the competence single-handedly to prescribe public policies for preventing eco-catastrophes:

> The greatest hazard in our path is inherent in Lyndon Johnson's acid query "Therefore, what?" which he is said to have thrown at a group of professors who had just briefed him on the Middle Eastern situation. The political interest in the environment demands proposals for *action*. . . . At present, we are not equipped to make such proposals.

The same must be said even more emphatically about the problem of counteracting the psychological pollution of groupthink, for much less is known about the causes and consequences of concurrence-seeking behavior than is known about environmental contaminants. Yet, as Hare points out, the researchers who have the deepest understanding of the problems are not acting in a socially responsible way if they attempt to withdraw completely from the arena of practical reform. Hare argues that "no important social problem is ever simple and none ever lies fully within the competence of a single academic discipline." He recommends that instead of evading the issue by repeating that "this is an interdisciplinary problem," everyone who knows something relevant should participate in developing a new discipline that will tackle the social and technical engineering problems. So great is the need for synthesis and multivariate analysis of theoretical and applied problems in all discplines, according to Hare, that a marked change is to be expected in the trend of basic sciences. Whereas the past century has been the era in which each subdiscipline dissected reality in fine detail, Hare foresees that in the next century scientists will try to understand how complex systems work and how they can be changed.

If we are to overhaul the machinery of policy-making in complex governmental, industrial, and welfare organizations, we must certainly apply Hare's advice and stop complaining about the interdisciplinary complexities of the problems and start creating a new discipline that synthesizes whatever is relevant from them all. What is urgently needed is a new type of intervention research, in which experienced executives familiar with the policy-making system from the inside and a variety of specialists familiar with various decision-making processes from the outside collaborate to develop viable improvements. If this type of enterprise materializes, one line of intervention research might be devoted to testing plausible recommendations, inferred from tentative generalizations about the conditions under which groupthink flourishes, for improving the quality of executive decision-making.

My answer to the acid-test question "Therefore, what?" is heavily influenced by many prior social psychological experiments and detailed observations bearing on group dynamics, including my own studies of task-oriented groups. In this field of research, we become sensitized to the vagaries of human response to seemingly straightforward treatments for improving the quality of group products—vagaries that often force the investigator to conclude that the remedy is worse than the disease. Furthermore, even if free from undesirable side effects, the new treatments are undoubtedly a long way from providing a complete cure. In most cohesive groups, concurrence-seeking tendencies are probably much too powerful to be subdued by administrative changes of the type to be proposed. At best, those changes might somewhat decrease the strength of concurrence-seeking tendencies, thereby reducing the frequency of error. But is it worthwhile, then, for an organization to expend effort, time, and money to try to introduce and assess improvements with such limited potentialities? The answer depends partly on how much damage can be expected from collective miscalculations by an organization's policy-making group. When there is no known antibiotic to cure a virulent respiratory disease, it is still worthwhile during an epidemic to find out whether some elementary precautions, such as staying away from crowded places, will lower significantly the chances of being infected. The prescriptions I am proposing are perhaps like those elementary precautions; they may sometimes help to keep us out of danger while the search for an effective cure continues. It is with considerable ambivalence, therefore, that I offer my suggestions for preventing groupthink.

Three prescriptions and their undesirable side effects

The three suggestions for preventing groupthink presented at the end of Chapter 7 have major drawbacks. One reason for dwelling on the drawbacks is to underline the fact that these prescriptive hypotheses, as well as others to be discussed shortly, must be validated before they can be applied with any confidence. In my opinion, despite potential drawbacks, they warrant the trouble and expense of being tested as potentially useful means for partially counteracting groupthink whenever a small number of executives in any organization meet with their chief executive to work out new policies. Certain of the anti-groupthink procedures might also help to counteract initial biases of the members, prevent pluralistic ignorance, and eliminate other sources of error that can arise independently of groupthink.

1. *The leader of a policy-forming group should assign the role of critical evaluator to each member, encouraging the group to give high priority to airing objections and doubts. This practice needs to be reinforced by the leader's acceptance of criticism of his or her own judgments in order to discourage the members from soft-pedaling their disagreements.*

If the proposed practice is wholeheartedly approved and reinforced by the chief executive and the other top executives in the organization's hierarchy, it might help to counteract the spontaneous group pressures that give rise to a premature consensus. This will not happen, however, unless the leader conveys to the members by his own actions that the task of critical appraisal is to be given precedence over maintaining traditional forms of deference. It is difficult for the members of an amiable executive group to adopt such a norm, but without this basic change in orientation, no other recommendation for improving the quality of group decision-making is likely to be successful because each can easily be subverted by a group intent on pleasing the leader. The leader must demonstrate that he can be influenced by those who disagree with him. He will fail to reinforce the new norm if he shows his displeasure by terminating a discussion when it is not moving in the direction he wants or if his facial expressions and other nonverbal communications belie his words.

The proposed leadership practice has some potential disadvantages that must be taken into account. Prolonged debates within the group can sometimes be costly when a rapidly growing international crisis requires an immediate policy solution in order to avert catastrophe. Open criticism can also lead to damaged feelings when the members resolutely live up to their role as critical evaluators and take each other's proposals over the bumps. Feelings of rejection, depression, and anger might be evoked so often when this role assignment is put into practice that it could have a corrosive effect on morale and working relations within the group. The critical-evaluator role assignment might have to be supplemented by an in-service training program to give executives special skills for avoiding the pitfalls of uninhibited debate. Further, a judicious chairperson would be needed, one whose talents as a mediator enable him or her to head off disruptive quarrels and demoralizing stalemates.

The effectiveness of a group of critical evaluators will depend on the background and personality of the members. A policy-making group of bristling curmudgeons might waste their time on endless reiterations of clashing points of view. Seldom, if ever, do we find in a policy-making committee the ideal type of genuinely reasonable people who can be counted on to function as constructive discussants, to take account of their colleagues' points of view, and to make judicious but principled compromises when the time comes for consensus. Nevertheless, many policy-making groups are probably made up of people who are capable of functioning more effectively in the desired direction if norms that foster critical evaluation are adopted.[1]

2. *The leaders in an organization's hierarchy, when assigning a policy-planning mission to a group, should be impartial instead of stating preferences and expectations at the outset. This practice requires each leader to limit his or her briefings to unbiased statements about the scope of the problem and the limitations of available resources, without advocating specific proposals he or she would like to see adopted. This allows the conferees the opportunity to develop an atmosphere of open inquiry and to explore impartially a wide range of policy alternatives.*

The expected benefit of this leadership practice is that it avoids setting a group norm that will evoke conformity with the leader's views. Among the hazards, however, is a potential cleavage between the leader and the members, which could become a disruptive power struggle if the chief executive regards the emerging consensus among the members as anathema to him. Having lost the opportunity at the outset to steer the group, an inflexible chief might fight with the others, reject their consensus, or disband the group entirely. Even if no rift develops, the chief may feel so frustrated that he becomes more directive than ever. Perhaps the proposed nondirective leadership practice will work only when the chief can be genuinely open-minded in all stages of decision-making and values the judgment of the group sufficiently to abstain from using his power when the others reach a consensus that displeases him.[2]

3. *The organization should routinely follow the administrative practice of setting up several independent policy-planning and evaluation groups to work on the same policy question, each carrying out its deliberations under a different leader.*

This practice—which many specialists in administrative sciences advocate for other reasons—would prevent insulation of an executive in-group from challenging information and independent judgments by well-qualified outsiders. Many executives object to it, however, on the grounds that the more people consulted, the greater is the risk of a security leak. This risk would have to be tolerated, or the security problem would have to be solved by adopting measures that could be applied to a larger number of participants without being inordinately costly in time, money, efficiency, and morale. Another drawback is that the more organizational units involved in policy formation, the greater is the opportunity for intraorganizational politics to play a determining role. Harold Wilensky has emphasized this drawback in *Organizational Intelligence:*

> President Eisenhower . . . made the National Security Council "the climax of a ponderous system of boards, staffs and interdepartmental committees through which national security policy was supposed to rise to the top" [Schlesinger wrote in *A Thousand Days*]. As a result, the NSC was converted into a forum for intramural negotiations; what Dean Acheson called "agreement by exhaustion" blurred policy discord. An ironic feature of such a system is that men of good will are moved to obfuscate their positions and overstate agreements with their rivals, on behalf of an ultimate consensus. . . . When they cannot cope with issues by glittering generalities representing the lowest common denominator of agreement, such supercommittees avoid controversial issues entirely, delay decisions, refer issues to other committees, or engage in logrolling, as when the Navy trades off support for more Air Force wings in return for Air Force support for more Navy carriers. Sharp questions, cogent arguments, minority positions, a clear calculation of gains and costs are lost to view.

Furthermore, when many different planning and evaluation groups deliberate, none of them feels responsible for making a careful assessment of the policy's drawbacks. These are the circumstances that encourage a "let George do it" attitude and the even more pervasive presumption that "George must have already done it." Warren Weaver speaks of an organization whose top administrators take great pride in the series of scheduled steps that each new proposal has to go through before reaching them, without realizing that they are allowing responsibility to be so diffuse that no one actually takes on the task of making a careful evaluation: "By the time the proposal reaches the higher levels of responsibility, the number of examinations and successive interim approvals is so impressive that there is an almost overwhelming temptation to assume that the real decision has already been made."

To minimize the risks, guidelines might be formulated that specify the responsibilities of each group and define the role of each participant, emphasizing that primary loyalty is expected to the organization as a whole rather than to a local unit. Further, it may be possible to select statesmenlike executives capable of surmounting the chronic rivalries that plague every large bureaucracy—men who can be counted on to assess objectively the potential gains and losses for each policy alternative without always giving priority to the special interests of their own unit in its power struggles within the organization. The ultimate success of a multiple-group procedure probably depends on whether these and other safeguards can be introduced. Otherwise the multiple-group antidote to groupthink could spawn a virulent form of politicking that is a worse disease than the one it is supposed to prevent.

More prescriptions to offset insulation

Additional prescriptive hypotheses based on inferences from the generalizations stated in Chapter 10 concerning the conditions under which groupthink is least likely to occur might help prevent groupthink. The costs and potential losses are essentially the same as those just described for the first three prescriptions; the reader will undoubtedly think of additional ones. Suffice it to say that all the recommendations pose obvious risks: The proposed procedures may lower group cohesiveness and correspondingly lower the morale of the participants, as consensus continues to elude them. They may also prove to be prohibitively costly in taking up the precious time of already overburdened executives. Nevertheless, these prescriptions seem to hold the promise of somewhat reducing the chances of groupthink at a moderate cost, if they are implemented flexibly by sensible executives who do not suffer fools gladly and who do not gladly allow themselves to be made into fools. Like the first three, the additional prescriptions offer only a partial cure.

The next three prescriptions take account of the need to offset the potentially adverse effects of insulation of the policy-making group; they would be especially applicable when the multiple-group structure cannot be implemented.

4. *Throughout the period when the feasibility and effectiveness of policy alternatives are being surveyed, the policy-making group should from time to time divide into two or more subgroups to meet separately, under different chairpersons, and then come together to hammer out their differences.*

The formation of subgroups might reduce the chances that the entire group will develop a concurrence-seeking norm and increase the chances that illusory assumptions will be critically examined before a consensus is reached. Subgrouping was one of the procedures used by the Executive Committee during the Cuban missile crisis, and it appears to have contributed to the effectiveness of that group's critical appraisals.

5. *Each member of the policy-making group should discuss periodically the group's deliberations with trusted associates in his or her own unit of the organization and report back their reactions.*

Here I am assuming that each policy-maker's circle of associates can be trusted to adhere to the security regulations that govern the policy-makers. I also assume that each circle will include persons with somewhat different types of expertise, outlooks, and values, so that they can be expected to make independent criticisms and perhaps offer some fresh solutions. In order for the home-office meetings to be effective, each policy-maker would have to conduct them in a nondirective style that encourages free discussion, taking on the role of information-seeker rather than of proselytizing boss. When reporting back to the group, each policy-maker would have to take on the role of information-transmitter and try to describe accurately all varieties of reactions, not specially singling out those that support his or her own views.

Consider what would have happened at the Bay of Pigs planning session if, instead of restricting discussions to the small group of advisers dominated by the two CIA leaders who had evolved the plan, Secretary Rusk had conducted a genuine evaluation meeting with trusted associates in the State Department, Secretary McNamara had done the same in the Defense Department, and each of the others had done likewise in his home office. Chances are that the members of the planning group would have been rudely shaken out of their complacency as they encountered strong negative reactions like the horror that Chester Bowles is reported to have experienced at the one planning session he attended. When Bowles submitted his criticisms in a memorandum and spoke privately to Rusk, his objections were quickly brushed aside; Rusk did not permit the memorandum to be shown to the President or to anyone else. Wouldn't a member of a policy-making group be much less likely to protect the group from such outside influence, to take on the functions of a mindguard, if he were to encounter strong objections to a preferred policy alternative from more than one colleague, especially when he knew that the policy-making group was expecting him to report back on what was actually said at the meetings in his home office?

6. *One or more outside experts or qualified colleagues within the organization who are not core members of the policy-making group should be invited to each meeting on a staggered basis and should be encouraged to challenge the views of the core members.*

In order to counteract a false sense of complacency about risky decisions, the visitors would have to be trustworthy associates carefully selected because of their capacity to grasp new ideas quickly, perspicacity in spotting hidden catches, sensitivity to moral issues, and verbal skill in transmitting criticism. Such outsiders were, in fact, deliberately brought into the Executive Committee's meetings during the Cuban missile crisis, and they were urged to express their objections openly. This atmosphere was quite different from the one that prevailed throughout the Bay of Pigs planning sessions, where, with rare exceptions, the discussants at every meeting were always the same men.

Additional safeguards might be needed to ensure that the objective of inviting well-qualified visitors is not neutralized or subverted. First, visitors who are likely to raise debate-worthy objections should be invited long before a consensus has been reached, not after most of the core members have made up their minds, as was the case when Senator Fulbright was invited to participate in the Bay of Pigs deliberations. Second, each visitor should be asked to speak out about his or her qualms and not brood silently, as Bowles felt constrained to do when he attended a Bay of Pigs planning session. Third, after the visitor speaks his piece, the chairman should call for open discussion of his objections instead of moving on to other business, as President Kennedy did after Senator Fulbright gave his rousing speech at the final planning session about the undesirable political and moral consequences of the Bay of Pigs invasion plan.

More prescriptions to offset leadership bias

These prescriptions are designed to help offset leadership practices that bias the group's deliberations and that establish concurrence-seeking as an informal group norm.

7. *At every meeting devoted to evaluating policy alternatives, at least one member should be assigned the role of devil's advocate.*

Whenever assigning the role of critical evaluator to every member of the group is not feasible, assigning the devil's advocate role to one or two members may be of some limited value. In recent years, however, use of a devil's advocate has become popular among high-level executives, and many go through the motions without any apparent effect. For example, President Johnson and other leading members of his Tuesday Lunch Group claimed that they had devil's advocates in their midst each time they decided to intensify the air war against North Vietnam. But those devils were not very devilish. James C. Thomson has informed us, on the basis of his observations during several years of service on the White House staff, that the devil's advocates in Johnson's inner circle quickly became domesticated and were allowed by the President to speak their piece only as long as they remained within the bounds of what he and other leading members of the group considered acceptable dissent. George Reedy, who was President Johnson's press secretary for a time, adds that within Johnson's councils ''[the official devil's advocate's] objections and cautions are discounted before they are delivered. They are actually welcomed because they prove for the record that decision was preceded by controversy.'' Alexander George also comments that, paradoxically, the institutionalized devil's advocate, instead of stirring up much-needed turbulence among the members of a policy-making group, may create the "comforting feeling that they have considered all sides of the issue and that the policy chosen has weathered challenges from within the decision-making circle.'' He goes on to say that after the President has fostered the ritualized use of devil's advocates, the top-level officials may learn nothing more than how to enact their policy-making in such a way as to meet the informed public's expectation about how important decisions should be made and "to project a favorable image into the 'instant histories' that will be written shortly thereafter.''

The problem, then, is how to avoid tokenism on the part of the chief executive, how to inject a genuine effort that will not belie the instant historians' reassuring picture of healthy controversy. If the leader genuinely wants the group to examine opposing arguments, he will have to give the devil's advocate an unambiguous assignment to present his arguments as cleverly and convincingly as he can, like a good lawyer, challenging the testimony of those advocating the majority position. This does not mean that the leader has to transform the meetings with his policy advisers into a kind of formal debate or that the devil's advocate should be strident, rude, or insolent in pressing for an alternative point of view. The most effective performers in the role are likely to be those who can be truly devilish by raising new issues in a conventional, low-key style, asking questions such as, "Haven't we perhaps overlooked . . . ?'' "Shouldn't we give some thought to . . . ?'' The chief executive must make it clear by what he or she says and does that the listeners are expected to pay close attention to all the devilish arguments and to take them up one by one for serious discussion. The group might adopt essentially the same supplementary procedures suggested for dealing with the points raised by outsiders who introduce fresh notes into the group's deliberations.

During the Cuban missile crisis, President Kennedy gave his brother, the Attorney General, the unambiguous mission of playing devil's advocate, with seemingly excellent results in breaking up a premature consensus. But the vehemence with which Robert Kennedy plunged into the role may have cost him a considerable amount of popularity among his colleagues on the Executive Committee, and had he not been the President's brother, this might have damaged his government career. Perhaps rotating the role among the most talented role-players in the group would help solve this problem and hamper the build-up of subtle pressures that induce domestication of the role. With one fresh contender after another on hand to challenge the consensus of the majority, the devil could get his due at the meetings and not afterward.[3]

8. *Whenever the policy issue involves relations with a rival nation or organization, a sizable block of time (perhaps an entire session) should be spent surveying all warning signals from the rivals and constructing alternative scenarios of the rivals' intentions.*

To counteract the members' shared illusions of invulnerability and their tendency to ignore warning signals that interfere with complacency, the leader may have to exert special efforts to induce himself and his colleagues to pay sufficient attention to potential risks to make realistic contingency plans. Even when executives have a role assignment requiring them to be vigilant, they are likely to disregard intelligence reports and warnings about a potential danger if there is a preexisting consensus among members of their reference group that the particular threat is improbable. Thomas Schelling speaks of the "poverty of expectations" that prevented the military commanders at Pearl Harbor from considering that the warning signals they were receiving during 1941 might point to an oncoming Japanese attack. "Unlike movies," he points out, "real life provides no musical background to tip us off to the climax."

When participants in a policy-planning group are being briefed about their rival's latest moves, audio-visual aids that provide the equivalent of melodramatic background music might overcome their poverty of expectations, especially when their complacency is grounded in unanimous agreement that the warning signals point only to minor threats that can be safely ignored.

Setting aside a block of time for thorough consideration of the potential risks probably has to be made an institutionalized requirement; otherwise any bearer of ill tidings is likely to meet the fate of Cassandra, whose accurate prophecies of catastrophe were never taken seriously. Briefings by intelligence specialists might be supplemented by films or illustrated talks prepared by a skilled scenario writer who deliberately takes on the role of *Cassandra's advocate,* calling attention as vividly as possible to alarming interpretations of the evidence at hand that might otherwise be overlooked.

I am not proposing that Hollywood-like productions become standard fare in high government counsels, which could bring us closer to the day when the Pentagon will routinely commission horror films for use along with other forms of scare propaganda to persuade congressional committees to increase their appropriations to the armed forces. What I have in mind is an occasional presentation of multiple scenarios as a stimulant to the imagination of the members of a policy-making group, which could arouse a state of constructive vigilance in an inert group that has been reposing in tranquil overconfidence. Perhaps the model for the presentation of multiple scenarios should be the great Japanese film *Rashomon,* directed by Akira Kurosawa. This film presents four entirely different scenarios successively, each explaining the same events (a sexual assault and a murder) in a different way, attributing entirely different motivations to the principals, yet accounting equally well for the known facts.

Of course if the most ominous interpretation of an enemy's activities is presented convincingly, a group of government policy-makers might overreact to relatively innocuous events and become all too ready to launch a preemptive first strike. In the series of Rashomon-like alternative scenarios there should always be at least one that plausibly attributes benign intentions to the enemy; this might help prevent such overreactions. To ensure careful weighing of the evidence, additional safeguards against precipitous judgment might be needed. For example, after bringing in outside experts to brief the policy-making group, the leader might assign several members the task of evaluating all warning messages and information about risks that need to be taken into account for contingency planning. In carrying out this task, the participants might find it useful to assume that there is some truth and also some exaggeration in every unwelcome message, before they begin any discussion that moves in the direction of either acting on it or dismissing it as irrelevant.

Psychodramatic role-play exercises might also be used to overcome the influence of stereotypes and to facilitate understanding of the rivals' warnings, enabling the group to predict more accurately the probable responses to one or another course of action. For example, after intelligence experts have given a factual briefing on, say, the Chinese Communists' ambiguous threats during a new international crisis in the Far East, the members of a foreign policy planning group who are most familiar with the beliefs and values of the Chinese leaders might try out a psychodramatic procedure in which they assume the role of their opposite numbers in Peking. The psychodrama might be enacted as a meeting during which the Chinese leaders talk over their options for dealing with the crisis and the countermoves they might make if the United States takes a hard line versus an ameliorative stance. Had this type of role-play exercise been conducted by Truman's advisers in the fall of 1950, they might have taken much more seriously the repeated warnings from Communist China and become reluctant to approve General MacArthur's catastrophic policy of pursuing the North Korean army to the Manchurian border.

The same type of role-playing might be useful in overcoming complacency in a group that collectively judges a series of warnings to be inapplicable and sees no reason to prepare contingency plans for dealing with the potential danger. Suppose that a role-play exercise had been carried out by the group of United States Navy commanders in Hawaii on December 2, 1941, the day that Admiral Kimmel, after being informed by the chief of naval intelligence that no one in the Navy knew where the Japanese aircraft carriers were, jokingly asked if they could be heading straight for Hawaii. If the exercise of playing the role of Japan's supreme military command had been carried out seriously, isn't it likely that at least a few of the high-ranking naval officers responsible for the defense of Hawaii would have argued against the prevailing view that the war warnings they had been receiving during the past week did not warrant the expense of a full alert at Pearl Harbor or a 360-degree air patrol around the Hawaiian Islands?

9. *After reaching a preliminary consensus about what seems to be the best policy alternative, the policy-making group should hold a "second chance" meeting at which the members are expected to express as vividly as*

they can all their residual doubts and to rethink the entire issue before making a definitive choice.

In order to prevent a premature consensus based on unwarranted expectations of invulnerability, stereotypes about the enemy, and other unexamined assumptions shared by members of the group, the second-chance session should be held just before the group takes a definitive vote or commits itself in any other way. At this special meeting, every member should be encouraged to become the devil's advocate and Cassandra's advocate, challenging his or her own favorite arguments and playing up the risks. Everyone should deliberately set himself the task of presenting to the group any objections he can think of that have not yet been adequately discussed. In order to stimulate a freewheeling, open discussion in which residual doubts are frankly expressed, the members might be asked to read in advance an eloquent document presenting opposing arguments prepared by opponents of the chosen policy. In giving out such an assignment on occasions when a consensus has been reached rapidly, the leader might take as a model the statement made by Alfred P. Sloan, a former chairman of General Motors who reportedly announced at a meeting of his fellow policy-makers:

> Gentlemen, I take it we are all in complete agreement on the decision here. . . . Then I propose we postpone further discussion of this matter until our next meeting to give ourselves time to develop disagreement and perhaps gain some understanding of what the decision is all about.

To encourage members to reveal vague forebodings, it might not be a bad idea for the second-chance meeting to take place in a relaxed atmosphere far from the executive suite, perhaps over drinks (as sometimes happens spontaneously anyhow). According to a report by Herodotus dating from about 45 B.C., whenever the ancient Persians made a decision following sober deliberations, they would always reconsider the matter under the influence of wine. Tacitus claimed that during Roman times the Germans too had a custom of arriving at each decision twice, once sober, once drunk. Some moderate, institutionalized form of allowing second thoughts to be freely expressed before the group commits itself might be remarkably effective for breaking down a false sense of unanimity and related illusions, without endangering anyone's reputation or liver.

Tooling up for innovations

Recognizing that each innovation in policy-making procedures can introduce new sources of error that might be as bad as or worse than groupthink, we can see why public administrators and executives in large private organizations might have solid reasons for resisting any change in their standard procedures. Nevertheless, innovative executives who know their way around the organizational maze may be able to figure out how to apply one or

another of the prescriptions successfully, without producing harmful side effects. If they were to invite well-qualified behavioral scientists to collaborate
with them, they might obtain something more than academic advice from the
sidelines. Some behavioral scientists (though, alas, not many) possess that
rare set of skills required for developing and making objective assessments of
new administrative procedures. A few specialists in administrative science,
for example, have developed ways of applying the most sophisticated
methods of assessment used in engineering and the behavioral sciences to
problems that arise in connection with executive functions in large organizations. They know a great deal about obtaining data from field studies to
evaluate innovations for coordinating the operations of the specific units of
an organization so as to determine whether the proposed changes will achieve
the goals of the organization as a whole. Research teams of specialists from
several different behavioral science disciplines have dealt with management
problems such as the allocation of available resources, the scheduling of sequential tasks, the replacement of facilities, and the development of effective
steps for carrying out information searches that will supply policy-makers
with the information they need at the lowest cost and with the fewest errors.
The same systematic methods used by research teams to deal with these problems—evaluating the effects of changing a given procedure in one unit of the
organization on every other aspect of the unit's functioning and on the
organization as a whole—might be applied to problems concerning the procedures used by an executive committee making its policy decisions.

   Imaginative workers in the new field of research on policy-making procedures might be able to develop the equivalent of a wind tunnel for a series of
trial runs to pretest various anti-groupthink procedures before going to the
expense of setting up a field test. For example, in recent studies of political
gaming, small groups of middle-level executives (who are thought to have the
potential for eventually becoming top-level executives) are given decision-
making exercises in simulated crises. In one exercise, conducted during a
three-day period at the Center for International Studies at the Massachusetts
Institute of Technology, two teams of executives met separately to arrive at
policy decisions in a simulated clash between the United States and the Soviet
Union centering around a Communist revolt in an underdeveloped country,
similar to the situations that led to United States intervention in Korea and
Vietnam. Both sides initially tried to avoid intervention and a direct confrontation, but these cautious strategies gradually gave way to military policies involving considerable risks, just as in real life. While these decisions were being
made, it was clear that each side was misunderstanding the intentions of the
other and was drawing incorrect inferences because of stereotyped images and
unexamined preconceptions about how the rival group would react. This too
resembles what has happened in groups making real-life decisions.

   One of the limitations of political game-playing is that it does not
generate the severe stress and intense need for social support that arise in real

international crises. Nevertheless, some symptoms of groupthink may regularly appear when group decision-making exercises are carried out in the context of simulated international crises. It should be possible to use them to try out various anti-groupthink prescriptions to see what the problems are, to find out how the problems can most easily be eliminated, and then to evaluate their success in preventing the worst effects of groupthink. The political gaming exercises might also be useful for training executives. Briefing sessions could be held afterward to enable them to become aware of symptoms of groupthink and other manifestations of group dynamics.

A collaborative team made up of practical executives from inside the organization working with behavioral scientists who spend enough time tooling up to understand what the insiders tell them ought to be able to find a relatively painless way to carry out field studies to assess the long-run effectiveness of the most promising innovative procedures. The objective evaluations made by a team of administrators and behavioral scientists could weed out ineffective and harmful procedures and provide solid evidence to keep the good ones going. By accumulating systematic evidence, they could contribute to the transformation of effective policy-making from a haphazard art into a cumulative science.[4] In the absence of sound evaluation studies, improvements in decision-making procedures have a chancy existence and often get lost in the shuffle of changing personnel at the top of the organization. Consider the promising innovations introduced by President Kennedy after the humiliation of the Bay of Pigs fiasco. We have seen that he made several major changes along the lines of some of the foregoing prescriptions for counteracting groupthink and improved the quality of decision-making on subsequent occasions, including the Cuban missile crisis. What happened to those innovations after Kennedy's death? Evidently they were regarded simply as part of Kennedy's personal style of leadership and were promptly dropped by his successor, who had his own way of doing things. If a solid body of evidence had been available to show that those procedures would generally be effective in various policy-making bodies headed by leaders other than Kennedy, there might have been strong pressures to retain the innovations. The better the evidence showing that a given innovation is effective in a variety of different organizations and at all levels of management, the more confidence everyone can have that the prescription is a valid generalization and the better the chances are that it will be retained when new top executives replace those who initiated the change.

The ethical issue

The type of innovation I have been discussing confronts us with a rather painful ethical issue that is a source of embarrassment for anyone who would like to see improvements in the policy-making procedures in our society: Suppose that knowledge about how to prevent groupthink turns out to have practical value for improving the effectiveness of policy-making groups. Who will benefit? Will it be good or bad for the Jews? For the Christians? For the blacks? For the whites? For the hawks? For the doves? For the men in power? For the oppressed who are striving for power? All along, I have assumed that many people are inadvertently victimized when war-and-peace decisions are dominated by groupthink, that many lives are unintentionally sacrificed as a result of ill-conceived nationalistic policies. In the back of my mind has been the expectation (and hope) that improving the efficiency of policy-making groups will increase the chances that they will fulfil their humanitarian goals along with their other goals.

But, of course, there is a rub. Suppose that a policy-making body talks about humanitarianism only for window dressing, while secretly believing that whatever is good for ''our group'' will be good for mankind.[5] For any exploitative, totalitarian, or criminalistic gang, wouldn't the prevention of groupthink be contributing to evil rather than good by helping them to be more successful? Yes, of course. Any improvement in the efficiency of decision-making, unfortunately, can be used for evil as well as for good. Prevention of groupthink cannot be expected to provide a cure for evils intentionally perpetrated by a policy-making group, any more than a cure for the infections afflicting patients in a cancer ward will restore them to full health.

Where does that leave us? My answer is that a cure for staphylococcus infection can be worthwhile even if it does not cure cancer. The evils that are deliberately perpetrated by policy-making groups must be fought as people have always fought them, through persistent political confrontations that challenge the legitimacy of bad policies and through concerted efforts to change public attitudes to win the support of large constituencies for good policies. This struggle is often carried out by small groups of dedicated men and women who are deeply committed to democratic and humanitarian values. One hopes that these groups are open to innovation and will want to avoid the unfortunate consequences of groupthink. Similarly, the policy-making groups in large organizations that take democratic and humanitarian values seriously might be less hidebound than those striving primarily to maintain traditional bureaucratic or conventional values. Maybe there are grounds, therefore, for being somewhat optimistic about the possibility that some groups with good values will take seriously the techniques for preventing groupthink in their own policy-making deliberations and make good use of those techniques.

Most of what I have just been saying boils down to a simple truism: Improving the quality of decision-making by eliminating certain sources of error that prevent a group from achieving its goals can be expected to have good social consequences for policy-making groups that have good goals; otherwise not. I hope that behavioral scientists will keep this in mind when they are deciding whether or not to collaborate with executives who want them to help improve the effectiveness of an organization's policy-making.

Is a little knowledge of groupthink a dangerous thing?

Even if we had more than a little knowledge of groupthink, my answer to this question would be a categorical "yes" if we have in mind a naive person in a position of power who might be led to believe that groupthink is the only major source of error in policy-making and therefore that decisions can be made better by just one man (notably himself) than by a group of colleagues. I would also answer "yes" if I thought that a substantial number of policy-makers might be misled into believing that preventing groupthink should be given high priority, so that all sorts of safeguards should be introduced into the decision-making process without regard for hidden costs. Finally, I would wearily say "yes" if I discovered that many executives were being subjected to a lot of nonsense from overly eager faddists on their staff who were taking up precious time trying to introduce some kind of group therapy in the conference room, like an earlier generation of faddists who tried to inflict parlor-room psychoanalysis on their friends.

But my answer is "no" for anyone who takes the trouble to examine the fragmentary evidence on which I have drawn inferences about the conditions that give rise to groupthink. My two main conclusions are that along with other sources of error in decision-making, groupthink is likely to occur within cohesive small groups of decision-makers and that the most corrosive effects of groupthink can be counteracted by eliminating group insulation, overly directive leadership practices, and other conditions that foster premature consensus. Those who take these conclusions seriously will probably find that the little knowledge they have about groupthink increases their understanding of the causes of erroneous group decisions and sometimes even has some practical value in preventing fiascoes. (If I didn't think so, I wouldn't have bothered to write this chapter.)

A little knowledge of groupthink might be valuable for anyone who participates in a group that makes policy decisions, whether it is the executive committee of an international organization, an ad hoc committee set up by a government agency, the steering committee of a local business, professional, or political organization, or a student committee at a college. Such knowledge can be especially useful if it inclines the participants to consider introducing antidote prescriptions, provided, of course, that they are aware of the costs in time and effort and realize that there are other disadvantages they must also watch out for before they decide to adopt any of them as a standard operating procedure.[6]

Sometimes it may even be useful for one of the members of the group to ask, at the right moment, before a decision is definitely made, "Are we allowing ourselves to become victims of groupthink?" I am not proposing that this question should be placed on the agenda or that the members should try to conduct a group therapy session. Rather, I have in mind making salient the realization that the desire for unity within the group can be discussed frankly and that agreement within the group is not always desirable. This open acknowledgment may enable some members to adopt a psychological set that inclines them to raise critical questions whenever there are signs of undue complacency or a premature consensus. One such question has to do with the consensus itself. A leader or a member who is aware of the symptoms of groupthink, for example, might ask to hear from those who have not yet said anything, in order to get all points of view onto the table before the group makes a final decision. In addition to this common-sense application, some ingenious procedures may be worked out or spontaneously improvised so that the symptoms of groupthink are counteracted by participants who know about the groupthink hypothesis, without constantly reminding the group of it.[7]

With these considerations in mind, I suggest that awareness of the shared illusions, rationalizations, and other symptoms fostered by the interaction of members of small groups may curtail the influence of groupthink in policy-making groups, including those that meet in the White House. Here is another place where we can apply George Santayana's well-known adage: "Those who cannot remember the past are condemned to repeat it." Perhaps a better understanding of group dynamics among government leaders will help them avoid being condemned to repeat the fiascoes of the recent past described in this book.

Notes

1 Introduction

1 In *Theories in Social Psychology,* Morton Deutsch and Robert Kraus point out that Kurt Lewin's "impact on social psychology continues to be felt in the work of his students and colleagues, including Back, Barker, Bavelas, Cartwright, Deutsch, Festinger, French, Heider, Horwitz, Kelley, Lippitt, Pepitone, Redl, Schachter, Thibaut, White, Willerman, Wright, Zander" (p. 61). They add, "Of Lewin's students, Festinger is the one whose work has had the broadest impact on social psychology . . . notably his theory of the process of social comparison and his theory of cognitive dissonance" (p. 62). Festinger's theory of social comparison, his greatest contribution to group dynamics, is based on two main assumptions: The first is that people strive to find out if their opinions and judgments are correct. The second is that when objective means are unavailable, people evaluate their opinions and judgments by comparing them with those of others who are similar to themselves (such as members of face-to-face groups). Such comparison produces pressure toward uniformity.

2 My observations of military combat units indicate that social pressures in cohesive groups can have favorable effects on morale and unfavorable effects on compliance with organizational standards of ethical conduct (Janis, 1945a, 1945b, and 1968). During the chaotic period following the end of World War II, many small cohesive units among the American occupying forces developed norms that were counter to those of the military organization and to the society at large; this development facilitated collective delinquent behavior (Janis, 1968). Other observational studies (Janis, 1966) show that therapy groups and self-help groups of would-be nonsmokers and dieters go through developmental stages conducive to uniform emotional responses of pride in membership and aggression toward outgroups. Recent field experiments (Janis, 1982; Janis and Hoffman, 1970; Miller and Janis, 1973) indicate that under certain conditions, increased social contact among group members increases not only the attractiveness of the group but also adherence to norms fostering self-improvement (for example, giving up smoking). Under other conditions, however, the informal norms that develop may subvert the original purposes for which the group was formed.

2 The Bay of Pigs

1 Dulles and Bissell evidently were misinformed by their operatives dealing with the brigade of Cuban exiles in Guatemala and neglected to check up on them to find out what they were really up to. The heads of the CIA also neglected to obtain a thorough, independent critique

of the invasion plan from military and political experts affiliated with their agency. Supporters of the CIA have claimed, however, that the original plan might have been successful if it had not been greatly weakened by the curbs imposed by President Kennedy, especially the requirement that there should be no active military participation by the United States armed forces. The plan that was approved called for the exiles to carry out the operation on their own. Had the plan called for direct intervention by United States military forces, it undoubtedly would have been rejected by the President's advisory group because it would have required the United States to openly engage in an act of unprovoked aggression against a neighboring country. Sorensen points out that "had the U.S. Navy and Air Force been openly committed, no defeat would have been permitted, a full-scale U.S. attack would ultimately have been required, and—assuming a general war with the Soviets could have been avoided—there was no point in beginning with a Cuban brigade in the first place" (p. 333).

Within the limits of the plan as approved by the President, a specific tactical decision has been singled out as a possible cause of the military debacle—the President's cancellation of the second air strike. Apprehensive about political attacks against the United States government touched off by the first air strike against Cuba, President Kennedy, after consultation with his advisers, canceled the second one, which had been scheduled to take place just before the landing party arrived on the beaches. It might conceivably have destroyed Castro's highly effective jet planes, which subsequently prevented ammunition and supplies from reaching the beleaguered invaders. On this point, however, Sorensen argues that "there is no reason to believe that Castro's air force, having survived the first [air strike] and then dispersed into hiding, would have been knocked out by the second" (p. 337). Schlesinger adds that "even on the most unlikely assumption that the second strike achieved total success and wiped out Castro's air force, it would still have left 1,200 men against 200,000" (p. 294). At best, in his judgment, the second air strike might have enabled the beachhead to be defended a few more days and perhaps would have made possible the evacuation of the survivors. Without the aid of the United States Navy or Air Force, Schlesinger concludes, the beachhead could have been sustained only if a successful internal uprising had prevented Castro's army from surrounding the invaders. But for this, there was practically no hope at all.

2 When asked by President Kennedy to look into the CIA's invasion plan about two months before the decision was made, the Joint Chiefs at first were skeptical about the prospects of a small band of exiles overcoming the two hundred thousand or more men in Castro's armed forces. Their view at that time was that if the United States did not intervene, a Cuban insurrection behind the lines was essential for success. During the subsequent weeks, however, General Lemnitzer, spokesman for the Joint Chiefs, confined his critical comments to specific details, such as doubting that two air strikes would be enough to destroy Castro's air power. But the Joint Chiefs never communicated any real opposition to the plan and, in fact, just one week before it was put into effect, gave it their written endorsement. Schlesinger reports that at all the meetings during the crucial period of decision—which took place over a ten-week period—"the Joint Chiefs seemed to go contentedly along" (p. 250). He surmises, as does Sorensen, that they were secretly assuming that once the enterprise was under way, the President would change his mind and allow United States armed forces to complete the job if necessary, rather than risk defeat.

After the debacle, the Joint Chiefs let it be known that from a military standpoint they had had serious doubts about the Bay of Pigs invasion all along but had assumed that the CIA could be relied upon to make sound estimates of Castro's military and political weaknesses. Perhaps before the invasion attempt the Joint Chiefs had felt that it would be better for them to avoid criticizing the CIA's military plan than to become embroiled in rivalry with another agency of the government. Schlesinger states (p. 255) that as holdovers from the Eisenhower administration, the Joint Chiefs were prepared to risk the world's growing faith in the new American President. He implies that the Joint Chiefs were assuming that if the mission succeeded they would share the glory but if it failed the blame would fall on the President and the CIA.

If they assumed they would escape responsibility, the Joint Chiefs were quite wrong. Although President Kennedy accepted full responsibility and the CIA was duly castigated for its defective intelligence, the Joint Chiefs received their full share of the blame, particularly within the government. During the days following the fiasco, the White House staff noted bitterly that the Joint Chiefs were releasing self-protective statements to the press. As soon as he felt able to do so, President Kennedy removed General Lemnitzer, chairman of the Joint Chiefs of Staff, replacing him with a military man of his own choosing, General Maxwell Taylor. President Kennedy did not hesitate to tell his close associates that he was disgusted with all three Joint Chiefs for endorsing the military plan without having examined it thoroughly. Nor did the Joint Chiefs of Staff escape blame in accounts of the fiasco by Schlesinger and Sorensen. The latter gives an additional reason for their failure. One of Sorensen's conclusions is that the Joint Chiefs, like the CIA, "were moved more by the necessity of acting swiftly against Castro than by the necessity for caution and success" (p. 342).

3 My conclusion, in effect, is that there is more to the defective Bay of Pigs decision than the four factors emphasized by Schlesinger, because groupthink also contributed to the misjudgments. Responding to this conclusion (presented in the first edition of this book published in 1972), Peter Wyden in his illuminating book, *Bay of Pigs* (1979, p. 314), has stated the same conclusion in reverse. He says, "There *had* to be more to the making of the Bay of Pigs disaster . . . than groupthink" and goes on to reemphasize the four other factors that contributed to the misjudgments. In some passages of his book, however, he implies that the other factors furnish a sufficient explanation and that the groupthink hypothesis is not needed at all.

    Most of Wyden's penetrating discussion (and most of the eyewitness interviews he conducted) pertain to the CIA's inept military planning of the invasion and its botched-up execution. With regard to the decision by the President and his advisers to approve the plan—which Wyden attributes to "the seeming mindlessness of the Kennedy group" (p. 314)—he places especially heavy emphasis on the "newness" of the Kennedy administration and the typical inhibitions in an unfamiliar hierarchy wherein each adviser is fearful of damaging his personal status and future prospects if he steps on the toes of other powerful personages or is regarded as a troublemaker by the President. As I indicate on pages 32 to 34, such factors undoubtedly contributed to the group's errors, but they do not adequately explain the lack of information-seeking and critical questioning of dubious assumptions on the part of the key advisers who were members of Kennedy's inner circle. They knew that in order to protect the President from a misguided, regrettable decision, they were expected to be skeptical and cautious about any plan that called for an unprovoked military attack against a neighboring country and especially one that everyone immediately could recognize as being risky. These same considerations also apply to another factor that Wyden suggests may have been a major cause of the "assumed consensus" among Kennedy's advisers—the persuasiveness of Richard Bissell, architect of the CIA plan, who shared with Kennedy a "drive for gutsy action" (p. 326) and "was allowed to become defendant, prosecutor, jury, and judge (subject only to Kennedy's veto from the appeals bench)" (p. 320).

    The only new evidence that Wyden offers in support of his explanation emerges from his interview with Roswell L. Gilpatrick, "who attended a number of their [the Kennedy group's] meetings in the Pentagon and in the Cabinet Room as Deputy Secretary of Defense" (p. 314). Gilpatrick told Wyden that Bissell was "a very effective advocate," and that at the meetings "I kind of got religion" (p. 315). As the interview is reported, Gilpatrick seems to have been implying that others at the group meetings "got religion," too. In any case, Gilpatrick explicitly said that "there was a paucity of questions" and that he himself wondered about the assumptions of Castro's weakness but remained silent. One reason he gave to explain why he did not "chide" himself for failing to speak up at the time was that he and the others were so new in their roles that they "didn't know how far" they could speak up (p. 315). It may well be that, as this quotation implies, some of the men in subordinate positions on the Kennedy team, like Gilpatrick, were keenly aware of the personal risks to their careers if they challenged the assumptions of the CIA leaders or openly raised critical questions about the judgment of the Joint Chiefs of Staff.

    Gilpatrick's statements in his interview with Wyden, however, do not preclude the possibility that as a peripheral member, he shared in the esprit de corps of the Kennedy team. In fact, Gilpatrick's vivid account of his own uncritical acceptance of the invasion plan (stating that he "got religion" and that he did *not* "chide" himself during the meetings for remaining silent about his doubts) suggests that he shared with others an unwarranted faith that the plan would work. If so, his self-censorship of doubts may have been the result of mixed motives—not wanting to impair the harmony of the group, which is a central feature of groupthink, as well as not wanting to get into personal trouble by stepping on the toes of any of the powerful personages who were present.

The testimony of Gilpatrick is the only substantial evidence cited by Wyden in support of the hypothesis that fear of recriminations, newness, and the other factors listed by Schlesinger fully account for the assumed consensus among the President's advisers. It might be a sufficient explanation for the silencing of peripheral members of the Kennedy team and outsiders like the Joint Chiefs of Staff. But it does not bear directly on and certainly does not preclude my hypothesis that groupthink was a dominant source of the consensus among the President's most trusted key advisers who were members of his inner circle—Robert Kennedy, Dean Rusk, Robert McNamara, and McGeorge Bundy. It is unlikely that these powerful men who were closest to the President would have a high degree of personal concern about being regarded as troublemakers and damaging their careers if they fulfilled their advisory role and blew the whistle on a plan they felt might be seriously defective.

All the evidence indicates that the key advisers failed to express any serious doubts about the faulty assumptions because they believed that the CIA plan was basically sound. They thought that even if the invasion did not succeed in overthrowing Castro, the infiltrations of the Cuban refugees would at least succeed in strengthening the anti-Castro forces without creating serious embarrassment for the United States. As the report by the official board of inquiry (headed by General Maxwell D. Taylor) asserted, they, like the President, believed that defeat was most improbable. If any one of the four key advisers had thought otherwise, he had sufficient power to obtain independent estimates from the government's intelligence community about Castro's strength, the likelihood of a Cuban uprising, the military soundness of the invasion plan, the ease or difficulty of retreating to the Escambray Mountains from the Bay of Pigs, and so on. Furthermore, each of the key advisers could have had direct access to the President to express his candid concerns even if he felt it inexpedient to do so at the formal meetings in the presence of the CIA chiefs and the Joint Chiefs of Staff.

Robert Kennedy, for example, could have raised serious doubts in his private discussions with the President during the week before the final decision was made. But according to his memorandum of June 1, 1961 (quoted by Schlesinger, 1978, p. 477), it was because he was so impressed by "the information that had been given . . . by Dick Bissell, Allen Dulles, the Joint Chiefs of Staff, Mac Bundy and the others" that he told the President "there really wasn't any alternative to accepting it." Evidently Robert Kennedy had the impression that there was just about a consensus among all the President's advisers except one. In an interview with John Bartlow Martin on March 1, 1964 (quoted by Schlesinger, 1978, p. 478), Robert Kennedy asserted that "the one person who was strongly against it was Arthur Schlesinger," whom he told to "remain quiet" because the "President had made up his mind" and "we should make all efforts to support him" (corroborating Schlesinger's account of this conversation, which I quote on p. 40).

Dean Rusk, as Secretary of State, had ample opportunity to check on his doubts and convey his frank opinion to the President. But instead of collecting relevant information to supply to the President, he deliberately withheld Chester Bowles's critical memorandum, and he turned down Roger Hilsman's urgent request to allow the Cuban specialists in the State Department to prepare critical appraisals. In an interview with Wyden (p. 148), Rusk said that he did not speak about his doubts at the crucial meeting in which the vote was taken because he was eager to "close ranks with the President." Rusk's explanation for withholding his doubts, which is in line with the groupthink hypothesis, appears to be more plausible than an alternative explanation cast in terms of the factors mentioned by Gilpatrick (being new to his role and not knowing how far he could speak up, implying fear of personal damage to his status).

There is at least one impressive piece of evidence concerning Rusk's lack of fear of recriminations in opposing the CIA and speaking his mind to the President during this period. Robert Kennedy's memorandum of June 1, 1961 (quoted by Schlesinger, 1978, p. 479) states that on the day after the Cuban invasion had started and the CIA asked for air cover, Rusk spoke up unequivocally against the position favored by the President, which undoubtedly contributed to the President's refusal of the CIA's request. The President, according to Robert Kennedy, "was in favor of giving it." But "Dean Rusk was strongly against it. He said that we had made a commitment that no American forces would be used and that the President shouldn't appear in the light of being a liar."

It seems equally improbable that McNamara felt too inhibited to raise critical questions because of the newness of his role as Secretary of Defense and personal concern about recriminations. It would certainly not be in keeping with this man's well-known record of telling presidents as well as generals, cabinet officers, and congressmen exactly what he thought of plans or policies he judged to be flawed. And in this instance, he had every reason to expect that his critical comments would be well received. During the first months of the Kennedy administration, according to Schlesinger (1978, p. 486), the President "counted on Robert McNamara to contain the military" and had feelings of "admiration and affection for the Secretary of Defense."

McGeorge Bundy is an equally unlikely candidate for suppressing doubts out of personal fear of recriminations. As Special Assistant to the President for National Security Affairs, his main job, according to Neustadt (p. 52), was to "review options" and keep the President informed about more than one perspective when facing policy decisions. Kennedy restored the type of relationship that Franklin D. Roosevelt had had with Harry Hopkins, according to Neustadt. "Kennedy made McGeorge Bundy a limited peacetime equivalent for Hopkins, assisting with the stream of presidential actions in diplomacy and defense" (p. 52). Neustadt adds that Bundy had a "strong substantive role" (p. 290). Wyden agrees that "he was very influential with the President" (p. 101).

From an interview with him, Wyden reports that Bundy felt that Castro was dangerous and that it was good to have a plan against him. Bundy had little doubt about the CIA venture because, like McNamara and others, he believed that the fall-back plan to resort to guerilla operations pretty much guaranteed success. Bundy told Wyden that he had thought "a substantial portion of the force would *almost certainly* be able to survive for a prolonged period in guerilla operations" (Wyden, p. 103, italics added). It seems most probable, therefore, that Bundy along with the other three key advisers in the President's inner circle, failed to raise critical questions and to obtain independent appraisals because all of them shared the consensus that basically, in one way or another, the CIA plan was going to be successful, and as Rusk put it, they were "closing ranks."

4 Wyden (1979) suggests the possibility that President Kennedy may have made his decision to approve the CIA's invasion plan independently of his advisers' influence. He says that the decision was "not made in a group," and that in mid-April 1961, Kennedy gave the final "go" order over the telephone to Bissell "after extensive lonely soul-searching" (p. 316). But it seems to me that the available evidence consistently indicates that Kennedy worked on and arrived at the decision in group settings, including informal as well as formal meetings with his advisers. Robert Kennedy and Schlesinger, from their own direct personal observations, have reported that the President was very strongly influenced by a consensus of his key advisers. McGeorge Bundy's memorandum, prepared right after the group meeting on March 11, 1961, implies that Kennedy was highly responsive to his advisers' acceptance of the invasion plan, even though he asked the CIA to modify the plan so as to reduce apparent U.S. involvement: "The President expects to authorize U.S. support for an appropriate number of patriotic Cubans to return to their homeland" (quoted by Wyden, p. 101). At the formal meeting on April 4, 1961, after allowing Senator Fulbright to state his objections, the President cut off any discussion of the questions raised by requiring his advisers to vote yes or no on the CIA invasion plan. Secretary of State Dean Rusk was not the only one there who felt that the President wanted to "close ranks" in the face of Fulbright's opposition; Paul Nitze and William Bundy told Wyden that they had much the same impression (see Wyden, pp. 148–149). Bissell left the meeting with "a sense of finality," believing that the chances were now very high that he would get presidential approval of his plan, especially since the President had required his advisers to vote, which put them on record as wanting to go ahead (Wyden, 1979, p. 150). During the next week, in informal talks with Robert Kennedy and other members of his in-group, the President continued to convey his positive responsiveness to the advice he was receiving.

Drawing on Sorensen's account, Wyden succinctly summarizes President Kennedy's appraisal of the CIA plan: Although he had had "grave doubts" about the Cuban operation, he felt it should not be "scrapped" for a number of reasons.

To the President, the plan seemed to entail no actual aggression by the U.S., no evident risk of U.S. involvement, *little risk of failure . . .*

When he did give the "go" order, "I really thought they had a good chance," he told Sorensen. Besides, it looked like a *no-lose solution.* If a group of Castro's own countrymen could, without overt U.S. help, establish a new government, rally the people and oust Castro, all Latin America would be safer. If the exiles were forced into the mountains as guerrillas, the operation was still a *net gain* [Wyden, p. 308, italics added].

Note that Kennedy's appraisal, as summarized by Wyden, is the same as that of the key members of his team who advised him to accept the plan (see the last half of Note 3). He shared with them the overoptimistic expectation that the risks of failure and of embarrassment to the United States government were so slight that they need not be a deterrent to approving the clandestine operation. Wyden also acknowledges that during this early period of his administration, Kennedy shared with the members of his team the buoyant sense of optimism that characterized "the flowering of Camelot" (p. 316). Wyden quotes Schlesinger's analysis ("Everyone around him thought he had the Midas touch and could not lose") and adds, "His confidence in his own luck was unbounded" (p. 316).

But what about Kennedy's "grave doubts," which would seem to contradict the conclusion that he shared in his team's optimism about the chances of success? Careful examination of the doubts and skeptical comments Kennedy made at meetings with his advisers reveals that those seemingly critical comments were limited to specific details of the overall CIA plan which he wanted to improve. He did *not* raise skeptical questions about the basic plan itself or ask for independent appraisals of any of its main assumptions. If he had, he and his advisers would have had the benefit of candid evaluations of the military prospects from the Joint Chiefs of Staff and candid evaluations of the key assumptions from the Cuban specialists in the CIA (who were never consulted) and in the State Department (who were also excluded).

What Kennedy was primarily concerned about in asking for specific changes was the visibility of United States involvement and the unfavorable political damage that could result from adverse publicity, especially if the United States were branded as an aggressor. Almost all of his skeptical and critical comments were in this category. Here are the five main instances of Kennedy's critical stance: (1) in early March 1961, he told the planners that the landing site they had selected (Trinidad) would make the operation "too spectacular" (Wyden, p. 100); (2) a few days later when the CIA planners changed the landing site to the Bay of Pigs, he wanted them to "reduce the noise level" by unloading the ships at night rather than in daylight (Wyden, p. 102); (3) on March 29 at another meeting, Kennedy was still troubled by the "noise level" and asked if the large-scale air strikes were really essential (Wyden, p. 139); (4) during the meeting on April 4 at which he asked his advisers to vote and was given a go-ahead consensus, his skeptical questioning of the military planners was confined to expressing "concern that the operation would look too much like a World War II invasion," and this prompted an answer that the assaults would be relatively small, spread over four separate beaches, and carried out at night, which "seemed to make the President feel easier" (Wyden, p. 150); and (5) at a meeting on April 12, he wondered if the planned air strikes, "even as modified, were still too noisy" (Wyden, p. 163).

This limited type of doubting, which led to cosmetic changes of the basic CIA invasion plan, is not inconsistent with Wyden's overall view that the plan entailed "little risk of failure." As a matter of fact, many commentators on the military aspects of the plan assert that the changes Kennedy asked for in order to lower the political risks had the effect of increasing markedly the already serious risks of military failure. But Kennedy was apparently oblivious to those consequences, as were the members of his inner circle. And also, like others on his team, he grossly underestimated the likelihood that, despite having cut down on the noise level, the invasion would still be reported by the news media as a United States government operation and would elicit worldwide condemnation. (The planned invasion by Cuban refugees was already exposed as a CIA operation in the United States press during the week preceding the actual event.) There were also at least three other important potential risks that Kennedy and his team overlooked or seriously underestimated—the risk of instigating a prolonged civil war in Cuba with the loss of many lives, the risk of alienating Latin American countries, and the risk of pushing Castro toward a protective military alliance with the Soviet Union, culminating in Cuba becoming armed with Soviet missiles directed against the United States. (This third potential actually materialized and led to the Cuban missile crisis in 1962.)

Minimizing the major risks of an ill-conceived plan is a central feature of the *illusion of invulnerability*. When this diagnosis is made, it does not necessarily mean that those who share the illusion are totally oblivious to the risks of a very hazardous venture. Rather, it means that to some extent the major risks are being minimized on the basis of a preconscious assumption that *everything is going to work out all right because we are a special group.* When combat flyers in a cohesive air crew are assigned a hazardous target, their shared illusion of invulnerability does not take the form of denying the dangers of aircraft on the mission being shot down (such denial would be psychotic). Rather, it takes the form of a preconscious belief that "others on this dangerous mission are likely to be killed, *but not us.*" Similarly, when statesmen in a cohesive policy-making group share an illusion of invulnerability in the face of a risky venture, their preconscious belief is "if others tried to do it they might fail, *but not us.*" I surmise from all that has been reported about the exuberant confidence of Kennedy and his team, as well as their minimization of the major risks, that the leader, as well as members of the inner circle, shared an illusion of invulnerability of this kind.

When the members of a cohesive group share an illusion of invulnerability they tend to display a collusive tendency to exclude from their meetings anyone who is likely to challenge their overoptimism by calling attention to the serious risks that are being soft-pedaled. Kennedy did, in fact, exclude many potentially valuable advisers who might have been nay-sayers. On the one occasion when he invited a nay-sayer (Senator Fulbright) to present his political and moral objections at a formal meeting of his large group of advisers, he did not give the group an opportunity to discuss the objections that were being raised. Instead, he immediately called for a vote on the CIA plan. This was the meeting at which Rusk and other participants felt it was essential to "close ranks with the President." William Bundy told Wyden that at that meeting he felt that he and the other members of the executive branch of the Kennedy administration were expected "to stand with the President against Fulbright's arguments to back up the presidential effort at 'rallying the troops' to deal with the lone nay-sayer" (Wyden, p. 149). In this instance, although the leader did arrange to have the group exposed to an outsider's opposing viewpoint, he did not take the essential steps to encourage the members of the group to openly discuss and evaluate the outsider's challenge to their assumptions about the moral acceptability and the political soundness of the plan to sponsor an unprovoked military attack against a small neighboring nation.

Wyden points out that Kennedy generally took pains to avoid exposing himself and others on his team to all such challenges:

> Kennedy . . . filtered the information that went into his decision-making by stifling protest and potential resistance. Schlesinger was finally told by Bob Kennedy outright to shut up. Other nay-sayers—Bowles, Murrow, Hilsman, Meeker—were silenced by nonadmission into the inner circle. Influential potential nay-sayers—Ted Sorensen, Clark Clifford, Adlai Stevenson—were left ignorant because they were generalists or too intellectual and therefore presumably not action-minded [Wyden, pp. 316–317].

It should be emphasized that at least three other members of the in-group participated actively in the process of excluding or silencing potential dissenters—Robert Kennedy (who silenced Schlesinger), Dean Rusk (who was responsible for preventing Bowles and Hilsman from presenting their objections to Kennedy and his team), and McGeorge Bundy (who told Edward R. Murrow, the director of the United States Information Agency, that his moral and political "objections were not without validity, but nothing could be done about them" [Wyden, p. 145]). If the various articulate nay-sayers mentioned in the above quotation from Wyden had not been silenced or excluded, the illusion of invulnerability shared by Kennedy and the members of his in-group might well have been dispelled (and perhaps along with it their unexamined assumption of the morality of the planned act of aggression). Had that happened, Kennedy and the members of his in-group would most likely have engaged in a much more vigilant information search, which would have greatly increased their chances of discovering the major flaws in the basic assumptions of the ill-conceived plan.

5 Schlesinger's somewhat self-abasing confession about his failure to present his objections at the group meetings might be a symptom of persisting loyalty to the dead leader and to the group. He appears to be saying, in effect, "Don't put all the blame on President Kennedy or on the other leading members of our team." This theme is not apparent in other portions of Schlesinger's account of the Bay of Pigs fiasco, which level many serious criticisms against

the Kennedy team and is far from a whitewash. Still, at present there is no way of knowing to what extent a protective attitude colors Schlesinger's description of how the CIA's invasion plan came to be accepted at the White House. The same problem arises, of course, for all accounts by pro-Kennedy authors, especially Sorensen (who has sought to gain political office on his record as a participant on the Kennedy team and his close personal ties with the Kennedy brothers). My only solution to the problem of subtle distortions and biased reporting is to take the position that *if* the facts reported by Schlesinger, Sorensen, and the other authors are essentially accurate, my analysis of the converging pattern of this "evidence" leads to the conclusion that the groupthink hypothesis helps to account for the deficiencies in the decision-making of the Kennedy team.

6 Bureaucratic political considerations might also have contributed to the group norm of trying to keep the two new members of the team happy. The President and his senior advisers may have realized that if they asked Dulles and Bissell too many embarrassing questions and appeared to be rejecting the work of their agency, the two chiefs of the CIA might be pushed in the direction of becoming allied with the military men in the Pentagon, who were already supporting them, rather than with the Kennedy team in the White House.

Another contributing factor might have been the President's personal receptivity to the idea of taking aggressive action against Castro. Although somewhat skeptical of the plan, Kennedy may have welcomed the opportunity to make good on his campaign pledge to aid the anti-Castro rebels. According to Sorensen, the opportunity to inflict a blow against Castro was especially appealing to the President: "He should never have permitted his own deep feeling against Castro (unusual for him) and considerations of public opinion—specifically, his concern that he would be assailed for calling off a plan to get rid of Castro—to overcome his innate suspicion" (p. 343).

Obviously, these ancillary political and psychological factors are not symptoms of groupthink. But they may have reinforced the group norms conducive to concurrence-seeking and thus could be regarded in the same general category as biased leadership practices—that is, as conditions that foster groupthink.

3 *In and Out of North Korea*

1 At times, the bad news from the war front was upstaged by a dramatic policy war being fought by the military and civilian leaders of the United States government. For five months, policy battles were waged between a minority of government leaders who supported General MacArthur's demands to broaden the war and a majority who refused to authorize an all-out war against China. Finally, on April 11, 1951, the President launched his ultimate bid for a policy victory. He took the extraordinary step of dismissing General MacArthur after the general had made public statements that appeared to be disrupting the administration's plans for peace negotiations. Following the abrupt and humiliating dismissal of America's popular military leader, at a time when the public was fed up with the stalemate in Korea, a wave of suspicion and indignation swept across the country. It set in motion a new era of domestic reaction, epitomized by the irresponsible accusations of Senator Joseph McCarthy, who gained immense popular support for his charge that the Truman administration was guilty of treason for being soft on communism. This charge was deeply resented by Truman and his advisers. Ironically, it was precisely because these men had wanted to be tough on communism that they had decided to send American forces to Korea in the first place and then had attempted to destroy the power of the Communist regime of North Korea by military occupation.

Among the political losses to the Truman administration stemming from the decision to invade North Korea was the marked public reaction of antipathy to "Mr. Truman's War" during 1951 and 1952. This contributed to the smashing defeat of the Democratic party in the presidential election of 1952. Provoking the intervention of Communist China gave rise to major setbacks for American foreign relations. Communist China gained control over North Korea and increased its influence on other countries in Asia, while the

United States lost prestige and wrecked its chances of establishing economic ties and friendly diplomatic relations with the Chinese government in Peking.

2 Truman says that the warning message received from Indian Ambassador Panikkar and similar messages from Moscow, Stockholm, and New Delhi were regarded as "no more than a relay of Communist propaganda." He adds that "Mr. Panikkar had in the past played the game of the Chinese Communists fairly regularly." Furthermore, the United Nations was about to vote on the resolution authorizing MacArthur to operate in North Korea, so "it appeared quite likely that Chou En-lai's 'message' was a bald attempt to blackmail the United Nations by threats of intervention in Korea" (vol. 2, p. 363).

De Rivera comments on the reaction of Truman and his advisers to the Chinese threats in this way:

> The fact that the Foreign Minister could be trying to influence the United Nations without necessarily bluffing; the fact that good ambassadors usually are sympathetic to nations they are dealing with—without necessarily "playing their game"; the fact that with initiative and darkness a river can be crossed; the fact that there were no other diplomatic channels open to the Chinese—that there was no other way for them to deliver their threat if they had been serious—these facts were not considered.
> . . . It is interesting to note that while the threats of the Chinese Foreign Minister and the intelligence reports of Chinese troops moving toward the Yalu alarmed neither the United Nations Commander in Tokyo nor the President in Washington, they did alarm the Eighth Army Headquarters in Korea. According to [General S. L.] Marshall, the headquarters believed that the Chinese would enter the war, and accurately forecasted the order of battle along the Yalu River [pp. 146–147].

3 The Washington policy-makers increased the risks of a military clash with Communist China during October 1950 by giving General MacArthur new directives that let him decide whether to attack Chinese forces in North Korea. In mid-September, MacArthur had been instructed to extend his operations north of the 38th parallel if there was no indication of threat of Soviet or Chinese Communist entry (Truman, vol. 2, p. 359). The same cautionary proviso was repeated in a directive he received two weeks later. But on October 9, three days after MacArthur's general advance into North Korea, he was given new instructions that failed to include the cautionary proviso. None of Truman's advisers balked at the abdication of presidential control, which left everything up to MacArthur's notoriously poor judgment. Neustadt has written, "In the weeks to come he would misjudge with tragic consequences, but it cannot be charged that he exceeded his instructions" (p. 133).

4 The assumption that North Korea, China, and the Soviet Union formed a homogeneous Communist bloc, with all three Communist countries acting in concert to carry out Russia's prearranged plan for dominating the Far East, was, according to De Rivera, "a grave conceptual error on the part of the administration." De Rivera suggests that early in the Korean War (in June 1950) this undifferentiated view of the Communist world contributed to the ill-considered decision to send the United States Seventh Fleet in support of Formosa, which meant abandoning America's long-standing policy of neutrality in the Chinese civil war: "By attributing a *North Korean* attack to 'communism,' the President justified intervening in the *Chinese* Civil War" (pp. 86–87). When the Formosa move was discussed at a meeting of President Truman and his advisers, no one seems to have raised the question of whether the Formosa action might interfere with the State Department's efforts to develop good relations with the Chinese Communist leaders in order to weaken their ties with the Soviet Union. The same misconception appears to have pervaded the thinking of Truman's advisers throughout the period when the decision was made to occupy North Korea.

5 In June 1950, when the Korean War crisis arose, Kennan agreed with Acheson and others in the State Department that the United States should intervene to help South Korea, but he felt strongly that the United States should act alone, without being encumbered by involving the United Nations. Later in the summer he prepared a strong set of arguments against authorizing MacArthur's forces to cross the 38th parallel.

De Rivera points out that Kennan's exclusion from the advisory group follows a familiar pattern for dealing with a "deviant" who is qualified for group membership but who holds views that would interfere with acceptance of the norms to which everyone else in the group wants to adhere. Numerous social psychological studies show how readily a deviant is rejected by the members of a group, even though he may be capable of performing a valuable function by challenging their unwarranted assumptions. In this case, Kennan's exclusion in advance evidently saved the group from the discomfort of having to debate a number of potentially disturbing issues concerning alternative ways of viewing the Communist countries and of dealing with the war in Korea.

6 Neustadt (pp. 212–214) claims that around the time of this meeting Acheson, Marshall, and the Joint Chiefs had become sufficiently worried to believe that MacArthur should be given a new directive to consolidate his forces and to call off his planned offensive. Neustadt, on the basis of a report by Martin Lichterman, says that the military chiefs asked Acheson to inform the President but he refused on the grounds that since it was a military matter the recommendation should come from them. General Collins (1969, p. 202) denies this story. "That just isn't so," Acheson told Collins. Acheson read Collins the letter he had sent to Lichterman, which was the supposed source of the story, and it did not say what Lichterman reported. On the basis of his own observations, Collins adds, "I am positive that no such request was made to Secretary Acheson by Secretary Marshall or the JCS at any meeting attended by me" (p. 202). McLellan argues that there was no reason to assume that these men would "engage in some kind of Gaston-and-Alphonse routine about who would be the first to break the [unpleasant] news to the President" (p. 33). He adduces documentary evidence to show that Acheson did not believe that any changes in MacArthur's orders were necessary. As for the military chiefs' being reluctant to tell the President about the military risks, McLellan says that there would be no reason for them to keep the President ignorant of serious risks of which they were aware "unless we are to assume the President is the equivalent of the pre-war Japanese emperor" (p. 30).

Although there is evidence against Neustadt's claim, nevertheless the military advisers could have been quite reluctant to talk about the risks, not out of fear of incurring the President's displeasure but for other reasons.

4 *Pearl Harbor Revisited*

1 The statement by Admiral King is quoted by Morison (p. 138). In this statement, Admiral King asserted that the feeling of immunity "pervaded all ranks at Pearl Harbor." But Morison cites evidence indicating that at least some of the junior officers in the fleet believed the ships at Pearl Harbor to be far from immune; they openly discussed the danger among themselves and took active steps on their own initiative to prepare their own ships for a possible air attack (see pp. 89–91). No instances are cited of any high-ranking Navy officers at Pearl Harbor displaying comparable concern about the threat. Kimmel testified that no one on his staff and none of his other advisers ever expressed any view indicating that an attack on Pearl Harbor might be expected (*Hearings,* part 6, p. 2639). Similar testimony was given by members of Kimmel's staff. Captain McMorris, for example, said, "I can recall no officer who felt that there was a serious probability [of an air raid on Pearl Harbor]" (*Hearings,* part 22, p. 527).

2 Military commanders in Hawaii took their lead from the policy statements and warnings sent to them from Washington. But they were free to make their own decisions concerning reconnaissance and anti-aircraft preparations for a surprise attack. As we look over the list of warnings received by the military commanders and their staffs during the six months prior to the event, it is difficult to imagine that anyone in a position of military responsibility could receive such messages and continue to believe that there was no realistic possibility of a destructive Japanese attack against Pearl Harbor.

In addition to the main war warnings in the last week of November 1941, there were many other warning messages. Most important are the following, all fully documented by Wohlstetter (pp. 5–70):

November 16, 1941: United States naval combat intelligence in Hawaii reported losing track of Japanese aircraft carriers. (All six of them were proceeding toward Hawaii for the planned attack on Pearl Harbor.) From this time on, constant efforts were made to pick up Japanese signal calls that might reveal the whereabouts of the carriers. On the basis of indirect, and admittedly undependable clues, the Hawaiian Naval District decided that the carriers were probably near the Marshall Islands, more than two thousand miles away. The Navy's combat intelligence unit in the Far East District disagreed with this surmise and informed Hawaii that the missing carriers were most likely in Japanese home waters.

December 6, 1941: A message from Admiral Stark in Washington to Admiral Kimmel ordered Kimmel to authorize the destruction of secret and confidential documents now, or under later conditions of greater emergency, in American bases on outlying Pacific islands. In addition, the FBI in Hawaii reported that the local Japanese consulate had been burning papers for the past two days. (The FBI had intercepted a local telephone call from the Japanese cook at the consulate who was excitedly telling a friend or relative that all major documents were being burned inside the building.) Admiral Kimmel and his staff regarded this information as somewhat puzzling, but none of them expressed the suspicion that Japan might be taking the final steps in preparing for an attack on Hawaii.

December 7, 1941: At 6:53 A.M. the harbor control post received a message from the *Ward* stating that a hostile submarine was spotted in the wake of a United States battleship and that "we have attacked, fired upon, and dropped depth charges upon submarine operating in defensive sea area." The junior officer at the control post that morning interpreted this message as meaning that "this is it, we're in it!" and desperately telephoned all the relevant naval officers he could think of. But none of the high-ranking officers he reached thought that it could possibly be a genuine emergency. According to Wohlstetter, "Everyone else refused to believe that it was a submarine, or that the encounter indicated any immediate danger" (pp. 16–17). Admiral Kimmel and several members of his staff doubted the report when they heard it and were still waiting for confirmation when the Japanese dive bombers began the attack.

The airraid broadcast and the accompanying sights and sounds of exploding bombs were the first emergency signals perceived as such by Admiral Kimmel and the others in his advisory group. All the preceding warnings had been dismissed either as unauthentic or as pertaining to the danger of a Japanese attack elsewhere, thousands of miles away. In addition to the unheeded warning messages, there were several last-minute emergency signals that the Navy at Hawaii failed to pick up because of lack of vigilance. For example, a last-minute warning could have been obtained from the radar centers operated by the Army's aircraft warning service. Admiral Kimmel's staff had failed to remind the Army that the Navy was depending upon the radar stations for information about hostile aircraft. As it turned out, one hour before the Japanese attack started on the morning of December 7, all seven mobile radar centers in the Hawaiian islands closed down officially for the day. (They were being operated mainly as a training operation, and their working hours were from 4 A.M. to 7 A.M.) By chance, two Army privates happened to stay late at one of the radar stations, located at the northern tip of Oahu, because one of them wanted further instruction in using the equipment. At 7:02 A.M. they spotted "something completely out of the ordinary" and began plotting the massive cluster of Japanese aircraft when the flight was 137 miles north of Oahu. Since it was a "fine problem" for practicing, they continued to plot the Japanese flight until 7:30 A.M., when it was 30 miles north of Oahu, at which time they were unable to discern a clear radar pattern, so the men closed the radar station and went home.

Twenty-five minutes earlier, one of the men had managed to reach a duty officer on the telephone. This officer was inexperienced and knew nothing about radar signals, but he did know that a flight of United States B-17s was expected from the mainland that morning and felt certain that this must be what the radar operators had picked up. So he told the radar operator to forget it. At 7:55 A.M., this duty officer stepped outside the door of the radar center and saw with his own eyes the planes starting to dive-bomb Pearl Harbor, but he believed they were American planes carrying out some kind of practice exercise. He was not unique. Wohlstetter states: "The noise of the explosion was necessary before anyone identified the aircraft as Japanese" (p. 68).

3 It is conceivable that out of loyalty to Kimmel the naval commanders testifying at the various
   inquiries may have exaggerated the extent of their agreement with his judgments. But it
   seems unlikely that a dozen of the nation's highest-ranking naval officers would deliberately give a false account of what they had said at the meetings they had attended during the
   fall of 1941. Unless we are to conclude that the senior officers in the Navy group at Hawaii
   were perjuring themselves at the hearings, it seems fairly conclusive that every one of them
   shared the conviction that the limited alert was all that was necessary.

4 Peffer points out in his history of United States–Japanese relations during 1941:

>   Japan had maneuvered itself into the necessity of a life-and-death choice. It
>   could not remain where it was. To do so was to accept with resignation sentence
>   of death by slow starvation. It had either to retreat entirely, renouncing all the
>   gains it had made, or to go forward. . . . It would not, of course, wait passively
>   to starve. No nation would, least of all Japan. It would not retreat. Again, the
>   army could not do so without surrendering its ascendancy in the Japanese
>   scheme. . . . And from July, 1941, it was certain . . . that, failing some
>   miraculous intervention, war would come in the Pacific [p. 396].

5 According to W. W. Smith, Kimmel's chief of staff, Admiral Kimmel and General Short had
   joint meetings at least twice a week with some members of their respective staffs (*Hearings,*
   part 26, p. 44). Admiral Anderson, in an interview with Brownlow, described the cordial
   relations between Kimmel and Short:

>   The papers said that Short and Kimmel were not on good terms, which was a
>   complete falsification. Now I was over to see Kimmel a very few days before this
>   attack and Short was announced. . . . I got up, of course, to get out because here
>   was the senior Army officer coming to call on the senior Naval officer. Kimmel
>   said, "Sit down, Andy, don't go. Stay here!" I sat down and Short came in and
>   they greeted each other in the cordial way that honest-to-God friends would, you
>   know" [p. 88].

6 As the crisis deepened during late November and early December, Admiral Stark became
   somewhat more cautious in his personal communications, but he blew both hot and cold,
   sometimes expressing optimism and pessimism in successive sentences. For example, in his
   letter of November 23, 1941, which Admiral Kimmel received on December 3, he stated that
   the situation is grave, that both President Roosevelt and Secretary Hull think the Japanese
   might launch a surprise attack. Surely this should have underlined the seriousness of the official warnings radioed on November 24 and November 27. But Stark went on to say, "from
   many angles an attack on the Philippines would be the most embarrassing thing that could
   happen to us. There are some here who think it likely to occur. I do not give it the weight the
   others do, but I include it because of the strong feeling among some people" (*Hearings,* part
   16, p. 2224).
        Given the climate of unconcern about the security of Pearl Harbor that pervaded the
   Navy group, Stark's final statements in this letter must have meant to Admiral Kimmel, and
   to those of his advisers with whom he discussed it, that the possible threat to Pearl Harbor
   need not be taken seriously. Why bother if the chief of naval operations, who has more inside information than anyone else in the entire Navy, regards even the Philippines as an
   unlikely target?

7 In their negotiations with Japan, according to Wohlstetter, Secretary Hull and other representatives of the United States government made uncompromising demands, which greatly
   underestimated Japanese desperation and readiness to take great risks. Like the naval officers in Hawaii, the members of the War Council smugly assumed that the Japanese were
   so impressed by America's military power and production potential that they would
   carefully avoid provoking the United States into entering the war. Critics of the Roosevelt
   administration point out that if the members of the War Council had given more consideration to the options that would have been attractive to the hard-pressed Japanese military
   elite, the negotiations during the months preceding the Pearl Harbor attack might have
   been directed toward working out a diplomatic settlement mutually satisfactory to Japan
   and the United States. The heads of both the Army and the Navy in Washington took the

position that war in the Pacific should be postponed as long as possible, to give top priority to helping America's allies in Europe defeat Nazi Germany. A more open-minded view of the alternative strategies that Japan might be considering would at least have led the members of the War Council to become worried when naval intelligence lost radio contact with the Japanese carriers at a time when diplomatic relations between the two countries had broken down. Wohlstetter suggests that if they had been more upset about this development, they undoubtedly would have sounded the alarm loud and clear in tactical warnings to the Army and Navy in Hawaii.

The War Council's lack of concern about the potential danger to the Pacific Fleet was most clearly shown by the group's failure to follow up on the warnings to find out what specific preparations were being made to protect Hawaii from a surprise attack. Army and Navy headquarters also neglected to inquire on their own whether a full alert had been put into effect, as the War Council had intended. Consequently, no one on the War Council found out until after December 7 that neither Army nor Navy leaders in Hawaii had issued orders for a full alert, that they had introduced no changes at all in air patrols or reconnaissance, and that they had continued to keep anti-aircraft guns manned at only one-fourth strength.

General Short gave several members of the War Council an opportunity to learn that he had misinterpreted the war warning of November 27 to mean that the only precautions needed at Hawaii were to watch out for sabotage. He had promptly radioed back an answer: "Report department alerted to prevent sabotage. Liaison with Navy." (Quoted by Buchanan, p. 56). His answer was received in Washington early on November 28 and was promptly distributed to Secretary Stimson, General Marshall, and General Gerow (head of the Army's war plans division). All three men routinely initialed the reply and sent it to be filed away.

The threat to Pearl Harbor was not recognized as a serious one by any member of the War Council until a few hours before the attack on the morning of December 7. That morning General Marshall and Admiral Stark learned from a message decoded by MAGIC that the Japanese ambassadors in Washington were directed to submit an ultimatum (tantamount to a declaration of war) to the United States at exactly 1 P.M. Eastern Standard Time. Colonel Bratton of G-2, who transmitted the decoded message, had recognized that the specified time in Washington was the time of sunrise in Hawaii, when a dawn attack might be launched. After some debate between the general and the admiral (Stark arguing that Hawaii had already been alerted by the earlier warnings), the two military chiefs agreed to send out a last-minute warning to Hawaii and other United States bases, ordering them to be on the alert for a massive attack. If the message had been radioed promptly, it would have given the Army and Navy in Hawaii two hours advance warning, but the War Department radio was unable to contact Army headquarters in Hawaii because the office was not open that Sunday morning. Two other direct radio communications to Hawaii were available, one handled by the Navy and the other by the FBI. But the message center signal officer did not know that the message was urgent because General Marshall, evidently in his haste, had neglected to mark it urgent. So the message was routinely sent by Western Union. It arrived in Honolulu at 7:33 A.M. and was still in the hands of the Western Union messenger, who was delivering it by motor bike to Army headquarters, when the bombs started to explode.

5 *Escalation of the Vietnam War*

1 Published accounts of the Vietnam War policy decisions made by the Johnson administration are sufficiently rich in partially authenticated details to yield at least some tentative answers to the central questions that can be posed in the light of what we have already learned about the symptoms of groupthink. It is precisely by formulating and attempting to answer such questions that the full meaning of the groupthink hypothesis can be grasped. Here I am using the term "meaning" in its technical sense, as used by Carl Hempel, Abraham Kaplan, Karl Popper, and other philosophers of science. By formulating the detailed questions that need to be answered by empirical evidence to see if the groupthink hypothesis applies to a particular historic decision or series of decisions, we are specifying how it can be tested, how

factual observations can be brought to bear to determine whether a psychological interpretation of a series of historical events in terms of groupthink tendencies is confirmed or
falsified.

2 We can see the reverse trend occurring in a number of psychiatric hospitals and clinics, where
the superintendent, the clinical director, and the staff of psychiatrists function as a policy-
making group on basic issues concerning the treatment of patients. Some psychiatrists, in
their role as executives, develop a degree of bureaucratic detachment to the human consequences of their decisions that matches the attitude of Washington bureaucrats in the Pentagon. (Such attitudes among psychiatric personnel are shockingly portrayed in a documentary film, *The Titicut Follies*.) Nevertheless, the psychiatrists in a policy-making group may
become aware of the detrimental consequences of this attitude and collectively agree that
they should avoid dehumanizing the patients. When this new group norm emerges, we see a
marked change in the vocabulary used by the policy-makers. "Patients" suddenly become
"men," "women," and "children," and correspondingly more humane considerations are
introduced into the planning discussions.

3 Hoopes claims that Clark Clifford, practically single-handedly, was responsible for convincing the members of the group that they had to change their policy. This point is disputed
by John P. Roche and others. According to the Pentagon Papers, one of the major considerations that led to President Johnson's decision to seek a new road to peace in March
1968 was "the conviction of his principal advisers, particularly Secretary of Defense Clifford, that the troops requested by General Westmoreland would not make a military victory
more likely" (quoted in Sheehan et al., p. 612).

6   *The Cuban Missile Crisis*

1 When the President was not present at the group meetings, his influence was still felt to some
extent, especially because his brother usually became the discussion leader. One participant
remarked, "We knew little brother was watching," but he added that this way of conducting the meetings "had a healthy effect in stimulating real discussion," probably because "it
was less inhibiting than having the President there" (Abel, p. 58). In short, having "little
brother" around is not the same as facing "big daddy."

2 Graham Allison (pp. 124–126, 204–210) asserts that "miscommunication" and "misinformation" contributed to the Executive Committee's choice of the blockade option instead of a
surgical air strike, because the group was misinformed about the limitations of the latter by
General Le May and other military experts. Nevertheless, Allison points out that the search
for accurate information about the probable effectiveness of an air strike continued even
after the group had tentatively decided on a blockade. For example, Allison says that "Kennedy seemingly reconsidered" by calling a special meeting with Air Force experts, at which
he was informed by the commander of the Tactical Air Command that no more than 90 percent effectiveness could be expected in a surprise air strike against the Cuban missile sites.
Allison makes much of the fact that the 90 percent estimate was an underestimate based on
defective intelligence that misled the Air Force experts to assume that the "mobile" Soviet
missiles could be moved during an attack and fired from a different position. It is not clear,
however, that the President and the members of the Executive Committee were in any way
remiss in accepting this misinformation. They could not be expected to challenge such intelligence estimates at that time, and in any case 100 percent effectiveness could hardly be
expected of a complicated military operation carried out by large numbers of men who had
never before carried out comparable missions under combat conditions.

   Members of the Executive Committee evidently did not rest content with the
discouraging estimates by the Air Force experts but continued their search for information
on the effectiveness of air strikes after the blockade option was chosen. They turned up
more optimistic estimates from civilian experts early enough to add surgical air strikes to

their list of options well before the missile crisis ended. Nor did the members of the Executive Committee fail to detect that the Air Force generals were giving misleading answers to questions about a *surgical* air strike because they were trying to sell the *massive* air strike they favored. "By the end of the first week," Allison says, "the misunderstanding became apparent to several of the leaders [in the Executive Committee]" (p. 125).

3 Albert and Roberta Wohlstetter suggest that President Kennedy's cautious, step-by-step efforts to put off a direct military confrontation with the Russians may reflect the effects of the "enormous consequences" that the President knew could issue from his chosen course of action (p. 19). The same consideration may apply to the members of the policy-making group. Nevertheless, awareness of the possibility of nuclear war does not necessarily induce in all high-level government groups a cautious choice of steps that will postpone a dangerous confrontation. The Joint Chiefs of Staff knew perfectly well about the "enormous consequences" of a military confrontation; nevertheless from the beginning to the end of the Cuban missile crisis they consistently urged a massive attack against Cuba and were willing to gamble that Russia would not retaliate with a nuclear attack against the United States. Allison (p. 206) calls attention to the fact that even on the Sunday the crisis ended, right after the Russians had agreed to remove the missiles from Cuba, the Air Force chief of staff still advised that the United States government should "attack Monday in any case" (R. Kennedy, p. 119).

 Nathan (1975) takes a position quite different from the Wohlstetters'. He believes that the psychological stress generated by the threat of nuclear war precluded sound decision-making. Nathan says that "the Kennedy Administrations' shimmering hour—the Cuban missile crisis—has just begun to have its luster tarnished by critics" (p. 256). He adds that most of the revisionist critiques "are rather polemical and thin" (p. 256). It seems to me that his own critique of the way the decision was arrived at suffers from exactly the same two shortcomings (although he makes some impressive points about how the Cuban missile crisis subsequently has been misused by Kennedy's successors as a model of crisis management for dealing with international conflicts). Nathan offers no evidence but infers that the members of the Kennedy group could not have done a very good job of weighing the alternatives because some of them have acknowledged that during those trying thirteen days, they were worried about what might happen and at times were not only apprehensive but also fatigued from the strain, the long hours, and the pressures. Men under stress, Nathan would have us believe, "are scarcely capable of considered judgment" (p. 259). The available evidence from behavioral science research, as well as from this case study of the Cuban missile crisis, does not bear out any such generalization. (See Janis and Mann, 1977.)

7 *The Making of the Marshall Plan*

1 The Truman Doctrine was widely praised in the American press as a constructive effort to insure the sovereignty of the so-called free countries of Europe, which desperately needed economic aid and were threatened by the growing coercive pressures of the Soviet Union. But it was also severely criticized. Political conservatives believed the Truman Doctrine gave carte blanche to conniving foreign politicians who would dupe America. Some liberals and leftists accused the Truman administration of trying to buy its way into a position of control over the small countries of Europe in the name of averting the alleged "Communist menace." Additional criticisms have subsequently been presented and documented by Williams and other revisionist historians (Barnet, Bernstein, Gardner, Kolko and Kolko, and La Febre), who retrospectively see the Truman Doctrine as a major step toward the polarization of Europe and as an ideological excuse for bolstering the ultra-rightist, reactionary regimes in Greece and Turkey in an effort to preserve and expand American foreign trade. Spanier and other historians dispute the revisionists' evidence and defend the Truman Doctrine as a justifiable countermove to Soviet postwar expansion.

 Whether the truth lies on the side of the critics or the supporters of the Truman Doctrine is not an issue that is likely to be easily settled. It suffices for our purposes to recognize that the doctrine inaugurated a period of innovative ferment in the United States government, especially in the State Department, and culminated in the formulation of the Marshall Plan.

2 In his account of how the Marshall Plan was evolved, Dean Acheson gives relatively little credit to Kennan or his group (perhaps as a consequence of long-standing disagreements between the two men on other policy issues). Acheson claims that he himself and Will Clayton were responsible for the main work done on the Marshall Plan in the State Department. He acknowledges that Kennan's group played a role but characterizes Kennan's report as "more cautious than Clayton's [memorandum], dwelling more on difficulties and dangers" (p. 231).

    Jones, who was also an insider, attributes considerably greater importance to the work of Kennan's group. He gives a picture that is similar to the one we get from Kennan's *Memoirs*. Clayton's major contribution, according to Jones, was to give a vivid account of the economic chaos in Europe, which imparted a sense of urgency for taking immediate action. When Secretary Marshall called a meeting for evaluating policy proposals, according to Jones, it was mainly "to consider with Kennan the Policy Planning Staff's memorandum on the problem of reconstruction in Europe" (p. 249). Jones also asserts that what the Kennan report said about long-term plans was "reproduced almost literally" in Secretary Marshall's Harvard speech, which launched the Marshall Plan (p. 250). In that speech, "Whole parts of the Kennan memorandum and many of Clayton's phrases and word-pictures are clearly visible" (Jones, p. 255).

3 Dean Acheson, who played a central role in initiating work on the Marshall Plan and in gaining congressional approval for its adoption, claims that Secretary Marshall was "wholly right" in stating that the purpose of the plan was to combat "hunger, poverty, desperation and chaos." But he adds that this type of statement was not sufficient to sell the plan to Congress and to influential members of the American public:

> I have probably made as many speeches and answered as many questions about the Marshall Plan as any man alive, except possibly Paul Hoffman, and what citizens and the representatives in Congress alike always wanted to learn in the last analysis was how Marshall aid operated to block the extension of Soviet power and the acceptance of Communist economic and political organization and alignment. Columnists and commentators might play with bloodless words and conceptions like projectors of silent moving pictures, but the bulk of their fellow citizens were unimpressed [Acheson, p. 233].

4 When asked what would happen if the Soviets decided to come in, Kennan recommended, according to his own account, just to "play it straight" (p. 360). But a number of historians suggest that in saying that, Kennan was not playing straight. There are numerous indications that the seemingly open invitation to the Soviet Union was little more than a propaganda device based on the shrewd calculation that the Soviet leaders would promptly refuse to cooperate. Their refusal would put the onus on them rather than on the Americans for whatever contentions might arise between the eastern and western sectors of Europe. Patterson, for example, says, "Many Europeans and Americans interviewed in the 'Marshall Plan Project' considered the American invitation a gesture and diplomatic finesse, placing the burden of rejection on the Soviet Union" (p. 101). Patterson's surmise is borne out by a candid statement in the memoirs of an insider, Charles E. Bohlen (p. 91). Nevertheless, these commentators do not question the genuineness of the open-ended invitation to Poland, Czechoslovakia, and other countries in the Soviet orbit.

5 Paul G. Hoffman, who filled the role of director of the Economic Cooperation Administration, the agency that implemented the Marshall Plan, has also commented on the excellent quality of the Harriman Committee's "well conceived" report and its "crucial" role in gaining acceptance for the plan from interested sectors of business, labor, agriculture, and the general public. Hoffman adds that one man associated with the Harriman Committee, more than anyone else, was responsible for the quality of the committee's report. That man was Richard M. Bissell, Jr., a professor of economics at the Massachusetts Institute of Technology, who was appointed the full-time executive secretary of the Harriman Committee and performed the heroic task of coordinating and synthesizing the work of the commit-

tee. This same man subsequently became deputy director of the Central Intelligence Agency and during the Kennedy administration was mainly responsible for coordinating (perhaps it would be more accurate to say miscoordinating) the work on the ill-conceived Bay of Pigs invasion plan. Here again we find that a hero in a group of critical evaluators can become an anti-hero in a group of consensus-seekers. The performance of a man with high capabilities evidently can deteriorate markedly when he becomes a member of a policy-planning group in which groupthink tendencies are dominant.

8   The Groupthink Syndrome

1 The study by Philip Tetlock (1980) sampled passages of speeches by the President of the United States and the Secretary of State for three of the groupthink decisions described in Chapters 2, 3, and 5 of this book—the Bay of Pigs invasion, escalation of the Korean War, and escalation of the Vietnam War. Using a systematic content analysis technique, he compared those speeches with the speeches made for the two nongroupthink decisions described in Chapters 6 and 7—the Cuban missile crisis and the Marshall Plan. Tetlock found that when the leaders were announcing and explaining the groupthink decisions, their speeches not only obtained significantly lower scores on a measure of cognitive complexity, but also showed a higher frequency of unqualified favorable comments about the United States and its allies, which suggests that they were manifesting the use of positive stereotypes about their own group and its supporters. There was no significant difference, however, in the relative number of unfavorable comments about Communist states and their allies that might be indicative of negative stereotypes of opponents. Although the first two findings support the groupthink hypothesis, the latter finding does not. There appears to have been an absence of negative stereotypes of rival nations in the thinking of the political leaders at the time when they were preparing their public speeches, even though the thinking that went into the policy decision itself may have been dominated by the symptoms of groupthink. It is conceivable, of course, that leaders are fairly skilled at public relations and, as diplomatic statesmen, deliberately avoid mentioning the negative stereotypes of opposing groups in the texts of their speeches. In any case, Tetlock's main findings imply that even if the leaders are striving to present themselves publicly as wise policy-makers who have looked into all the complexities of the issues involved, they nevertheless are unable to avoid being relatively simple-minded in what they say to the entire world about their decision when it is a product of groupthink.

   Tetlock's study is a pioneering contribution that provides a model for carrying out comparative case studies in a systematic and objective way. Such studies can supply dependable evidence pertinent to hypotheses about the causes of groupthink as well as its consequences.

2 Among the examples of the reassurance Chamberlain received from members of his inner circle are several described in his diary entries for September 1938, when he and the other members were planning for a summit conference with Hitler to settle the Czechoslovak crisis. Chamberlain reports that he was not sure at first that the plan would succeed. After Horace Wilson suggested it to him, Chamberlain talked it over with Simon, Hoare, and Halifax. According to Chamberlain's private diary, Halifax, unlike the others, was hesitant: The plan was "so unconventional and daring that it rather took Halifax's breath away" (Feiling, p. 357). But then, Chamberlain adds, he decided not to abandon the plan because the response from Henderson, the member of the inner circle stationed in Berlin, encouraged him to pursue it. On September 3, 1938, with Halifax's unencouraging reaction still in mind, Chamberlain was far from enthusiastic about the new plan: "I hope all the time," he wrote in his diary, "that it won't be necessary to try it" (Feiling, p. 357). But by September 11, after further discussions with members of the inner circle, he was eagerly looking forward to "the opportunity for bringing about a complete change in the international situation." By that time, the only risk he mentions in his diary is that "Hitler might act so unexpectedly [against Czechoslovakia] as to forestall it" (Feiling, pp. 360–361).

9   *The Watergate Cover-up*

1 The participants have consistently disagreed with each other about who approved of the
Watergate break-in plan. Mitchell, for example, contradicts Magruder and LaRue by
claiming that Liddy's wild plans had to do only with surveillance at the Democratic Conven-
tion in Miami and were not accepted at any of the meetings. Haldeman (1978, pp. 220–222),
who was President Nixon's Chief of Staff, speculates that Liddy was originally delegated to
work on the plans by his former boss, Charles Colson, one of Nixon's White House aides,
who, in turn, had been given a direct order by the President to get information about
Democratic Party Chairman Larry O'Brien (whose Watergate office was bugged).
Specifically, according to Haldeman, Nixon wanted to find out what O'Brien might be
doing in exchange for an alleged retainer of $180,000 from multimillionaire Howard
Hughes. But since Liddy was currently working for the Committee to Re-elect the President, he would have had to obtain approval from the Committee's Chairman, John Mitchell, or his delegate in order to obtain the tens of thousands of dollars needed to finance his
mission. At that particular time, according to Haldeman, Mitchell was beset by personal
problems concerning his wife's acute depression and alcoholism as well as by the complicated political problems posed by his new post, and he may have carelessly authorized
Liddy to use his team of ex-CIA agents to carry out the Watergate break-in without checking into the details of the foolhardy mission.

2 The other six contributors to *Harper's* October 1974 symposium on "Rulers v Reality" were
James Boren, Art Buchwald, Victor Gold, Michael Novak, Murray N. Ruthbard, and
Peregrine Worsthorne.

3 Theodore H. White in *Breach of Faith* (1975), a detailed history of Watergate and the fall of
Nixon, discusses a number of causal factors but says almost nothing at all about group
dynamics. The closest he comes to this type of explanation is when he mentions, in the context of talking about the "mean side" of Nixon's character, that Haldeman, Colson, and
other of Nixon's associates in the White House may have brought out the worst in him. For
example, White quotes without comment the following remark by Leonard Garment,
which vaguely hints at the possibility that group processes may have played a role in the
cover-up decisions: "There were people around him who brought out in him and each
other . . . a set of negative qualities which, instead of cancelling each other out, multiplied
each other" (White, p. 163). Such remarks suggest that it is worthwhile to examine the
cover-up decision made by the Nixon team from the standpoint of group dynamics.
        In a popular book, *Before the Fall* (pp. 272–277), William Safire discusses my group-
think hypothesis. His observations, however, are limited to the period before 1972 and pertain to decisions about issues other than the Watergate cover-up. He claims that during the
pre-Watergate period, symptoms of groupthink were sometimes but not always manifested
by Nixon and his group (by which he apparently means not just the top group of policy-
makers but the extended staff, including men like Herbert Klein, Daniel Patrick Moynihan,
Patrick Buchanan, and Safire himself, all of whom he says were labeled as "house
oddballs" and "indulged as iconoclasts"). Safire emphasizes that symptoms of groupthink
were *not* displayed on certain issues. For example, Nixon's team did not have an illusion of
invulnerability with regard to winning the next election (they felt that they were "winners by
an eyelash in 1968" and "we would likely win or lose by an eyelash in 1972"). On foreign
policy issues, according to Safire, there was also a great deal of realistic vigilance. On the
other hand, the dangers of "starting a 'plumbers' unit to protect secrecy" and the "unseen
risks of letting an antiscoundrel force turn into a personal secret police" were regularly
overlooked. Haldeman, according to Safire, helped to prevent groupthink on foreign
policy issues and also on certain domestic issues by guarding against one-sided presentations that left out conflicting views about the available options. But Safire goes on to say
that Haldeman did not function as "a guardian of open options" when it came to handling
leaks and various excesses in the use of presidential power to attack political opponents:

> Where the inner circle's groupthink and paranoid style did reinforce each other
> disastrously was on attitudes, but nobody thought to guard against that.
>   The attitude that fire had to be fought with fire, "leaks" with "plumbers,"
> political opponents with the full range of Government pressures, that threats

were of such magnitude that they called up the most severe response—unfortunately, this was never "staffed out," to use Haldeman's favorite phrase, and there is where the programmers needed "input" above all.

What Safire says about groupthink during the period preceding the Watergate break-in is compatible with my assumption that the illusion of invulnerability and other symptoms of groupthink can be displayed when a policy-making group is dealing with one type of issue (such as undermining the power of a set of political opponents) and not necessarily on other issues (such as foreign policy). My theoretical analysis of groupthink, as represented in Figure 10–1 (page 244) indicates that the same group can be expected to show groupthink at one time and not at another time, depending upon whether certain conditions are present that facilitate or counteract collective uncritical thinking.

4 All of Nixon's key aides who participated in the Watergate cover-up were judged by courts of law to be responsible for their illegal actions and were given jail sentences.

5 Raven (1974) surmised that four factors in addition to groupthink contributed to the White House group's readiness to pursue a risky cover-up policy. One was the factional disputes, especially between Haldeman's subgroup in the White House and Mitchell's subgroup in the Department of Justice, which contributed to their lack of moral restraint as well as their willingness to take extreme risks in order to attain tactical political gains. Another factor was an excessive sense of authorization for whatever actions the White House group regarded as expedient, derived from the long-standing tradition of emphasizing the legitimacy of their political goals. A third factor was the routinization of expedient political actions to such a degree that moral issues were not raised in the group discussions. The fourth contributing factor was the habitual tendency of the group members to dehumanize outsiders, which reinforced their propensity to manipulate other people without regard for legal, ethical, or humanitarian constraints. All four of these factors, it seems to me, are important causal factors in their own right but they are likely to exert their influence most powerfully in the decision-making activities of a group when the members are striving for concurrence, as manifested by the symptoms of groupthink.

In his account of three of the contributory factors—authorization, routinization, and dehumanization—Raven draws upon a theoretical analysis by Herbert Kelman (1973) of the conditions under which moral restraints against antisocial actions are reduced. Although Kelman's analysis is derived from studies of extreme deviations from elementary humanitarian standards, such as the Nazi extermination camps and the My Lai massacre, it is formulated in general terms that would apply also to deviations on the part of democratic governments and any other type of group or organization.

Raven and Rubin (1977) point out that in groups characterized by strong conformity pressures there is likely to be a "runaway norm," which leads the members to adopt more and more extreme positions.

With respect to runaway norms . . . it appears that the decisions of the Nixon group were often characterized by pressures to at least equal, and preferably exceed, the group average. One norm that had to be equaled or exceeded was taking a tough stand against Nixon's "enemies." One could not appear to be softer than the group average or more concerned about the moral implications of the issue of dealing with the press, liberals, intellectuals, or other such groups. Exceeding the norm was the path to success, while appearing softer than the group average was the road to exile from the Nixon group [pp. 431–432].

The runaway norm phenomenon was especially prominent among Nixon's men before and after the Watergate break-in, according to Raven and Rubin, because the members of each faction were attempting not only to be tougher than each other but also to be tougher than the rival faction.

6 In Wong-McCarthy's coding scheme, comments bearing on the interests of Nixon as an individual rather than as President and leader of the group, or pertaining to the goals of just one particular individual in the group, are not considered as pertinent and therefore are not included in his agreement scores. Also excluded are pseudoagreements, such as "right" and "okay" in response to either purely factual statements or utterances that contain nothing to agree or disagree about.

Wong-McCarthy reported that during the first month of "bombshells," when the group was cohesive and the members were participating in concerted action in response to external threats of exposure, the overall measure of concurrence shows that the relative percentage of agreements increased. This was during the month from late February to late March 1973. In contrast, during the next month, as the group was disintegrating the measure of concurrence shows a marked decline. The overall difference in concurrence scores between the first and second of the two months that are being compared proved to be statistically significant.

7 Ulrich Neisser (1981) made a study of Dean's memory by examining errors in the testimony he gave under oath in 1973 to the Senate Watergate Committee. The study deals with Dean's recall of two of the most crucial Oval Office conversations (September 15, 1972, and March 21, 1973). When Neisser assessed the accuracy of Dean's testimony by comparing it with the objective verbatim records obtained from the unedited transcripts of the White House tapes, he found that Dean had misremembered dates and many important substantive details. Sometimes Dean did not recall correctly the gist of what Nixon had said or of what he himself had said. Nevertheless, Neisser observed that the main story line of Dean's testimony was basically correct.

In this book, I do not make any use of Dean's 1973 testimony from memory about the White House conversations; rather, I rely on the unedited transcripts. I do, however, make some incidental use of Dean's book, published in 1977, in which he corrected many of the memory errors in his earlier testimony by consulting the unedited transcripts, by conducting interviews with other participants, and by examining pertinent notes and documents that had not been available to him in 1973.

8 It is conceivable that, despite the absence of any explicit discussions of the morality of their actions, Nixon and his aides shared a belief in the inherent morality of their group which is difficult to discern because it was manifested only indirectly. For example, Colson seems to have alluded to a basic assumption of inherent morality that never needed to be talked about or even privately thought about:

> I believed what I was doing was right. The President, I am convinced, believed he was acting in the national interest. . . . While I thought I was serving him well and faithfully, I now recognize I was not—at least in the sense that I never really questioned whether what he wanted done was right or proper. [Quoted in *Newsweek,* July 1, 1974, p. 17.]

There are a few statements in the records that appear to be moralistic rationalizations implying that the President and his men are on the side of the angels. For example, on the evening of March 21, 1973, the day Dean gave his "cancer within the presidency" report to Nixon and told him that Haldeman, Ehrlichman, and Dean might be sent to jail for various criminal actions, Nixon, dictating his daily diary into a recording machine while alone, made a comment that could be construed as a rationalization to the effect that their illegal actions were morally justified: "I feel for all the people involved here, because they were all, as I pointed out to them in the meeting in the EOB this afternoon, *involved for the very best of motives."* (Quoted by White, p. 202. Italics added.)

The next day, when Nixon and Haldeman were discussing one of the obstructions of justice that Dean had so forcefully brought to their attention—using the White House slush fund to pay the Watergate burglars to keep silent—they told each other that there is nothing wrong with doing so. "God damn it," Nixon said, ". . . it's only right for people to raise money for them . . . we're sorry for them. We do it out of compassion . . . There's no report requirement or any kind of requirement [for such payments]." Haldeman vehemently agreed: ". . . it doesn't seem to me that we are obstructing justice, for Christ sake" (Transcript, March 22, 1973, A.M.).

About two weeks later, when Nixon, Haldeman, and Ehrlichman were deciding to make a public statement that John Dean was the only one in the White House responsible for the cover-up, the President stated a similar rationalization implying that Dean's crimes on behalf of the Nixon team were excusable on moral grounds: "What Dean did, he did with all conscience in terms that the higher good . . ." (*Presidential Transcripts,* April 14, 1973, quoted by White, p. 212; the edited *Presidential Transcripts* attributes this statement to Haldeman rather than Nixon). In any such instance, one cannot be sure whether their vehement assertions about the higher good and about humanitarian values like compassion are moral judgments being sincerely expressed with righteous indignation, or are just another one of their self-serving public relations scripts that they think ought to put a stop to hostile critics who are annoying the powerful personages in the White House with accusations of illegality.

Theodore H. White, having described Nixon's successful reelection campaign in *The Making of the President—1972,* attempts in a sequel on the unmaking of the President (*Breach of Faith*) to explain why Nixon and his aides became criminals. He discusses and documents many specific contributing factors, but the main answer he comes to at the end of his book is speculative; it focuses on the shared conviction of the men in the inner circle that whatever they did for the good of the team was morally good. This is the way White formulates his conclusions:

> To trace the answers to the question of "Why?" one must accept the political reality that Richard Nixon and his men were . . . carrying on an ideological war. Because they felt their purpose was high and necessary and the purpose of their enemies dangerous or immoral, he and his men believed that the laws did not bind them—or that the laws could legitimately be bent [p. 328].

From my own reading of the transcripts, I can see that there is some basis for White's surmise, although the evidence is far from convincing. Each time the group was deciding to carry out one or another of the cover-up activities, the members seem to have taken it for granted that they were justified in taking "tough" actions, irrespective of whether outside judges might regard them as unethical or breaking the law. But inferences about the group's alleged tacit assumptions of morality cannot be well documented with a series of unequivocal quotations from the White House transcripts because, as I have already stated, the members hardly ever spoke about the moral justifications for any of their actions except when they were figuring out their public relations tactics to prevent or mollify public criticism.

9 Perhaps Haldeman was simply helping Nixon to "let off steam" and had no intention of pursuing Nixon's suggestion to engage in the criminal action of using "thugs" to beat up the protesters. In his memoirs, *The Ends of Power,* Haldeman says that he sometimes managed to control "the dark impulses in Nixon's mind" (p. 92) by talking to the President as though he was going along with his hostile orders without actually implementing them:

> I soon realized that this President had to be protected from himself. Time and again I would receive petty vindictive orders. "Hugh Sidey is to be kept off Air Force One." (Sidey was *Time's* man.) Or even, once or twice, "All the press is barred from Air Force One." (Pool representatives of the press accompanied the President on every trip.) Or, after a Senator made an anti–Vietnam War speech: "Put a 24-hour surveillance on that bastard." And on and on and on. If I took no action, I would pay for it. The President never let up. He'd be on the intercom buzzing me ten minutes after such an order. "What have you done about Sidey?" I'd say, "I'm working on it," and delay and delay until Nixon would one day comment, with a sort of half-smile on his face, "I guess you never took action on that, did you?"
> "No."
> "Well, I guess it was the best thing."

There is no way to tell whether Haldeman's elaborations of Nixon's plan to call in "thugs" on May 5, 1971, is another such instance or whether he was genuinely considering the plan without regard for its illegality and inhumanity. One cannot even be certain that Haldeman's claim that he merely played along with Nixon's dark impulses is not a self-serving falsehood designed to explain away some of the nasty conversations that he knew were on the tapes and that might subsequently be made public, like the conversation in question.

Even if we assume that Haldeman did not really mean what he was saying about murderous thugs and that Nixon knew that Haldeman would not implement his wild and destructive plan, it is still instructive to consider the implications of the hostile fantasy they were constructing together. Implicit in that conversation, even if it is sheer fantasy, is the notion that they relished the idea of getting away with murderous attacks against domestic groups that opposed their policies.

10 A weak version of the groupthink hypothesis would assert that groupthink (or the set of conditions for concurrence-seeking) was one of several major causes of the series of lawless and self-defeating decisions that led to the downfall of the Nixon team. A stronger version, which I believe is fairly well supported by the case study evidence presented in this chapter, would assign a more primary causal role to groupthink. According to the stronger version, the Watergate cover-up fiasco would be interpreted as follows: With all the predispositional, subcultural, and other background factors operating, Nixon and his key aides might well have initiated the first steps in the cover-up during the summer of 1972 without adequately considering the potentially adverse consequences. Those predispositional and background factors might also have inclined them to persist in the cover-up as long as it seemed expedient. But if the conditions making for groupthink had not been present, the group would not have continued to regard the unsuccessful containment policy as expedient in the face of increasingly threatening events, to the point where they would suffer completely disastrous consequences. Because the conditions making for concurrence-seeking were present, according to this interpretation, the group failed to change its policy and to cuts its losses long before the end of March 1973, when it should have been apparent to the White House trio, as it was to John Dean, that their cover-up attempts could no longer be expected to succeed.

10   *Generalizations*

1 Figure 10–1 indicates that when consequential policy decisions are being made, groupthink can be expected to have unfavorable effects from the group's own standpoint because it leads to outcomes that are not likely to be successful with regard to attaining the group's objectives (box E). Longley and Pruitt (1980) call attention quite correctly to the potentially positive effects of concurrence-seeking under certain very special conditions, which are entirely different from the circumstances of the groupthink-dominated decisions I have been talking about. Their point is that when consensus is reached *after careful deliberations,* the *brief* appearance of symptoms of groupthink could enable the group to stop discussing the problem they have just finished solving and move on to other pressing matters. This point is essentially the same as a view presented by Janis and Mann (1977) about what happens to vigilant decision-makers when they reach the final stage of commitment, after they have already gone through all the essential earlier stages for sound decision-making—carefully surveying alternatives, exhaustively searching for information, examining the pros and cons for each alternative in an unbiased way, and finally, facing up to the question, "which course of action will best meet all the essential requirements to solve the problem?" After doing all that, according to Janis and Mann (p. 194), a vigilant decision-maker is likely "to bolster, in a highly biased way, the one [alternative] he regards as best"; "the decision-maker's pattern of vigilance may give way to defensive avoidance at the point where he loses hope of finding a better solution" than the one he has so painstakingly arrived at. Janis and Mann (pp. 284–286) add that the bolstering (or cognitive dissonance reduction) that occurs as a result of the defensive avoidance pattern in this final stage, just prior to implementation of a new decision, can have the functional value of stabilizing the decision, enabling the decision-maker to become more fully committed to it, to implement it wholeheartedly, and to continue to act in accordance with it despite the deterrence of minor setbacks.

Since Janis and Mann state that groupthink can be "a collective form of defensive avoidance" (p. 129), their position is compatible with the point emphasized by Longley and Pruitt: the symptoms of groupthink would have a positive function if they were to occur after a *mature* consensus has been reached at the end of thorough deliberations that include vigilant search and appraisal of the alternatives. But I must emphasize that the model of groupthink in Figure 10–1 (which is based on a figure in Janis and Mann, p. 132) pertains *only to instances where the symptoms of groupthink pervade most or all of the group's deliberations on the problem at hand, which makes for premature consensus characterized by the symptoms of defective decision-making* (box D in Figure 10–1).

In their discussion of the detrimental effects that occur when groupthink contributes to premature consensus, Longley and Pruitt make use of an important distinction developed by Lawrence and Lorsch (1969) between "differentiation" (which involves proliferation of ideas and debate within the decision-making group) and "integration" (which involves efforts of the decision-making group to achieve unity), both of which are needed for effective policy-making. Groupthink, according to Longley and Pruitt, can be thought of as a decision process that suffers from too much integration too soon, at the cost of too little differentiation.

Longley and Pruitt also emphasize the obvious point that premature consensus as a result of groupthink is not necessarily detrimental to a group's objectives and could even be helpful for certain trivial or routine decisions—minor problems of the type described by Katz and Kahn (1978) that can easily be solved by applying a readily available frame of reference, a past precedent, or an existing general policy, in contrast to major dilemmas requiring reformulation of policy and innovative solutions. It seems plausible to assume that the more trivial the issue, the greater the likelihood that groupthink will have the beneficial effect of making for a speedy consensus on an acceptable, or at least harmless, solution, which can avoid wasting the precious time of high-level executives. Longley and Pruitt agree with my main point, however, that groupthink has detrimental effects when it pervades the group's deliberations about *consequential* issues that implicate vital group goals and values, which is the only type of decision with which this book is concerned. Figure 10–1 is not intended to be applicable to the two types of exceptions they talk about—groupthink only during the final phase of deliberations about consequential alternatives (after vigilant search and appraisal) and groupthink throughout all the deliberations on relatively trivial issues. Rather, the figure is designed to summarize the causes and consequences of the groupthink syndrome *when it pervades the group's deliberations on a consequential policy choice.* It is for such choices that the figure indicates that when a chief executive and his advisers engage in defective decision-making (box D) as a result of the symptoms of groupthink (box C), their failure to engage in adequate search and critical appraisal is likely to have the *detrimental* effect of decreasing the group's chances of attaining its goals and of avoiding fiascoes (box E).

2 Some of the implications of the distinction between deliberate conformity based on fear of recrimination and nondeliberate conformity based on concurrence-seeking tendencies are illustrated in the diagram below.

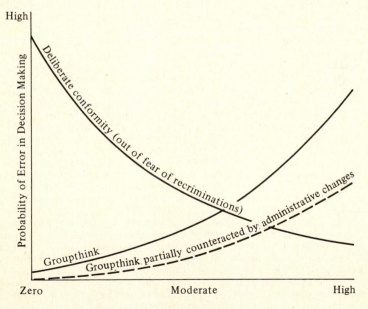

Hypothetical curves showing expected relationships between cohesiveness of the group and errors from deliberate conformity and from groupthink tendencies.

The inverse relation between cohesiveness and deliberate conformity out of fear of recrimination is represented by the descending curve in the diagram. In contrast, a positive relation between groupthink tendencies and cohesiveness is represented by the ascending (solid-line) curve. The assumption that groupthink tendencies can be partially counteracted is represented by the dashed line, which shows the expected decrease in groupthink tendencies from various administrative changes that meet the conditions for preventing or counteracting concurrence-seeking tendencies. (The dashed line could also represent the lower degree of concurrence-seeking expected when cohesiveness is based on enhancement of competence and other task-oriented values rather than on purely social rewards of friendship and prestige.) When none of the conditions that counteract groupthink are present, the combination of the two conformity curves (deliberate conformity out of fear of recrimination and concurrence-seeking) will produce a U-shaped curve, with the optimal level falling somewhere in the middle range of cohesiveness, where deliberate conformity is substantially lower than at zero cohesiveness but where concurrence-seeking tendencies have not yet become very strong. By optimal level, I mean the degree of cohesiveness that gives rise to the fewest errors in decision-making. The optimal level corresponds to the lowest point on the combined U-shaped curve, which, for two combinable curves like those shown in the diagram, occurs near the point where they intersect. When groupthink is partially counteracted, the combination of the curve for groupthink tendencies (the dashed line) with the curve for deliberate conformity results in a U-shaped curve whose lowest point is much farther to the right; that is, the optimal level is at a higher level of cohesiveness. Theoretically speaking, if groupthink could be eliminated, there would be nothing to add to the curve for deliberate conformity, and the optimal level would be at the highest possible degree of cohesiveness. The main point is that the more effectively groupthink is counteracted, the higher will be the optimal level of cohesiveness.

3 Myers and Lamm (1977) discuss the dozens of laboratory experiments carried out during the 1960s that purported to demonstrate that the average individual was more prone to take risks after participating in a group discussion than when making a decision on his or her own. They emphasize that more recent findings and analyses call into question the generality of the so-called risky-shift tendency. Their analysis of the accumulated evidence points to a group polarization tendency such that the group decision enhances whichever point of view, risky or conservative, is initially dominant within the group. They add the following comment about groupthink:

> Some of the literature cited presents experimental demonstrations of groupthink processes which Irving Janis . . . has proposed to help explain decision fiascoes . . . For example, his suggestion that group members "show interest in facts and opinions that support their initially preferred policy and take up time in their meetings to discuss them, but they tend to ignore facts and opinions that do not support their initially preferred policy" . . . is confirmed by a recent finding that discussion arguments more decisively favor the dominant alternative than do written arguments [Myers and Lamm, 1977].

4 One implication of the speculative notions about elation and the sense of omnipotence is that members of a cohesive policy-making group would actually enjoy undergoing an external crisis requiring drastic action against an enemy. But obtaining evidence of such reactions among government policy-makers is difficult because no responsible government official would be likely to admit publicly that he enjoys having his country plunged into a crisis that brings it to the brink of war. However, positive reactions of elation have occasionally been reported by leading participants in nonmilitary battles over social issues. Romain Rolland, for example, has described his elation in response to the upsurge of protest among French liberals who displayed a remarkable degree of unity in attacking the French military establishment at the time of the Dreyfus affair. In February 1898, when the Dreyfusards were mobilized by the opening of the sensational trial of Emile Zola, who had accused the French military authorities of a frame-up, Romain wrote in his diary: "I would rather have this life of combat than the mortal calm and mournful stupor of these last years. God give me struggle, enemies, howling crowds, all the combat of which I am capable." Senator Ranc, another supporter of Dreyfus, recalled that during that period, "It was exciting; one felt alive; nothing is so good as a time of action, in combat in the consciousness of the cause" (quoted in Tuchman, 1966, pp. 204–205).

5 The explanatory hypothesis implicitly assigns a secondary role to the structural faults of the organization (box B–1 in Figure 10–1). Those structural features can be regarded as moderating variables involving the presence or absence of organizational constraints that could counteract the concurrence-seeking tendency when it is evoked in a cohesive policy-making group by the incentives arising from the provocative situational conditions of external or internal stress (box B–2).

The explanatory hypothesis, with its emphasis on the primary role of internal or external sources of stress, has an important implication concerning instances of groupthink in situations of relatively low stress from external threats. Here I am referring to such examples as Admiral Kimmel's complacent group of naval commanders at Pearl Harbor when they ignored ominous warning signs during the late summer of 1941 and Nixon's complacent White House group when they engineered the Watergate cover-up in June 1972. For these and any other instances of groupthink occurring under conditions of apparently low external stress, the explanatory hypothesis leads us to expect that the incentives for concurrence-seeking must have arisen from low self-esteem induced in the members of the group by one or another of the three types of provocative circumstances—recent failures, excessive difficulties on current decision-making tasks, or moral dilemmas. If careful examination of instances of groupthink in situations of low stress from external threat fail to confirm this expectation, the proposed hypothesis will have to be regarded as an inadequate explanation of the incentives for groupthink. According to the explanatory hypothesis, there should be no instances of groupthink when the level of stress from internal sources (involving potential lowering of self-esteem) as well as external sources of threat (involving fear of failure or defeat) is *consistently low* among the members of a cohesive policy-making group.

If it turns out that well-documented examples can be adduced of the groupthink syndrome occurring under conditions of consistently low internal and external stress, the explanatory hypothesis might have to be discarded as untenable. Before discarding it on such grounds, however, it may be worthwhile to examine all known examples of groupthink to see if something could be added to the hypothesis to provide a more complete explanation. It is possible that when groupthink occurs under conditions of high stress from either internal or external sources, the hypothesis does, in fact, provide an adequate explanation of the main incentives; whereas, when groupthink occurs under conditions of low stress from both internal and external sources, other incentives are the effective ones. In short, subsequent research might show the need for either a new or a more complete explanation and might ultimately provide a more adequate set of explanatory hypotheses.

Obviously, even if the explanatory hypothesis stands up well to the first test I have just discussed (involving investigations of decisions by cohesive policy-making groups under conditions of low stress from both internal and external sources), other modifications may well be needed to fit new facts as they emerge. For example, there is an asymmetry in the formulations of the two sources of stress (items 1 and 2 in box B–2 in Figure 10–1) that might prove to be unwarranted: High stress from external threats is combined with another variable (low hope of a better solution than the leader's); but temporarily lowered self-esteem, which I refer to as an internal source of stress, is not. My reason for this asymmetry is that there are indications from psychological research that people tend to cope with the two sources of stress in somewhat different ways (see Janis and Mann, 1977, pp. 142–147). When worried about external threats, the members of a policy-making group become highly motivated to find a solution to the problem that enables them to foresee success in keeping the threatened utilitarian losses to a tolerable minimum. Along with an increase in their need for social support from the group is an increase in reliance on the leader's wisdom to guide them to a safe course of action. But they are still open to clear-cut opportunities for arriving at a better solution than the one favored by the leader to ward off the impending external danger. For example, if the top business managers of a factory are confronted by the threat that everyone in their factory could be poisoned by polluted air unless the air conditioning system is drastically improved soon, they are likely to have a greater hope of learning about the most feasible solution to the problem from ventilation engineers, air pollution experts, and other outside experts, than from their budget-minded leader, no matter how respected and revered he is as the head of their business enterprise. In such circumstances, the level of stress from external threat is high; but because the hope of finding a better solution than the leader's is also high, the chances of groupthink are expected to be low. The members are likely to engage in vigilant search for and appraisal of alternatives without necessarily impairing group cohesiveness (if the leader does not foolishly insist on fighting against the outside experts).

When the source of high stress is internal, however, I do not expect to find any such instances of high hope of finding a better solution than the leader's unless group cohesiveness has been so greatly impaired that this necessary condition for groupthink is no longer present. When the provocative circumstances generate a high level of stress from temporary loss of self-esteem but with only a low level of external threat present, as when a policy-making group is confronted with a distressing moral dilemma about continuing to exploit loopholes in the law to save money on corporation taxes, an essential requirement of the solution that each member is seeking is to obtain the acceptance and approval of the admired leader as well as the rest of the group. In a depressed mood dominated by feelings of shame and guilt, policy-makers will have little interest in what outside experts, such as tax account-ants, have to say about the acceptability of the tax-evasion policy, unlike situations in which there are strong threats of being sent to jail or other external dangers that need to be warded off. I expect that people in a temporary state of lowered self-esteem will have little hope of alleviating their shame or guilt unless they rely on the solution endorsed by the leader on whom they project the power to exonerate deviations from ethical standards, as the arbiter of morality. In those circumstances, a heightened need for esteem and moral support from the leader is much more pressing than finding a feasible solution to maximize utilitarian gains or to minimize utilitarian losses. Consequently, the members of a policy-making group beset by provocative circumstances that lower self-esteem tend to rely on the leader's moral judgment unless the leader does something outlandish that breaks the affiliative bond—for example, expressing moral condemnation of the members or withdrawing from contact in a manner that is interpreted as desertion. If the affiliative bond is broken, the members will seek elsewhere to satisfy their need for esteem and moral approval, the cohesiveness of the policy-making group will sharply decline, and the probability of group-think will correspondingly decrease.

These somewhat speculative theoretical assumptions about differential responses to external and internal sources of stress among policy-making groups will undoubtedly re-quire sharper formulations and perhaps considerable modification as new evidence ac-cumulates pertaining to the effects of provocative situational circumstances on groupthink tendencies.

6 How can the hypotheses about causes and consequences of groupthink (represented in Figure 10–1) be tested? My answer is that the full range of behavioral research methods could be used, including comparative case studies, experiments in social psychological laboratories, and field experiments in natural settings.

In limited ways, comparative case studies can provide pertinent evidence. Studies based on existing records of a few historic policy decisions, such as those presented in this book, are of value primarily for the *discovery phase* of the research, to suggest plausible hypotheses about the conditions under which high-quality policy-making is impeded or facilitated. In order to pursue the most promising hypotheses with larger numbers of cases, as the first step in the *verification* phase of the research, it might be feasible to build up a data bank that includes sizeable samples of both low-quality and high-quality policy deci-sions.

What I have in mind for the data bank is to test the hypotheses embodied in Figure 10–1 by obtaining correlational evidence from fairly large samples of policy decisions. For example, the three types of antecedent conditions (boxes A, B–1, and B–2 in Figure 10–1), which were inferred as causes of groupthink from a small number of comparative case studies, might be tested systematically by comparing thirty high-quality decisions with thirty low-quality decisions made by governmental committees. A series of comparisons could focus on blind ratings of the degree of group cohesiveness, the degree of insulation of the group, the extent to which the group had previously developed norms requiring methodical procedures, and the other variables specified by the model, as well as blind ratings of the symptoms of groupthink. An essential step would be to index and code the material in ways that can be useful for comparative analysis.

For blind coding of the quality of the decision-making procedures, the seven major criteria (shown in box D of Figure 10–1) could be used by taking account of specified in-dicators to rate the degree to which each criterion is met. These ratings could enable in-vestigators to test hypotheses about the consequences of groupthink in a more sophisticated way by subdividing the case studies into three main categories—policy decisions arrived at by (1) high-quality procedures (high or moderate scores on all seven criteria), (2) medium-quality procedures (mixed scores), and (3) low-quality procedures (low scores on all seven criteria). Systematic correlational investigations using these ratings should enable us to determine the degree to which specific antecedent conditions (and interacting sets of conditions) are related to the quality of policy-making procedures. They might also be useful for cross-cultural and cross-national studies, to see to what extent the consequences, as well as the causes, of groupthink tend to be the same or different under varying social conditions.

These comparative studies using blind rating procedures with fairly large samples should provide us with dependable evidence on situational and structural factors that make a difference. This type of research ought to enable investigators not only to test hypotheses concerning the effects of situational factors we already know something about but also to discover new circumstances present when the quality of a group's decision-making is adversely affected by groupthink and absent when the same group (or a comparable group) functions effectively as a decision-making body. Comparative investigations might also provide evidence concerning the interactions of predispositional factors (personality, social background, training) and situational or structural factors (e.g., type of risks, organizational subculture, role assignments), so that we could gradually build up our knowledge of the sorts of persons most vulnerable to each type of circumstance that promotes groupthink.

The evidence needed to test hypotheses about the causes of groupthink must ultimately come from field experiments and other systematic investigations specifically designed to pin down causal sequences, rather than from historical case studies. The comparative studies I have been discussing are correlational and suffer from a number of obvious disadvantages with regard to achieving control over the independent variables under investigation. But they have the great advantage of high external validity because they deal with real-life decisions by policy-makers. The reverse advantages and disadvantages are to be expected, of course, for laboratory experiments, where a relatively high degree of control over the variables can be achieved but at the expense of obtaining findings for hypothetical or relatively nonconsequential decisions that may prove to have little validity outside the laboratory. Controlled field experiments on consequential decision-making in actual organizational settings might be feasible, in which case we can hope to observe cause-and-effect relationships that will have a high degree of external validity. If the field experiments as well as the laboratory experiments and comparative case studies of historic decisions all point to the same general conclusion when we are testing a hypothesis about the conditions that foster groupthink, we can feel reasonably confident about the generality of the findings.

When I speak of controlled field experiments, I have in mind studies in which the investigator (1) introduces an experimental intervention under natural conditions with policy-planners making real decisions and (2) determines the effects of the intervention by comparing groups assigned on a random basis to the experimental and control conditions. The interventions would, of course, pertain to the antecedent conditions that are presumed to contribute to groupthink, including the various factors listed in the first column of Figure 10–1. But laboratory experiments, employing complex analysis of variance designs, might have to be relied upon for investigating the interacting effects of the antecedent variables. This is an important adjunct because my main hypotheses about the causes of groupthink predict interaction effects. The type of interaction to be expected can be described as follows: Whenever one of the structural factors that foster groupthink (listed in box B–1 in Figure 10–1) is present and cohesiveness of the decision-making group is *low,* that factor may increase the chances slightly that certain symptoms of defective decision-making (listed in box C) will occur. For example, lack of norms requiring methodical procedures in noncohesive groups of policy-makers might generally produce about a 10 percent increase in failure to examine risks of the preferred choice and a similar increase in poor information searches (with little or no effect on the other symptoms of defective decision-making). When the group is *moderately or highly cohesive,* however, a much more marked increase is to be expected *in all the symptoms of defective decision-making.* For example, lack of norms requiring methodical procedures in a *cohesive* group of policy-makers, as compared with noncohesive groups that are equivalent in all other respects, might significantly increase the incidence of failure to examine risks and the incidence of poor information search from about 10 percent to about 35 percent and also significantly increase the incidence of each of the other five symptoms of defective decision making from close to zero to about 20 percent. A similar interaction effect would also be expected for *symptoms of groupthink,* such that the effect of lack of norms requiring methodical procedures might have little or no effect on the eight symptoms (listed in box C in Figure 10–1) when the decision-making groups are noncohesive but would significantly increase the incidence of those symptoms when the groups are cohesive.

Everything that I have just said about the way group cohesiveness is expected to interact with each structural factor that fosters groupthink (box B–1 in Figure 10–1) applies equally to the way group cohesiveness is expected to interact with each of the provocative situational context factors, such as those that temporarily lower the self-esteem of the decision-makers (box B–2 in Figure 10–1).

It is difficult to imagine that it would ever be feasible to test the complex interaction hypotheses of the type I have just described in field experiments with policy-makers working on consequential decisions in an organizational setting because a large number of executive committees would have to be assigned on a random basis to many different conditions. Consequently, investigators may have to resort to laboratory experiments that involve simulations of policy-making. Such experiments can also deal with certain variables that for ethical or practical reasons cannot be investigated in field experiments. For example, the combined influence of the level of stress and the degree of hope for a better solution than the one favored by the leader could be investigated in laboratory studies by varying the severity of simulated external threats and by varying information about whether the leader's pertinent wisdom is superior or inferior to that of available outside experts. One way to reduce the potentially low external validity of the results of laboratory experiments on groupthink would be to conduct the experiments in workshops where large numbers of executives are given training in management techniques, using simulated but realistic decisions of the type that the executives actually have to deal with in their jobs. Such experiments could provide pertinent evidence about the main effects and interaction effects of the antecedent conditions specified in Figure 10–1, and could help investigators to pose more sharply the issues to be pursued in the much more costly field experiments dealing with real-life decisions by policy-making groups in natural organizational settings.

11 *Preventing Groupthink*

1 No organization can be expected to do very much about preventing the provocative situational contexts that promote groupthink (listed in box B–2 of Figure 10–1 on page 244) because these factors are largely determined by uncontrollable events, such as the occurrence of recent failures, or by the nature of the problem requiring a policy decision, such as moral dilemmas. But any organization should be able to do something to eliminate or at least to minimize administrative or structural faults (the factors listed in box B–1 in Figure 10–1). In Chapter 11, the main suggestions for preventing groupthink are in this category.

One way to foster critical evaluation and to prevent premature consensus is to introduce methodical procedures for search and appraisal. Janis and Mann (1977, Chapter 14) describe a number of relevant interventions that have been found to be at least partially successful in preventing defective decision-making procedures in individual decision-makers. These include the balance-sheet procedure and stress inoculation for post-decisional setbacks. The same basic procedures, which could easily be modified for use in group meetings, might prove to be effective in promoting vigilance among members of decision-making groups.

Another suggested methodical procedure involves the use of scenarios to project future consequences of alternatives. ''By generating 'best case' and 'worst case' scenarios the group can foresee the potential positive and negative consequences of the leading alternatives'' (Wheeler and Janis, 1980, p. 202).

The tendency of problem-solving groups to avoid planning and discussion of procedural methods has been pointed out by Hackman and Morris (1975). They describe the assumptions, apparently made by many decision-makers in public and private institutions, that everyone already knows how to go about the task and that discussion about how to tackle the problem is a waste of time. It is therefore unlikely that methodical procedures will be used unless the leader sees to it that they are on the agenda. Even so, any such procedure can easily be subverted by the group members if they regard it as useless or annoying.

Consequently, before any changes in standard operating procedure are put into operation, they need to be fully explained in a way that will motivate the participants to give them a fair trial. In-service training courses and management workshops might be useful contexts for conveying the rationale behind such changes.

Janis and Crow (1975) have proposed a brief training program for executives to provide a desirable educational background for introducing various antigroupthink procedures in policy-planning committees. On the assumption that appropriate information about the causes and consequences of groupthink can have a beneficial deterring effect, their curriculum includes impressive case studies illustrating the symptoms and harmful effects of groupthink together with recommendations for prevention. Janis and Crow suggest that such an in-service training program precede application of any of the nine prescriptive hypotheses to any policy-making or planning group on the verge of changing its operating procedures. A consultant or instructor starts by presenting to the members the twenty-minute film *Groupthink* (in the Psychology Today training films series, 1974), which depicts a typical policy-planning group in action and describes the symptoms of groupthink and their detrimental consequences. This is followed by a group discussion of the film, with special reference to its application to the group's own purposes and procedures. In a second session, the specific recommendations contained in the prescriptive hypotheses are explained to the group in terms of the conditions that make for groupthink . . . This briefing is again followed by a group discussion, during which the instructor gives special attention to the members' objections and qualms about adopting the new procedures. The instructor may also provide additional information and suggestions in an attempt to counteract whatever sources of resistance become manifest. But he will not deny that there are potential costs in terms of time, effort, and frustration. In fact, it would be part of his role to make the participants aware of the possible disadvantages that might arise, so that they could watch out for them and try to mitigate their effects [Janis and Mann, 1977, pp. 400–401].

Another way to increase the chances that the participants in a policy-making group will adopt the role of critical evaluators of whatever alternatives are proposed is to include members who represent divergent viewpoints within the organization. In the earlier discussion of the homogeneity factor as a structural fault (Chapter 10), I mentioned that Alexander George (1974, 1980) has proposed a system of "multiple advocacy" such that sincere advocates of differing policy options will be selected for membership in a policy-planning committee. He describes various special features of the system that could give those who represent minority positions within the organization the full opportunity and resources needed to present their case to the others as effectively as those who represent the majority position. In order to work the way the multiple-advocacy system is intended, the members selected for the planning committee would have to be a good mix of divergent viewpoints. All of them would have to have sufficient expertise and access to inside information so that everyone's comments are taken seriously by the others. Special precautions may be needed to reduce the risks of bickering and smoldering animosities, which could interfere with effective policy-making.

The use of methodical procedures and a multiple-advocacy system can take up a great deal of time and lead to hesitation when rapid decisions may be urgently required. However, all the fiascoes discussed in this book were actually planned piecemeal over a long period of time, often with one small commitment growing out of another. Ironically, of all the foreign policy crises I have studied, the one that put the policy-makers under the greatest time pressure was the Cuban missile crisis. The policy-makers knew that if United States action was delayed, the installations would be completed and the missiles would be armed with atomic warheads, posing a tremendous threat to American cities. Nevertheless, the group debated the issues thoroughly and examined critically many alternatives. This suggests that if the members of a policy-making group give priority to critical scrutiny of alternatives, they can somehow find the time to do so during a crisis.

2 Some experimental evidence has been reported on the effectiveness of impartial leadership that fosters open inquiry. Flowers (1977), in "a laboratory test of some implications of Janis's groupthink hypothesis," divided forty teams of students into different treatment groups and asked all of them to work on the same hypothetical decision (imagining that they were a group of school administrators deciding what to do about a formerly good teacher who as a result of illness had become incompetent). Group leaders were trained to conduct meetings according to two different leadership styles: (1) using an *open* style—in line with prescriptive hypotheses about preventing groupthink, the leader avoided stating his own position on the issue until after the others in the group had discussed their own solutions, continually encouraged free discussion of alternatives, and explicitly conveyed the norm of airing all possible viewpoints, versus (2) using a *closed* style—the leader stated his own position at the outset, did not encourage free discussion of alternatives, and explicitly conveyed the norm that the most important thing was for the team to agree on its decision. Flowers found that, as predicted, the teams exposed to the open leadership style offered significantly more solutions to the problem and during their discussion cited significantly more facts from the information made available to them before arriving at a consensus than the teams exposed to the closed leadership style.

Longley and Pruitt (1980) have criticized Flowers's study on the grounds that the instructions to the directive leaders confounded another variable with the instructions to state their own opinions at the outset of the discussion: they were also encouraged to curtail the group discussion, which, in and of itself, could be responsible for the group producing fewer proposed solutions and introducing fewer facts into the discussion.

Another variable investigated in Flowers's laboratory experiment was cohesiveness of the groups, which she manipulated by comparing groups of acquaintances with groups of strangers. The teams made up of acquaintances, who were assumed to be more cohesive, did not differ significantly from the teams made up of strangers on either measure of decision-making activity. This negative finding, if taken at face value, is in line with my assumption that cohesiveness is not a sufficient condition for groupthink. Flowers did not find, however, the predicted interaction effect of high versus low cohesiveness with open versus closed style of leadership, which implies that cohesiveness is not a necessary condition for groupthink. But here again, as Longley and Pruitt (1980) point out, there were serious shortcomings of the procedures used in the experiment, which makes Flowers's data questionable as a test of the interaction hypothesis.

Flowers acknowledges that the leaders and the student groups she studied differ on many dimensions from the groups described in my case studies of groupthink—such as degree of consequentiality of the decision, salience of real rivals or enemies, length of time the group worked together, and quality of interaction among the members. She also calls attention to the lack of power of the leaders in the experiment: "Janis's groups had powerful leaders who could exercise reward and punishment as well as legitimate, expert, and perhaps referent power . . . over their members, whereas the leaders in this experiment held only certain legitimate power" (p. 895). In addition, I would add that the two levels of cohesiveness she compared may be at the lower end of the cohesiveness continuum. When a leader lacks impartiality, the differences in decision-making activities at relatively low levels of cohesiveness (strangers versus mere acquaintances) may be too slight to be detected; whereas differences between a low and a high degree of cohesiveness (for example, strangers versus friends who are somewhat dependent upon one other for self-esteem enhancement) might emerge quite clearly.

If we were to take at face value Flowers's positive finding on the effects of open leadership practices, her experimental evidence suggests that when groups of students are working on problem-solving tasks, they are very responsive to the cues given by the appointed leader as to whether he or she wants the group to move in one particular direction or wants open inquiry into alternatives. Perhaps the same kind of responsiveness to leaders' cues will be found in many policy-making groups. If so, it might be helpful for leaders not only to abstain from stating their preferred solution to the policy problem at hand but also to absent themselves from the first few meetings of the policy-planning group (after having briefed the members about the dimensions of the problem) so as to avoid conveying by tone of voice, facial expressions, and other nonverbal cues the policy alternative that they prefer. But this leadership practice has obvious disadvantages. For example, a leader who absents himself from some of the meetings, as President Kennedy did during the Cuban missile crisis, might become somewhat perturbed when he returns to discover that the group has moved toward a consensus on adopting a policy alternative to which he objects. This puts him on the spot because if he feels strongly that the group's judgment is wrong, he is at a disadvantage at that late date in trying to persuade the members otherwise, unless he glaringly uses his power, which might impair his relations with his advisers and even create a permanent rift with those who feel resentful that the chief has devalued their judgment. After one traumatic experience of this type, a chief executive might thereafter attend all meetings and try to steer his advisers in the direction he wants them to go.

3 Longley and Pruitt (1980) call attention to the following additional advantages and disadvantages of appointing a devil's advocate to help prevent groupthink. On the positive side, the devil's advocate could not only present arguments in a way that stimulates the others to think more deeply about the pros and cons of each alternative but could also encourage other potential dissenters within the group to speak up for the first time. But on the negative side, these advantages could sometimes become disadvantages: the devil's advocate might wield *too much* influence if he or she is so impressive in refuting others' arguments that some of the members become inhibited about expressing their genuine opinions for fear of being "shot down."

In order to avoid the danger of appointing a devil's advocate who will wield either too much or too little influence, Longley and Pruitt propose that the devil's advocate should be someone who has neither very high nor very low status. They also suggest that when the main danger is that of too little influence, the devil's advocate should be someone who is capable of presenting the opposing view in a consistent and confident manner. Since a devil's advocate who spontaneously emerges within the group is more likely to be effective than an appointed one, these authors suggest that decision-making groups should establish the norm that anyone who is in disagreement with an emerging consensus should speak up vigorously against it. This suggestion could be regarded as equivalent to my first prescriptive hypothesis, which proposes that everyone in the group should be expected to function as a critical evaluator who will air objections and doubts. If this prescription is followed, it might be unnecessary to appoint a devil's advocate because everyone in the group would be set to take on that role.

4 Elsewhere (Janis, 1981) I have described three lines of research that can be useful for developing and testing prescriptions that are expected to help prevent groupthink: (1) decision-simulation experiments to develop new interventions and to test them in a preliminary way; (2) field experiments with ad hoc policy-planning groups (for example, with advanced trainees in the policy sciences who volunteer to prepare a position paper on proposed means for dealing with a current national or international problem, to be circulated within appropriate government agencies); and (3) field experiments in organizational settings, starting with aides who are relatively low in the organizational hierarchy and then, if the evidence shows that certain interventions are effective, replicating the study by moving up the hierarchy to higher-level policy-planners.

Prior to attempting to carry out field experiments in order to test any of the interventions specified by the prescriptive hypotheses, I think it is sensible to develop and test them first in laboratory experiments. For example, some pertinent evidence was obtained by Crow and Noel (1975) in a simulation experiment of the historical decision by Mexican authorities that led to the Alamo episode. Groups of subjects in this study displayed some symptoms of groupthink. When consensus was induced prematurely as an experimental condition, the groups tended to choose a more risky course of action than many individual members initially preferred. Such experiments can help investigators to pose more sharply the issues to be pursued in the much more costly field experiments dealing with real-life decisions by policy-making groups in natural settings.

Laboratory experiments have the advantage of control over the manipulation of independent variables and therefore more certain identification of cause-and-effect relations than is the case with most field studies. However, the many background variables that are held constant by the nature of the experimental setting potentially could affect the extent and direction of the relationships observed between the independent and dependent variables. Often these "interactions" contribute to the failure of observed relationships to hold up in new, untested situations. A research strategy that may help to solve this problem without going to the enormous expense in time and effort of doing field experiments in large organizations is to carry out small laboratory-like experiments using ad hoc groups of advanced trainees (or retired executives) who are qualified policy-planners and who agree to cooperate with a research team in exchange for having the opportunity to participate in policy-planning on an issue about which they are deeply concerned. Enough volunteers are needed to set up two equivalent groups, one of which can be given the procedures of the antigroupthink program developed earlier in laboratory experiments, while the other can serve as a control group. Using several different issues as replications in an analysis of variance design, the effectiveness of the intervention procedures can be determined. Because of the educational value of the antigroupthink research program, cooperation of management training workshops can be expected.

In all such studies, the seven criteria for high-quality decision-making could be used as dependent measures. Other measures could also be obtained to ascertain the effectiveness of the antigroupthink program. These might include, in addition to manifestations of the eight symptoms of groupthink, blind ratings by well-qualified judges of the quality of the policy recommendations and the arguments for them in the "white papers" produced by each of the policy-planning groups.

If sufficient progress is made from such experiments with ad hoc groups, I see no reason why the necessary arrangements could not be made to test the most promising interventions in a few organizations interested in improving the quality of policy-making procedures. Ultimately the same type of field research on prescriptive hypotheses might be carried out in many different organizations in different countries so as to accumulate evidence on the generality of the conclusions in different organizational and national contexts.

By testing the prescriptive hypotheses in controlled laboratory and field experiments we can expect to gain some further information about the effects of the antecedent conditions listed in Figure 10–1 (p. 244). Insulation of the group, for example, is counteracted by prescriptive hypotheses 5 and 6, which involve consultation with "home-base" colleagues and having outside experts at each meeting. The antecedent condition of lack of methodical procedures for search and appraisal may prove to be counteracted to some extent by prescriptive hypotheses 1, 4, 7, 8, and 9, as well as by special techniques, such as the balance-sheet procedure (see Note 1). Also, leadership bias and low hope of finding a better solution than the leader's should be counteracted by prescriptive hypothesis 2, which requires the leader to be impartial in stating the problem and to avoid expressing a preference for a particular solution. Consequently, basic research on the effects of these antecedent conditions might be advanced by applied research on the effectiveness of the prescriptive hypotheses that are intended to counteract the conditions that are expected, according to the theoretical analysis, to facilitate groupthink.

5 In many instances, the consequences of preventing groupthink in a policy-making group of powerful government officials who are inclined to resort to illegal actions for the sake of their political "cause" could have either a detrimental or beneficial effect for the nation, depending partly on the circumstances, such as whether or not a criminalistic solution to their problems appears to be expedient. Suppose, for example, that President Richard M. Nixon and his chief aides in the White House were able to counteract their groupthink tendencies in March 1973. They might have decided at that point to destroy the White House tapes containing evidence of their Watergate cover-up conspiracy (before anyone else learned about their existence) and to issue clever public relations statements in line with a new deceitful policy of a "limited modified hang-out." This nongroupthink decision might well have enabled them to survive in office with enough residual power to damage the nation by perpetuating their antidemocratic repressive measures against political opponents on their "enemies list." But the net effect might have been quite different if they had been able to prevent groupthink in their earlier deliberations about the Watergate break-in shortly after it happened, say in late June or July 1972. At that point in time, to use one of their phrases, they might have decided that from a tough, strictly expedient point of view (never mind the moral issues involved), they would be better off not to cover up the involvement of higher-ups in the Watergate caper, but rather to pursue a genuine hang-out policy and to avoid implementing any other illegal plans that could result in impeachment and jail sentences. In such a case, would the effect of counteracting groupthink in a powerful group with a strong criminalistic propensity necessarily be a bad thing for the nation or for the cause of democracy and the rule of law?

6 Management training programs might profitably include a unit on prevention of groupthink. See Note 1 for a proposed curriculum.

7 Wheeler and Janis (1980) raise the following question: In the absence of standard operating procedures to promote critical assessment of the pros and cons of each viable alternative, what could an individual member do if he or she begins to surmise that the policy-making group might be in the grip of groupthink? Their answer is not a very optimistic one because they argue, in light of what little evidence is available, that standard operating procedures and appropriate norms endorsed by the leader are probably essential for fostering critical evaluation:

> If you suggest a critical analysis session, most of the criticism will be directed at you for disrupting the group spirit. If you try the devil's advocate role, the other members will react as though you were disloyal. If you tell the others of your diagnosis and point out the symptoms of groupthink, they are likely to resent your psychologizing because they feel you are accusing them of being incompetent.
>
> We cannot be very encouraging about the likelihood of success. The best approach is probably to state your reservations about the group's plan as clearly and logically as you can, without mentioning groupthink at all. Present your evidence in a straightforward manner and avoid being drawn into name calling or other personal attacks. You may succeed in raising enough doubts in enough minds to get support from some of the other members in moving away from groupthink long enough to reconsider the alternatives.
>
> In any group the members are allowed only a limited amount of "idiosyncrasy credit." Each member can argue his or her own pet points up to a certain limit. Beyond that the group stops listening [p. 208].

Curing groupthink, according to Wheeler and Janis, is more difficult than preventing it by means of standard operating procedures that help to counteract premature consensus.

> Once groupthink sets in, censorship within the group will block the recognition of the fact that groupthink is occurring and members will resist any efforts to change toward multiple advocacy. Furthermore, in crisis situations when prompt action is required the members of a group are unlikely to take the trouble to institute new procedures just for that crisis, especially since to do so would appear to increase the time and effort required for making the decision. Therefore, we recommend that groups adopt anti-groupthink procedures when they are making important noncrisis decisions and follow the procedures regularly. These standard operating procedures are then more likely to be maintained for those critical decisions in which groupthink might otherwise lead to devastating errors. Standard operating procedures are also useful for avoiding other sources of defective group decision making, such as excessive bickering over territorial rights among representatives of different departments within an organization and fear of being fired by the top boss if one disagrees with his pet ideas [p. 195].

Sources

1 Introduction

page
2   Policy decisions and computers: Shepard, 257–263.

4   Lewin's prerequisites for effective group decisions: Lewin (1947).

4   Importance of group cohesiveness: Lewin (1952), 145–169.

4   "Other things . . . self esteem": Cartwright, 105.

5   Group solidarity and the stresses that beset policy-makers: see George (1974).

5   Group cohesiveness and members' inclination to reject a nonconformist: Schachter, 165–181, and Schachter et al. (1954).

5   Norms of different work groups: Vroom, 223–227 summarizes field research on group productivity by French and Zander, Likert, Seashore, and others. See also Homans.

5   Stereotyped images that dehumanize outgroups: see Ashmore, 318–339; Sherif et al.; Zimbardo.

5   Shift toward riskier courses of action: see Brown; Dion, Baron, and Miller; Myers and Lamm; Pruitt; Wallach, Kogan, and Bem.

6   "presuming always . . . rational manner": Morgenthau, 5.

7   "The best . . . their explanations": Allison, 258–259.

7   "Most theorists . . . and models": *Ibid.*, 273.

8   Mutual dependency and resistance to termination of group: Janis (1966).

9–10   Major defects in decision-making: Based on Janis and Mann, 10–14.

11   French and German military errors during World War I: see Tuchman, 45–62, 242–261, 487–488.

2 The Bay of Pigs

The main reference used in preparing this chapter was Arthur M. Schlesinger Jr.'s *A Thousand Days*, which presents a detailed account of the meetings at which President Kennedy and his advisers discussed and approved the Bay of Pigs invasion plan. In addition to having access to official records, Schlesinger was able to draw on his personal observations as an insider. He attended most of the meetings of the advisory committee and frequently discussed the issues with the President and with fellow members of the White House staff. Another major source of information was Theodore Sorensen's *Kennedy*. Although Sorensen did not participate in any of the meetings, he had extensive discussions with the President and with other participants during the weeks immediately following the Cuban fiasco. Additional details were obtained from books by

Hilsman, Guthman, Meyer and Szulc, Salinger, and Wyden, cited in the bibliography. I have also drawn heavily from an unpublished paper by my daughter, Charlotte Janis, prepared partly under my supervision, which presented an analysis of the group processes that entered into the Bay of Pigs decision on the basis of material culled from most of the above-mentioned references.

page
14   The quote "Perfect failure" is from T. Draper, cited by Meyer and Szulc, 146.
15   "use of . . . the United States": Sorensen, 332.
15   "the nearest . . . to write": This statement from the *New York Times* is quoted on the cover of the Bantam Book edition of Sorensen's *Kennedy* (1966).
16   "How could . . . same question": Sorensen, 346.
16   "Kennedy would . . . and adventure": Schlesinger, 292.
16   "still troubled . . . and haggard": *Ibid.,* 295.
16   McNamara's statement about misadvising Kennedy: *New York Times,* February 5, 1968.
16   "a shocking . . . process": Sorensen, 338.
16–19   Most details about qualifications of members of Kennedy's advisory group are from Opotowski.
19   "was a brilliant . . . retired": Hilsman, 30.
20   "I can't believe . . . for him": Salinger, 194.
20   "somehow the idea . . . actual fighting": Schlesinger, 249.
21   "there will not . . . inside Cuba": Sorensen, 334.
21   "the integrity . . . jeopardize that": Schlesinger, 271.
23   "The President . . . capability": Sorensen, 340.
23   "ultimate success . . . from outside": Schlesinger, 238.
24   Kennedy's expectation that Cubans would revolt against Castro: Sorensen, 332.
24   "We all . . . the CIA": Schlesinger, 247.
26   "No coordinated . . . or possible": Sorensen, 339.
26–27   "I don't . . . and jungle": Schlesinger, 250.
27   Castro's bargain with the U.S. for releasing 1200 prisoners: *New York Times. The Kennedy Years* (1964), 238.
27   "for all . . . bowels of government": Schlesinger, 295.
30   "With hindsight . . . decision-making process": Sorensen, 338.
30   "failed in . . . the nation": Schlesinger, 256.
31   "we can't . . . have been doing": *Ibid.,* 242.
31   Rusk's avoidance of charges of State Department softness: Sorensen, 303.
31   "that the military . . . ordinary mortals": Schlesinger, 258.
32   "The same men . . . was afoot": *Ibid.,* 248.
35   "It seemed . . . challenged us": Guthman, 88. Italics added.
35   "Everything . . . not lose": Schlesinger, 259.
35   "affected by . . . new day": *Ibid.,* 259.
35   "*Euphoria . . . unlimited*": *Ibid.,* 214. Italics added.
36–37   "although . . . underground": *Ibid.,* 293.
38   "No strong . . . were presented": Sorensen, 341.
38   "the massed . . . against it.": Schlesinger, 258–259.
38   "Our meetings . . . *assumed consensus*": *Ibid.,* 250. Italics added.
38   "Rusk asked . . . our position": Hilsman, 58.
38   "they are . . . risk Guantánamo": Schlesinger, 257.
39   "doubts were . . . their colleagues": Sorensen, 343.
39   "In the months . . . *discussion*": Schlesinger, 255. Italics added.
40   "Virile poses" of the CIA representatives and the Joint Chiefs of Staff: *Ibid.,* 256.
40   "we seem . . . basis": *Ibid.,* 256.
41   "I'm sorry . . . tightly held.": Hilsman, 31.
41–42   Judgment made without benefit of advice from intelligence experts: Hilsman, 31.
42   "sensible and strong" speech by Fulbright: Schlesinger, 252.
43   Well-known experiments on conformity in small groups: See Elms, 136–146, for a review of research by S. Asch, R. Crutchfield, S. Milgram, M. Sherif, and other social psychologists.

43–44   Bowles' reaction to the group's acceptance of the CIA's invasion plans: Schlesinger, 250.
44   "I can't . . . *nice* man": *Ibid.,* 436.
45   "a man . . . intellectual gifts": *Ibid.,* 241.
46   "had become . . . of the plans": Hilsman, 31.

3   *In and Out of North Korea*

This chapter draws mainly on the work of four social scientists—George, DeRivera, McLellan, and Neustadt—each of whom has analyzed the available historical materials on the Truman administration's decision to authorize the invasion of North Korea. The latter two accounts are partly based on interviews of Secretary of State Acheson and President Truman, respectively. These two leading participants in the policy-making group and a third participant—General Collins, who was one of the Joint Chiefs of Staff—have published their personal memoirs, from which I have extracted numerous observations. Additional details were obtained from Hersey's eyewitness account of President Truman's reactions on the day he received the news that Communist China had entered the war. Some relevant background material was obtained from publications by DeWeerd, Higgins, Leckie, Lichterman, Marshall, and Paige, and from an unpublished paper by Gale Tenen prepared for one of my graduate seminars.

page
48   "The momentum . . . administration": George and Smoke, 208–209.
49   Series of emergency decisions in response to the collapse of South Korea's military forces: Paige, 79–280.
49   "one of the most . . . decision makers": *Ibid.,* 331.
49   "the finest . . . ever known": *Ibid.,* 179.
49   "with minimal conflict": *Ibid.,* 320.
51   "General Bradley . . . generals": McLellan, 37.
51   Civilian advisers in agreement with Joint Chiefs: George and Smoke, 219–224.
51   "carried . . . Defense": Collins, Preface, vii.
51   "full understanding . . . and respect": *Ibid.,* 6.
51   "I came . . . fearless decision": *Ibid.,* 14.
51   "disliked . . . personally": De Rivera, 215.
52   "revered . . . chief": Acheson, 441.
52   "No change . . . to me": *Ibid.,* 441.
52   "art of . . . compelled respect": *Ibid.,* 441.
52   "History . . . has had": Truman, 429.
52   "Among . . . public interest": Acheson, 729.
52   "little . . . and loved.": *Ibid.,* 730.
53   "the longest . . . history": S. L. A. Marshall, 1.
53   "in the wrong . . . wrong enemy": Quoted in Leckie, 214.
53   "a passing fancy . . . news changed": Neustadt, 195.
55   "The trouble . . . had warned.": Acheson, 454.
55   "In White House . . . as a cause": Neustadt, 207.
56   "if the U.N. . . . North Koreans": *Ibid.,* 203.
56   "Chou's words . . . disregarded": Acheson, 452.
56   "With the military . . . any sort": Neustadt, 204.
56   "a general . . . in Asia": McLellan, 23.
56   "As I look . . . frank enough": Acheson, 468.
57   MacArthur allowed to advance to the border of Communist China: Truman, 378–381.
57   Truman's advisers worried about risk to MacArthur's forces: George and Smoke, 224–230.
57   "It is not . . . activity": George and Smoke, 222–223, 229.
57   "It was not . . . from it": DeWeerd, 451.
57   "supported . . . risk-taking": De Rivera, 148.
57   "collaborating . . . situation": *Ibid.,* 148.

58	"is a prime example . . . to others": McLellan, 39.
59	Stereotypes shared by Truman's advisory group about Red China: McLellan, 35–36; Neustadt, 209–211.
59	"all previous experience . . . *a will of its own*": McLellan, 36. Italics added.
59	"Moscow . . . restraint": Neustadt, 210.
60	The policy planning staff's opposition to occupation of North Korea: Acheson, 451.
60	"a 'floating kidney' . . . decisions": Kennan, 514.
60	"relegated . . . White House level": *Ibid.,* 513.
60	"All through . . . schooled minds": Kennan, 526–527.
61	"The United States . . . ever since": McLellan, 36–37.
61	"we needed . . . Korean moves": This quotation and other details about the meeting of the National Security Council on November 28, 1950 are from Truman, 385–388.
61	The Chinese move "a ruse": *Ibid.,* 380.
61	Truman insists U.S. would not abandon Europe for Asian entanglements: *Ibid.,* 381.
62	"Here, I believe . . . to be served": Acheson, 466.
62	Agreement that MacArthur's directive should not be changed: Truman, 380.
62	"something strangely . . . this meeting": McLellan, 32.
62	"prevailing confidence . . . the Yalu": *Ibid.,* 33.
62	Change in expectations and concern about Chinese intervention: George and Smoke, 227–230. George and Smoke point out that in all probability the dramatic change in mood was partly a response to the disappearance of the Chinese units, which McLellan does not mention.
63	Strength of MacArthur's forces: McLellan, 32; and Truman, 376–377.
63	"if we find . . . negotiation": McLellan, 31.
63	"The time . . . a success": McLellan, 32.
63	Secretary Marshall's minutes on Acheson's agreement: McLellan, 31.
63	"shared with . . . wishful thinking": *Ibid.,* 33.
64	MacArthur's optimistic announcement: Truman, 381.
64	"They all agree . . . this thing": Hersey, 53.
65	Truman displays "anguish" and "irritability and disgust" when announcing bad news to his staff: *Ibid.,* 53.
65	"Well the liars . . . this morning": *Ibid.,* 54–55.
66	Comments made at the meeting of the National Security Council on November 28, 1950: Truman, 385–388.
66	"Did MacArthur . . . indiscretion": *Ibid.,* 386.
67	"vilification . . . Soviets had": *Ibid.,* 388.
67	"reckless charges . . . campaign": *Ibid.,* 388.
68	Truman pursuing the most balanced approach: *Ibid.,* 345.
68	"I said . . . to be drawn": *Ibid.,* 335.
68	"I told . . . world-wide war": *Ibid.,* 337.
68	Truman intent on not withdrawing: *Ibid.,* 340.
69	"Time was all important": *Ibid.,* 343.
70	"I *accepted* . . . declined.": *Ibid.,* 343. Italics added.
70	Truman's leadership style: Paige, 290.
70–71	"The President's . . . advised": Neustadt, 205.
71	"By November . . . to unification": *Ibid.,* 214–215.

4   *Pearl Harbor Revisited*

The main reference work used in this chapter is Roberta Wohlstetter's *Pearl Harbor: Warning and Decision* (1962), a masterful analysis of the testimony and intelligence reports concerning America's greatest military blunder. I also examined the bulk of the testimony by Kimmel and by leading members of his advisory group published in the *Hearings Before the Joint Committee on the Investigation of the Pearl Harbor Attack* (1946), cited as *Hearings*. Additional bits of information were culled from other standard sources, including historical analyses by A. Russell

Buchanan, Herbert Feis, Samuel Eliot Morison, Nathaniel Peffer, and John Toland. Some specific details about meetings and conversations of members of Kimmel's advisory group were obtained from *The Accused* (1968), the biography of Kimmel by Donald Grey Brownlow, who presents new information from his interviews of several members of the advisory group.

page

72   "She was . . . *she was crazy*": Brownlow, 128. Italics added.
73   "The prevalent . . . *of security*": *Hearings,* Part 26, 398–399. Italics added.
73   "There was . . . naval command": *Ibid.,* 398–399.
73   "we all . . . air attack": *Ibid.,* 398–399.
73   Captain J. B. Earle as a friend and admirer of Admiral Kimmel: Brownlow, 91 and 141.
73   "Yes . . . take that chance": *Hearings,* Part 26, 412.
74   "gave an almost . . . Japanese government": Feis, 305.
74   "Never before . . . the enemy": Wohlstetter, 382.
74   "It was . . . American history": Peffer, 399.
74   "close to ideal": Wohlstetter, 70.
75   "Chances of favorable . . . a possibility": *Hearings,* Part 14, 1405.
75   "This dispatch . . . in WPL 46 [the Naval war plan]": *Ibid.,* 1406.
75   "there was no . . . particular time": Wohlstetter, 66.
75   "I guess . . . put it in": *Hearings,* Part 10, 4807.
75   High costs of full alert with 360-degree air reconnaissance: See *Hearings,* Part 6, 2534; and Kimmel, 71.
76   The Naval officers' willingness to unload seemingly unimportant defense responsibilities: Roberta Wohlstetter, private communication.
76   "Again and again . . . Pearl Harbor": Wohlstetter, 46.
77   Admiral Kimmel's "senior advisers": Most of the information about Kimmel's advisers in this section comes from *Hearings,* Part 6, 2608–2609 and 2896–2900; Part 26, 41–45 and 397–398; Part 7, 3361; and Part 8, 3553.
77   "most distinguished . . . man's command": *Hearings,* Part 6, 2899.
77   Admiral Kimmel's visits to Admiral Bloch's home: *Hearings,* Part 26, 45.
77   Personal relations between Admiral Kimmel and Captain and Mrs. Earle: Brownlow, 91.
77–78 Personal relations between Admiral Kimmel and Captain W. W. Smith: Brownlow, 91, 124–126; and *Hearings,* Part 6, 2608.
79   "Was grand . . . understanding": Brownlow, 78.
79   "From that time . . . been shaken": *Ibid.,* 94.
79   "the Japanese . . . Asiatic operations": *Ibid.,* 127.
79   "We finally decided . . . stick to it": *Ibid.,* 127.
79   "put his worries aside": *Ibid.,* 127.
79   "They both . . . would happen": *Ibid.,* 139.
79   The Navy group's attempt to cheer up "ol' Kimmel": *Ibid.,* 140–141.
80   Japanese smoke screens and deceptions: *Ibid.,* 129–130; and Whaley, A-260.
81   "The history . . . intelligent men": Wohlstetter, 397.
81   "as efficient . . . could find": *Ibid.,* 392.
81   "very human . . . popular hypotheses": *Ibid.,* 392–393.
81   "may have . . . 'cry wolf' ": *Ibid.,* 56.
81   "What was . . . eventualities": *Ibid.,* 55.
82   "After every allowance . . . 7 December": Morison, 138.
82   "There is . . . been attacked": Wohlstetter, 397–398.
83   "that a power . . . United States": *Ibid.,* 349.
84–85 "the only problem . . . way down": *Hearings,* Part 10, 4859.
85   "there seems . . . tentative percentage": Wohlstetter, 69.
85   "If we . . . ten minutes warning": *Hearings,* Part 22, 540.
86   Admiral Ingersoll's statement about lack of safety from torpedo plane attack: *Ibid.,* Part 33, 1317.
86   "all my staff . . . danger negligible": *Ibid.,* Part 6, 2592.
87   "What, you don't . . . know it?" *Hearings,* Part 36, 128.
87   "atmosphere of geniality and security": Wohlstetter, 42.
87   "I did not . . . wish I had": *Hearings,* Part 10, 4840.

89   "because of . . . prompt alert": Morison, 107.
91   Army confidence in the Navy: Wohlstetter, 27.
91   "that the Navy . . . that area": *Hearings,* Part 28, 972.
92   Admiral Stark's letters to Admiral Kimmel: Wohlstetter, 146–147, 255–256.
93   "*the Island* . . . in the world": *Ibid.,* 69.
93   "Presence . . . major attack": *Ibid.,* 69.
94   "the war warnings that failed to protect": Feis, 324.
94   "an all-out . . . dramatic suddenness": Buchanan, 48.
94   Awaiting Japan's next piece of "deviltry": Wohlstetter, 277.
95   "get around . . . must not be allowed": *Hearings,* Part 11, 5435f.
95   "My God . . . Philippines": Toland, 34.

5   Escalation of the Vietnam War

In preparing Chapter 5, I made extensive use of the Pentagon Papers, both the *New York Times* single-volume work prepared by Neil Sheehan and his collaborators and the full twelve-volume edition published by the United States government. One of the main sources of information about the attitudes, expectations, and norms shared by the members of Johnson's advisory group is an eye-opening inside account published in 1968 by James C. Thomson, Jr., a historian on leave from Harvard who spent five years as an observing participant, first as an East Asia specialist in the State Department and then as an assistant to McGeorge Bundy in the White House. Similar inside information was obtained from *The Lost Crusade,* a book of memoirs by Chester Cooper, who was an official in the State Department during the Johnson administration and participated in the aborted attempts at peace negotiations during 1965–1968.

Additional material on peace negotiations and on the military courses of action considered by Johnson's advisory group was drawn from *The Secret Search for Peace in Vietnam,* by David Kraslow and Stuart Loory, two journalists who interviewed many government officials involved in forming United States policies concerning the Vietnam War. *The Limits of Intervention,* by Townsend Hoopes, former undersecretary of the Air Force, describes the social and political pressures put on Secretary of Defense McNamara and other high officials who, toward the end of the Johnson administration, became disillusioned and began to favor deescalation of the war. Additional observations bearing on attitudes of the members of Johnson's inner circle were obtained from *The Tuesday Cabinet,* by Henry F. Graff, a historian who was given the opportunity to interview President Johnson and his principal advisers during each of four critical phases in the Vietnam War between 1965 and 1968. I also made use of Lyndon B. Johnson's book of memoirs (*The Vantage Point*) and two published interviews with Bill Moyers. Background material was obtained from publications by Leslie Gelb, Phillip Geyelin, Roger Hilsman, Daniel Ellsberg, Ithiel Pool, George Reedy, Tom Wicker, Ralph K. White, and others.

page
98   "It is hard . . . we are defending": Pool, Introduction to *Reprint of Publications on Viet Nam 1966–1970,* 2.
98   "a rather narrow . . . for consideration": Department of Defense, Book 4, iv.
98   "the study indicates . . . [the] analysis": Sheehan et al., 332.
98   Little chance of breaking the will of Hanoi: *Ibid.,* 330–332.
98   "seems to have . . . *their favor*": *Ibid.,* 344. Italics added.
98   "With but rare . . . of the process": Janeway, 31.
99   "its work . . . at a time": Graff, 3.
101   "The men . . . week out": *Ibid.,* 6.
101   "loyalty with . . . entertained": *Ibid.,* 178.
101   "they turned . . . natural friends": *Ibid.,* 24.
101   Influence of the Tuesday Cabinet on the President: *Ibid.,* 24.
101   "one of the significant . . . a consensus": Sidey.
102   "holding actions . . . was concerned": Ellsberg, 233.
102   "political and . . . on to Communism' ": *Ibid.,* 242.
102   "This is not . . . to Communism": *Ibid.,* 246.

102	"tattooed on . . . over Saigon": *Ibid.,* 252.
103	"when U.S. . . . military victory": *Ibid.,* 264.
103	"Self-deception" . . . "over-optimistic expectations": *Ibid.,* 258, 261–262, 264.
103	"flaws and . . . process": *Ibid.,* 261.
103	"drift in . . . invalid optimism": *Ibid.,* 262.
103	"Fear of . . . risks to be": *Ibid.,* footnote, 252. Italics added.
103	"In the spring . . . deadly errors": *Ibid.,* 269.
104	"draft and . . . will propose": *Ibid.,* 269.
104	"to break . . . North Vietnam": Sheehan et al., 468.
104	"The idea . . . *colossal misjudgment." Ibid.,* 469. Italics added.
104	"official hopes . . . to wane": Dept. of Defense, Book 4, IV.C.5, 4.
105	"Several officials . . . *after sixty-four." Wicker,* 250. Italics added.
105	"the major . . . the consequences": Sheehan et al., 416. Italics added.
105	"was *not* . . . in the South": Sheehan et al., 416–417. Italics added. See also Department of Defense, Book 4, IV, C.5, 7.
105	"no one really . . . consistently underrated": Sheehan et al., 459. See also Department of Defense, Book 5, IV, C.6 (a), 41.
106	"The program . . . South Vietnam": Sheehan et al., 472.
106	"persistent skepticism . . . frank, cogent": Ellsberg, 234.
106	"tended toward a pessimistic view": Sheehan et al., 331. See also *Ibid.,* 329.
106	"cripple . . . operations": *Ibid.,* 459.
107	"bring the enemy . . . lack of support": *Ibid.,* 462.
107	"Lyndon Johnson's slow-motion Bay of Pigs": Thomson, 52.
110	Bureaucrats' quip about the extra minutes McNamara had to do his homework: Cooper, 255.
110	Research on heightened need for affiliation produced by external stress: See Cartwright and Zander, Janis, Schachter.
111	The policy-maker's black-and-white picture of the Vietnam War: White, 123–134.
112	"united both . . . since 1964": Hoopes, 150.
113	Research on effects of commitment to a decision and disinclination to look at unfavorable consequences: See Chapters 36–39 (by Zimbardo, Kiesler, Gerard, and Aronson) in Abelson et al. and Janis and Mann, Chapter 11.
113–114	"another result . . . either direction": Thomson, 53.
115	The "effectiveness trap": *Ibid.,* 49.
115	"the inhouse . . . remained intact": *Ibid.,* 49.
118	"gathering of homogeneous hawks": Hoopes, 52.
118	"Mr. McNamara's disillusionment . . . Secretary of Defense": Hedrik Smith in Sheehan et al., 510.
118	McNamara's turmoil after he concluded that the North Vietnamese could not be bombed into negotiating: Hoopes, 86.
118	"that military genius . . . on me": *Ibid.,* 90.
118	"Venting his . . . the basement": *Ibid.,* 90.
119	"confident that . . . in silence": *Ibid.,* 91.
119	Clifford selected as a dependable hawk: Cooper, 390–391.
120	"from the . . . against the North": Sheehan et al., 310. See also Department of Defense, Book 4, IV, C.2. (b), v.
120	"another of those . . . at night": Johnson, 237.
120	Unanimous agreement of the group on major escalation decisions: *Ibid.,* 120, 124–125, 128, 148–149, 242–245, and 371.
120	"All my advisers . . . acceleration": *Ibid.,* 37.
120	"The one thing . . . current policies": Graff, 73.
120	"History will salute us": *Ibid.,* 143.
120	"There was a confidence . . . would fold": Janeway, 29–30.
121	"to last two . . . to yield": Sheehan et al., 327.
121	"The optimistic predictions . . . up decisions": Cooper, 424.
121	Tuesday Lunch Group's avoidance of peace negotiations: Department of Defense, Book 4, 61ff.
122	"As a result . . . not being exceeded": Kraslow and Loory, 48.
123	"a remarkable document . . . the strikes": Sheehan et al., 479.

123–125   "For months afterward . . . to sleep": Kraslow and Loory, 12–13.
125   "In the summer . . . December 6, 1966": Johnson, 251.
125–126   William P. Bundy's choice of flower names for peace initiatives: Kraslow and Loory, 27.
126   Destruction of Marigold peace initiative: Cooper, 324–341; Kraslow and Loory, 3–74.
126   "The Poles claimed . . . suggested meeting": Johnson, 251.
126   "If Lewandowski . . . talks began": *Ibid.,* 251.
126   "The major result . . . from Hanoi": Smith in Sheehan et al., 523.
127   "marked . . . fumbling": Cooper, 324.
127   "Stopping or moderating . . . North Vietnamese": *Ibid.,* 432–433.
127   "the issue . . . the discussions": *Ibid.,* 336.
129   "buoyed by . . . his advisers": Hoopes, 113.
129   "the victim . . . discouraging word": *Ibid.,* 218.

6   *The Cuban Missile Crisis*

Chapter 6 draws mainly upon five accounts of the Cuban missile crisis: Abel (1966), Hilsman (1967), R. Kennedy (1969), Schlesinger (1965), and Sorensen (1965). Robert Kennedy and Theodore Sorensen were key members of the Executive Committee and attended practically all sessions. These two men also had private conversations with President Kennedy and were privy to his personal deliberations, some of which they included in their accounts of the crisis. Hilsman, as director of intelligence for the State Department, was familiar with the private views of Secretary Rusk and of several other members of the committee with whom he was in close contact. He also reports on what was said at several crucial meetings of the Executive Committee that he attended. Schlesinger's account in *A Thousand Days* is based mainly on documentary evidence and personal discussions with the participants. Schlesinger was not present at the Executive Committee meetings during the first five days, when the decision to institute a naval blockade was being made, but he was brought in to help carry out the plans and was in the White House as a direct observer of the later events of the crisis. Abel, an eminent journalist (later director of Columbia University's School of Journalism) who was in Washington during the crisis, brought together the documentary evidence as well as the personal accounts of participants in his attempt to reconstruct what happened in the White House during each of the thirteen days of the crisis. I have also drawn upon Alexander George's insightful analysis (1971) of the strategy of coercive diplomacy used in the Cuban missile crisis and Graham Allison's intriguing book (1971) containing three different analyses of the crisis, each based on a different theoretical model. Finally, I was greatly aided in evaluating relevant observations by an excellent discussion of the available historical materials concerning the deliberations of the Executive Committee presented in a term paper by Miss Gale Tenen as part of her work in one of my graduate seminars.

As usual, we are confronted with the fact that almost all the observations of what went on during the Executive Committee's deliberations come from participants who have a stake in presenting the group's actions in a favorable light. This bias, which we encounter in all case histories of policy-making groups, becomes most serious when we are dealing with supposedly well-worked-out decisions rather than with the erroneous ones that led to fiascoes. All I can say about this problem, other than referring to the caveats I presented in Chapter 1, is that after reading all the pertinent accounts, I am impressed by the consistency in what the participants have said about the decision-making procedures used by the Executive Committee and the social atmosphere in which their deliberations took place. I am left with the impression that to be *that* consistent, the participants must be either describing accurately what they actually observed or presenting a myth that they have collectively worked out in a conspiracy to mislead the public about what really went on.

page
132   "the most critical in our nation's history": Sorensen, 328.
132   "the greatest danger . . . nuclear age": Kennedy, 13.
132   Russian troops sent to Cuba: Sorensen, 813.

134   "the President . . . impossible": Schlesinger, 803.
134   "the President . . . from the outset": Sorensen, 770.
136   "If Eisenhower . . . dangerous circumstances": George (1971), 90.
136   Major criteria for sound decision-making: See the discussion of defective decision-
            making in Chapter 1, pp. 9–10.
137   Kennedy's dangerous "game of chicken": Horowitz, 284–287.
137   "emerged from . . . political consequences": *Ibid.,* 286.
138   McNamara's advocacy of the naval blockade to "maintain the options": Kennedy,
            34; Abel, 81.
139   "The President . . . act soon": Sorensen, 780.
139   "that we are not serving . . . much either": *Ibid.,* 780.
140   Kennedy's reactions to the defeat of the Cuban invaders: *Ibid.,* 345; Schlesinger, 285.
141   Kennedy's innovations in decision-making procedures: George (1974); Schlesinger,
            296–297.
142   "away from . . . Cabinet Room": Schlesinger, 297.
142   "I felt . . . in line": Abel, 60.
143   "we'll have to do . . . inoperable": *Ibid.,* 36.
143   "action was imperative": Sorensen, 761.
143   "a prompt . . . of action": *Ibid.,* 761.
143   "Surely . . . doing nothing": Schlesinger, 803.
144   Arguments concerning the Soviet Union's capability for launching a nuclear attack:
            Abel, 59–60; Allison, 200–202; and Hilsman, 195.
144   "one of the remarkable . . . his mind": Sorensen, 765.
144   "They, no more . . . do nothing": Kennedy, 36.
145   "would not voluntarily . . . articulate men": Sorensen, 766.
145   "discussions within . . . waste of time": Acheson ("Homage . . . "), 76.
146   Fulbright's stand, urging stronger "military action . . .": Kennedy, 54.
147   "nothing . . . was overlooked": *Ibid.,* 60.
147   "In no other period . . . or fighting": Sorensen, 767.
147   Dean Rusk's reference to "nuclear incineration" and surprise at being "still
            alive": Abel, 110.
147   "the most intense . . . operated under": McNamara, 13.
147   "forges bonds . . . close association": *Ibid.,* 16.
148   "And so we argued . . . running out": Kennedy, 35.
148   "The next morning . . . are understandable": *Ibid.,* 44.
148   Members' discussion of possibility that blockade might fail and leave U.S. more vul-
            nerable: Abel, 89; Sorensen, 767–768.
149   "the difficulty . . . once started": *Ibid.,* 768.
149   "There isn't any . . . least objectionable": *Ibid.,* 783.
149   "the danger and concern . . . anything but that": Kennedy, 70.
149   "For a few fleeting . . . hear anything": *Ibid.,* 70.
149   Dissociation and recall of past traumatic experiences under severe stress: Janis (1958),
            179–188.
151   "what changed . . . so eloquently": Abel, 80–81.
151   "maintain . . . control of events": Kennedy, 34.
151   "His contributions . . . never forgive us": McNamara, 14–15.
151   "We spent . . . troubled us all": Kennedy, 39.
151   "Rusk spoke out . . . uncertain man": Allison, 199.
152   "The fact . . . brainstorming": Abel, 6.
152   "Each of us . . . action to take": Sorensen, 767.
152   "Thinking aloud . . . to another": Schlesinger, 803.
152   "none was consistent . . . each day": Kennedy, 31.
154   "that we were going . . . from them": *Ibid.,* 82.
154   Time allowed for Soviet leaders to weigh consequences: Hilsman, 213.
154   "it was . . . the crisis": *Ibid.,* 220.
155   "I guess . . . my salary": Schlesinger, 818.
155   "I have read . . . the arms race": U.S. Department of State, *Bulletin,* Vol. 47,
            No. 1220, November 12, 1962, pp. 742–743.
155   "if they . . . the next day": Kennedy, 109.

155	The United States' tacit ultimatum: George (1971), 105 and 125.
156	"offered not only . . . removed soon": *Ibid.,* 101.
156	"foreboding and gloom": Kennedy, 94.
156	"a fateful step": Hilsman, 221.
156–157	"awesome to contemplate . . . atomic weapons": *Ibid.,* 227.
157	"flexibility . . . wisdom and restraint": *Ibid.,* 227.
157	"coercive diplomacy . . . coercive threats": George (1971), 132.
157	"A final lesson . . . country's shoes": Kennedy, 124.
157	"what was in . . . of mankind": *Ibid.,* 128.

7   The Making of the Marshall Plan

One of the main references used in preparing this chapter is Jones' *The Fifteen Weeks,* which gives a detailed account of the making of the Marshall Plan, based on Jones' direct observations as an insider in the State Department and the internal documents to which he had access. Another major source of information about the policy-planning is George F. Kennan's *Memoirs (1925–1950).* Additional material was obtained from the memoirs of two other participants, Dean Acheson and Charles E. Bohlen, and from a book by Harry B. Price, who interviewed Secretary George C. Marshall, Averell Harriman, and other leading participants. I also consulted the sections on the Marshall Plan in a number of historical analyses of the policies of the Truman administration, including books or papers by Barnet, Bernstein, Gardner, Kolko and Kolko, La Febre, Neustadt, Patterson, Perkins, Spanier, and Williams.

page
159	"the most unsordid act in history": Jones, 256.
159	"Revisionist" historians' views on the Marshall Plan: See Williams and Bernstein.
159	"there can be . . . that region": Williams, 176.
159	"literally . . . life and death": *Ibid.,* 199.
160	Committees set up to grapple with the European economic crisis: Jones, 199; Acheson, 226.
161	"to support free . . . outside pressures": Jones, 12.
161	"The Truman Doctrine . . . Marshall Plan": *Ibid.,* 117.
161	"the most compelling . . . of peace": *Ibid.,* 9.
161	"The patient . . . deliberate": *Ibid.,* 223.
162	"was supposed . . . the recommendations": Kennan, 343.
162	"to beat . . . head": Price, 21.
162	"Avoid trivia.": Kennan, 343.
162	"intellectually hard-headed . . . are used)": *Ibid.,* 345.
162, 164	"We were indebted . . . features of it": *Ibid.,* 361.
164	"the disruptive effect . . . and vigor": *Ibid.,* 353.
164	"not against . . . and chaos": Jones, 34.
166	Characteristics of Policy Planning group—"stout in argument" and in constant "sweat": Kennan, 345–346.
166	"the sort . . . Marshall Plan": *Ibid.,* 368.
166	"You say . . . we're off again": *Ibid.,* 367–368.
167	"[They] put me . . . complications": *Ibid.,* 345.
167	"force me . . . previously experienced": *Ibid.,* 345. Italics added.
167	"So earnest . . . entire building": *Ibid.,* 345, footnote.
168	The "hottest fight" of all, on availability of America's crude steel resources: Jones, 45.
168	"a body . . . sound undertaking": *Ibid.,* 46–47.
171	"I have . . . Mrs. Marshall": Acheson, 213.
171	"lost no opportunity . . . the cause": Neustadt, 59.

8   *The Groupthink Syndrome*

page

174–175   The familiar features of cohesive groups—overestimates of the group, closed-mindedness, and pressures toward uniformity—are discussed in numerous books that
report either case observations or experimental findings (or both) in the field of
group dynamics. See, for example, Bion, Cartwright and Zander, De Rivera,
Elms, Hare, Raven and Rubin, Shaw, Thelen.

178   The General Accounting Office report on the Ford administration's failure to pursue
diplomatic negotiations before launching a military attack to rescue the Mayaguez
and its crew: *New York Times,* October 10, 1976, 40; *Time,* October 18, 1976, 18.

178   "Machismo diplomacy": Editorial, *Nation,* May 31, 1975, 642.

178   Minutes before the surprise attacks were launched, Cambodia started broadcasting an
announcement that it was releasing the Mayaguez and its crew: *New York Times,*
May 16, 1975, 14.

178   Library research on details of the Mayaguez decision relevant to the groupthink
hypothesis was originally carried out by a number of undergraduate students for a
seminar discussion in one of my advanced courses in social psychology at Yale.
One of the students, Jay Winik, summarized the material and added to it in a case
study of the Mayaguez decision, which he presented as part of a term paper.

178–180   "Running through . . . the last decade" and "Washington operated . . . in Indo-
china": R. Morris, "What to make of Mayaguez," *New Republic,* June 14, 1975,
9–10.

180   "Even if the militants . . . unworkable": Drew Middleton, "Going the Military
Route": *New York Times Magazine* (special issue on "America in Captivity:
Points of Decision"), May 17, 1981, 111.

180   The report prepared by the staff of the Senate Armed Forces Committee concluded
that "major errors" were made in planning the Iranian rescue mission: *New York
Times,* June 6, 1980, 1.

182   "to study . . . own offices" and "the hostage . . . observers": Quoted from the
report to the Joint Chiefs of Staff in the *Los Angeles Times,* August 24, 1980, 2.

182   Vance regarded it as "ill-conceived": *New York Times,* April 29, 1980, A14.

182   Roger Fisher concluded, "The belief that diplomatic options for influencing Iran
have been exhausted is wrong": "Dealing with Iran" (guest column), *New York
Times,* April 27, 1980, E23.

182   "When he finished . . . serious questions": Tom Wicker, "A tale of two silences,"
New York Times, May 4, 1980, E23.

182   Was Secretary Vance "treated as a deviant who is violating group norms"?: Irving
Janis, "In rescue planning how did Carter handle stress?" (guest column), *New
York Times,* May 18, 1980.

184   "No one disputes . . . next year": *New York Times,* "The Nation: In Summary,"
May 17, 1981.

184   President Reagan's proposal suffered a "stunning" defeat in the Senate and Republicans admitted it was a "blunder": Hedrik Smith, *New York Times,* May 30,
1981, 1.

184   Months later, Republican Congressmen were still worried about adverse effects of
President Reagan's proposal to cut Social Security benefits: G. F. Will, "Reagan's
economic arcana," *International Herald Tribune,* September 29, 1981, 4.

184   "once solid grip . . . loosening"; "slippage"; "unhappiness . . . Social Security":
New York Times Service, news story by Adam Clymer in *International Herald
Tribune,* September 30, 1981, 3.

184   "premature and ill-considered": High Sidey, "The Presidency," *Time,* August 17,
1981, 37.

184   "Social security flap"; "to get . . . than anyone believed"; "it is easy . . . the negatives"; "Ronald Reagan plainly . . . *realistically*": *Washington Post* Service,
news story by Art Pine, *International Herald Tribune,* May 25, 1981, 3. Italics
added.

186   For some well-known examples of defective business decisions that are potential candidates for groupthink analysis, see Wilensky.
187   Accounts of how major European powers entered the first World War: Buchan; Holsti; Joffre; North; Tuchman.
187   "the most . . . English history": Trevor-Roper, 153.
188   "surrender . . . weaker nation": Rock, 338.
188   Summit conference with Hitler suggested to Chamberlain by Horace Wilson: Moseley, 36.
188   "much of the initial . . . German demands": Rock, 118.
188   "the historian . . . largely unmoved": Ibid., 33–34.
190   Assumption that British would be arbiter of Europe and capable of successful fighting: Ibid., 331; Feiling, 360–361.
190   "As early . . . with hope": Rock, 332.
190   German generals urging the British government to a firm stand against Hitler: The evidence concerning the messages sent by the German generals is mainly in captured German Foreign Office memoranda and German army documents, cited by Gilbert and Gott, 139; Shirer, 515–518; and other writers.
191   "The moment . . . twist of the screw": Gilbert, 109–110.
191   "if we two . . . the decision": Gilbert and Gott, 133.
194   "people consistently . . . how they turned out": Fischoff and Beyth-Marom, 391.
194   "everything seems stupid when it fails": Fyodor Dostoyevsky, quoted by G. F. Will, "Reagan's economic arcana," International Herald Tribune, September 29, 1981, 14.
196   "flaws and limitations . . . courses of action": Janis and Mann, 16.
196   "overestimating . . . biased samples": Wheeler and Janis, 93. This is a summary of the major types of errors in drawing inferences described by Nisbett and Ross.

9   The Watergate Cover-up

For this chapter, the primary sources—in both senses of the term—are verbatim excerpts bearing on the Watergate cover-up from the unedited transcripts of tape recordings of twenty-one meetings, held between June 23, 1972, and April 25, 1973, of President Nixon with one or more of his top aides. Unedited transcripts of two lengthy phone conversations of Nixon with Haldeman in April 1973 were also used. In the list below, "Transcript" refers to the unedited transcripts of the meetings and telephone conversations—which inserted a number of incriminating statements that had been left out along with all the deleted expletives in the laundered White House version. Eight of these unedited transcripts were made by members of the staff of the House Judiciary Committee and were published in a volume entitled Transcriptions of Eight Presidential Conversations. (These include the transcript for September 15, 1972, and the following transcripts during 1973: February, 28, March 13, March 21 A.M. and P.M., March 22 P.M., April 16 A.M. and P.M.) The others were prepared by Department of Justice personnel for use by the Watergate prosecutors in criminal court trials. They were published in an appendix to Watergate: Chronology of a Crisis by the Congressional Quarterly. (These include the transcripts for June 23, 1972, A.M. and P.M., and the following transcripts during 1973: January 8, March 17, March 20, March 22 A.M., April 17, and multiple sessions on April 19 and April 25.)

Another major source of documentary evidence is The Final Report of the Committee on the Judiciary, House of Representatives: Impeachment of Richard M. Nixon, President of the United States. This report includes excerpts from subpoenaed White House records.

Because of the availability of the unedited transcripts, it was unnecessary to depend upon any of the sworn testimony published in the New York Times and in the final report of the Senate Watergate (Ervin) Committee from the men who participated in the cover-up conspiracy. Some of this testimony was false and led to perjury convictions; most of it is probably trustworthy only for the general thrust, but not for details about what was said in specific conversations because of memory errors, as Neisser (1981) found when he compared John Dean's testimony about two crucial White House meetings with the unedited transcripts. (See Note 7 of Chapter 9 for a discussion of Neisser's study.)

A few noncrucial meetings and telephone calls for which only Nixon's edited transcriptions of the tape recordings have been published were examined for background purposes. Because the edited transcriptions probably have some omissions and occasional imprecisions in the wording of statements embarrassing to Nixon, I did not rely on excerpts from those edited transcriptions as the main evidence for any of my conclusions.

For indications of subjective reactions of the White House conspirators to various dilemmas and events during the nine months following the Watergate break-in, I examined carefully the books of memoirs published by three of the main participants in the cover-up conspiracy—Nixon, Haldeman, and Dean. Although none of these men established a record for veracity during the years they were in the White House, some of the material subsequently published in their memoirs (especially private diary notes made immediately after meetings) is used as low-level evidence that might indicate what they were thinking and feeling when they participated in making the cover-up decisions. For the same purpose, I also used articles containing quotations of subjective comments by the two other main participants—Ehrlichman and Colson. (Ehrlichman's book of memoirs, which was published in 1982, came out after this chapter was in press, too late to be used.)

Of the numerous historical and journalistic accounts of Watergate that have been published, the one I found to be most valuable as a source of well-documented background material, observations, and interpretations is Theodore H. White's *Breach of Faith: The Fall of Richard Nixon*. Additional secondary sources that provide some noteworthy commentaries are the publications by Blanchard, Lukas, and Jaworski.

Three papers by social psychologists—Duane and Conolley, Raven, and Wong-McCarthy—provide valuable leads concerning symptoms of groupthink manifested in the White House conversations. Raven's sociometric analysis of the Nixon group and Wong-McCarthy's data from his content analysis of the unedited transcripts are so cogent that I give detailed summaries of them.

page
200   Details from the congressional inquiries concerning the three meetings held by John Mitchell on Liddy's plans for surveillance of the Democratic party and the disagreements in the testimony of the participants about what had been decided at those meetings are presented in the *Final Report of the Committee on the Judiciary, U.S. House of Representatives* (1974), 56 ff.
200   "a gun loving . . . patriotism": White, 156–157.
200   "Black bag . . . mugging": Transcript of what Dean told Nixon about the meetings in Mitchell's office, March 21, 1973.
200   One of the Watergate burglars was still an active CIA agent: Chester et al., 186, Haldeman, 184.
201   "all of us . . . each wrong": Haldeman, 14–15.
201   "*failure* . . . every stage": *Ibid.,* 62. Italics added.
201   "things were compartmentalized" and "One necessarily regrets . . . I didn't see": Interview with Ehrlichman quoted in *Time,* December 1, 1975, 21.
201   "screwed up . . . the rest of my life": David Frost's television interview with Richard Nixon, published verbatim in the *New York Times,* May 5, 1977.
204   The chronology of Watergate events is based on the *Congressional Quarterly*'s *Watergate: Chronology of a Crisis,* 1973; *Time,* "Watergate Retrospective," August 19, 1974, 54; *Washington Post,* "Outlook: The Year of Watergate," June 17, 1973, C1–C4; *New York Times,* "The continuation of Doar summary of the impeachment inquiry," July 23, 1974, C14–C24; *London Sunday Times* team, *Watergate: The Full Inside Story,* 1973; and T. H. White's *Breach of Faith: The Fall of Richard Nixon,* 1975.
204   "The hell with it . . . stonewall it": Transcript, June 20, 1972.
205   "Watergate is all but forgotten": *Time,* Watergate Retrospective, August 19, 1974, 54.
208, 210 "Dean shifted . . . consequence": Haldeman, 317.
210   The new set of aides, after April 1973, felt no personal loyalty to Nixon and were wary of each other: White, 221 and 241–245.

210 For details about Nixon's decision resulting in "the Saturday night massacre," see White, 257–268.
210 For a description of the hypervigilant pattern of decision-making, see Janis and Mann, 59–61 and 245–246.
210 "Haldeman and Ehrlichman . . . rather than suggesting": *Congressional Quarterly,* 341.
210 "Behind the closed door . . . take the lead": *Newsweek,* May 13, 1974, 10.
211 Haldeman told Nixon, "the only way . . . further on it": Transcript, June 23, 1972.
211 "at least two . . . one another": Raven, 310.
213 "John is one . . . he would": Transcript, September 15, 1972.
213 "one of the protectors of the President": Haldeman, 317.
213 "was enormously impressed with him" and "had the kind of steel . . . needed": Nixon's diary for September 15, 1972, quoted by Nixon, 682. Italics added.
213 "Ehrlichman and I decided . . . Dean": Nixon, 779.
214 "Dean . . . is really the one . . . advice": Nixon's diary for March 25, 1973, quoted by Nixon, 807.
214 Dean's "firefighting" enabled him "at last [to] make the first team": Dean, 88.
214 Dean cherished the "ego-boosting badges of intimacy": *Ibid.,* 1977.
214 Dean transferred his loyalty to the White House and would not tell Mitchell what was going on: *Ibid.,* 106.
214 "I became possessed . . . the overall effort": *Ibid.,* 126.
214 "I was not prepared . . . collegially received": *Ibid.,* 134–135.
215 Gray was expected to be "one hundred percent loyal . . .": Haldeman, 300.
215 Dean was "furious at Gray": Dean, 212.
215 "He may be dead . . . shoot him": Transcript, March 22, 1973.
215 "Ehrlichman: Hi . . . slowly in the wind": Transcript of a phone call at the end of the first week in March, 1972, quoted by Chester et al., 233–234.
215 "closer . . . professionally" and "an extension . . . alter ego": Haldeman, 99.
216 "I have . . . less stupidly": Nixon, 646.
216 "The cover-up collapsed . . . the gains": Haldeman, 402.
216 "It was not planned . . . growth": *Ibid.,* 408.
217 "Orthodox political scientists . . . news on television": M. N. Rothbard in section of "Commentary: Rulers vs. Reality" in *Harper's,* Oct. 1974, 80.
217 "an entirely avoidable quagmire": Editor's introduction to *Harper's* special issue on Watergate published in October, 1974.
218 "The groupthink phenomenon . . . in the Nixon group": Raven, 297.
219 "The Nixon 'team' . . . day by day": Lukas, 306.
219 Disintegration of the White House group during April 1973 and objections of Haldeman and Ehrlichman to Nixon's proposal that they should leave the government: Haldeman, 324–367; Nixon, 820–822; Transcripts for April 1973.
220 "Whatever the problems . . . hurt him now": Haldeman, 29–30.
220 "There is an unreality . . . accomplished": White, 168.
221 "faith . . . wisdom": Dean, 186.
221 "the way you . . . sprung there": Transcript, September 15, 1972.
221 "I wouldn't want . . . would you?" . . . "No, no": Transcript, September 15, 1972.
221 "I felt sure . . . public relations solution": Nixon, 773.
221 "I felt at my toughest . . . the cover-up": Dean, 139.
221 "deflated my confidence . . . open": *Ibid.,* 141.
221 "they offered me confidence": *Ibid.,* 186.
221 "began to lose faith": *Ibid.,* 186.
221 Dean sought refuge in heavy drinking at home: *Ibid.,* 173 and 185.
221 "optimistic front": *Ibid.,* 183.
222 Dean's reassurances and "we have made it . . . anything serious": Transcript, February 28, 1973.
222 "to snap . . . his benefit": Dean, 200.
222 "They are . . . looking most for" and "I don't think . . . frankly": Transcript, March 21, 1973.
222 "damn soon . . . bottle": Transcript, March 21, 1973.
222 "Maybe he *is* right . . . thing": Dean, 207.

222   "What are *your* feelings . . . options" and "soft spots" and "not confident that we
         can ride through this": Transcript, March 21, 1973. Italics added.
223   Dean felt guilty and worried: Dean, 207.
223   "John's point . . . whatever the cost": Transcript, March 21, 1973.
223   "was later . . . my presidency": Nixon, 799.
223   "I left the meeting . . . not look so defensive": *Ibid.,* 800–801.
223   "As far as the day . . . talk with Dean": Transcript of Nixon's diary entry on Dic-
         tabelt recorded March 21, 1973, quoted by White, 201–202; italics added. Addi-
         tional sentences in this diary entry are quoted by Nixon, 799–800.
224   "out of compassion": Transcript, March 22, 1973, A.M.
224   "Again . . . *It may not be the worst*": Transcript, March 22, 1973, A.M. Italics added.
224   "In fact . . . was the worst": *Ibid.*
224   "Who do you . . . down" and "totally cut off" and "The White House . . . the
         Watergate thing": *Ibid.*
224   "to hide . . . White House": *Ibid.*
224   "He's awfully close . . . Haldeman now" and "Mitchell will . . . good route for us
         to go": *Ibid.*
224   "Haldeman . . . we're under rules . . . can't go fishing . . .": *Ibid.*
225   "What we're fighting . . . battle": Transcript, March 22, 1973, P.M.
225   Dean's decision to save his "own ass": Dean, 229–233.
225   Dean's feeling that he was being set up to be the next fall guy: *Ibid.,* 214–220.
226   "Looking back . . . our own vulnerabilities": Nixon, 799.
226   "These differing perceptions . . . minuets around the problem": *Ibid.,* 799.
227   "Shit . . . as a matter of fact": Transcript, March 13, 1973.
227   "the last gasp . . . they have to squeal on": *Ibid.*
227   Nixon's tapes "destroyed him": Haldeman, 267.
227   Jaworski's considered opinion that Nixon could have survived in office if he had
         destroyed his tapes: Jaworski, 328–329.
227   "Nixon did not destroy . . . too late": *Ibid.,* 329.
228   Nixon discussed destroying the tapes in April 1973 and never again raised the issue:
         Haldeman, 260–261.
228   "the President . . . to trip him up": *Ibid.,* 261.
228   Ehrlichman's suggestion to use the tapes, Haldeman's and Nixon's concurrence, and
         the subsequent telephone call after Haldeman had listened to the March 21, 1973
         tape: Transcripts of two meetings and a telephone conversation on April 25, 1973,
         and Haldeman, 345–349. Italics added in the quotation from Nixon's telephone
         call: "I always wondered . . . aren't you?"
229   "It'll be . . . affects them": Transcript, March 13, 1973.
229   Dean's characterization of the Senate Committee as a Kennedy conspiracy and
         Nixon's response, "Yeah . . . make their move": Transcript, February 28, 1973.
230   "You certainly can't . . . ammunition": Transcript of April 15, 1973, quoted by
         Haldeman, 334.
230   "I just wonder if the son-of-a-bitch . . . on him": Transcript, April 25, 1973, P.M.
230   Nixon was plagued by the obsessional idea that Dean may have made recordings:
         Haldeman, 358 and 388.
230   "basically . . . *blackmail* by him": Transcript of a telephone call of Nixon to Halde-
         man, April 25, 1973. Italics added.
230   "I think . . . deeply in it" and "to handle it . . . he deserves": Transcript of a tele-
         phone call of Nixon to Haldeman, April 25, 1973; italics added.
230   Dean characterized as acting "in desperation," "panicked," and "shafted": Halde-
         man, 330–331.
231   "potentially subject . . . not" and "*you* have no problem": Transcript, March 17,
         1973. Italics added.
231   "I said the containment theory . . . realistically": Transcript, April 16, 1973, P.M.
         Italics added.
232   Before March 1973, Dean did not discuss with others in the White House group his
         worries concerning obstructions of justice: Dean, 152–171.
232   Ehrlichman's and Haldeman's expectations about not being asked to resign: Halde-
         man, 342–343.
232   "The President said . . . The unthinkable had been uttered": *Ibid.,* 344–345.
234   ". . . there is ample evidence . . . the Nixon group": Raven, 311.

235 "disciplined, lawyer-like fashion": Haldeman, 321.
235 "the transcripts . . . sequential minds": White, 211.
235 "The transcripts . . . his own innocence": *Ibid.,* 209.
236 Haldeman's account of the telephone call on June 20, 1972 that set the pattern for the cover-up: Haldeman, 50–52.
236 "it never occurred to me . . . concept": *Ibid.,* 51.
236 "with no personal motivation . . . campaign": *Ibid.,* 402.
236 "when I told Nixon . . . his approval of it": Ehrlichman's review of Haldeman's book in *Time,* March 1, 1976, 26.
237 "My reaction . . . its illegality": Nixon, 628–629.
237 Nixon did not want questions asked of Mitchell: *Ibid.,* 636.
237 "a desire . . . unpleasant": *Ibid.,* 809.
237 "The president . . . 'aware' of the details": Blanchard, 228.
237 "I, I have tried . . . personal problems": Transcript, April 16, 1973, A.M.
237–238 ". . . the president's conversations . . . details of Watergate": Blanchard, 229.
239 "PR . . . the name of the game": White, 55.
239 Dean was a "white collar striver" and "conniver": *Ibid.,* 142.
239 "through hard-hats and Legionnaires," "thugs," "go in . . . heads off" "Sure . . . Murderers . . . smash some noses": Seymour M. Hersh, "Tape Reveals Nixon Wanted 'Thugs' Used Against Anti-War Protesters in 1971," *New York Times* Service, reprinted in *International Herald Tribune,* September 25, 1981. The news story asserts that there is no evidence that the "thugs" plan was put into operation. It quotes Mr. Nixon's attorney, R. Stan Mortinson, as stating that the transcript in possession of the *New York Times* appears to be one prepared by the Special Watergate Prosecution Force or another investigative group, but does not conform to the transcript prepared for official court procedures.

10   *Generalizations*

page
242 Research on conformity in persons fearful of disapproval and rejection: See Berkowitz; Janis (1982); Marlowe and Gergen.
246 Compliance among group members out of fear of recriminations when there is little solidarity: See Argyris; McGregor.
246 Errors in decision-making in noncohesive groups: see Argyris.
247 Research on social rewards that increase group cohesiveness: See Back; Hare; Raven and Rubin.
248 "High-cohesive groups . . . consistent": Shaw, 229.
249 "When the cohesiveness . . . group norm": Janis and Mann, 131.
250 "[This pair] specifies the prime conditions . . . made by the leader.": *Ibid.,* 131.
252 "What the hell . . . blow something." (Nixon) Transcript, March 21, 1973.
257 "The out-group's . . . toward it": Campbell, 825.
259 "We can . . . frustrated it": Scriven, 115. (I have inserted a few qualifying phrases that are in line with Scriven's caveats presented elsewhere in his paper—[apparently] and [seem to]—in order to emphasize the uncertainty of inferences from historical studies.)

11   *Preventing Groupthink*

page
260 Excellent summaries of the social psychological research literature bearing on the conditions under which groups have positive versus negative effects on constructive thinking can be found in Davis, Kowitz and Knutson, and Raven and Rubin.

260   Pretzel-shaped questions and answers: Irving Sarnoff (in a widely quoted but unpub-
            lished commentary) is the psychologist who has enriched our vocabulary with
            "pretzel-shaped" questions and answers.
261   "the greatest hazard . . . such proposals": Hare, 352.
261   "no important . . . academic discipline": *Ibid.*, 357.
264   "President Eisenhower . . . lost to view": Wilensky, 54.
265   "By the time . . . been made": Weaver, 267.
267   Claim that the Tuesday Lunch Group contained devil's advocates: Graff, 46–51,
            69–73, 87, 125, 136–137; Reedy, 11: Thomson, 49.
267–268   "[the official devil's advocate's] objections . . . by controversy": Reedy, 11.
268   "comforting feeling . . . circle": George (1974).
268   "to project . . . thereafter": *Ibid.*
269   "Unlike movies . . . the climax": Schelling, viii.
271   "Gentlemen . . . all about": Drucker, 148.
272   Research teams dealing with management problems: See Ackoff; Miller and Starr.
272   Political gaming exercise at Center for International Studies, MIT, simulating clash
            between U.S. and S.U. over a revolt in an underdeveloped country: Bloomfield,
            1–6.

Bibliography

Abel, E. *The missile crisis.* New York: Bantam Books, 1966.

Abel, E., and Kalb, M. *Roots of involvement.* New York: Norton, 1971.

Abelson et al. (Eds.) *Theories of cognitive consistency.* Chicago: Rand McNally Co., 1968.

Abelson, R. P. Script processing in attitude formation and decision making. In J. S. Carroll and J. W. Payne (Eds.), *Cognition and social behavior.* New York: Lawrence Erlbaum Associates, 1976.

Acheson, D. *Present at the creation.* New York: Norton, 1969.

Acheson, D. Homage to plain dumb luck. *Esquire,* February, 1969.

Acheson, D. D.A.'s version of Robert Kennedy's version of Cuban missile affair. *Esquire,* February, 1966.

Ackoff, R. Operations research. In D. L. Sills (Ed.), *International encyclopedia of the social sciences.* Vol. 2, 290–294.

Allison, G. T. *Essence of decision: Explaining the Cuban missile crisis.* Boston: Little, Brown, 1971.

Argyris, C. *Interpersonal competence and organizational effectiveness.* Homewood, Ill.: Irwin & Dorsey Press, 1962.

Argyris, C. *Organization and innovation.* Homewood, Ill.: Irwin & Dorsey Press, 1965.

Ashmore, R. Solving the problem of prejudice. In B. Collins, *Social psychology.* Reading, Mass.: Addison-Wesley, 1970, 298–339.

Back, K. W. Influence through social communication. *Journal of Abnormal and Social Psychology,* 1951, *46,* 9–23.

Barnet, R. J. *Intervention and revolution.* New York: World, 1968.

Barnet, R. J. *The economy of death.* New York: Atheneum, 1969.

Berkowitz, L. Social motivation. In G. Lindzey and E. Aronson (Eds.), *The handbook of social psychology.* Vol. 3, 50–135. Reading, Mass.: Addison-Wesley, 1969.

Bernstein, B. J. (Ed.) *Politics and policies of the Truman administration.* Chicago: Quadrangle Books, 1970.

Bernstein, B. J., and Matuso, A. J. (Eds.) *The Truman administration: A documentary history.* New York and London: Harper & Row, 1966.

Bion, W. *Experiences in groups.* London: Tavistock Publications, 1961.

Blanchard, W. H. *Aggression American style.* Santa Monica, Calif.: Goodyear Publishing Co., Inc., 1979.

Bloomfield, L. P. Some policy observations based on Polex II. Center for International Studies, MIT. (Dittoed), June 1, 1961.

Bohlen, C. E. *The transformation of American foreign policy.* New York: W. W. Norton, 1969.

Brown, R. *Social psychology.* New York: Free Press, 1965.

Brownlow, D. G. *The accused.* New York: Vantage, 1968.

Buchan, J. *A history of the great war.* Vol. 1. London: Nelson, 1922.

Buchanan, A. R. *The United States and World War II.* (2 vols.) New York: Harper & Row, 1964.

Campbell, D. T. Stereotypes and the perception of group differences. *American Psychologist,* 1967, *22,* 817–829.

Cartwright, D. The nature of group cohesiveness. In D. Cartwright and A. Zander (Eds.), *Group dynamics: Research and theory* (3rd ed.). New York: Harper & Row, 1968.

Cartwright, D., and Zander, A. (Eds.) *Group dynamics: Research and theory* (3rd ed.). New York: Harper & Row, 1968.

Chester, L., McCrystal, C., Aris, S., and Shawcross, W. (the *London Sunday Times* team). *Watergate: The full inside story.* New York: Ballantine Books, 1973.

Collins, J. L. *War in peacetime.* Boston: Houghton Mifflin, 1969.

Cooper, C. L. *The lost crusade.* New York: Dodd, Mead & Co., 1970.

Crow, W. J., and Noel, R. C. An experiment in simulated historical decision-making. In M. G. Hermann and T. W. Milburn (Eds.), *A psychological examination of political leaders.* New York: Free Press: 1975.

Dean, J. W. *Blind ambition.* New York: Simon & Schuster, 1976.

Department of Defense, *United States–Vietnam relations 1945–1967.* (12 vols.) Washington, D.C.: U.S. Government Printing Office, 1971.

De Rivera, J. *The psychological dimension of foreign policy.* Columbus, Ohio: Merrill, 1968.

Deutsch, K. W. *The nerves of government.* New York: Free Press, 1963.

Deutsch, M., and Kraus, R. M. *Theories in social psychology.* New York: Basic Books, 1965.

De Weerd, H. H. Strategic surprise in the Korean War. *Orbis,* 1962, *6,* 435–452.

Dion, K. L., Baron, R. S., and Miller, N. Why do groups make riskier decisions than individuals? In L. Berkowitz (Ed.), *Advances in experimental social psychology.* Vol. 5, 306–377. New York: Academic Press, 1970.

Dittes, J. E., and Kelley, H. H. Effects of different conditions of acceptance upon conformity to group norms. *Journal of Abnormal and Social Psychology,* 1956, *53,* 100–107.

Drucker, P. F. *The effective executive.* New York: Harper & Row, 1966.

Ellsberg, D. The quagmire myth and the stalemate machine. *Public Policy,* Spring 1971.

Elms, A. *Social psychology and social relevance.* Boston: Little, Brown, 1972.

Feiling, K. *The life of Neville Chamberlain.* London: Macmillan, 1946.

Feis, H. *The road to Pearl Harbor.* New York: Atheneum, 1962.

Festinger, L. A theory of social comparison processes. *Human Relations,* 1954, *7,* 117–140.

Fischhoff, B., and Beyth-Marom, R. Failure has many fathers. *Policy Sciences,* 1976, *7,* 388–393.

Flowers, M. L. A laboratory test of some implications of Janis's groupthink hypothesis. *Journal of Personality and Social Psychology,* 1977, *35,* 888–896.

Gardner, L. C. *Architects of illusion.* Chicago: Quadrangle Books, 1970.

Gelb, L. H. Today's lessons from the Pentagon Papers. *Life,* Sept. 17, 1971.

George, A. The Cuban missile crisis, 1962. In A. George et al., *The limits of coercive diplomacy.* Boston: Little, Brown, 1971, pp. 86–143.

George, A. Adaptation to stress in political decision making: The individual, small group, and organizational context. In G. V. Coelho, D. A. Hamburg, and J. E. Adams (Eds.), *Coping and adaptation.* New York: Basic Books, 1974.

George, A., and Smoke, R. *Deterrence in American foreign policy: Theory and practice.* New York: Columbia University Press, 1974.

George, A. *Presidential decisionmaking in foreign policy: The effective use of information and advice.* Boulder, Colo.: Westview, 1980.

Geyelin, P. L. *Lyndon B. Johnson and the world.* New York: Praeger, 1966.

Gilbert, M. *The roots of appeasement.* New York: New American Library, 1966.

Gilbert, M. and Gott, R. *The appeasers.* Boston: Houghton Mifflin, 1963.

Graff, H. *The Tuesday cabinet.* Englewood Cliffs, N.J.: Prentice-Hall, 1970.

Green, D., and Conolley, E. S. "Groupthink" and Watergate. Paper presented to annual meeting of the American Psychological Association, 1974.

Guthman, E. *We band of brothers.* New York: Harper & Row, 1971.

Hackman, J. R., and Morris, C. G. Group tasks, group interaction process, and group performance effectiveness: A reveiw and proposed integration. In L. Berkowitz (Ed.), *Advances in experimental social psychology.* Vol. 8. New York: Academic Press, 1975.

Haldeman, H. R. (with DiMona, J.). *The ends of power.* New York: Dell, 1978.

Halperin, M. H. *Bureaucratic politics and foreign policy.* Washington, D. C.: Brookings Inst., 1974.

Hamilton, D. Cognitive biases in the perception of social groups. In J. S. Carroll and J. W. Payne (Eds.), *Cognition and social behavior.* New York: Lawrence Erlbaum Associates, 1976.

Hare, A. P. *Handbook of small group research* (2nd ed.). New York: Free Press, 1976.

Hare, F. K. How should we treat environment? *Science,* 1970, 352–357.

Hearings before the Joint Committee on the Investigation of the Pearl Harbor Attack, 79th Congress. (39 vols.) Washington, D.C.: U.S. Government Printing Office, 1946.

Hersey, J. Profiles: Mr. President II—Ten o'clock meeting. *New Yorker,* April 14, 1951.

Higgins, P. *Korea and the fall of MacArthur.* New York: Oxford University Press, 1960.

Hilsman, R. *To move a nation.* New York: Doubleday, 1967.

Holsti, O. R. The 1914 case. *American Political Science Review,* 1965, *59,* 365–378.

Homans, G. Group factors in worker productivity. In H. Proshansky and L. Seidenberg (Eds.), *Basic studies in social psychology.* New York: Holt, 1965, 592–604.

Hoopes, T. *The limits of intervention.* New York: McKay, 1969.

Horowitz, I. L. Deterrence games: From academic casebook to military codebook. In Swingle, P. (Ed.), *The structure of conflict.* New York: Academic Press, 1970, pp. 277–296.

House of Representatives. *The final report of the Committee on the Judiciary House of Representatives: Impeachment of Richard M. Nixon, President of the United States.* New York: Bantam Books, 1975.

House of Representatives. *Transcripts of eight recorded Presidential conversations.* Washington, D.C.: Committee on the Judiciary, House of Representatives, 93rd Congress, 2nd session. May–June 1974.

Janeway, M. Bill Moyers talks about L.B.J., power, poverty, war, and the young. *Atlantic Monthly,* July, 1968.

Janis, I. L. Psychodynamic aspects of adjustment to army life. *Psychiatry,* 1945, *8,* 159–176.

Janis, I. L. Objective factors related to morale attitudes in the aerial combat situation. In S. Stouffer et al., *The American soldier.* Vol. 2. Princeton, N.J.: Princeton University Press, 1949.

Janis, I. L. *Psychological stress.* New York: Wiley, 1958.

Janis, I. L. Field and experimental studies of phases in the development of cohesive face-to-face groups. A paper presented at the 18th International Congress of Psychology in Moscow, U.S.S.R. Mimeo., August, 1966.

Janis, I. L. Group identification under conditions of external danger. In D. Cartwright and A. Zander (Eds.), *Group dynamics: Research and theory*. New York: Harper & Row, 1968, 80–90.

Janis, I. L. *Stress and frustration*. New York: Harcourt, Brace & Jovanovich, 1971.

Janis, I. L. Counteracting the adverse effects of concurrence-seeking in policy-planning groups: Theory and research perspectives. In H. Brandstätter, J. H. Davis, G. Stocker-Kreichgauer (Eds.), *Group decision making*. London: Academic Press, 1981.

Janis, I. (Ed.) *Counseling on personal decisions: Theory and research on short-term helping relationships*. New Haven, Conn.: Yale University Press, 1982.

Janis, I. L., and Crow, W. J. Improving the quality of decisions in planning groups. Unpublished grant application submitted to Department of Health, Education, and Welfare, 1975.

Janis, I. L., and Hoffman, D. Facilitating effects of daily contact between partners who make a decision to cut down on smoking. *Journal of Personality and Social Psychology,* 1970, *17,* 25–35.

Janis, I. L., and Mann, L. *Decision making: A psychological analysis of conflict, choice, and commitment*. New York: Free Press, 1977.

Jaworski, L. *The right and the power: The prosecution of Watergate*. New York: Pocket Books, 1977.

Joffre, J. *Memoirs*. Vol. 1 (translated by T. B. Mott). New York: Harpers, 1932.

Johnson, L. B. *The vantage point: Perspective of the presidency, 1963–1969*. New York: Holt, Rinehart & Winston, 1971.

Jones, J. M. *The fifteen weeks*. New York: Viking, 1955.

Kalb, M., and Abel, E. *Roots of involvement*. New York: Norton, 1970.

Katz, D., and Kahn, R. L. *The social psychology of organizations* (2nd ed.). New York: Wiley, 1978.

Kelman, H. Violence without moral restraint: Reflections on the dehumanization of victims and victimizers. *Journal of Social Issues,* 1973, *29,* 25–61.

Kennan, G. F. *Memoirs (1925–1950)*. New York: Bantam, 1969.

Kennedy, R. F. *Thirteen days*. New York: Norton, 1969.

Kimmel, H. E. *Admiral Kimmel's story*. Chicago: Regnery, 1955.

Klein, H. G. The fall began when deceit replaced truth. *Los Angeles Times,* August 16, 1974.

Kolko, J., and Kolko, G. *The limits of power: The world and United States foreign policy, 1945–1954*. New York: Harper & Row, 1972.

Kowitz, A. C., and Knutson, T. J. *Decision making in small groups*. Boston: Allyn & Bacon, 1980.

Kraslow, D., and Loory, S. H. *The secret search for peace in Vietnam*. New York: Vintage, 1968.

La Febre, W. *America, Russia, and the Cold War, 1945–1966*. New York: Wiley, 1968.

Langer, E. J. The illusion of control. *Journal of Personality and Social Psychology,* 1975, *32,* 311–328.

Lawrence, P. R., and Lorsch, J. W. *Organization and environment: Managing differentiation and integration*. Homewood, Ill.: Irwin, 1969.

Leckie, R. *Conflict: The history of the Korean War*. New York: Putnam, 1962.

Lewin, K. Group decision and social change. In T. Newcomb and E. Hartley (Eds.), *Readings in social psychology*. New York: Holt, 1947, pp. 197–211.

Lewin, K. *Field theory in social science*. London: Tavistock Publications, 1952.

Lichterman, M. To the Yalu and back. In H. Stein (Ed.), *American civil-military decisions: A book of case studies*. Montgomery: University of Alabama Press, 1963.

Lindblom, E. The science of "muddlingthrough." In A. Etzioni (Ed.), *Readings on modern organizations.* Englewood Cliffs, N.J.: Prentice-Hall, 1969, pp. 154–165.

Longley, J., and Pruitt, D. G. Groupthink: A critique of Janis's theory. *Review of Personality and Social Psychology,* 1980, *1,* 74–93.

Lukas, J. A. *Nightmare: The underside of the Nixon years.* New York: Viking, 1976.

McGregor, D. *The human side of enterprise.* New York: McGraw-Hill, 1960.

McLellan, D. S. Dean Acheson and the Korean War. *Political Science Quarterly,* 1968, *83,* 16–39.

McNamara, R. Introduction to R. F. Kennedy's *Thirteen days.* New York: Norton, 1969.

Marlowe, D., and Gergen, K. Personality and social interaction. In G. Lindzey and E. Aronson (Eds.), *The handbook of social psychology.* Vol. 3. Reading, Mass.: Addison-Wesley, 1969, pp. 590–665.

Marshall, S. L. A. *The river and the gauntlet.* New York: Morrow, 1953.

Meyer, K. E., and Szulc, T. *The Cuban invasion.* New York: Praeger, 1962.

Miller, D. W., and Starr, M. K. *Executive decisions and operations research.* Englewood Cliffs, N.J.: Prentice-Hall, 1960.

Miller, J. C., and Janis, I. L. Dyadic interaction and adaptation to the stresses of college life. *Journal of Counseling Psychology,* 1973, *3,* 258–264.

Mollenhoff, C. R. The problem was Haldeman's iron control. *Los Angeles Times,* August 16, 1974.

Morgenthau, H. *Politics among nations* (4th ed.). New York: Knopf, 1970.

Morison, S. E. *The Rising Sun in the Pacific: 1931–April, 1942.* Vol. 3 of *History of United States naval operations in World War II.* Boston: Little, Brown, 1950.

Moseley, L. *On borrowed time: How World War II began.* London: Weidenfeld & Nicolson, 1969.

Myers, D. G., and Lamm, H. The polarizing effect of group discussion. In I. L. Janis (Ed.), *Current trends in psychology: Readings from the American Scientist.* Los Altos, Calif.: Kaufmann, 1977.

Nathan, J. A. The missile crisis: His finest hour now. *World Politics,* 1975, *27,* 256–281.

Neisser, U. John Dean's memory: A case-study. *Cognition,* 1981, *1,* 1–23.

Neustadt, R. E. *Presidential power: The politics of leadership with reflections on Johnson and Nixon.* New York: Wiley, 1976.

The New York Times, *The Kennedy Years.* New York: Viking, 1964.

Newsweek, The secret history of Vietnam, June 28, 1971.

Nisbett, R. E., and Ross, L. *Human inference: Strategies and shortcomings of informal judgment.* Englewood Cliffs, N.J.: Prentice-Hall, 1980.

Nixon, R. M. *RN: The memoirs of Richard Nixon.* New York: Grosset & Dunlap, 1978.

North, R. Perception and action in the 1914 crisis. *Journal of International Affairs,* 1967, *21,* 103–122.

Opotowsky, S. *The Kennedy government.* New York: Dutton, 1961.

Osgood, R. E., Tucker, R. W., Dinerstein, H. S., Rourke, F. E., Frank, I., Martin, L. W., and Liska, G. *America and the world.* Baltimore: Johns Hopkins Press, 1970.

Paige, G. D. *The Korean decision.* New York: Free Press, 1968.

Patterson, K. G. The quest for peace and prosperity: International trade, communism, and the Marshall Plan. In B. J. Bernstein (Ed.), *Politics and policies of the Truman administration.* Chicago: Quadrangle Books, 1970, pp. 78–112.

Peffer, N. *The Far East.* Ann Arbor: University of Michigan Press, 1958.

Perkins, D. *The diplomacy of a new age.* Bloomington: Indiana University Press, 1967.

Pool, I. *Reprint of publications on Viet Nam, 1966–1971.* MIT, May, 1971.

Price, A. B. *The Marshall Plan and its meaning.* Ithaca, N.Y.: Cornell University Press, 1955.

Pruitt, D. Choice shifts in group discussion: An introductory review. *Journal of Personality and Social Psychology,* 1971, *20,* 339–360.

Pruitt, D. Conclusions: Toward an understanding of choice shifts in group discussion. *Journal of Personality and Social Psychology,* 1971, *20,* 495–510.

Raven, B. H. The Nixon group. *Journal of Social Issues,* 1974, *30,* 297–320.

Raven, B., and Rubin, J. Z. *Social psychology: People in groups.* New York: Wiley, 1977.

Reedy, G. E. *The twilight of the presidency.* New York: World, 1970.

Roche, J. P. The jigsaw puzzle of history. *New York Times Magazine,* January 24, 1971.

Rock, W. R. *Appeasement on trial.* Hamden, Conn.: Anchor Books, 1966.

Salinger, P. *With Kennedy.* New York: Avon Books, 1966.

Schachter, S. *The psychology of affiliation.* Stanford, Calif.: Stanford University Press, 1959.

Schachter, S. Deviation, rejection, and communication. In D. Cartwright and A. Zander (Eds.), *Group dynamics: Research and theory.* New York: Harper & Row, 1968.

Schachter, S. et al. Cross-cultural experiments on threat and rejection. *Human Relations,* 1954, *7,* 403–439.

Schelling, T. Foreword to R. Wohlstetter's *Pearl Harbor.* Stanford, Calif.: Stanford University Press, 1962.

Schlesinger, A. M., Jr. *A thousand days.* Boston: Houghton Mifflin, 1965.

Schlesinger, A. M., Jr. *Robert Kennedy and his times.* New York: Ballantine Books, 1978.

Scriven, M. Objectivity and subjectivity in educational research. In L. G. Thomas (Ed.), *Philosophical redirection of educational research.* Chicago: University of Chicago Press, 1976.

Senate Select Committee on Presidential Campaign Activities. *The Watergate hearings: Break-in and cover-up.* Proceedings as edited by staff of the *New York Times.* New York: Viking Press, 1973.

Shaw, M. *Group dynamics.* New York: McGraw-Hill, 1971.

Sheehan, N. et al. *The Pentagon Papers as published by The New York Times.* New York: Bantam, 1971.

Shepard, R. N. On subjectively optimum selections among multi-attribute alternatives. In W. Edwards and A. Tversky (Eds.), *Decision making.* Baltimore: Penguin Books, 1967, pp. 257–283.

Sherif, M., Harvey, O. J., White, B. J., Hood, W. R., and Sherif, C. W. *Inter-group conflict and cooperation: The robbers cave experiment.* Norman, Okla.: University of Oklahoma Press, 1961.

Shirer, W. *The rise and fall of the Third Reich.* New York: Crest, 1963.

Sidey, H. White House staff vs. the cabinet. *Washington Monthly,* February 1969.

Simon, H. A. *Administrative behavior: A study of decision-making processes in administrative organization* (3rd ed.). New York: Free Press, 1976.

Slovic, P., Fischhoff, B., and Lichtenstein, S. Cognitive processes and societal risk taking. In J. S. Carroll and J. W. Payne (Eds.), *Cognition and social behavior.* New York: Lawrence Erlbaum Associates, 1976.

Smith, G. *The aims of American foreign policy.* New York: McGraw-Hill, 1969.

Smith, G. The limits of power. *New York Times Book Review,* Feb. 27, 1972.

Sorensen, T. C. *Kennedy.* New York: Bantam, 1966.

Spanier, J. W. *American foreign policy since World War II* (3rd rev. ed.). New York: Praeger, 1968.

Tetlock, P. E. Identifying victims of groupthink from public statements of decision makers. *Journal of Personality and Social Psychology, 1979, 37,* 1314–1324.

Thelen, H. A. *Dynamics of groups at work.* Chicago: Phoenix Books, University of Chicago Press, 1963.

Theobald, R. A. *The final secret of Pearl Harbor.* New York: Devin-Adair, 1954.

The presidential transcripts—with commentary by the staff of the Washington Post. New York: Delacorte Press, 1974.

The White House transcripts. New York: New York Times Co., 1974.

Thomson, J. G., Jr. How could Vietnam happen? An autopsy. *The Atlantic Monthly,* April 1968.

Toland, J. *But not in shame: The six months after Pearl Harbor.* New York: Random House, 1961.

Trevor-Roper, H. R. Munich—Its lessons ten years later. In F. L. Loewenheim (Ed.), *Peace or appeasement? Hitler, Chamberlain, and the Munich crisis.* Boston: Houghton Mifflin, 1965, pp. 150–157.

Truman, H. S. *Memoirs: Years of trial and hope.* Vol. 2. New York: Doubleday, 1956.

Tuchman, B. *The guns of August.* New York: Dell, 1963.

Tuchman, B. *The proud tower.* New York: Macmillan, 1966.

Tversky, A., and Kahneman, D. Judgment under uncertainty. *Science, 1974, 185,* 1124–1130.

United States Department of State *Bulletin* (on the Cuban Missile Crisis), v, 1.47, No. 1220, Nov. 12, 1962.

Vroom, V. H. Industrial social psychology. In G. Lindzey and E. Aronson (Eds.), *The handbook of social psychology.* Vol. 5. Reading, Mass.: Addison-Wesley, 1969, pp. 196–286.

Wallach, M. A., Kogan, N., and Bem, D. J. Group influence on risk-taking. In D. Cartwright and A. Zander (Eds.), *Group dynamics: Research and theory* (3rd ed.). New York: Harper & Row, 1968, pp. 430–443.

Watergate: Chronology of a crisis (2 vols.). Washington, D.C.: Congressional Quarterly, 1973, 1974.

Weaver, W. The moment of truth. *Science,* Jan. 1960, 27.

Whaley, B. *Stratagem: Deception and surprise in war.* Cambridge, Mass.: Center for International Studies, MIT, 1969.

Wheeler, D. D., and Janis, I. L. *A practical guide for making decisions.* New York: Free Press, 1980.

White, R. K. Misperception and the Vietnam War. *Journal of Social Issues, 1966, 22,* 1–164.

White, T. H. *Breach of faith: The fall of Richard Nixon.* New York: Atheneum, 1975.

Wicker, T. *JFK and LBJ.* New York: Morrow, 1968.

Wilensky, H. *Organizational intelligence: Knowledge and policy in government and industry.* New York: Basic Books, 1967.

Williams, W. A. *The tragedy of American diplomacy.* New York: Dell, 1962.

Wohlstetter, R. *Pearl Harbor: Warning and decision*. Stanford, Calif.: Stanford University Press, 1962.

Wohlstetter, R. Cuba and Pearl Harbor. *Foreign Affairs,* July 1965.

Wohlstetter, A., and Wohlstetter, R. Controlling the risks in Cuba. *Adelphi Papers,* No. 17, Institute of Strategic Studies, London, April 1965.

Wong-McCarthy, W. A content analysis of the unedited White House transcripts. Unpublished research report, 1976.

Wong-McCarthy, W. A qualitative analysis of excerpts from unedited presidential conversations. Unpublished research report, 1977.

Wyden, P. *Bay of Pigs: The untold story*. New York: Simon & Schuster, 1979.

Zimbardo, P. The human choice: Individuation, reason and order versus deindividuation, impulse, and chaos. *Nebraska Symposium on Motivation 1969,* Vol. 17, 237–307. University of Nebraska Press.

Index

Photo Credits

ABCDEFGHIJ-A-898765432